T0316315

E-Serials Cataloging:
Access to Continuing
and Integrating Resources
via the Catalog and the Web

E-Serials Cataloging: Access to Continuing and Integrating Resources via the Catalog and the Web has been co-published simultaneously as *The Serials Librarian*, Volume 41, Numbers 3/4 2002.

E-Serials Cataloging:
Access to Continuing and Integrating Resources via the Catalog and the Web

Jim Cole
Wayne Jones
Editors

E-Serials Cataloging: Access to Continuing and Integrating Resources via the Catalog and the Web has been co-published simultaneously as *The Serials Librarian*, Volume 41, Numbers 3/4 2002.

Routledge
Taylor & Francis Group
New York   London

First published by
The Haworth Information Press, 10 Alice Street, Binghamton, NY 13904-1580 USA

The Haworth Information Press is an imprint of The Haworth Press, Inc., 10 Alice Street, Binghamton, NY 13904-1580 USA.

This edition published 2013 by Routledge

Routledge   Routledge
Taylor & Francis Group   Taylor & Francis Group
711 Third Avenue   2 Park Square, Milton Park
New York, NY 10017   Abingdon, Oxon OX14 4RN

Routledge is an imprint of the Taylor & Francis Group, an informa business

E-Serials Cataloging: Access to Continuing and Integrating Resources via the Catalog and the Web has been co-published simultaneously as *The Serials Librarian*™, Volume 41, Numbers 3/4 2002.

The development, preparation, and publication of this work has been undertaken with great care. However, the publisher, employees, editors, and agents of The Haworth Press and all imprints of The Haworth Press, Inc., including The Haworth Medical Press® and Pharmaceutical Products Press®, are not responsible for any errors contained herein or for consequences that may ensue from use of materials or information contained in this work. Opinions expressed by the author(s) are not necessarily those of The Haworth Press, Inc. With regard to case studies, identities and circumstances of individuals discussed herein have been changed to protect confidentiality. Any resemblance to actual persons, living or dead, is entirely coincidental.

Cover design by Thomas J. Mayshock Jr.

Library of Congress Cataloging-in-Publication Data

E-Serials Cataloging: Access to Continuing and Integrating Resources via the Catalog and the Web / Jim Cole and Wayne Jones, editors.
    p. cm.
    "Co-published simultaneously as The serials librarian, v. 41, nos. 3/4 2002."
    Includes bibliographical references and index.
    ISBN 0-7890-1710-5 – ISBN 0-7890-1711-3 (pbk.)
    1. Cataloging of electronic journals. 2. Cataloging of computer network resources. I. Cole, Jim E. II. Jones, Wayne, 1959- III. Serials librarian.
Z695.712 .E84 2001
025.3′44–dc21
                        2001059412

ABOUT THE EDITORS

Jim Cole is Principal Serials Cataloger and Acting Head of Serials Cataloging at Iowa State University in Ames. Among his research interests are European trends and practices in serials management. Mr. Cole is the author of a variety of scholarly articles, book reviews, and columns and is the co-editor of several volumes, among them *Serials Cataloging: The State of the Art* (The Haworth Press, Inc., 1987), *Serials Cataloging: Modern Perspectives and International Developments* (The Haworth Press, Inc., 1992), *Serials Management in the Electronic Era* (The Haworth Press, Inc., 1996), and *Serials Cataloging at the Turn of the Century* (The Haworth Press, Inc., 1997). Editor-in-chief of *The Serials Librarian,* he has served on several committees of the American Library Association.

Wayne Jones is a freelance editor in Toronto (canEdit.ca). He is the editor of *Serials Canada* (The Haworth Press, Inc., 1995) and *E-Serials* (The Haworth Press, Inc., 1998, and forthcoming in a second edition in 2002), the chief editor of *Cataloging the Web: Metadata, AACR, and MARC 21* (Scarecrow Press, 2002) and of several articles and book reviews in professional journals. Mr. Jones has been active on committees of the American Library Association, notably CC:DA and the Networked Resources and Metadata Committee, and served for many years as co-convenor of the Serials Interest Group of the Canadian Library Association. He is Senior Editor of *The Serials Librarian.*

In memory of Crystal Graham, a colleague and friend

E-Serials Cataloging:
Access to Continuing
and Integrating Resources
via the Catalog and the Web

CONTENTS

Preface

Over the years, *The Serials Librarian* has published a number of collections of articles devoted to serials cataloging, beginning in 1987 with *Serials Cataloging: The State of the Art* and continuing through the 1997 *Serials Cataloging at the Turn of the Century*. The articles in these collections hint at a change that was taking place–while one probably cannot find mention of the Internet in the 1987 volume, the 1997 volume contains an article about CONSER on the Internet, and still another on practical issues and concerns related to the cataloging of Internet resources. Since 1997, however, the Internet (and specifically the World Wide Web) has become a standard source of serials as publishers rush to develop electronic versions of their print publications–and cataloging them has become a fact of life in most libraries. The present collection, *E-Serials Cataloging: Access to Continuing and Integrating Resources via the Catalog and the Web*, is a recognition of that fact.

E-Serials Cataloging is arranged in several sections: General; Standards; Education and Training; Policies and Procedures; National Projects and Local Applications; and Books, Serials, and the Future. As stated in the introduction to *Serials Cataloging: The State of the Art*, however, any classification scheme is to some extent arbitrary, and other groupings of the papers would have indeed been possible. The editors therefore must once again beg the indulgence of the reader in this matter.

The first section opens with Jean Hirons's tribute to Crystal Graham, to whose memory the collection is dedicated. Next, Ann Copeland sets the stage with a comprehensive survey of the professional literature on e-serials cataloging in the 1990s, reviewing the major themes in a volatile decade of ideas and

[Haworth co-indexing entry note]: "Preface." Cole, Jim, and Wayne Jones. Co-published simultaneously in *The Serials Librarian* (The Haworth Information Press, an imprint of The Haworth Press, Inc.) Vol. 41, No. 3/4, 2002, pp. xxiii-xxv; and: *E-Serials Cataloging: Access to Continuing and Integrating Resources via the Catalog and the Web* (ed: Jim Cole, and Wayne Jones) The Haworth Information Press, an imprint of The Haworth Press, Inc., 2002, pp. xvii-xix. Single or multiple copies of this article are available for a fee from The Haworth Document Delivery Service [1-800-HAWORTH, 9:00 a.m. - 5:00 p.m. (EST). E-mail address: getinfo@haworthpressinc.com].

xvii

action. Then, under "Standards," one finds two articles. Françoise Pellé, Director of the ISSN International Centre, discusses the ISSN in the context of the evolving re-definition of seriality in the AACR, ISBD, and ISSN communities, and focuses particular attention on its use as a persistent identifier of resources on the Internet. Following this, Sten Hedberg describes the development and features of the International Standard Bibliographic Description for Electronic Resources, and also looks at the catalysts for change that are impacting the ISBD family.

In "Education and Training," Taemin Park first presents the results of her study of the programs of forty-five American schools of library and information science, and the extent to which instruction about the cataloging of Web resources has been integrated into their curricula. Arlene Taylor then discusses the difficulty of teaching students the differences between serials and monographs, and examines the partial solution to this problem in the proposed rule changes dealing with seriality. Elena Romaniuk next provides a Canadian perspective on training for serials cataloging, as she relates the experiences of various trainers and trainees in CONSER's Serials Cataloging Cooperative Training Program. Finally, Danielle Hinton describes the University of Leicester's Electronic Journals Tutorial, one of the first online tutorials attempting to support and promote e-journal access.

Next comes "Policies and Procedures," which consists of six articles. Here, Wayne Morris and Lynda Thomas offer a convincing case for creating separate catalog records for each version of an e-journal. John Blosser, Tim Hagan, and Yvonne Zhang then review a selection of Web sites that support the cataloging of electronic serials and continuing resources. Following this, Jeanne Boydston and Joan Leysen examine the types of Internet resources that are being cataloged in ARL institutions, the level of staff performing the cataloging, and the impact this has made on cataloging departments. Next, for catalogers looking for practical guidance on making notes in MARC records about e-serials, Bea Caraway provides a categorized list of examples, demonstrating the content and wording in typical (and not-so-typical) situations. Following this, Gregory Wool discusses the use of structured metadata for collocation and browsing capability. In the last article in this section, Michael Wright takes a brief look at OCLC's CORC service.

The reader will find a variety of topics addressed in "National Projects and Local Applications." First, Ross MacIntyre discusses an experiment within the United Kingdom's National Electronic Site Licence Initiative in which sample MARC records were produced for e-journals using data provided by Swets Blackwell. Juha Hakala then explains how Uniform Resource Names based on Serial Item and Contribution Identifiers can be resolved using the ISSN register as a way station pointing to the article databases; Rob Cameron describes a model based on the Web-based bibp protocol for making persistent references to e-journals and e-books; and Michael Miyazaki talks about efforts at Cambridge Scientific Abstracts to provide links between bibliographic records and the corresponding full-text e-resources. Next, Nicole Hennig provides a detailed overview of the development of "Vera," the MIT Libraries' FileMaker-backed interface to journals and databases, and Evelinde Hutzler and Gerald Schupfner discuss the Elektronische Zeitschriftenbibliothek (Electronic Journals Library), a service offering user-friendly access to a large number of e-journals, both free and licensed, within a single user interface. Finally, David King describes the types of access the Kansas City Public Library provides for electronic serials and other continuing resources, showing that both public and academic libraries are reaching many of the same decisions in this area.

In the last section, "Books, Serials, and the Future," Susan Cleyle writes about the other major element of the electronic universe–the e-book–and discusses the basic technology as well as who are the current players in the field, and what the future possibly holds for this resource. In the concluding article, Gerry McKiernan looks not only at the evolution of the electronic journal and the emergence of functionalities that expand and extend it, but also at new forms and formats of scholarly communication likely to arise in the not-so-distant future.

The editors wish to express their sincere gratitude to these authors who, through their time and talent, have made possible this collection detailing the current state of e-serials cataloging.

Jim Cole
Wayne Jones

GENERAL

Crystal Graham, 1952-2000:
A Personal Tribute

Jean L. Hirons

The serials community lost one of its stars with the death of Crystal Graham in August 2000. During the past quarter century, Crystal was involved with every important issue regarding serials, from multiple versions and microforms to format integration, and then to electronic serials and the revision of AACR2. Crystal played a pivotal role in all of these, and she gave generously of her time and energy to the library community. Crystal was the head of the Digital Information and Serials Cataloging Section at the University of California, San Diego (UCSD), where she had worked in various positions since 1986. She had battled a crippling form of arthritis for many years and her courage and determination were an inspiration to all who knew her.

Serials were always her passion. Crystal was a part of CONSER (the Cooperative Online Serials Program) long before I was. Indeed, she was one of the first participants, serving as Cornell's Associate CONSER Project Director from 1977 to 1979. Subsequently, she served as a serials cataloger at New York University from 1979 to 1985. She served as science cataloger and Latin

Jean Hirons is Coordinator of the Cooperative Online Serials Program (CONSER) at the Library of Congress, 101 Independence Avenue SE, Washington, DC 20540-4160.

[Haworth co-indexing entry note]: "Crystal Graham, 1952-2000: A Personal Tribute." Hirons, Jean L. Co-published simultaneously in *The Serials Librarian* (The Haworth Information Press, an imprint of The Haworth Press, Inc.) Vol. 41, No. 3/4, 2002, pp. 1-6; and: *E-Serials Cataloging: Access to Continuing and Integrating Resources via the Catalog and the Web* (ed: Jim Cole, and Wayne Jones) The Haworth Information Press, an imprint of The Haworth Press, Inc., 2002, pp. 1-6. Single or multiple copies of this article are available for a fee from The Haworth Document Delivery Service [1-800-HAWORTH, 9:00 a.m. - 5:00 p.m. (EST). E-mail address: getinfo@haworthpressinc.com].

1

American studies cataloger at UCSD, finally returning to serials in 1996. I remember her telling me how happy she was.

Crystal will be well remembered for her efforts to find pragmatic solutions to the still-troublesome area of multiple versions. She began her efforts when versions were limited to microforms and print. She was a speaker and participant at the Airlie House conference on multiple versions in 1989 and during that time served as a Visiting Program Officer for the Association of Research Libraries. She authored ARL's *Guidelines for Bibliographic Records for Preservation Microform Masters* and wrote extensively on the topic. With the emergence of electronic resources, multiple versions took on a whole new dimension. She became a staunch supporter of CONSER's single-record approach and advocated it for the California Digital Library, which UCSD was helping organize.

The integration of the MARC formats, which occurred during the mid-1990s, gave great concern to serialists because of the emphasis on physical format. With the growing proliferation of electronic journals, it was important that the computer file aspects not preclude regular serials processing in local systems. Crystal was instrumental in convincing MARBI and the MARC Network Development and MARC Standards Office content should be primary over carrier and coding was subsequently changed as a result. Crystal lectured extensively on the topic and participated with me in an ALCTS institute, "Serials in the Age of Format Integration."

The growing proliferation and varying forms of electronic resources also pointed out the weaknesses in the *Anglo-American Cataloguing Rules*. Ever the wit, Crystal dubbed resources that are neither monograph nor serial, such as loose-leafs, databases, and Web sites, as "bibliographic hermaphrodites." In 1995, Crystal was invited to give a paper, "What's Wrong with AACR2: The Serials Perspective," at the AACR 2000 preconference to the American Library Association annual meeting. In addition to citing the lack of rules for the above-mentioned "hermaphrodites," Crystal claimed that the rules were also not sufficient for traditional serials as well. This, of course, led to our collaboration in writing and presenting the paper "Issues Related to Seriality" at the Conference on the Principles and Future Development of AACR, held in Toronto, October 1997. Crystal claimed that this was one of the greatest honors of her career.

Another honor came in 1998 when she received the Bowker/Ulrichs Serials Librarianship award for her many contributions to the serials community. Unfortunately, she was too ill to attend ALA and only her immediate colleagues could celebrate with her.

The lists of activities, papers, and honors cannot possibly do Crystal justice. For it was her spirit and drive, her indomitable quest to improve cataloging, and her great sense of humor that made her so special. Even when she was facing great pain or recovering from yet another operation, Crystal was there, arguing her points, making us all listen. And she was heard. Her work will benefit the library community for many years to come. She will long be remembered.

PUBLICATIONS AND PRESENTATIONS BY CRYSTAL GRAHAM, 1977-1997

The following list of articles and speeches was compiled by Crystal.

"JSC Conference Addresses Seriality," with Jean Hirons and Sara Shatford Layne. *CONSERline* 11 (Dec. 1977). Available online: http://lcweb.loc.gov/acq/conser/consln11.html

"Cataloging of the Electronic Kind," with Rebecca Culbertson. OCLC Pacific Workshop, Rancho Cucamonga, Calif., Nov. 21, 1997. Bibliography available on the Internet: http://tpot.ucsd.edu/Cataloging/Formats/ebibliography.html

"Issues Related to Seriality," with Jean Hirons. In *The Principles and Future of AACR: Proceedings of the International Conference on the Principles and Future Development of AACR, Toronto, Ontario, Canada, October 23-25, 1997*, ed. by Jean Weihs (Chicago: American Library Association, 1998), 180-212.

"Redefining Seriality: A Cataloger's Perspective." Paper presented at the Association for Library Collections & Technical Services Serials Section Program "At Issue: Dimensions of Seriality in an Electronic World," June 29, 1997, San Francisco, Calif.

"UC San Diego Uses New CONSER Guidelines to Enhance CONSER Records." *CONSERline* 9 (Jan. 1997). Available online: http://lcweb.loc.gov/acq/conser/consln9.html

"ISSN Addition Project Completed at UCSD," with Julia Blixrud. *SISAC News* 44 (winter 1996/spring 1997): 26-27.

Review of: *The John Foster Dulles Oral History Collection. Microform and Imaging Review* 25:4 (fall 1996): 175-176.

"Format Integration and Serials Cataloging." Presentation to the North American Serials Interest Group, Albuquerque, N.M., June 21, 1996. Judith Johnson, reporter. Recorded in *The Serials Librarian* 31:1/2 (1997): 279-287.

"Hermaphrodites & Herrings," with Rebecca Ringler. In "Old Wine in New Bottles? Defining Electronic Serials," edited by Ellen Finnie Duranceau. *Serials Review* 22, no. 1 (spring 1996): 73-76.

"Preservation Microfilming and Bibliographic Control." Chapter 5 of *Preservation Microfilming: A Guide for Librarians and Archivists*, ed. by Lisa L. Fox (Chicago: American Library Association, 1996), 225-262.

Review of: **Mann, Thomas.** *Library Research Models: A Guide to Classification, Cataloging, and Computers. The Serials Librarian* 27, no. 4 (1995): 100-103.

"Special Topics in Cataloging: Format Integration," with Kathryn Glennan and Joy Wanden (OCLC Pacific training materials), February 1996. A booklet prepared in conjunction with OCLC Pacific programs on format integration.

"Serials Computer Files Under Format Integration," with Rebecca Ringler. Position paper submitted to the CONSER Task Force on Electronic Resources. Available online at: http://tpot.ucsd.edu/Cataloging/Current/cg1.html

"Format Integration." Presentation to the Third Greater San Diego Paraprofessional Development Workshop, August 11, 1995, California State University, San Marcos, Calif.

"What's Wrong with AACR2: A Serials Perspective." In *The Future of the Descriptive Cataloging Rules: Papers from the ALCTS Preconference, AACR2000, American Library Association Annual Conference, Chicago, June 22, 1995*, ed. by Brian E. C. Schottlaender (Chicago: American Library Association, 1998), 66-83.

"Commonsense Cataloging for Your Local System." Presentations at the Association for Library Collections & Technical Services Institutes on Serials Cataloging in the Age of Format Integration, Atlanta, Ga., April 8, 1995, and San Francisco, Calif., October 7, 1995.

Guidelines for Bibliographic Description of Reproductions. Prepared by the ALA Committee on Cataloging: Description and Access, Multiple Versions Task Force. Bruce Chr. Johnson, principal editor. Chicago: American

Library Association, 1995. [Crystal served as the ALCTS Reproduction of Library Materials Section's representative to the task force.]

"Microforms," with Cecilia Botero, Ruth Haas, and Jean Hirons. Module 32 of *CONSER Cataloging Manual*, ed. by Jean Hirons. Washington, DC: Library of Congress, Cataloging Distribution Service, 1994.

"Multiple Versions & Format Integration." Presentation at a workshop on Computer Files Cataloging, Heads of Cataloging, California State University Southern Campuses, Fullerton, Calif., Oct. 22, 1993.

"Microform Reproductions and Multiple Versions: U.S. Cataloging Policy and Proposed Changes," in *Serials Cataloging II: Modern Perspectives and International Developments*, ed. by Jim E. Cole and James W. Williams (New York: The Haworth Press, Inc., 1992), 213-234. (Also published as *The Serials Librarian* 22, no. 1-2 (1992): 213-234.)

"Bibliographic Control of Microforms: A Bibliography of Reports and Articles." *Microform Review* 20, no. 3 (summer 1991): 106-111.

"Issues in Microform Cataloging." Paper presented at the Seminar on the Acquisition of Latin American Library Materials, San Diego, June 5, 1991 and published as "Microform Cataloging: Current Issues and Selected Bibliography," in *Latin American Studies into the Twenty-First Century: New Focus, New Formats, New Challenges: Papers of the Thirty-Sixth Annual Meeting of the Seminar on the Acquisition of Latin American Library Materials, University of California, San Diego and San Diego University, San Diego, California, June 1-6, 1991* (Albuquerque, N.M.: SALAM Secretariat, General Library, University of New Mexico, 1993), 393-407.

Association of Research Libraries Guidelines for Bibliographic Records for Preservation Microform Masters. Washington, DC: Association of Research Libraries, 1990. Reprinted in *Microform Review* 21, no. 2 (spring 1992): 67-73, and as Appendix E of *Preservation Microfilming* (Chicago: American Library Association, 1996), 335-345.

"Microform Cataloging Rules, Formats, and Practices." Paper presented at the Preconference on Bibliographic Control of Microforms, Chicago, Ill., June 22, 1990.

"Definition and Scope of Multiple Versions." Paper presented at the Multiple Versions Forum, Airlie, Va., Dec. 6, 1989, and published in *Cataloging & Classification Quarterly* 11: no. 2 (1990): 5-32.

"Guidelines for Cataloging Microform Masters (Serials)." *RTSD Newsletter* 14:6 (1989): 53-54.

"ARL Guidelines for Bibliographic Control of Microform Masters." Presentation to California Library Association, Technical Services Chapter, Cerritos, Calif., Sept. 18, 1989.

"Direct vs. Indirect Local Subdivision: Pros and Cons and Impact on Local Databases." Presentation to the California Library Association, Technical Services Chapter, Cataloging Discussion Group, Spring Meeting, Pomona, Calif., April 16, 1987.

"Rethinking National Policy for Cataloging Microform Reproductions." *Cataloging & Classification Quarterly* 6, no. 4 (summer 1986): 69-83.

Review of: **Whiffen, Jean.** *Union Catalogues of Serials. Information Technology and Libraries* 3, no. 2 (June 1984): 220-221. Reprinted in *Newsletter of the IFLA Section on Serials Publications* 4 (Nov. 1984).

"Serials Cataloging on RLIN and OCLC: A Comparison." Paper presented at the American Library Association, Copy Cataloging Discussion Group, Philadelphia, Pa., July 10, 1982. Published in "Copy Cataloging of Serials," *The Serials Librarian* 8, no. 2 (winter 1983): 32-35.

Latin American Studies Research Guide, with Jean Hawkins Coffin. Bloomington, Ind.: Latin American Studies Program, Indiana University, 1977. (Latin American Studies Working Paper; no. 8). 139 pp.

E-Serials Cataloging in the 1990s:
A Review of the Literature

Ann Copeland

SUMMARY. The published literature specific to electronic serials cataloging over the decade of the 1990s and the work of CONSER, MARBI, the ALCTS Committee to Study Serials Cataloging, and others were reviewed to identify issues and developments. The proliferation and the changing nature of e-serials were challenges to catalogers throughout the period examined. Policies and procedures were offered by CONSER and its members. Multiple versions, revising AACR2, metadata, and aggregator databases were among the issues actively discussed at the close of the decade. *[Article copies available for a fee from The Haworth Document Delivery Service: 1-800-HAWORTH. E-mail address: <getinfo@haworthpressinc.com> Website: <http://www.HaworthPress.com> © 2002 by The Haworth Press, Inc. All rights reserved.]*

KEYWORDS. Electronic serials, serials cataloging

With the explosion of electronic journal publications over the past decade, serials catalogers have had to adapt to new and varied forms and devise strategies and policies for coping with them. In the first half of the nineties, the cata-

---

Ann Copeland is Special Collections Cataloging Librarian at Penn State University, State College, PA (E-mail: auc1@psu.edu). She was formerly Serials Team Leader at the University of Illinois, Urbana-Champaign.

[Haworth co-indexing entry note]: "E-Serials Cataloging in the 1990s: A Review of the Literature." Copeland, Ann. Co-published simultaneously in *The Serials Librarian* (The Haworth Information Press, an imprint of The Haworth Press, Inc.) Vol. 41, No. 3/4, 2002, pp. 7-29; and: *E-Serials Cataloging: Access to Continuing and Integrating Resources via the Catalog and the Web* (ed: Jim Cole, and Wayne Jones) The Haworth Information Press, an imprint of The Haworth Press, Inc., 2002, pp. 7-29. Single or multiple copies of this article are available for a fee from The Haworth Document Delivery Service [1-800-HAWORTH, 9:00 a.m. - 5:00 p.m. (EST). E-mail address: getinfo@haworthpressinc.com].

loging of electronic journals had only emerged as a new topic in the literature.[1] By the latter half of the decade, numerous articles were written not only on how to catalog e-serials, but also on numerous related issues, chief among them: why catalog e-serials, multiple versions, aggregator databases, MARBI discussions, seriality, inadequacy of AACR2 for electronic resources, harmonization, metadata, tools and training. At the close of the decade, the cataloging for e-serials was noted to be "as unsettled as the terminology" with "a kind of limbo in the serials cataloging universe where it is generally recognized that new policies (and changes to existing ones) are necessary, but they are still some time away . . . this is a very busy and exciting time."[2]

Judging by the titles of articles in recent years, such as "Keeping the Jell-O Nailed to the Wall,"[3] and "Taming the Octopus,"[4] it is clear that librarians have felt challenged by managing such intangible forms as e-journals. Titles like "A Square Peg in a Round Hole"[5] and "Old Wine in New Bottles?"[6] further reveal the frustration of catalogers over the difficulties posed by applying a static cataloging code to dynamic electronic forms. This review surveys these and other concerns and activities of the serials cataloging community relating to the changing nature of e-serials publishing through the decade.

EARLY DAYS

Jim Williams's fine article reviewing serials cataloging literature from 1991-1996[7] covers the period during which the cataloging of electronic journals first emerged as a topic in the literature. He notes that new discussion groups were created, and committees were organized within ALA and other task forces charged. The *CONSER Cataloging Manual* Chapter 31 on Remote Access Computer File Serials[8] and the addition of field 856 for the URL in MARC greatly aided catalogers in 1994. Catalogers in 1993 had complained about rules being "in a state of flux,"[9] having to choose between cataloging an e-journal with the computer file format or with the serial format, the lack of interpretations in AACR2, frustration with terminology and rapidly changing computer technology. Early advice urged "creativity on the part of the cataloger."[10]

"WE NEED THOSE E-SERIAL RECORDS"[11]

In Priscilla Caplan's 1996 article, "U-R Stars: Standards for Controlling Internet Resources," she remarks that since her earlier talk at the 8th NASIG annual conference, "It has been very gratifying to see the level of discourse rise from 'why would anyone want to catalog this stuff?' " to debating practice.[12] Indeed, during the mid-1990s, numerous articles were written in the literature on the question of "Why catalog?" In 1994, Diane Vizine-Goetz made a presentation at the Seminar on Cataloging Digital Documents[13] in which she highlighted the benefits, obstacles and progress made on cataloging remotely accessible resources. Among the benefits: controlled access points and indexing vocabularies, standardized description, and the MARC record structure which facilitates indexing, retrieval and exchange of bibliographic data. Among the obstacles: impermanence, preservation, instability, location, versions, services, problems in authentication and attribution.[14] Looking back at the decade, Vinh-The Lam traced the decade-long history of librarians' efforts to effectively answer the "Why, What, How?" questions pertaining to cataloging Internet resources.[15] Kristin Gerhard looked at these same questions in terms of an individual institution's (Iowa State University) practice and policy.[16]

Regarding electronic serials specifically, a collection of articles in a 1995 "Balance Point" column of *Serials Review* entitled "Cataloging Remote-Access Electronic Serials: Rethinking the Role of the OPAC," presented five varying perspectives on the issue of why and what to catalog.[17] Martha Hruska noted that catalogers who know their mission is to provide quality access in the OPAC wonder, "So why the question? Why not 'just do it?'[18] Time, labor supply and policy are some of the answers given in the negative. Wayne Jones emphatically called for cataloging in "We Need Those E-Serial Records,"[19] arguing that proliferation of e-serials will result in the "likely co-existence of printed and electronic serials" and that "without OPAC records the loss of access for library users is terrible."[20] Regina Reynolds cautioned about changing the clarity of the "old" catalog by including records for items "pointed to" and suggested alternatives for cataloging.[21] Eric Lease Morgan argued that we should extend our concept of the OPAC from inventory list to finding aid,[22] and Alison Mook Sleeman[23] reviewed events in 1994 as evidence that cataloging electronic materials is "an idea whose time has come."[24]

Janet Swan Hill wrote about remotely accessible electronic information resources using the metaphor of the three blind men and the elephant, calling these materials the "newest of cataloging's elephants": one can't see the entire beast, it may move or change following description, and the person who described it may have no control or ownership of it.[25] Regardless of these obstacles, Hill emphatically affirms our obligation to catalog these beasts: "library users more and more expect to have access to these resources, so the option of leaving them undescribed and thus excluding them from the catalog is becoming indefensible."[26] In looking at how catalogers have dealt with other similar challenges in the past, including cataloging other things not owned, seen, or touched, Hill concludes that "the trend is against exclusion": "No matter how understandable it may be, however, resistance to adding new types of information to the catalog will almost certainly be seen as inadequacy, inflexibility, or obstructionism in the cataloging department."[27]

Over against the criticisms–too expensive to catalog fully, too few staff resources for so many electronic resources, database maintenance and dead URLs in the catalog[28]–are the many advantages of having access through the catalog. CONSER affirms "the need of a library to record in one place–the catalog–all of the materials that are available to its users, regardless of their format."[29] Landesman hailed the advantages of the "hook to holdings" through citation sources facilitated by having holdings in the catalog.[30] Steve Shadle pointed out that cataloging e-journals is "consistent with the long-standing premise that a library's catalog should provide access to materials regardless of their format. Adding Web-based serials allows the Web OPAC to function as an Internet gateway offering users the full range of access points, subject analysis and search functionality available for other types of materials."[31] Erik Jul, who wrote several articles over the decade on OCLC's initiatives to catalog e-resources, lists the typical arguments against cataloging–nothing valuable on the Internet, instability warrants against it, and cataloging is too labor intensive/expensive–but states these should not preclude cataloging: "Big mistakes will be thinking that cataloging is the answer, and thinking that it is not."[32]

It is CONSER's philosophy that the library community should take the lead in organizing and providing pathways to information on electronic networks all over the world. Internet publishers can't provide the precision of a controlled vocabulary or the variety of search capabilities that a MARC cataloging record in an online catalog can.[33] Further, while cataloging locally points to resources for a particular community, "those same records stored in a national database can also provide universal access to electronic resources of interest to the larger research and information community."[34]

The alternatives to cataloging e-serials were examined in the literature as well. Ford and Harter in "The Downside of Scholarly Electronic Publishing: Problems in Accessing Electronic Journals through Online Directories and Catalogs" examined four online directories and two online union catalogs (OCLC and RLIN).[35] They concluded that directories and catalogs serve different functions. Directories provide few but working URLs, while catalogs provide many more URLs and entries to a work, but there is a greater chance that they will not work.[36] Luise Hoffman and Ronald M. Schmidt wrote of the problems with linking from a Web home page, noting the "sheer number of serials involved" that would need "presentation within a subject tree organized according to the library's classification scheme," and the amount of effort required to guide patrons to the home pages from outside the OPAC.[37] Such an effort, combined with the fact that if items were not in the OPAC they probably would not be included in printed catalogs or current awareness lists, advised against using this approach.[38] Comparing a typical library's practice of arranging print journals in broad subject categories alphabetically, Ann Schaffner suggested creating Web pages for electronic journals that would be organized similarly, a list with broad subject classification to facilitate electronic browsing.[39] She noted that in the future the subject coding for such Web pages could be created from cataloging records.[40]

From the government documents perspective, alternatives to cataloging noted included relying on specialized Websites maintained by others, offering printed lists of Websites, and creating one's own Website.[41] However, each of these was reported to have problems for documents research. In the case of the first, sites would not be tailored to users of the local collection. With one's own Website, constant updating and URL checking, and the fact that users of the catalog would fail to consult the site, were negatives.[42] Recognizing that "many studies have shown that cataloged document collections get used more than uncataloged ones" and that if cataloged, individual issues can be checked in, Treff-Gangler and MacArthur affirmed a combination of methods and found cataloging of electronic government documents to be "desirable and useful."[43]

MULTIPLE VERSIONS

In general, serials catalogers writing in the literature over the decade assumed Landesman's "just do it!" philosophy.[44] With the marked rise in e-journal publishing mid-decade, discussions and policy-making moved into high gear. CONSER queried e-mail discussion lists in early 1995 concerning the desirability of creating one record that would represent all formats or separate records for formats that were significantly different.[45] Jean Hirons, Acting CONSER Coordinator, detailed her experience surveying the cataloging community through the OCLC Internet Cataloging Project's discussion list InterCat, CONSERLST and SERIALST asking: Should we really have separate records for the same title in different online versions?[46] Subsequently CONSER made the decision to allow the use of a single record, usually for the print title, that would note the existence of additional versions.

Hirons explained the rationale of taking such a big step in a speech before NASIG: e-versions are growing and resources shrinking, CONSER did not want to repeat the path of microforms (patrons care little about publishing details of the facsimile version), and public services staff made it clear that multiple records for physical versions of the same work are not user friendly.[47]

Hirons made it very clear what a single record is and isn't: it is not a composite record–there are no MARC 007's describing electronic characteristics in a single record for the print title, and no multiple ISSNs. The only data elements added to the record would be: notes about the existence of the electronic version in the 530 field (additional physical versions note); a different title would go in the 730 field; access to the electronic serial would be provided via the 856 field.[48]

While CONSER would favor using separate records in the national databases to reflect the bibliographic universe, the single-record approach served the local needs for an intelligible single display of holdings and the desire to do more with less.[49] The response from CONSER members was very appreciative. In one article, catalogers at the University of Texas at Austin expressed gratitude at having an allowable alternative, given pressure from their public services faculty.[50] Indeed, the following caption from an article by Jim Holmes explains the prevailing attitude at UT: "Public Services response: We don't care for you or your rules. We want what we want and that is what the public wants. Don't clutter the catalog with lots of records."[51] Holmes noted that having lobbied hard to include electronic journals in the catalog, Technical Services staff embraced the single-record approach as an appropriate response "to the desire of Public Services staff to have succinct and clear bibliographic search results and displays in the catalog."[52]

Burnett and TerHaar also described public services concerns at the University of Michigan's University Library in "Can I Get It or Not? A Public Services View of Cataloging Electronic Journals."[53] Detailing a series of illustrations from their OPAC, they highlighted problematic content and holdings information for multiple versions, voicing the opinion that CONSER has responded to user needs with the single-record option and that as things change they should continue to do so. Thomas A. Downing, discussing the Federal Depository Library Program (FDLP), praised the usefulness of the single-record option which had allowed the FDLP to be "the leading contributor of URL data to existing records."[54] The government documents community uses the single record for three versions–print, microform and electronic–of a title.

To further examine the interim guidelines for a single-record approach, CONSER established a Working Group in 1999.[55] The Working Group ultimately recommended that it be accepted as standard practice, and provided guidance for its use.[56] Revisions were incorporated into the *CONSER Editing Guide*[57] and *CONSER Cataloging Manual*, Update Fall 2000.[58] The ongoing discussions of the interim policy to keep the single-record policy were recorded by the ALCTS Serials Section Committee to Study Serials Cataloging.[59] Jeanne Baker wrote a list of reasons for which the single-record approach might not be the best approach, including the appropriateness of using a print cataloging record with information added about the e-serial when a library doesn't own the print; the question of whether a holdings symbol should be added to a print record when the library only owns the electronic version; ease of maintenance and problems with journals when manifestations are not exact reproductions.[60] Many libraries created policy decisions and posted them on the Web.[61]

Having removed the provisional status of the "Interim Guidelines" for multiple-format versions, the proliferation of reproductions and electronic versions of serials by multiple publishers, producers and aggregators has resulted in another CONSER interim policy for multiple distributors of electronic text. In the fall 2000 update to Module 31 of the *CCM*, sections 31.3.4 and 31.3.5 were completely rewritten to include not only the policy but "Guidelines for specific fields in separate online serial records for aggregator versions."[62] The work of a PCC task force formed in May 2000 will result in further recommendations on long-term policies on the matter of multiple manifestations of electronic resources.[63]

That aggregators are a specific concern within the single-record discussion was clear in the literature as well. Wayne Jones began "E-SCape: a Column About E-Serials Cataloging" in *The Serials Librarian* with the theme of "E-Packages."[64] Jones observed that they have volatile content, titles come and go as publisher agreements change, and that this impacts decisions to catalog. Often it is hard to tell if they are a "monographic agglomeration–a database–of serial titles or a simple website interface to those titles." Cataloging decisions are greatly impacted if it is a question of creating 1 or 700 records. Further, holdings updates may be confined to a recent issue or back issues.[65] Yumin Jiang presented a workshop at NASIG on her experience at Cornell, cataloging titles in *ProQuest Direct* by employing the single-record approach with heavy use of macros to add information about holdings.[66] Jiang recommended that vendors provide detailed information about title and holdings coverage, that before embarking on a project libraries investigate all access options and staff resources, and that each aggregator collection be considered individually. Jeanne Baker, member of the PCC Task Group on Journals in Aggregator Databases,[67] spoke at NASIG about the work of the task force and its survey to libraries concerning the expressed interest in vendor-supplied record sets. An expanded task group assumed responsibility for recommending vendor-record content and for communicating specs to appropriate vendors, and worked with EBSCO to mount a test file.[68]

USMARC FORMAT AND MARBI:
DEVELOPMENTS OVER THE DECADE

With format integration mid-decade, catalogers now had one integrated bibliographic format and standard. Practically speaking, this meant that cataloging decisions were no longer restricted to format-specific workforms in USMARC. As Crystal Graham noted, because of format integration "all elements of the bibliographic description can be recorded without restriction . . . a primary material type is recorded in the 008 field, with additional characteristics recorded in the 006 field."[69] For electronic serials, this meant coding for computer file, with all elements of the 008 relating to the computer file characteristics (character positions 18-34); seriality would then be described using the 006 of the MARC format: "the basic procedure is that the cataloguer chooses a code for leader/6, then chooses the appropriate 008 corresponding to the leader/6 code, and finally chooses the 006 (or 006s) which correspond to the additional characteristics of the item."[70] The 006 to describe the file's serial characteristics corresponds to the character positions 18-34 for a serial 008.

A further definition for cataloging computer file serials came in June 1997 when MARBI redefined leader/06 code "m" and limited its usage. At the time of format integration, type "m" for computer file was defined as:

> Code m indicates that the content of the record is for a body of information encoded in a manner which allows it to be processed by a computer. The information in the computer file may be numeric or textual data, computer software, or a combination of these types. Although a file may be stored on a variety of media (such as magnetic tape or disk, punched cards, or optical character recognition font documents), the file itself is independent of the medium on which it is stored.[71]

MARBI's Discussion Paper No. 97, "Coding Digital Items in Leader/06 (Type of Record) in the USMARC Bibliographic Format,"[72] proposed a change in this definition. It notes that any digitized item would be coded as a computer file, regardless of its digitized type, and poses the question: "Does the GMD and the existence of a computer file 006 suffice to determine what is the actual physical form of the item? For instance, if the Leader/06 were coded 'e' for cartographic material and there is a field 006 for computer file, could one determine whether this record represents a paper map with accompanying computer disk or a computer file that displays maps?"[73] The paper recommends coding for content rather than carrier in the case of computer files. The new definition for "m" was implemented in OCLC in March 1998. The narrower use of this code in USMARC and MARC 21 has meant that almost all records for electronic serials that are textual in nature have code "a" for "language material" in leader/06, a serial 008 field, and a computer file 006 field.[74]

Additionally, code "s" for "electronic" in the serial 008 was implemented in spring 2000 for "form of item" (008/23) and "form of original item" (008/22).[75] This allows the coding of records to indicate the original as a textual material that exists in electronic form, as "an item intended for manipulation by computer": It is used in the same way that codes for microfilm and microfiche are currently used in those 008 bytes. The current practice for coding records for textual electronic serials is:

    008/22 (Form of item):   s
    008/23 (Form of original):   s
    006/00 (Form of material):   m

CONSER has added a page on its Website to help sort out the relationships of 006, 007 and 008 "m" and form "s."[76]

Each of these adaptations by USMARC and MARC 21 has greatly aided the cataloger's ability to describe the textual content, serial characteristics, and the electronic nature of the item. The USMARC Advisory Group also discussed URLs throughout the decade. Shadle and Hawkins noted the numerous MARC fields that could reasonably contain a URL (037 Source of Acquisition, 270 Primary Address, 307 Hours, and 506 Restrictions on Access Note) and a 538 Systems Details Note.[77]

MARBI's Discussion Paper No. 87, "Addition of Subfield $1 for Linking Entry Fields 76X-78X in the USMARC Bibliographic Format,"[78] responded to requests to add URLs to linking fields in the negative, noting that the changeable nature of URLs makes revision extremely difficult in 856's, let alone in linking entry fields. However, another proposal resurfaced in 1998 in Discussion Paper No. 112, "Defining URL/URN Subfields in Fields Other Than Field 856 in the MARC Bibliographic/Holdings Formats."[79] This paper took up the expressed need for the definition of a URL subfield in the following fields:

    Field 037 (Source of Acquisition)
    Field 583 (Action Note)

The Network Development and MARC Standards Office of Library of Congress issued "Guidelines for the Use of Field 856 Revised August 1999"[80] based on new definitions for subfields in the 856 and the concatenation of previously used subfield u's.

CSB'S AND LCRI'S

There was very little change in the LCRIs for electronic serials through the decade. In the chapter for serials, rule 12.7B3 Source of Title Proper recorded:

> LC/CONSER practice: For electronic serials issued remotely, in addition to providing the source of the title proper (cf. AACR2 9.1B2), give also, in parentheses, the date the title was viewed: 500 ## $a Title from title screen (viewed on July 18, 1997).[81]

Cataloging Service Bulletin #66 (fall 1994) added computer files to 25.5B–conflict resolution for serials. Perhaps the biggest change to occur was the decision by LC to expand LCRI 1.11A to include electronic manifestations as reproductions, announced in *Cataloging Service Bulletin* #89 (summer 2000, p. 12). The revised LCRI includes the following directions for cataloging an electronic journal considered to be a reproduction: transcribe for the original, use GMD for the format of the reproduction, use reproduction information in 533 field, use a physical description fixed field (007) for elements relating to the reproduction, and, for electronic reproductions, also supply information about the electronic location and access (856).[82] CONSER decided *not* to follow this LCRI, which treats some electronic serials as reproductions, because "once a serial is available in an online version, the publisher may go back and 'reproduce' back issues as well. Thus, when cataloging such titles, making distinctions between 'versions' and 'reproductions' is generally not practical."[83]

SERIALITY AND AACR2

In the latter years of the decade, there was much discussion in the literature about the inadequacy of AACR2 to describe electronic serials and, indeed, electronic resources generally.[84] With electronic manifestations taking on new and unusual characteristics, adhering to cardinal AACR2 rules became problematic. Two discussions were taking place in the literature and overlapped organically: how to work with the current codes and standards to describe electronic serials given their inadequacies, and how to revise the code to address the reality of continuing and integrating electronic resources.

AACR2 and MARC

The OCLC Research Project in 1991-1992, which investigated the nature of electronic textual information on the Internet and the feasibility of creating records using MARC and AACR2, concluded that with a few changes the

USMARC for Computer Files Format and Chapter 9 of AACR2 would work; guidelines for modifications were forwarded to CC:DA.[85] The implementation of the 856 field was key in making these work. Quickly the limitations of the 856 as defined were apparent to authors like Landesman: "The values defined in the first indicator of the 856 field for the access method are: Email, FTP, Remote login (Telnet), and 'Method specified in subfield 2'–i.e., 'Other.' The access methods defined do not represent the majority of the resources we are cataloging today."[86]

Shadle and Hawkins gave a workshop at NASIG on how to apply current rules to describe the transitory aspects of remote-access titles, advising catalogers to use the most stable address as the main URL, adding additional URLs to point to other levels and advising liberal use of 246 (varying form of title).[87] Shadle noted that CONSER libraries keep the 538 (Systems Details Note) as general as possible because of the changeable nature of online access systems; the wording from the CC:DA Task Force on Cataloging Internet Resources prefers "Mode of access: Internet <URL> ."[88]

Shadle suggested that there are notes that can be added to help identify such resources in the catalog, such as "516 Electronic journal available in ASCII, Acrobat and Post Script file formats."[89] He also noted the addition of two newly approved ISBD(ER) Specific Material Designations–"computer journal" and "computer newsletter"–that will hopefully be eventually used in the Computer File Characteristics field (USMARC 256).[90] Landesman offered suggestions for an expanded list of descriptors of file characteristics to include terms such as "electronic journal" and "bibliographic database," and a more accurate GMD than the only one authorized for electronic resources, "computer file"–a term that does "not necessarily evoke the nature of what we are cataloging . . . nor represent the majority of the resources cataloged today."[91] CONSER, however, recommended: "In lieu of a commonly accepted GMD, continue to use [computer file]."[92]

Another criticism of AACR2 for computer files was that inadequate terminology affects not only description, but identification and retrieval in a catalog. Shadle noted that there are many clues in the description indicating that something is an electronic journal: "MARC 516, 007, GMD, 530 (physical format), 130 (Online) but these 'hooks' are not access points."[93] Several catalogers noted the restrictiveness of LCSH which doesn't allow a specific form subdivision, "–Electronic journals," as MESH does: "SCM H 1580.5 (Electronic serials) and H 1520 (Databases) basically allow form subdivision '–Periodicals' and '–Databases' but certain exceptions make application confusing."[94]

Shadle conducted a survey on local practice and found that of 108 responses, most libraries identified strategies to provide identification and retrieval.[95] They employed the following techniques: local call numbers to collocate e-journals; a generic phrase or URL as a location for "shelf" search; e-journal package as call number (gives the example PROJECT MUSE); routine assignment of a qualifying term in a 130 uniform title; descriptive notes that would be found in keyword searches.[96] Carroll Davis concluded that this is the natural time to "study and redefine categories we need since the context of forms has changed so substantially over the past few years."[97]

Seriality

As serials change so much in the Web environment they have been noted in the literature as "behaving in new and different ways, to the point where Crystal Graham has jokingly characterized electronic serials as 'serials on drugs.'"[98] Often e-serials are updated with new articles and new titles, losing traces of the original altogether. Versions can change from one viewing to another and lose their "serial" properties of successive issuance and numeric designation in the process. Then, according to AACR2, they need to be cataloged as databases. Similar problems deriving from the way in which the new formats repackage and bundle information have resulted in a fundamental reexamination of AACR2 definition of seriality.

Mid-decade, four authors contributed to a "Balance Point" article for the *Serials Review* describing particular views on "whether electronic serials are old wine in new bottles, or whether they are *new* wine in new bottles."[99] Erik Jul looked at several "serials" in the OCLC InterCat catalog and at the ways they have been "Freed from the physical limitation of print on paper,"[100] and suggested "letting go of chronology and enumeration." Marilyn Geller examined the permutations of several online serials and how they challenge AACR2 definitions.[101] Crystal Graham and Rebecca Ringler proposed adding a new chapter to AACR2 for such bibliographic "hermaphrodites"[102] and provided specific examples of how MARC cataloging could work. Ed Jones argued for keeping the current definition of serial and applying it to e-serials until it is no longer possible.[103]

Les Hawkins published an annotated list of WWW serials and tracked specific instances confronted in cataloging when articles are added on a continuous basis, titles and designs change, and print is replaced entirely by an electronic version.[104] Shadle published "A Square Peg in a Round Hole: Applying AACR2 to Electronic Journals," which presented strategies used by the serials cataloging community to address the inadequacies of AACR2. In this article he reviewed developments in cataloging for Internet resources and noted inherent differences in these items: they are often organized in distributed files or databases, they are mutable, they don't follow the same standards for display of bibliographic information and they often have additional functionality.[105] At the close of his paper he refers the reader to "Issues Related to Seriality," a paper written by Jean Hirons and Crystal Graham for the International Conference on the Principles and Future Development of AACR in Toronto in 1997. That paper prompted the Joint Steering Committee for Revision of AACR (JSC) to charge Hirons and CONSER with establishing rule revisions, and began the momentum for changing the code now in full swing.

Four working groups were set up to work on aspects of this charge[106] and over the course of their work and much feedback, Hirons reported that people commented that it would not work for various kinds of materials: "A major problem was the reliance on a distinction between publications that are intended to continue indefinitely and those that are not, and this may not always be a reasonable, or even possible, distinction to make."[107] Reynolds and Hirons then went back to a broader concept of "ongoing publications"–Model C–in which the "bibliographic universe" consisted now of "monographic entities" and "ongoing entities," each subdivided further. In this model, Graham and Ringler's "hermaphrodites"–materials that are not truly monographic and not truly serial–are acknowledged as having a broad potential for change. The model recognizes seriality and accommodates "integrating entities."[108]

In 1999 Hirons submitted her report, *Revising AACR2 to Accommodate Seriality: Report to the Joint Steering Committee for Revision of AACR*[109] and released it for worldwide review. This was hailed by Wayne Jones to be the most important recent initiative in e-serials cataloging; although not only about e-serials, "to some extent it can be said to have been inspired by the urgent need for the cataloging rules to address the inadequate provisions in the rules for dealing with the wide array of e-resources of various shapes and sizes that institutions are attempting to catalog."[110] The JSC has mounted "Selected Documents" at its Website.[111] The ALCTS Serials Section Committee to Study Serials Cataloging (CSSC) posts minutes of twice-yearly meetings with discussions at each meeting of the progress of these issues,[112] as does the CONSER Operations Committee Meeting.[113]

Hirons and Les Hawkins led a workshop at NASIG entitled, "AACR2 and You: Revising AACR2 to Accommodate Seriality," describing the goals of the proposed revision, and discussing the four major areas of change:

1. type of publication (defining continuing resources) and defining new rules for new types of resources;
2. the concept of major and minor changes in relation to the need to create a new catalog record;
3. description (chief source and prescribed sources, titles, publishing statement, item described); and
4. organization of the code.[114]

Due to the problem of chief source with electronic journals, the entire online resource would be used in cataloging, "with preference given to titles presented in association with the latest article or issue."[115] Some title changes would be considered minor, others major, and earliest and latest publisher information would be noted. MARBI's "Discussion Paper No. 119" takes up five specific areas of MARC 21 that could potentially be affected by serials-related changes to AACR2.[116] Further discussions are available by both Hirons and Reynolds in the literature.[117]

Hirons, speaking to NASIG,[118] described another major change for electronic serials, the concept of "Incorporating Entry," first proposed by Sara Shatford Layne.[119] "Incorporating Entry" or, as Layne herself called it, "Successive Latest Entry," addresses the problems that arise when a change of title occurs but the publisher puts the current title on all the old issues as well. Under the concept, a new record would be created for a title change but each title "would begin with the first issue of the entire publication, and a note would explain that the new title incorporates the former title."[120] The concept has been compared to analytic entry, "where there exist individual records for parts and a record for the whole."[121] While the NASIG discussion received a mixed response, Hirons maintained that it would have the advantages of maintaining the identity of earlier titles, "would allow us to describe in the national database what happens to the publication over time, but would not need to result in latest entry's problem of having a single record that lives on in the local catalog even when a subscription is discontinued."[122] Further, it addresses the problem of publishers replacing old titles with current titles: "someone looking at the journal for the first time during one of the later titles might think it has carried only that title."[123]

The CC:DA also created a task force on 0.24[124] to discuss the primacy of this rule in AACR2. The rule itself gives primacy to the physical carrier aspect, instructing us to catalog by physical format rather than the content. The content vs. carrier problem has been called the "underlying cause of AACR2's ineffectiveness in serials cataloging . . . identifying the physical form of the item-in-hand as the starting point for description . . . obviously inapplicable to electronic media with no physical format."[125] The CC:DA has recommended that the rule be rewritten so that all aspects of a document are brought out, including its content, carrier, type of publication, and relationship to other expressions of the same work, with no one aspect taking precedence. The approach has been criticized by some,[126] but all agree that the time has come for a change to this rule.

The need for "harmonization" of cataloging codes internationally is of great concern as we close the decade. With the overlapping conversations of the structure of AACR2, issues of seriality, and rule 0.24, there are also reexaminations of international codes. A CC:DA Task Force on Harmonization of ISBD(ER) and AACR2 was charged with a detailed review of the ISBD(ER): International Standard Bibliographic Description for Electronic Resources–specifically, with noting areas in which Part 1 of AACR2 (and Chapter 9 and Appendix D (Glossary) in particular) are not in conformance with the ISBD(ER) and, if necessary, proposing rule revisions to harmonize AACR2 with the ISBD(ER).[127] As Reynolds notes, "In a rare alignment of bibliographic planets, three key standards: AACR2, ISBD (S) and the ISDS Manual are all currently undergoing revision."[128] While the harmonization of standards presents an enormous challenge, Reynolds points out that "harmonization in one or two key areas, such as seriality and extent of the record, would go a long way towards facilitating record sharing and merging of databases."[129]

METADATA

Toward the latter half of the decade, discussions of metadata as an alternative to full MARC cataloging for e-resources, and OCLC's CORC project in particular, swell in the literature. The birth of the *Journal of Internet Cataloging*[130] attests to the growth in the conversation from cataloging e-serials to the various dimensions of cataloging and organizing e-resources on the Web. An ALCTS summary on recent literature on various topics noted that "Writing a summary of the library literature on metadata from 1995 to the present is a little like trying to drink from a fire hose."[131] The explosion of literature on this topic was published in large part on the Web, such as Jessica Milstead's "Metadata: Cataloging by Any Other Name";[132] Erik Jul wrote about new developments in cataloging Internet resources, including serials, as alternatives to AACR2 and MARC, providing the background to the development of the Dublin Core.[133]

The Dublin Core was the subject of a combined issue of the *Journal of Internet Cataloging* with one of the articles specifically addressing "Dublin Core and Serials."[134] Wayne Jones considers that the Dublin Core was developed in the context of a move at the national level toward the core standard for cataloging. He suggests that because of the explosion of "sites or 'knowledge objects' or things to control bibliographically . . . if there is any hope of gaining that control over a reasonably sized subset of them, then the philosophy of the cataloging scheme should be simple and basic."[135] Jones deems that DC is useful as it describes essential information through its fifteen elements. Two issues stand out however: volume/date designation and dates. Jones notes that there is no equivalent of the MARC 362 (Designation) field, and that there are some problems in the way Dublin Core expresses dates in accordance with the ISO standard that uses the form YYYY-MM-DD. Jones offers two areas of concern: the mapping from DC to MARC for Coverage which neglects the 362, and use of ISO standard dates rather than four-digit dates–but asserts that DC serves serials well.[136] MARBI is at the time of this writing looking at "Types of Dates for Electronic Resources in MARC 21 Formats" and specifically those used as qualifiers in the Dublin Core Metadata Element Set and their mapping to MARC 21 in Discussion Paper 2001-DP03.[137]

OTHER TOPICS

Cataloging tools were also a big factor mentioned in the literature. Landesman referred to them in 1997 as "the enabling infrastructure for cataloging electronic resources . . . at last moving from anguished debate into implementation."[138] Included in the list of cataloging tools to develop for electronic resources over the decade are the *CONSER Cataloging Manual, Module 31: Remote Access Computer File Serials* on the Web; the *CONSER Editing Guide*; Nancy Olson's *Cataloging Internet Resources: A Manual and Practical Guide*;[139] *Draft Interim Guidelines for Cataloging Electronic Resources (DCM B19)* from the Library of Congress;[140] two new sections, Q and R, in the second edition of Liheng and Chan's *Serials Cataloging Handbook*;[141] individual libraries' cataloging policies on the Web; and shared records. Several authors anticipated hypertext links between AACR2 and the LCRIs and MARC formats as "creating a virtual cataloging tool that integrates what is now inconveniently dispersed"[142] and which AACR2-e (available in CD-ROM and on the *Catalogers Desktop*) made a reality. The Serials Cataloging Cooperative Training Program (SCCTP) offered training materials which include a chapter on electronic resources.[143] The need for serials cataloging training generally and the growth of same via the SCCTP were mentioned as well as the hope that the future might hold in store "a Web-based course on e-journals and an advanced course that might be called 'special problems in serials cataloging.'"[144]

Case studies occupied much of the literature of e-serials cataloging over the course of the decade. In addition to those noted above and those listed in Williams's essay from the first half of the decade,[145] representatives from the University of Michigan, University of Washington, and Virginia Tech presented their efforts at NASIG.[146] "Eeee!-Serials: Providing Access to Online Serials," a workshop at the 1998 NASIG, discussed original cataloging done at the MIT core level, "a standard just below the CONSER core."[147] At MIT, all serials catalogers participate in cataloging electronic serials and "Serials cataloging has determined that automatic URL checking is the responsibility of the systems office and is not in the purview of cataloging or acquisitions."[148]

Dajin Sun wrote about his experience with a cataloging experiment of Chinese remote-access electronic serials at the University of Pittsburgh and the great number of challenges, such as disappearing titles and the need for dual entries of MARC fields in Chinese and English, that he encountered in this project.[149]

This was a dynamic decade for serials catalogers and serials librarians trying to manage electronic formats. The many problems involved with cataloging these new "beasts" were voiced in the literature only to be answered by CONSER, its members, and numerous other authors carefully thinking through the specifics and big pictures pertaining to serials and catalogs. The swell of activity on both national and international fronts currently makes this a very intriguing and hopeful time.

NOTES

1. Jim Williams, "Serials Cataloging, 1991-1996: A Review," *The Serials Librarian* 32, no. 1-2 (1997): 3-26.

2. Wayne Jones, "E-Packages: E-SCape: A Column About E-Serials Cataloging," *The Serials Librarian* 39, no. 1 (2000): 15-18.

3. Betty Landesman, "Keeping the Jell-O Nailed to the Wall: Maintaining and Managing the Virtual Collection," *The Serials Librarian* 30, no. 3-4 (1997): 137-147.

4. Donnice Cochenour, "Taming the Octopus: Getting a Grip on Electronic Resources," *The Serials Librarian* 38, no. 3-4 (2000): 363-368.

5. Steve Shadle, "A Square Peg in a Round Hole: Applying AACR2 to Electronic Journals," *The Serials Librarian* 33, no.1-2 (1998): 147-166.

6. Ellen Finnie Duranceau, Column Editor, "Old Wine in New Bottles?: Defining Electronic Serials," *Serials Review* 22 (spring 1996): 69-79.

7. Jim Williams, op cit.

8. *CONSER Cataloging Manual: Module 31, Remote Access Computer File Serials*, updated fall 2000 with the assistance of the CONSER E-serial Specialist Group, http://www.loc.gov/acq/conser/module31.html.

9. Pamela Morgan, Recorder, "Cataloging Computer Files That Are Also Serials," *The Serials Librarian* 23, no. 3-4 (1993): 265-266.

10. Margaret Mering, Recorder, "Cataloging Serial Computer Files," *The Serials Librarian* 23, no. 3-4 (1993): 229-230.

11. Wayne Jones, "We Need Those E-Serial Records," *Serials Review* 21 (winter 1995): 74-75.

12. Priscilla Caplan, "U-R-Stars: Standards for Controlling Internet Resources," *The Serials Librarian* 28, no. 3-4 (1996): 238-239.

13. Diane Vizine-Goetz, "Cataloging Internet Resources," in *Proceedings of the Seminar on Cataloging Digital Documents, October 12-14, 1994, University of Virginia Library, Charlottesville and the Library of Congress*, http://lcweb. loc.gov/catdir/ semdigdocs/goetz.html.

14. Ibid.

15. Vinh-The Lam, "Cataloging Internet Resources: Why, What, How," *Cataloging & Classification Quarterly* 29, no. 3 (2000): 49-61.

16. Kristin H. Gerhard, "Cataloging Internet Resources: Practical Issues and Concerns," *The Serials Librarian* 32, no. 1-2 (1997): 123-137.

17. Ellen Finnie Duranceau, Column Editor, "Cataloging Remote-Access Electronic Serials: Rethinking the Role of the OPAC," *Serials Review* 21 (winter 1995): 67-77.

18. Martha Hruska, "Remote Internet Serials in the OPAC?" *Serials Review* 21 (winter 1995): 68-70.

19. Wayne Jones, "We Need," op. cit.

20. Ibid., 75.

21. Regina Reynolds, "Inventory List or Information Gateway? The Role of the Catalog in the Digital Age," *Serials Review* 21 (winter 1995): 75-77.

22. Eric Lease Morgan, "Adding Internet Resources to our OPACS," *Serials Review* 21 (winter 1995): 70-71.

23. Allison Mook Sleeman, "Cataloging Remote Access Electronic Materials," *Serials Review* 21 (winter 1995): 72-74.

24. Ibid., 73.

25. Janet Swan Hill, "The Elephant in the Catalog: Cataloging Animals You Can't See or Touch," *Cataloging & Classification Quarterly* 23, no. 1 (1996): 5-25.

26. Ibid., 5-6.

27. Ibid., 19.

28. Charlotte E. Ford and Stephen P. Harter, "The Downside of Scholarly Electronic Publishing: Problems in Accessing Electronic Journals through Online Directories and Catalogs," *College and Research Libraries* 59, no. 4 (July 1998): 335-346.

29. *CCM*, op. cit.

30. Landesman, op. cit.

31. Steve Shadle, quoted in Patricia French, Recorder, "Cataloging Electronic Serials," *The Serials Librarian* 34, no. 3-4 (1998): 385-389.

32. Erik Jul, "Why Catalog Internet Resources?" *Computers in Libraries* 16, no. 1 (Jan. 1996): 8, 10.

33. *CCM*, op. cit.

34. Ibid.

35. Ford and Harter, op. cit.

36. Ibid.

37. Luise Hoffmann and Ronald M. Schmidt, "The Cataloging of Electronic Serials in the Union Catalog of the North Rhine-Westphalian Library Network," *The Serials Librarian* 35, no. 3 (1999): 123-129.

38. Ibid., 124.

39. Ann Schaffner, "Lost In Cyberspace? Subject Access to Electronic Journals," *Serials Review* 24, no. 2 (summer 1998): 102-103.

40. Ibid.

41. Wayne Jones, Recorder, "Access to Government Serial Information in a Digital Environment," *The Serials Librarian* 36, no. 3-4 (1999): 441-447.

42. Ibid., 444.

43. Ibid., 445.

44. Landesman, op. cit, 141.

45. *CCM*, 31.3.4.

46. Jean Hirons, "One Record or Two? The Online Discussion and the CONSER Interim Approach," *Journal of Internet Cataloging* 1, no. 2 (1997): 3-14.

47. Jean Hirons, "Interim Guidelines for Online Versions," *The Serials Librarian* 34, no. 1-2 (1998): 159-164.

48. Ibid.

49. Ibid.

50. Jim Holmes, "Cataloging E-Journals at the University of Texas at Austin: A Brief Overview," *The Serials Librarian* 34, no.1-2 (1998): 171-176.

51. Ibid., 175.

52. Ibid., 176.

53. Thomas C. Burnett and Linda K. TerHaar, "'Can I Get It or Not?' A Public Services View of Cataloging Electronic Journals," *The Serials Librarian* 34, no. 1-2 (1998): 177-185.

54. Thomas A. Downing, "G.P.O. and the Interim Guidelines," *The Serials Librarian* 34, no. 1-2 (1998):165-170.

55. "CONSER Working Group: Single or Separate Records? What's Appropriate and When," http://wwwtest.Library.ucla.edu/libraries/cataloging/sercat/conserwg/right.htm.

56. "CONSER WG: Single v. Separate Records Draft Report," http://wwwtest. Library.ucla.edu/libraries/cataloging/sercat/conserwg/.

57. *CONSER Editing Guide*, Fall 1999 Update 11, B6: 14.

58. *CCM*, 31.3.4, 31.3.5.

59. ALCTS Serials Section Committee to Study Serials Cataloging, "Minutes of the ALCTS Serials Section Committee to Study Serials Cataloging at the 1999 ALA Midwinter Conference in Philadelphia, PA," http://www.ala.org/alcts/organization/ss/serialscat99mw.html.

60. Jeanne Baker, "Single v. Separate Record Approach: PRO," Feb. 11, 1999, http://wwwtest.library.ucla.edu/libraries/cataloging/sercat/conserwg/baker.htm.

61. "CONSER WG: Bookmark File of Policies," http://wwwtest.library.ucla.edu/libraries/cataloging/sercat/conserwg/right2.htm.

62. *CCM*.

63. "PCC Task Force on Multiple Manifestations of Electronic Resources," http://lcweb.loc.gov/catdir/pcc/tgmuler.html.

64. Wayne Jones, "E-Packages,"18.

65. Ibid.

66. Lynda S. Kresge, "Toward Better Access to Full-Text Aggregator Collections," *The Serials Librarian* 38, no. 3-4 (2000): 291-297.

67. PCC Task Group on Journals in Aggregator Databases, *Interim Report*, http://lcweb.loc.gov/catdir/pcc/aggupdrpt.html.

68. Kresge, op. cit., 294.

69. Crystal Graham, "Hermaphrodites & Herrings," *Serials Review* 22 (spring 1996): 74.

70. Wayne Jones and Young-Hee Queinnec, " Format Integration and Serials Cataloging," *The Serials Librarian* 25, no. 1-2 (1994): 83-95.

71. MARBI, "Discussion Paper No. 92: Change in Definition of Computer File in Leader/06 (Type of Record) in the USMARC Bibliographic Format," http://lcweb.loc.gov/marc/marbi/dp/dp92.html.

72. MARBI. "Discussion Paper No. 97: Coding Digital Items in Leader/06 (Type of Record) in the USMARC Bibliographic Format," http://lcweb.loc.gov/marc/marbi/dp/dp97.html.

73. Ibid.

74. *CCM*.

75. OCLC, *Technical Bulletin 236: OCLC-MARC Bibliographic Update 2000*, http://www.oclc.org/oclc/tb/tb236/.

76. CONSER, "Use of Fixed Fields 006/007/008 and Leader Codes in CONSER Records," http://www.loc.gov/acq/conser/ffuse.html.

77. French, op. cit.

78. MARBI, "Discussion Paper No. 87: Addition of Subfield $l (Uniform Resource Locator) in Linking Entry Fields 76X-78X in the USMARC Bibliographic Format," http://lcweb.loc.gov/marc/marbi/dp/dp87.html.

79. MARBI, "Discussion Paper No. 112: Defining URL/URN Subfields in Fields Other Than Field 856 in the MARC Bibliographic/Holdings Formats," http://lcweb.loc.gov/marc/marbi/dp/dp112.html.

80. "The Network Development and MARC Standards Office Library of Congress Issued Guidelines for the Use of Field 856 Revised August 1999" < http://www.loc.gov/marc/856guide.html>.

81. Library of Congress, *Catalogers Desktop* (Washington, D.C.: Cataloging Distribution Service, 1994-).

82. *Cataloging Service Bulletin* 89 (summer 2000): 12.

83. *CCM*, 31.3.4

84. Arlene G. Taylor, "Where Does AACR2 Fall Short for Internet Resources?" *Journal of Internet Cataloging* 2, no. 2 (1999): 43-50.

85. Vinh-The Lam, "Cataloging Internet Resources: Why, What, How," *Cataloging & Classification Quarterly* 29, no. 3 (2000): 49-61.

86. Landesman, op. cit., 142.

87. Ibid.

88. Ibid.

89. Steve Shadle, "Identifications of Electronic Journals in the Online Catalog," *Serials Review* 24, no. 2 (summer 1998): 104-107.

90. Shadle, "A Square Peg," op. cit.

91. Landesman, op. cit.

92. Steven Shadle, Bill Anderson, Thomas Champagne, Leslie O'Brien, "Electronic Serials Cataloging: Now That We're Here, What Do We Do?" *The Serials Librarian* 30, no. 3-4 (1997): 109-127.

93. Shadle, "Identifications."

94. Carroll N. Davis, "Problems in Defining '–Periodicals' (Electronic or Otherwise)," *Serials Review* 24, no. 2 (summer 1998): 107-109.

95. Shadle, "Identifications."

96. Ibid.

97. Davis, op. cit., 109.

98. Regina Romano Reynolds, "Harmonizing Bibliographic Control of Serials in the Digital Age," *Cataloging & Classification Quarterly* 28, no. 1 (1999): 3-19.

99. Ellen Finnie Duranceau, Column Editor, "Old Wine in New Bottles?: Defining Electronic Serials," *Serials Review* 22 (spring 1996): 69-79.

100. Erik Jul, "Revisiting Seriality and Periodicity," *Serials Review* 22 (spring 1996): 70-71.

101. Marilyn Geller, "A Better Mousetrap Is Still a Mousetrap," *Serials Review* 22 (spring 1996): 72-73.

102. Crystal Graham and Rebecca Ringler, "Hermaphrodites & Herrings," *Serials Review* 22 (spring 1996): 73-76.

103. Ed Jones, "Serials in the Realm of the Remotely-Accessible: An Exploration," *Serials Review* 22 (spring 1996): 77-79.

104. Les Hawkins, "Serials Published on the World Wide Web: Cataloging Problems and Decisions," *The Serials Librarian* 33 no. 1-2 (1998): 123-145.

105. Shadle, "Square Peg," op. cit., 152.

106. CONSER AACR Review Group 1, *Final Report*, Jan. 19, 1999, http://lcweb. loc.gov/acq/conser/aacr1report.html; CONSER AACR Review Group 2A. *Description, (Chapter 12)*, http://StaffWeb.lib.washington.edu/Serials/cat/Procedures/group2Fin.htm (viewed June 24, 1999; inactive Apr. 13, 2001); CONSER AACR Review Group 2B, *Final Report*, Jan. 22, 1999, http://lcweb.loc.gov/acq/conser/aacr2breport.html; CONSER AACR Review Group 3, *Report to the CONSER Task Force on AACR*, http://www.humnet.ucla.edu/humnet/clarlib/acc/group3.htm (viewed June 24, 1999; inactive Apr. 13, 2001).

107. Kevin M. Randall, Recorder, "The Latest on Latest (Entry) and Other Hot News on Seriality." *The Serials Librarian* 36, no. 3-4 (1999): 483-490.

108. Jean Hirons and Regina Reynolds, "Proposal to Adopt a Modified Model C," http://lcweb.loc.gov/acq/conser/ModelC.html.

109. Jean Hirons, *Revising AACR2 to Accommodate Seriality: Report to the Joint Steering Committee for Revision of AACR*, Apr. 1999, http//www.nlc-bnc.ca/jsc/ser-rep0.html; Jean Hirons and members of the CONSER AACR Review Task Force, *Revising AACR2 to Accommodate Seriality: Rule Revision Proposals*, Feb. 2000, http://www.nlc-bnc.ca/jsc/docs.html#seriality.

110. Wayne Jones, "E-Packages," 16.

111. Joint Steering Committee for Revision of AACR, "Selected Documents," http://www.nlc-bnc.ca/jsc/docs.html.

112. ALCTS Serials Section Committee to Study Serials Cataloging, "Minutes of Meetings," http://www.ala.org/alcts/organization/ss/serialscat.html.

113. "Summary of the 1999 CONSER Operations Committee Meeting, April 22, 1999" for instance includes "Seriality Issues," a report by Jean Hirons on the Report and records relevant discussions: http://www.loc.gov/acq/conser/conop99.html.

114. Pat French, Recorder, "AACR2 and You: Revising AACR2 to Accommodate Seriality," *The Serials Librarian* 38, no. 3-4 (2000): 249-256.

115. Ibid., 254.

116. MARBI, "Discussion Paper No. 119: Seriality and MARC 21," http://lcweb. loc.gov/marc/marbi/dp/dp119.html.

117. Jean Hirons, "The 'Ongoing' Umbrella: Rethinking the Redefinition of 'Serial,'" *Serials Review* 23, no. 3-4 (1998): 107-117; Reynolds, "Harmonizing."

118. Randall, op. cit., 487.

119. See the "Minutes of the ALCTS Serials Section Committee to Study Serials Cataloging at the 1998 Annual Meeting in Washington, D. C.," http://www.ala.org/alcts/organization/ss/serialscat98annual.html.

120. Randall, op. cit., 487.

121. Ibid.

122. Ibid., 488.

123. Ibid.

124. See CC:DA Task Force on Rule 0.24, *Report to CC:DA 1999 Annual,* http://www.ala.org/alcts/organization/ccs/ccda/tf-024g.html.

125. Crystal Graham, "What's Wrong With AACR2: A Serials Perspective," recorded in the "Minutes of the ALCTS/Serials Section Committee to Study Serials Cataloging," http://www.ala.org/alcts/organization/ss/serialscat95annual.html.

126. Matthew Beacom, "Crossing a Digital Divide: AACR2 and Unaddressed Problems of Networked Resources," in *Bicentennial Conference on Bibliographic Control for the New Millennium,* Nov. 15-17, 2000, http://lcweb.loc.gov/catdir/bibcontrol/beacom_paper.html; Amy K. Weiss and Timothy V. Carstens provide a fine review of the related discussion, in their summary of "The Year's Work in Cataloging, 1999," *Library Resources and Technical Services* 45, no. 1 (2001): 47-58.

127. *Committee on Cataloging: Description and Access Task Force on the Harmonization of ISBD(ER) and AACR2,* http://www.ala.org/alcts/organization/ccs/ccda/tf-harm1.html.

128. Reynolds, "Harmonizing."

129. Ibid.

130. *Journal of Internet Cataloging,* The Haworth Press, Inc., 1997- .

131. Patricia M. Dragon, "Metadata Systems," http://ala8.ala.org/alcts/organization/ccs/prc-summ2.html, includes an extensive bibliography.

132. Jessica Milstead and Susan Feldman, "Metadata: Cataloging by Any Other Name . . . ," *Online* 23, no.1 (Jan. 1999), http://www.onlineinc.com/onlinemag/OL1999/milstead1.html.

133. Erik Jul, "Cataloging Internet Resources: An Assessment and Prospectus," *The Serials Librarian* 34, no. 1-2 (1998): 91-104.

134. Wayne Jones, "Dublin Core and Serials," *Journal of Internet Cataloging* 4, no. 1-2 (2001): 143-148.

135. Ibid., 144.

136. Ibid., 147.

137. MARBI, "Discussion Paper 2001-DP03: Types of Dates for Electronic Resources in MARC 21," http://lcweb.loc.gov/marc/marbi/2001-2001-dp03.html.

138. Landesman, op. cit.

139. Nancy B. Olson, Editor, *Cataloging Internet Resources: A Manual and Practical Guide,* 2nd ed., http://www.purl.org/oclc/cataloging-internet.

140. Library of Congress, *Draft Interim Guidelines for Cataloging Electronic Resources,* http://lcweb.loc.gov/catdir/cpso/dcmb19_4.html.

141. Carol Liheng and Winnie S. Chan, *Serials Cataloging Handbook,* 2nd ed. (Chicago, Ill.: American Library Association, 1998).

142. Daniel V. Pitti, "Standard Generalized Markup Language and Transformation of Cataloging," *The Serials Librarian* 25, no. 3-4 (1995): 243-253.

143. Cameron J. Campbell, *Basic Serials Cataloging Workshop* (Washington, DC: Library of Congress Cataloging Distribution Service, 1999).

144. Jean Hirons, "SCCTP–Continuing Education for Continuing Resources," *The Serials Librarian* 37, no. 4 (2000): 113-121.

145. Williams, op. cit.

146. Shadle et al., "Electronic."

147. David R. Rodgers, "Eeee!-Serials: Providing Access to Online Serials," *The Serials Librarian* 36, no. 3-4 (1999): 467-73.

148. Ibid.

149. Dajin Sun, "Issues in Cataloging Chinese Electronic Journals," *Journal of Internet Cataloging* 1, no.1 (1997): 65-82.

STANDARDS

ISSN:
An Ongoing Identifier
in a Changing World

Françoise Pellé

SUMMARY. The ISSN system, which was established in the 1970s for the identification of printed serial publications, is also a powerful system for the identification of electronic resources, thanks to a number of changes which reflect new publishing practices. The evolution of the concepts (from serials to continuing resources), the broadening of the scope for ISSN assignment, the harmonisation of cataloguing rules among the AACR, ISBD and ISSN communities and the *ISSN Manual* revision are presented in this paper. Particular attention is paid to the use of the ISSN as a persistent identifier on the Internet, through the implementation of resolution systems using the URN framework. *[Article copies available for a fee from The Haworth Document Delivery Service: 1-800-HAWORTH. E-mail address: <getinfo@haworthpressinc.com> Website: <http://www.HaworthPress. com> © 2002 by The Haworth Press, Inc. All rights reserved.]*

Françoise Pellé is Director of the ISSN International Centre (pelle@issn.org).
The author would like to thank Jean Hirons, Regina Reynolds, Werner Schwartz and Juha Hakala for their useful comments on various drafts of this paper.

[Haworth co-indexing entry note]: "ISSN: An Ongoing Identifier in a Changing World." Pellé, Françoise. Co-published simultaneously in *The Serials Librarian* (The Haworth Information Press, an imprint of The Haworth Press, Inc.) Vol. 41, No. 3/4, 2002, pp. 31-42; and: *E-Serials Cataloging: Access to Continuing and Integrating Resources via the Catalog and the Web* (ed: Jim Cole, and Wayne Jones) The Haworth Information Press, an imprint of The Haworth Press, Inc., 2002, pp. 31-42. Single or multiple copies of this article are available for a fee from The Haworth Document Delivery Service [1-800-HAWORTH, 9:00 a.m. - 5:00 p.m. (EST). E-mail address: getinfo@haworthpressinc.com].

KEYWORDS. ISSN, seriality, continuing resources, serials, ISST, URN, persistent identifiers

The ISSN system, created in the 1970s, is a well-known and well-established system for the identification of serial publications. Almost one million records, 73 member countries, 40,000 to 50,000 new records a year, truly international and used by all actors interested in serial publications–it was recognised a long time ago as the identification system for print publications. In the electronic era, the ISSN is also a powerful identification system–thanks to the changes that have been adopted by the ISSN Network and that are currently being implemented.

Those changes raise a number of interesting questions regarding the evolution of publishing practices, the definitions, the scope of the ISSN system, and of course the implementation of the changes at the operational level.

CHANGES IN PUBLISHING PRACTICES

A few years ago, like all actors interested in serial publications, the ISSN Network was facing a completely new situation. Unidentified electronic objects were flying through the Internet, looking sometimes like well-known objects–serial publications–and sometimes not. But were they monographs, or entirely new "resources"? They were continuously changing: the content was updated at any time, titles and presentation changed, links were added to other objects, addresses moved and suddenly you couldn't access them. They had no recognised identifier, but we all needed to identify them in a reliable and persistent way, especially as they were moved so often from one place to another. Should they be assigned "legacy" identifiers (ISSN, ISBN) at all?

It was crucial to try to identify the main changes occurring in publishing practices and information dissemination in order to be able to define the future of the ISSN system. A new strategic plan had to be adopted, and recognised experts were asked to provide the ISSN Network with their visions for the future. Several experts[1] agreed to present and discuss their views during the meeting of the Directors of ISSN National Centres held in Paris in 1999. Some of those views can be briefly summarised as follows:

- Publishing of print serials is not going to stop in the foreseeable future, and relatively little print publishing will move completely towards electronic publishing.

- Many print serials are already moving into dual print and electronic publication modes–in some cases, the print journal is simply duplicated in the digital medium; in other cases digital products extend the printed publication in various ways, but may also omit some of the content that is to be found in the print edition. Multiple print editions may be targeted for specific geographic or industry audiences, and only a single electronic version may be published which may or may not correspond exactly to one of the printed editions. The relationships between the electronic and the print editions are complex–they are seldom relationships of simple equivalence.
- For electronic serials, the dominant model today is to run a Web site that is continually (or at least regularly) updated with new content. Content is overwritten or revised, not only cumulated as a series of immutable units. Web sites often represent a serial in all its issues, or amalgamate many different serials.
- A serial in the digital world is conceptually not only an object or even a sequence of distinct objects–it is a process that is embodied in an object such as a Web site, and the process aspect of continued publication of content, of being a serial, is a critically important aspect of the Web site's behaviour and properties which is important to capture.

EVOLUTION OF THE CONCEPTS

Clearly, one of the main changes in publishing practices is in the form of issuance: increasingly, online resources are being continuously updated with new content, and are ignoring the need for issues. Nevertheless, we intuitively consider a number of those resources as "serials"–at least, there is some idea of "seriality" behind the scenes, for publishers as well as for librarians.

What is a serial? The traditional definition of a serial publication has worked well for many years: "a publication, in any medium, issued in successive parts, usually having numbered or chronological designations, and intended to be continued indefinitely."[2] Today, however, the first part of the definition ("issued in successive parts") does not encompass the new types of resources. It is also true that the concept underlying the phrase "intended to be continued indefinitely," which is the core concept of "seriality," encompasses both serials and the new types of resources.

All communities interested in serial publication identification and description (AACR, ISBD and ISSN) were facing the same fundamental questions and needed to revise their definitions and their rules. The AACR community had made the most progress, undertaking the revision of the chapter dealing with serials, and very important work was being accomplished. Crystal Graham, Jean Hirons and Regina Reynolds contributed in a decisive way to the establishment of a conceptual framework enabling one to characterise the different types of resources, including the new ones.[3]

Perhaps not all readers–especially outside the AACR community–are familiar with this framework and, given its importance, it will be briefly summarised below. Figure 1 below represents the model. In this model, the bibliographic world is divided into finite and continuing resources. Finite resources are complete as issued or intended to be complete in a predetermined number of parts. "Continuing" is a broad category, divided into two sub-categories which are defined in terms of their publication pattern–their "form of issuance" (Hirons-Graham). The first sub-category–successively issued resources–corresponds to serials–this includes, among others, series and electronic journals. The second sub-category–integrating–includes those resources into which new material is seamlessly integrated, so that there are no divisions into issues or parts. Examples of integrating continuing resources include loose-leaf services, databases and Web sites.

The strength of this model is that it relies on a few formal characteristics corresponding to the form of issuance, enabling us to get a better understanding of what "seriality" is, and providing us with a very powerful framework, both at the conceptual and practical levels. It was adopted by the ISSN Network for those reasons some three years ago as a tool for discussion, and has become today a common framework for the network.

FIGURE 1. AACR Types of Publication Model

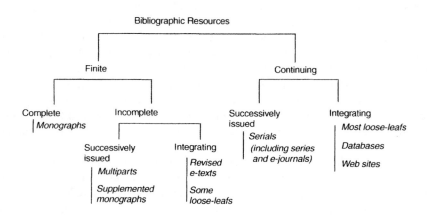

A NEW STRATEGIC PLAN FOR THE ISSN

The changes in publishing modes and concepts raised a number of questions about the future of the ISSN system, and the ISSN Network undertook a revision of its Strategic Plan,[4] which was adopted at the General Assembly meeting in May 2000.

Broadening the Scope: From Serials to Continuing Resources

Obviously, the new vision raises a major question regarding the scope of ISSN assignment : are all continuing resources "ISSNable"?

With regard to serials, there is no doubt: as before, all serials (in printed and electronic forms) should be assigned an ISSN. There is also no doubt that finite integrating resources are excluded. It is undoubtedly "continuing integrating resources" which represent the most difficult category.

The difficulty is both conceptual and practical. At a conceptual level, we still lack a typology that would enable us to define in more detail the main characteristics of those resources. At a practical level, the enormous amount of resources which fall under the definition–which encompasses most databases and most Web sites–excludes exhaustive identification and raises important questions about identification procedures, which might become more automatic–this raising another set of questions about some basic ISSN principles for ensuring reliable, persistent and unique identification.

These difficult questions are under discussion today, and the ISSN Network is working in two directions: the first involves trying to progressively establish a more detailed typology for continuing integrating resources; the second is more operational and involves establishing priorities as well as a few selection criteria. Indeed, the actual scope of application of ISSN will progressively be determined, taking the context into account and especially the developments in publishing modes, as well as the experience gained by the network. The basic rule, nevertheless, is that all continuing resources are "ISSNable," with a principle of exhaustivity for serials and a principle of selectivity for integrating resources.

The broadening scope has important consequences for the ISSN Network. However, there is another change that should be highlighted: the shift from identification to access. Identification systems such as the ISSN are mainly used, in the printed world, in the distribution chain, and all actors of the distribution chain need a shared identifier in order to ensure reliable transactions. In the online context, distribution modes have changed: users want to access the content directly. Indeed, this fact makes identifiers more necessary, but it also demands that the functionalities of those identifiers be expanded, so that they become a more active part of the access process, as well as playing their role of persistent identifier to the full. This aspect is presented in more detail below.

THE NEED FOR HARMONISATION (AACR, ISBD AND ISSN) AND THE ISSN MANUAL *REVISION*

Harmonisation

We have already mentioned the pioneering work of the AACR community and the fact that all communities interested in identification and description of serials were facing the same questions. Both the IFLA community and the ISSN community had undertaken the revision of their cataloguing codes, creating a unique opportunity for a broad harmonisation of cataloguing rules.

The three communities agreed that harmonisation is important for one main reason: it would allow existing records to be more widely reused, and would therefore save resources and improve bibliographic control–for the benefit of all. Significant progress was made, especially during a meeting which was held at the Library of Congress in November 2000 and which was attended by representatives of the AACR, ISBD(S) (now ISBD(CR)–Serials and Other Continuing Resources) and ISSN communities. Although we should bear in mind that the experts who met in Washington agreed on proposals which are still to be approved by the different communities and are therefore still subject to changes, three of those proposals should be highlighted:

- At a global level, the fact that the representatives of the three communities agreed on the same set of definitions is obviously fundamental (the definitions themselves, as endorsed by the ISSN Network, are given below).
- Another important goal for harmonisation is that the rules should allow a given entity to be represented by one record. In this respect, the harmonisation of both the definitions and the rules for the creation of new records is crucial. This goal is almost within reach: for instance, the three communities agreed on the rules for title changes, as well as on other points such as the establishment of a new record when the publication medium changes.
- Finally, satisfactory harmonisation cannot be reached if descriptions remain too different: in this respect, the harmonisation of the title transcription rules also represents an important improvement, especially for identification purposes.

Nevertheless, further harmonisation is needed, particularly with regard to the description of continuing integrating resources. For those resources, the ISSN

Network decided to apply the logic of successive entries, whereas both the AACR and the ISBD decided in favour of the latest entry principle. For the time being, the ISSN thinks that the purpose of identification will be better served by successive records, but recognises that this decision may be reviewed in the future if it appears that evolution is needed. Harmonisation is making significant progress—enough, one hopes, to enable the reuse of records in a majority of cases.

ISSN Manual *Revision*

Having described the context, we will give here below a more detailed view of the most important changes that are supported by the ISSN Network. All these changes are to be included in the *ISSN Manual*, which is currently under revision.

The first change regards the definitions, which now stand as follows:

- *Bibliographic resource:* a manifestation of a work that forms the basis for bibliographic description. A bibliographic resource may be in any medium or combination of media and may be tangible or intangible.
- *Continuing resource:* a bibliographic resource that is issued over time with no predetermined conclusion. Continuing resources include serials and ongoing integrating resources.
- *Integrating resource:* a bibliographic resource that is added to or changed by means of updates that do not remain discrete and are integrated into the whole. Examples of integrating resources include updating looseleafs and updating Web sites.
- *Serial:* a continuing resource issued in a succession of discrete parts, usually bearing numbering, that has no predetermined conclusion. Examples of serials include journals, magazines, electronic journals, continuing directories, annual reports, newspapers and monographic series.

A second important change for the ISSN Network regards the rules for title changes. In order to limit new ISSN assignments to the most significant title changes, a distinction between major and minor title changes has been adopted, with a basic principle: only major changes require the assignment of a new ISSN and the establishment of a new record. The basic rule for determining what is a major title change is the "first five words" rule: when a change occurs within the first five words of a title (the first six words if the title begins with an article), this should be considered as a major change. Changes occurring after those first words are generally considered to be minor title changes and therefore do not require the assignment of a new ISSN and the establishment of a new record. Two additional rules state that two other cases should also be regarded as major changes: when the change occurring after those first words changes the meaning of the title or indicates a different subject matter, and when a corporate body, named anywhere in the title, changes.

Significant additions to the list of minor title changes will reduce the number of new records and ISSN needed for irrelevant and careless changes, such as the name of the issuing body being added or dropped at the beginning of the title. Both publishers and ISSN National Centres should benefit from this new set of rules.

However, the most fundamental change probably concerns the scope for ISSN assignment, which, as already mentioned, encompasses now all continuing resources and applies a principle of exhaustivity for serials and of selectivity for continuing integrating resources. One of the main consequences of broadening the scope is a huge increase in the number of resources that may be assigned an ISSN. As the number of serial publications (both in printed and in electronic forms) also increases, it is unlikely that the present identification procedures will be sustainable in the long run, and the question of reorganising those procedures is now open. There is probably more than one answer to this question. In addition to more automated procedures and to a broader reuse of records, the solution will probably rely, at least partly, on new cooperation. In this respect, the ISST project opens up interesting possibilities.

THE ISST

The International Standard Serial Title project is being developed, under the auspices of the IFLA ISBD (CR) working group led by Ingrid Parent, by a sub-group which includes representatives of AACR, ISBD and ISSN.[5] The main objectives, here also, are to increase both international record sharing and bibliographic control. As currently defined, the ISST would act like the ISSN as the main identifier for a continuing resource. It would unify the purposes of the key title and uniform title in order to eliminate redundancy, and would serve as a benchmark for title changes, therefore allowing a one-to-one match between ISSN and cataloguing records. The ISST, if adopted, would be a title similar to key titles and uniform titles, consisting of the title proper and, when needed, a qualifier. It would accompany the ISSN, but would be created, at least in a provisional form, by all cataloguers–not only by the ISSN National Centres, which would nevertheless remain the authority for ISSN assignment and for the validation of ISST.

This project involves a number of challenges, for instance, regarding data flows, access to the whole set of ISST, and the establishment of corporate bodies, which is not standardised today throughout the different cataloguing codes. Many other questions are raised by the project, and further work is needed in order to estimate the feasibility of implementation more effectively. Nevertheless, both the goal and the project arouse interest among the communities concerned with serial cataloguing, and preliminary studies should progress during the next few months.

ISSN: WHAT DOES IT IDENTIFY?

The IFLA *Functional Requirements for Bibliographic Records* (FRBR)[6] provides the concepts and terminology to analyse a growing problem: how to treat multiple versions of the "same" serial. The FRBR model is four-tiered: a "work" is "a distinct intellectual or artistic creation" (an abstract entity); an "expression" is "the intellectual or artistic realisation of a work"; a "manifestation" is " the physical embodiment of an expression of a work"; an "item" is "a single exemplar of a manifestation."

Regarding serial publications (continuously updated or added to), the FRBR concepts raise some interesting questions about the definition of a work–and therefore about the definition of what is "the same" and what is "different." Do two separate manifestations (e.g., print and electronic) embody the same work if the contents are different, e.g., if version A does not contain exactly the same articles as version B, or if version A contains more articles than version B? At the operational level, determining whether the contents of two different versions are identical or not is in itself a challenge for continuously updated publications.

An ISSN identifies a manifestation of a work, and does not identify a work. Therefore, two different manifestations (or versions) of a "same" serial (e.g., the printed and the electronic versions) have two different ISSN and are represented by two different records, with each of these records including links to the other one. This practice meets the needs of a majority of the ISSN users (especially the actors of the distribution chain), but obviously fails to meet the need for the identification of works. A solution might be found thanks to the ongoing work undertaken under the auspices of ISO/TC46/SC9: the International Standard Textual Code (ISTC), a new standard for the identification of textual works.[7] Regarding continuing resources, further work still needs to be done on the definition of what a work actually is at the title level, and about the definition of the data elements which are needed to ensure the identification of continuing works.

ISSN: A PERSISTENT IDENTIFIER ON THE INTERNET

Readers interested in the use of existing bibliographic identifiers (such as ISBN, ISSN and SICI) as Uniform Resource Names will find in-depth discussion in RFC 2288[8] and in "Uniform Resource Identifiers and Online Serials."[9]

If we focus on the ISSN as an identifier in the electronic world, some characteristics of the system deserve to be highlighted. An ISSN is (and always has been) a persistent identifier for a resource. It is independent of information such as protocol, host, port, etc. Today, the ISSN system maps identifiers to URLs. The ISSN system identifies the entire population of continuing resources and therefore is a "Name Space" as defined by the IETF.[10] In addition, each ISSN is, following the same set of definitions, a persistent name for a continuing resource. Indeed, the ISSN system meets almost all requirements of Uniform Resource Names as defined by the IETF, and it was decided to experiment with the implementation of a resolution system, based on this framework and using the ISSN register as the basic tool for resolving ISSN into the corresponding electronic resource, and to register the ISSN as a Name Space Identifier.[11] The fundamental idea here is to use the ISSN as a persistent name on the Internet, in other words to use a name which never changes to enable access to the resource, whatever the changes in URLs for this resource may be.

The resolution system implemented at the ISSN International Centre relies on four main components: a mapping system (which maps ISSN to one or several URLs); a resolution system (which resolves an ISSN into one or several URLs); a checking system (which controls all URLs every day and updates redirected URLs); and a plug-in.

In practice, the user types in the browser command line a chain built as follows: "urn:issn:9999-999X" (e.g., urn:issn:1560-1560), and accesses the online resource (and other associated services, if any). Clicking on an ISSN in an HTML page gives the same result. Today, it is necessary to download the plug-in developed at the ISSN IC to benefit from this facility.[12] This implementation (which is reader-oriented) demonstrates the huge potential there is on the Internet for existing identifiers.

There are many other possible uses of the ISSN if we view it as a piece of the networked information infrastructure, as a piece of computer-oriented applications. An interesting development, for instance, is the use of the ISSN resolution system as an intermediary tool for the re-direction of URNs based on the Serial Item and Contribution Identifier. This experiment is being carried out within the framework of the European project DIEPER,[13] and the first results were successfully presented at the end of March 2001. The principle relies on the use of SICIs for the identification and retrieval of electronic articles. As SICIs are based on ISSN, SICI-based URNs will be sent to the ISSN resolver, which will parse the SICI and identify the appropriate final resolution service, the article itself being provided to the user by the server within the DIEPER architecture. By applying accepted standards this architecture is devised to be non-proprietary and open for use by other systems.

These new uses of the ISSN at least demonstrate that efficient linkage can be accomplished through the use of existing identifiers. In the two examples above, global and effective resolution is demonstrated or under development, and of course many other possibilities exist for applications in more local environments such as library catalogues or union catalogues, and for co-operation with other players interested in offering resolution services on the Internet, or in developing linking technologies.

CHALLENGES AND OPPORTUNITIES

We have tried to summarise some of the major changes occurring in the serials world and in the ISSN system. This new situation creates both challenges and opportunities. A key challenge is certainly the huge increase in the number of resources to be identified, requiring further thinking from the ISSN Network about identification processes. Another challenge is probably the shift from identification to access, which is very new for the ISSN Network and which will probably bring new developments at different levels. But there are also huge opportunities, especially regarding the uses of the ISSN in the electronic environment and the development of new partnerships.

NOTES

1. Clifford Lynch, Cecilia Preston, Leslie Daigle, Rollo Turner (Association of Subscription Agents), Stuart Ede (The British Library), Brian Green (EDItEUR).
2. International Organization for Standardization, *Information and Documentation–International Standard Serial Number (ISSN), ISO 3297*, 3rd ed. (Geneva: ISO, 1998), http://www.nlc-bnc.ca/iso/tc46sc9/standard/3297e.htm#3.
3. Jean Hirons and Crystal Graham, "Issues Related to Seriality," in *The Principles and Future of AACR: Proceedings of the International Conference on the Principles and Future Development of AACR: Toronto, Ontario, Canada, October 23/25, 1997*, edited by Jean Wiehs (Chicago: American Library Association, 1998), 180-212; Jean Hirons and Regina Reynolds, *Proposal to Adopt a Modified Model C Approach*, Apr. 1998, http://lcweb.loc.gov/acq/conser/ModelC.html; Regina Reynolds, "Harmonizing Bibliographic Control of Serials in the Digital Age," paper presented at the IFLA International Conference on National Bibliographic Services, Copenhagen, Nov. 25-27, 1998.
4. ISSN Network, *Strategic Plan for the ISSN Network 2000-2004*, http://www.issn.org/official/Strategic_Plan_2000.html.
5. The group is comprised of Ingrid Parent, Marg Stewart, Reinhard Rinn, Jean Hirons, Regina Reynolds, Alain Roucolle and Françoise Pellé.
6. IFLA Study Group on the Functional Requirements for Bibliographic Records, *Functional Requirements for Bibliographic Records: Final Report* (München: Saur, 1998).

7. ISO/TC 46/SC 9 Working Group 3, *Project 21047: International Standard Textual Work Code (ISTC)*, http://www.nlc-bnc.ca/iso/tc46sc9/istc.htm.

8. Clifford Lynch, Cecilia Preston and Ron Daniel, "Using Existing Bibliographic Identifiers as Uniform Resource Names," RFC 2288,   Feb. 1998, ftp://ftp.isi.edu/in-notes/rfc2288.txt.

9. Leslie Daigle, Ron Daniel Jr. and Cecilia Preston, "Uniform Resource Identifiers and Online Serials," *The Serials Librarian*, 33, no. 3-4 (1998): 325-341.

10. K. Sollins and L. Masinter, "Functional Requirements for Uniform Resource Names," RFC 1737, Dec. 1994, http://www.ietf.org/rfc/rfc1737.txt?number=1737.

11. Slawek Rozenfeld, "Using the ISSN (International Standard Serial Number) as URN (Uniform Resource Names) within an ISSN-URN Namespace," RFC 3044, Jan. 2001, ftp://ftp.isi.edu/in-notes/rfc3044.txt.

12. *ISSN-URN Demonstrator, Version 0.3 Beta, http://urn.issn.org/.*

13. *DIEPER: Digitised European Periodicals*, http://www.sub.uni-goettingen.de/gdz/dieper/.

ISBD(ER) and Its Role
in the Management of Electronic Resources

Sten Hedberg

SUMMARY. The development of the ISBD family has been an organic process that is itself linked to developments in both publishing and librarianship. This article describes the evolution of ISBD(ER)–the International Standard Bibliographic Description for Electronic Resources, which had its beginnings in ISBD(NBM), a standard devoted to non-book materials. Although new understandings and new technologies are challenging the established roles of cataloguing, the ISBDs will continue to be important tools for the visual presentation and availability of bibliographic information. *[Article copies available for a fee from The Haworth Document Delivery Service: 1-800-HAWORTH. E-mail address: <getinfo@haworthpressinc.com> Website: <http://www.HaworthPress.com> © 2002 by The Haworth Press, Inc. All rights reserved.]*

KEYWORDS. International Standard Bibliographic Description, descriptive cataloguing, electronic resources, Anglo-American cataloguing rules

THE BEGINNINGS

The idea of a standardized layout for the bibliographic description is a child of the late 1960s, being first envisioned at a meeting in Copenhagen in 1969.

Sten Hedberg is a member of the ISBD(CF) Review Group and is an authority on standards and cataloguing at Uppsala University Library, P.O. Box 510, S-751 20 Uppsala Sweden (e-mail: sten.hedberg@ub.uu.se).

[Haworth co-indexing entry note]: "ISBD(ER) and Its Role in the Management of Electronic Resources." Hedberg, Sten. Co-published simultaneously in *The Serials Librarian* (The Haworth Information Press, an imprint of The Haworth Press, Inc.) Vol. 41, No. 3/4, 2002, pp. 43-56; and: *E-Serials Cataloging: Access to Continuing and Integrating Resources via the Catalog and the Web* (ed: Jim Cole, and Wayne Jones) The Haworth Information Press, an imprint of The Haworth Press, Inc., 2002, pp. 43-56. Single or multiple copies of this article are available for a fee from The Haworth Document Delivery Service [1-800-HAWORTH, 9:00 a.m. - 5:00 p.m. (EST). E-mail address: getinfo@haworthpressinc.com].

Through the devoted support of the IFLA bodies, a rapid development took place. So, as is commonly known, the first half of the 1970s saw the emergence and the general acceptance of the International Standard Bibliographic Description for printed monographs, ISBD(M), and also progress toward its counterpart for serial publications, ISBD(S). The Swedish cataloguing rules published in 1974 were one of the first national codes to reflect both these sets of guidelines, bringing along with them a revised thinking regarding the cataloguing workflow.

The deciding step towards true comprehensiveness was the work on the general ISBD, ISBD(G), started in 1975 and eventually published in 1977. While this work was carried on, there was a parallel compilation of the guidelines for the description of cartographic material (ISBD(CM), 1977) and what was called "non-book material" (ISBD(NBM), 1977). Somewhat later another ISBD appeared, covering printed music (ISBD(PM), 1980). In the meantime, ISBD(M) and ISBD(S) had been issued in their first standard texts (1978 and 1977, respectively). With the various ISBDs, it was theoretically possible to find consistent guidance for the description of any document that could be expected within a library. The second edition of the *Anglo-American Cataloguing Rules* (AACR2) in 1978 followed suit and gave these standards for description the support they needed in the form of cataloguing rules.

Which of the ISBDs at that time covered computer materials? By elimination, they belonged to the NBM sphere. There was indeed in the 1977 edition of ISBD(NBM) one example in paragraph 1.5.2 of what was then called "Machine readable data." Paragraph 5.1.8 also advised the cataloguer to give the extent of the item as "the number of logical records or statements." Any remarks on format and physical carriers were omitted, "since change of form is a characteristic of the medium."[1] One did not find any notes on system requirements, and area 3, the Material specific area, was not used. These guidelines thus left much to the decision of the librarian, and no real standardization could be expected from the few instances at hand.

AACR2 was in principle based on the ISBD family. Either by remarkable foresight (or perhaps through access to profound background information) the chapters on description did not bundle non-book media together as the ISBD family then did. Specific chapters were, as we all know, developed for sound recordings, motion pictures and videos, graphic materials, three-dimensional objects, and machine-readable data files. It is even uncertain if the explicit restriction of the ISBD(NBM) to materials published in multiple copies, excluding "specimens or found objects . . . as well as original works of art" was applicable under AACR2. But of course the guidelines regarding the layout and the contents of the record were strictly observed, for better or worse.

INDEPENDENCE

In 1977 IFLA had decided that five years was to be the normal period for an ISBD to stand before it was considered for revision. Accordingly, with four ISBDs issued around 1977, a major revision exercise was due in 1982, and the necessary apparatus was established in 1981. New editions of the four oldest texts appeared in 1987 and 1988, the time-span being a sign of the extent of the work required to reach the consistency and the user-friendliness desired. Furthermore, technological advances also made themselves felt, perhaps more so in the electronic area than elsewhere. So, citing the rapid changes in the characteristics of computer files, the second (1987) edition of ISBD(NBM) explicitly referred to a separate ISBD for computer files then in progress: a committee had convened in March 1986, a final draft was circulated in late 1988, and the text was published as ISBD(CF) in 1990. The most important features of ISBD(CF) were, however, incorporated into the 1988 revision of AACR2, relying on expert reports that had been published in 1984. Who influenced whom can now only be guessed at; in any case, it was a piece of remarkable foresight by the editors of AACR2.

ISBD(CF), the first ISBD specifically written for computer files, incorporated two important features:

- A concentration on the microcomputer (later called the personal computer) as the chief equipment for access to electronic resources
- A recognition of remote access as a method of using machine-readable information, in which context it was stressed that the term *remote* "does not necessarily imply the usual meaning of 'distance.' "[2]

Earlier, the typical computer resource to be described could consist of several physical parts, such as a program file, a file of data and one or more manuals. The carriers could be tape reels or punched cards, later various sizes of floppy disks, and access meant mounting the resource on a computer that was reached from a terminal.

It is interesting that ISDB(CF) had inherited from the ISBD(NBM) the recognition that "the term *bibliographic* . . . is used in full awareness of its inappropriateness in this context."[3] The authors evidently had had some difficulty in applying this term to anything other than books and book-like objects. This was mentioned as a feature or a witness of the state of the art, somewhat strange after the introductory statement that one of the reasons for a separate ISBD was the fact that " . . . the development of programs and data files for smaller computers . . . resulted in physical items roughly comparable to other library materials to be more widely added to library collections, with bibliographic control needed for them."[4]

CHARACTERISTICS AND PECULIARITIES

The most important technical novelty of the independent ISBD(CF) was the application of area 3 (Material specific information) to record information on the type of resource and also on the logical size of the files. Area 5 (Physical extent) was set aside for the description of any physical carriers connected with the resource. In addition, one needed to include more extensive technical information about the resource. This led to the development of a priority note regarding the technical requirements for the hardware, such as capacity of the processor, amount of free memory, name of operating system, or necessary peripherals.

However, not all types of resources were treated alike in these contexts. A distinction was made between resources available by remote access and those accessed locally, that is, those distributed in physical carriers and mounted on a local personal computer. For the former, area 3 was declared mandatory, while area 5 was not allowed; the latter category had to use area 5, since one had to describe the carriers, but by some remarkable compensatory thinking, area 3 was declared optional. Area 1 (Title) also provided for an optional General material designation (GMD). It must be said, though, that only a few terms were permitted in each of the areas:

Area 1, Title: GMD (optional)

- Computer file

Area 3, Type and extent (optional for resources in local use)

- Computer data

- Computer program

- Computer data and program

Area 5, Physical description of the carrier (mandatory for resources for local use, prohibited or non-applicable for remote-access resources)

- Computer chip cartridge

- Computer floppy disk

- Computer optical disk

- Computer tape cassette

- Computer tape reel

If one omitted the optional elements from the description of an electronic resource (to use the later name for this medium) distributed on physical carriers, it would look like an ordinary book until you got to area 5, where the information "2 computer optical disks" would tell you that the item in question was something special. On the other hand, if one chose to apply the various options, one would have a record like this:[5]

> Oxford English dictionary [Computer file] : the original Oxford English dictionary on compact disc. – Computer data and program. – Oxford : OUP, 1987. – 2 computer optical disks ; 4 3&/4 in. + user's guide (loose leaf). – System requirements: IBM PC compatible; 640 RAM; CD-ROM player

Here, with three occurrences of the word *computer*, the electronic aspect cannot be easily overlooked. On the other hand, since area 5 was not allowed in the description of remote-access files, there was no possible place other than the notes area to report the occurrence of sound and of coloured illustrations.

In addition, the guidelines gave instructions regarding two other important matters:

- the permitted sources for each part of the description
- the management of different formats of the same resource

but these must be acknowledged as being too hard for the occasional user to apply and requiring a rather extensive exegesis. These issues will be treated below, in the context of ISBD(ER).

REVISION AGAIN

As early as 1993 the IFLA Section on Cataloguing decided once again to revise ISBD(CF), for the following reasons: "Electronic resources are products of volatile technology that continues to generate changes at a very rapid pace. Specific among recent advances are the following: emergence of interactive multimedia; development of optical technology; availability of remote electronic resources on the Internet and World Wide Web; and reproductions of electronic resources."[6] Today one would be tempted to add that electronic formats have become immensely popular among libraries that want to make their older or special holdings less vulnerable and more easily accessible to the public. This has led to projects for the retrospective digitization of library material equal to or surpassing the similar microfilming programs of earlier decades. In addition, it may not have been foreseen even in 1993 that "availability . . . on the Internet" would soon become a dominant method of distributing major scholarly journals. In all, electronic resources were on their way to becoming a normal part of the information output, and the libraries had to adjust.

The new revision was undertaken together with the IFLA Section on Information Technology. There was a three-day committee meeting in May 1995, during which an early political decision confirmed the view that everything that was stored on a public-access server on the Internet was to be considered as "published." After an extensive draft procedure the text was finalized and published in 1997.

THE LATEST VERSION: CHARACTERISTICS AND NOVELTIES

The most visible novelty of the new version is the change of the GMD from the former "Computer file" to "Electronic resource," a term judged more appropriate given the array of materials intended to be covered. Another important item is the recognition of the Internet address, expressed by placing that piece of information as one of the first two notes, preceded only by the System requirements note.

Other changes or new features perhaps appear more important than they really are. ISBD(ER) does provide more detailed rules for the handling of remote-access resources and has improved the internal economy of the record. In addition, it takes into account and explains the new terms that are the products of technological progress. The main step forward is the detailed analysis of the resource designations, intended for area 3 (Type and extent of resource), and their relationship to the GMD and the special material designations in area 5 (Physical description). Thus the former

- Computer data
- Computer program
- Computer data and program

of ISBD(CF) have now been subdivided into the following eleven types of resource designations, arranged in three categories (some of the eleven groups are themselves further divided into still more specific terms):

Data (or "Electronic data" if the GMD is not used–see below)

- Font data
- Image data
- Numeric data (with two subspecies)
- Representational data

- Sound data
- Text data (with four subspecies)

Program(s)

- Application program(s) (with six subspecies)
- System program(s) (with three subspecies)
- Utility program(s)

Data and program(s)

- Interactive multimedia
- Online service(s)

For the management of the designations, some important rules must be observed. First if the GMD is not given, *Electronic* should be added as the first word in area 3. Second, if neither the GMD nor area 3 is given, the special designation in area 5 should contain the word *electronic*. Thus the word *electronic* must appear at least once in each description, but for the sake of economy and style, editing rules may–or perhaps even should–prescribe that it occur once and *only* once, and then at the earliest opportunity. Also, if the list of terms in Appendix C does not give anything that can be applied in areas 3 or 5, the cataloguer is free to use "a term that is currently well established, in use by both the producers and users of the particular type of program, and is mutually exclusive of other terms used as designations."[7] This reduces the need for future frequent revisions of ISBD(ER) merely to keep pace with new terminology resulting from advances in technology.

OUTSTANDING ISSUES: SOURCES OF INFORMATION, VERSIONS

So, at last, the ISBD for electronic resources has accommodated technological development. In this process, to render it more practical, it has also incorporated changes regarding the choice of sources of information and techniques for handling versions and/or editions.

Originally, the primary source for the priority parts of the description, especially area 1 (Title), was the title screen of the resource, as it appeared when the user first accessed the resource. This would imply that a cataloguer had to mount the resource in order to describe it. Otherwise, one would have to use brackets. The technique eventually adopted recognizes internal sources such as the title screen, but also gives equal importance to information found on physical carriers, containers or accompanying materials. A mandatory note names the source used for the title area, and for the edition area if different from that of the title area.

The handling of versions and/or editions involves a decision whether one description may cover more than one version of a monographic resource or if you have to describe each of the versions separately, in which case area 2 (Edition) is used to distinguish them. It was important to decide that mere differences in format (such as disk or cassette, Macintosh or Windows) do not constitute new editions, although these cases can be managed by individual records, while terms such as *edition, release* or *update* normally constitute a true edition statement. It is even permitted to repeat area 5 (Physical description) if the same version is distributed in a variety of physical carrier formats, as long as the layout of the presentation inserts a line break before each occurrence of the area, starting with the point-space-dash group. So, one description could contain these two lines:

> . – 1 electronic optical disc ; 12 cm
> . – 1 videodisc ; 30 cm

Other such version information is referred to the notes area, and a repetition of the physical description can also require a repetition of the Systems requirements note.

THE PRESENT STATUS

The cataloguer will thus find sufficient guidance to formulate the description of an electronic resource that meets the needs of the intended bibliographic service, where

- the electronic character of the resource usually appears early in the record, not later than area 3
- the title and other identity elements can be recorded from an accessible source
- the notes area (albeit rather extensive) presents supplementary information in a predictable order, the most important notes being mandatory and given first.

The more important constraints are that

- the only GMD permitted, if applied, is "Electronic resource"
- there is no easy way to tell that a remote-access resource incorporates sound or colour, that information being relegated to the notes area.

With some common sense on the part of the cataloguer, the guidelines will accommodate technological change for a considerable time into the future.

CHANGES IN THE ENVIRONMENT

The process of arriving at ISBD(ER) has taken twenty years at least, and during that time many other things have changed in the library environment. Some of these have helped alter the scope and the role of the ISBDs as such, while others have affected only ISBD(ER). Catalysts for change include such things as the *Functional Requirements for Bibliographic Records* (FRBR), the MARC format, AACR2 and the libraries using it, and–perhaps the most important–metadata and the Dublin Core (which, however, will be the topic of other contributions in this collection).

FRBR is the report of an IFLA project that succeeded in analyzing information at four levels according to the stages of production and management:

- *work*–the abstract concept of the original idea
- *expression*–the medium and technique chosen to present the work, still an abstraction
- *manifestation*–the edition or the physical item presenting the expression
- *item*–a single copy of the manifestation

In connection with the various above-mentioned projects to transfer older material to an electronic format, it is evident that while one may encounter the category "electronic" on the abstract levels, one definitely finds it on the manifestation or item levels.

MARC, the MAchine Readable Cataloguing, dominated by the MARC 21 format and its predecessors, has recently taken one step in the direction given in the FRBR. The type of publication code for electronic resource, the code "m" in record label character position 06, is now applicable only for software, multimedia resources, numerical information and online services. Electronic versions and electronic distribution of works of other types are to be coded for their respective type, meaning that an electronic text document is coded "a," a map "e" (or "f" if it is the digitized version of a manuscript map). The code tag 008 follows suit but may be complemented by a repeatable tag 006 covering the electronic characteristics of those resources.

AACR2, so far, is remarkably stubborn or rigid. The most recent version, the 1998 revision, does not take ISBD(ER) into account at all but still bases its description of electronic resources on the 1990 ISBD(CF). Thus we have the strange situation where the description of an electronic text document contains the GMD "computer file" after the title proper, but the underlying MARC 21 bibliographic record fails to give equal emphasis to the work's electronic format. However, *libraries*, the users of AACR2, have found the code's comprehensiveness to be well justified: the term *document* can encompass many things, any unit of information with an independent value, be it in a museum, an archive, or a library. And the holdings in electronic form have continued to grow, both absolutely and relatively, a fact that has changed the behaviour and expectations of patrons.

Lastly, work on a new AACR has begun. Here it should be noted that certain parties involved question the use of area 3 (Type of resource) for electronic resources and want to record the information in the notes area instead. Their main reason seems to be that the designations describe what amounts to simple genre-like categories. More interesting, perhaps, is the recent work done on redefining the concept of "serial," but that is a special topic in itself.

The *metadata activities*, exemplified by the Dublin Core Metadata Initiative, are offering a real alternative to MARC, so far without having done anything noteworthy about cataloguing rules. They promise a more simplified input and a more flexible output, using general text mark-up technology, but they are more dependent on well-established cataloguing practice than they admit (some of them even seem to reinvent cataloguing).

IMPLICATIONS

What do these developments mean to ISBD(ER) in general now and in the future, and especially, how has this process (and what is to come) affected the bibliographic treatment of serial publications?

General Structure

We dare now say with certainty that there will be no real use for specialized sets of descriptive guidelines based on the physical format of an object. As was already evident in the 1997 Toronto International Conference on the Principles and Future Development of AACR and stressed again in the Library of Congress's Bicentennial Conference on Bibliographic Control for the New Millennium in 2000, rule 0.24 of AACR2 must be reworded. Indeed, the logical model set up by the FRBR project should be adopted, leading to, among other things, the establishment of dedicated authority records for agents, works and subjects. Several of these record schemes will have to support networks for international identification codes.

The simplest example of this change is that the remarkable mixture in AACR2 rule 1.1C1 of terms for works or expressions (among them cartographic material, motion picture, sound recording, text) and terms for manifestations or items (Braille, microform) must be restructured. "Computer file" in the present code can be both, and has to be coped with accordingly. A "General work designation" (GWD) that would allow for the possible addition of a term for the manifestation within parenthesis (e.g., [Music (Braille)]) could do as an interim solution.

The ISBD family has all along offered the general advice that cataloguers may need to consult several ISBDs when describing an item that extends beyond the scope of a single ISBD. Similarly, paragraph 0.23 of AACR2 directs the cataloger to

> Use the chapters in part I alone or in conjunction as the specific problem demands. For example, a difficult problem in describing a serial sound recording may lead the user to consult chapters 1, 6, and 12.[8]

Making this process as cataloguer-friendly as possible should be seen as a challenge for the new AACR.

Descriptions in Cross-Domain Searching

In this context, it must be stressed that the change of definition implemented by MARC 21 for "electronic resource" in the coded tags must be accepted in the cataloguing code for display purposes. On the other hand, the fact that an expression or a manifestation of a text (or any other work not covered by the new concept "electronic resource") is in an electronic format must be early and clearly displayed in the description in order to help the user select what versions to use. It is thus extremely disturbing to try to downplay area 3 as the natural place for this information.

This can be illustrated with a record for a large Swedish map in electronic form, first given in the ISBD(ER) format as it now stands:

Gröna kartan [Electronic resource] : CD-ROM för Windows och Macintosh /

Lantmäteriverket. - Map data. - Scale 1:50 000. - Gävle, 1996- - 20 disks : col.

Without area 3, you have no hint that it is a map until you reach "Scale":

Gröna kartan [Electronic resource] : CD-ROM för Windows och Macintosh /

Lantmäteriverket. - Scale 1:50 000. - Gävle, 1996-. - 20 disks : col.

Without the GMD, the same two records would be:

> Gröna kartan : CD-ROM för Windows och Macintosh / Lantmäteriverket. - Electronic map
>
> data. - Scale 1:50 000. - Gävle, 1996- - 20 disks : col.

and

> Gröna kartan : CD-ROM för Windows och Macintosh / Lantmäteriverket. - Scale 1:50 000.
>
> - Gävle, 1996- - 20 electronic disks : col.

Here one sees nothing regarding the format until one encounters the term *electronic*.

If the map were described according to the new MARC 21 practice, the record would be:

> Gröna kartan [Cartographic material] : CD-ROM för Windows och Macintosh /
>
> Lantmäteriverket. - Electronic map data. - Scale 1:50 000. - Gävle, 1996-. - 20 disks : col.

or, without the area 3,

> Gröna kartan [Cartographic material] : CD-ROM för Windows och Macintosh /
>
> Lantmäteriverket. - Scale 1:50 000. - Gävle. 1996-. - 20 electronic disks : col.

However, one might feel inclined to admit that the following layout is the most elegant and economic for the electronic version alone, and it is in fact one of the options already supported by the present rules:

> Gröna kartan : CD-ROM för Windows och Macintosh / Lantmäteriverket. - Electronic
>
> map data. - Scale 1:50 000. - Gävle, 1996-. - 20 disks : col.

It is important to point out, however, that this map is also available in a paper edition. In a combined catalogue, covering all sorts of material, the following two records would be the most suitable, since the important information about the material is presented earlier and more clearly in the record. A user can easily distinguish between them, they file together, and both are quite understandable even without the latter parts of area 1 (Title and statement of responsibility):

> Gröna kartan [Cartographic material] : topografiska kartan skala 1:50 000 /
>
> Lantmäteriverket. - Skala 1:50 000. - Gävle, 1983- . - 690 maps : col. ; 50 x 50 cm.
>
> Gröna kartan [Cartographic material] : CD-ROM för Windows och Macintosh /
>
> Lantmäteriverket. - Electronic map data. - Scale 1:50 000. - Gävle, 1996-. - 20 disks : col.

This leads us to the recommendation that the doubling of information between the General Work Designation and area 3 (Cartographic material–Map) should be permitted with some generosity, meaning also that the GWD should be allowed to retain its present place in catalogue procedures.

Serials

In serials cataloguing, the early warning "Electronic journal" in area 3 immediately after the title area is valued information to users, alerting them to what is to be expected in the record (no physical holdings, an Internet address, etc.). In the case of parallel print and electronic versions with identical titles, library practice may choose to cover them both in the same record, just adding the alternative ISSN and the alternative availability in the latter parts of the record. However, one still has to be able to describe the two versions of the publication separately, and then the regular ER-oriented technique is to be preferred.

THE FUTURE

In conclusion, the focus of this essay has to be somewhat changed. We must remember that the ISBDs, just as AACR2 and its forerunners, are products of what might be termed the "fixed formats era," when cataloguers had cards or printed bibliographies as their goal. Confidence in the fixed format went as far as saying that one of the reasons for ISBD punctuation was that the resulting record could be mapped by computer into a MARC format (but has that actually ever occurred in MARC cataloguing?). A residual of this approach is found in the MARC format and even permitted to reside in the most recent of them, MARC 21, revealed by the totally outdated handling of punctuation prescribed there. But normally now cataloguers produce records for computerized files. The data elements of the description are tagged, and the precision required by the computer has at last given the issues surrounding authorized forms of search elements the priority status they should have had all along.

Of course there will be a certain production of bibliographies in fixed formats, but from databases, and the designers of those presentation formats will hopefully turn to the provisions of the ISBD family for guidance as to the selection of information elements, internal order and punctuation. That will definitely facilitate universal intelligibility, and trained librarians are still aware of this. Also, for the same reason, presentation on OPAC screens might be designed to adopt at least the internal punctuation patterns given by the ISBDs for each area, even when the record is made more user-friendly through the use of captions. On the whole, however, efforts in the development of cataloguing should be directed not toward revising rules to accommodate presentation but toward facilitating the input of high-quality data into relational or object-oriented computer applications.

The ISBDs were a useful exercise, extremely important for cataloguing development, and they will stand for a long time without more far-reaching maintenance. The ongoing revision of ISBD(S) may seem more far-reaching, but that is due to progress in the analysis of the concept of seriality. Their relative importance has already started to diminish, however, and that is life, even in librarianship.

REFERENCES

1. *ISBD(NBM): International Standard Bibliographic Description for Non-Book Materials* (London: IFLA Universal Bibliographic Control and International MARC Programme, 1977), 33.

2. *ISBD(CF): International Standard Bibliographic Description for Computer Files* (London: IFLA Universal Bibliographic Control and International MARC Programme, 1990), 1 (footnote 3).

3. *ISBD(CF)*, 1 (footnote 2).

4. *ISBD(CF)*, ii.

5. *ISBD(CF)*, 93, slightly abridged.

6. *ISBD(ER): International Standard Bibliographic Description for Electronic Resources* (München: Saur, 1997), viii.

7. *ISBD(ER)*, 51-52.

8. *Anglo-American Cataloguing Rules*. 2nd ed., 1998 revision (Ottawa: Canadian Library Association, 1998), 8.

The Integration of Electronic Resources into Cataloging Instruction in the LIS Curriculum

Taemin Kim Park

SUMMARY. Basic, advanced, and related cataloging courses were examined to demonstrate the extent of integration of electronic Web resources into cataloging instruction in LIS programs in the U.S. Forty-five library school programs are analyzed to determine the extent of integration of Web resources, the major and sub-topics covered in full courses in cataloging Web resources, the methods of teaching, and the extent of integration of Web tools and standards into cataloging instruction. Seven full courses devoted to the instruction of cataloging electronic resources were identified. An early stage of cataloging instruction in electronic resources and some of the challenges in teaching are presented. *[Article copies available for a fee from The Haworth Document Delivery Service: 1-800-HAWORTH. E-mail ad-*

Taemin Kim Park is Associate Librarian, Indiana University Libraries and Adjunct Associate Professor, School of Library and Information Science, Indiana University, 1320 E. 10th Street, Bloomington, IN 47405 (e-mail park@indiana.edu).

The author would like to thank Dr. Thomas E. Nisonger, School of Library and Information Science, Indiana University, for helpful comments.

[Haworth co-indexing entry note]: "The Integration of Electronic Resources into Cataloging Instruction in the LIS Curriculum." Park, Taemin Kim. Co-published simultaneously in *The Serials Librarian* (The Haworth Information Press, an imprint of The Haworth Press, Inc.) Vol. 41, No. 3/4, 2002, pp. 57-72; and: *E-Serials Cataloging: Access to Continuing and Integrating Resources via the Catalog and the Web* (ed: Jim Cole, and Wayne Jones) The Haworth Information Press, an imprint of The Haworth Press, Inc., 2002, pp. 57-72. Single or multiple copies of this article are available for a fee from The Haworth Document Delivery Service [1-800-HAWORTH, 9:00 a.m. - 5:00 p.m. (EST). E-mail address: getinfo@haworthpressinc.com].

57

*dress: <getinfo@haworthpressinc.com> Website: <http://www.HaworthPress.com>
© 2002 by The Haworth Press, Inc. All rights reserved.]*

KEYWORDS. Cataloging, Internet, electronic resources, networked resources, digital resources

INTRODUCTION

The cataloging and classification curricula in the schools of library and information science appear to be strong. A recent survey reports that an introductory course in cataloging and classification was offered by all programs in the U.S. and Canada.[1] Rapid growth of the Internet and the World Wide Web has brought a substantial amount of electronic resources to libraries and information centers and increasingly raised the question of how we can best organize and integrate these resources into the existing print-based collection. A recent announcement from *The Directory of Scholarly Electronic Journals and Academic Discussion Lists, 2000* reported that there are over 3,900 peer-reviewed journal titles available electronically.[2] A major portion of scholarly electronic publications are digitized progressively and aggregated by various parties involved with Web publishing and delivery. For example, there are the traditional commercial publishers (e.g., Reed Elsevier, Academic Press, Wiley InterScience), vendors (EBSCO Information Services, Bell & Howell, Catchword), university-based projects (Johns Hopkins University's MUSE, Oxford University Press, Cambridge University Press, Stanford University Library's HighWire Press), and the JSTOR project. OCLC is also a major information provider for electronic journal collections. NetLibrary provides access to e-books for more than 5000 libraries.[3]

Increasingly users expect and prefer to have electronic resources easily available at their fingertips. Andrew Odlyzko reports that usage of online scholarly material is growing rapidly because of its easy access, even surpassing the usage expected with traditional print journals.[4]

Recent position descriptions for cataloging areas show a similar trend and call for new skills and knowledge in metadata standards for digital resources in addition to the existing bibliographic standards such as AACR2, MARC, LC subject headings and classification, among others. Bibliographic utilities like OCLC have taken initiatives in cataloging Internet resources (e.g., InterCat Project, CORC) and developing bibliographic standards such as Dublin Core. A journal devoted to the cataloging issues and problems of Internet resources, *Journal of Internet Cataloging*, was launched in 1997.

Despite the rapid growth in electronic resources and its uses, there has been relatively little written in the library literature concerning the problems and issues of educating and preparing practicing librarians and students for those challenges. In this paper, available courses, major topics, and methods of teaching and instruction regarding electronic-resource organization and access are reported. A survey was conducted to gain first-hand knowledge regarding the nature and extent of the courses and instructions in the LIS programs in the U.S.

LITERATURE REVIEW

Studies of the education for cataloging and classification have examined course content, course names, the number of courses available, theory-versus practice-based instruction, teaching methods, and cognitive requirements of the profession. By analyzing cataloging and classification courses and other related courses listed in the sixteen graduate library schools' bulletins offering a post-master's program, McAllister-Harper classified them into twelve general areas.[5] The twelve areas are: Advanced Cataloging and Classification, Analytical Bibliography, Automation, Bibliographic Organization, Cataloging and Classification, Classification Systems, Collection Development, Indexing, Organization of Special Types of Materials, Special Problems and Policies of Library Cataloging, Subject Analysis and Searching, and Technical Services. Automation and Cataloging and Classification courses were represented as 20.34% and 16.10 % of total courses, respectively.

Discussing the teaching of cataloging courses, Saye emphasized the problem-solving skills which are necessary in the cataloging process.[6] Three levels of cataloging instructions were suggested: basic, advanced, and related courses. For example, the following topics of study were identified as core course content: descriptive cataloging, access points, authority work, Dewey Decimal Classification, MARC format, OCLC, filing, and treatment of non-book materials. The elements for an advanced cataloging course were listed as: descriptive cataloging, Library of Congress Rule Interpretations, non-book material cataloging, additional classification work, MARC formatting, OCLC input and editing experience, antiquarian-materials cataloging, and serial cataloging. Courses for specialized and managerial knowledge were recommended: management of technical services operations, system analysis, database management, library automation, abstracting and indexing, theory of classification, collection development, government publications, serial publications, online searching, and history of the book.

By surveying cataloging educators and practitioners, Sheila Intner identified the seven most frequently selected theoretical topics and the ten most often selected practical topics.[7] The theoretical topics were: theoretical bases for subject heading/indexing, classification, descriptive cataloging, bibliographic networks, Cutter's objects, history of subject heading/indexing, and classification. The most-selected practical topics were: LCRIs, rules of applying subject headings, LC classification, DDC schedules, LC subject headings, bibliographic networks, AACR2, MARC formats, other classification systems, and construction of notes.

Noting the changes in the traditional functions of cataloging departments in libraries, Callahan and MacLeod urge educators to incorporate administrative skills and knowledge into the cataloging curriculum.[8] Hope A. Olson suggests a holistic approach in teaching cataloging courses, including critical knowledge and critical thinking.[9]

Sherry L. Vellucci examined bulletins of 52 library schools in the U.S. and Canada and reported the current trends in cataloging instruction.[10] Cataloging courses were categorized into introductory, advanced, and other related courses. The survey reported that an introductory cataloging course was offered by all programs. Courses in cataloging and classification were offered by 92% of the programs while 38% offered courses in information organization. The topics listed in Saye's core course content are all included except for filing. However, the strong shift toward a broader and more theoretical approach to information organization was noted in these more generic course titles: Theory of Organization of Information, Information Structure, and Organization and Representation of Knowledge and Information. Broader topics such as information transfer theory, bibliographic and document description, indexing and abstracting principles, natural-language processing, organization of records, document mark-up, and information retrieval theory were also noted. Advanced cataloging courses remained strong and covered such areas as Advanced Cataloging, Advanced Subject Analysis, Classification Theory, Advanced Descriptive Cataloging, Non-Print Cataloging, and Other Cataloging Electives. Topics identified by Saye remained the same in advanced cataloging courses. New topics such as metadata standards were noted in some advanced courses. Cataloging components were also identified in related courses in specific formats or types of librarianship. The total number of all cataloging-related courses was 156, with a range from 1 to 7 and with a mean of 3 courses per program. Related courses which contain technological components were identified: Networks, Library Automation, Systems Analysis, Information Storage and Retrieval, and Information System Design. Considering all the changes in the information environment and information technology, a syndetic structure for cataloging education and identification of related links within the existing LIS programs was suggested.

In light of the continued decline in cataloging education and the number of professional catalogers during the last thirty years, Janet Swan Hill and Sheila S. Intner urge today's cataloging professionals to be prepared as knowledge managers because the library catalog functions as a powerful gateway to the world of knowledge.[11] Ingrid Hsieh-Yee introduced a strategy for teaching the Organization of Internet Resources adopted at Catholic University of America's LIS program.[12] Three levels of cataloging courses were reported: the awareness of Internet-resources cataloging and metadata in basic cataloging courses; the application of cataloging standards and Dublin Core to Internet resources in the advanced cataloging course; and providing hands-on practice in creating electronic pathfinders and in the use of metadata standards such as the Dublin Core, Text Encoding Initiative (TEI) headers, and Encoded Archival Description (EAD) in the advanced Internet-resources organization course.

RESEARCH QUESTIONS

To be responsive to the growing collection of electronic resources in libraries and information centers and to the increasing demand from the professional community, cataloging curricula were examined to answer the following questions:

- To what extent are electronic resources covered in the cataloging and classification and organization of information courses in the LIS curriculum in the U.S.?
- What are the main topics in courses fully devoted to cataloging electronic resources? How are electronic resources viewed by faculty members and what teaching methods are used for them?
- To what extent are cataloging resources available on the Internet utilized and integrated in the cataloging instruction? Which resources are most often used?

DATA COLLECTION

Data for this study were collected in two phases: Website visits and an e-mail survey. The researcher visited the Websites of schools of library and information science programs in the U.S. during the fall and winter 2000 to identify the courses that cover the organization and access aspects of electronic resources. The list of 48 schools in LIS maintained on the homepage of the Association for Library and Information Science Education was accessed.[13] Except for 3 schools, online course syllabi or lists of courses were available at the school's Website. Therefore, 45 schools are used for data collection and analysis.

E-mail and Website analysis has been used by others as a method for surveying the education for Digital Libraries.[14] Survey research has been used in assessing the instruction of online searching in library education.[15,16,17] Those studies were instrumental in designing this research. After the preliminary Website analysis, a survey asking 7 questions was mailed in December 2000 to the JESSE listserv, the leading listserv in library and information science education. As the initial response from the e-mail survey was very low, the same questionnaire was sent again in January 2001 to the JESSE listserv and the listserv of the American Society for Information Science and Technology. The same questionnaire was also sent to a dozen educators in LIS who teach the courses relating to cataloging electronic resources.

DATA ANALYSIS

The school Websites reveal the courses available and the online syllabi in the curricula of LIS programs. Courses covering cataloging were identified first. Particular attention was paid to the course titles and descriptions that include Internet, digital, or electronic resources. When the online syllabus was not available for review, the brief description of the course title was used for data collection. Reviewed courses are categorized as full or as courses that include aspects of organizing and accessing electronic resources. Following Vellucci's categorization of cataloging and classification courses, courses that include electronic resources were further categorized under basic cataloging courses, advanced cataloging courses, or cataloging-related courses.

FINDINGS AND DISCUSSIONS

Full cataloging courses offered in the 45 LIS programs showed a total of 226 courses overall in basic, advanced, and cataloging-related courses. The number of courses offered by a given program ranged from 1 to 13, with a mean of 5 courses per program. The higher average number appears to be a result of the recent curriculum expansion in specialized librarianship in archiving resources and multimedia.

Electronic resources are integrated into 54 unique course titles in cataloging and classification or organization of information, and in cataloging-related courses. The list of course titles is presented below. The following topics are emphasized: the extent of integration of electronic resources into basic, advanced cataloging, and cataloging-related courses; major topics in the cataloging of electronic resources; teaching methods; and the challenge of teaching electronic resources.

Integrated Approach:
Basic Cataloging and Information Organization Courses

Electronic resources are integrated into the basic and advanced cataloging courses. A trend toward broader and generic titles is evident as the title names in the following list demonstrate:

Titles of Introductory Cataloging Courses

Bibliographic Access and Control

Bibliographic Control

Cataloging and Classification

Cataloging and Classification of Library Materials

Catalogs, Cataloging and Classification

Content Representation

Descriptive Cataloging

Information Organization and Access

Information Organization and Records Control

Organization and Control of Information Resources I

Organization of Information

Organization of Information and Resources

Organization of Information in Collections

Organization of Knowledge I

Organization of Material

Organizing and Providing Access to Information

Organizing Information

Principles of Information Organization

Representation and Organizing Information Resources

Titles of Advanced Cataloging Courses

Advanced Bibliographic Control

Advanced Cataloging

Advanced Cataloging and Classification

Advanced Cataloging and Organization of Information

Advanced Representation and Organization of Information Resources

Cataloging and Classification II

Knowledge Structure II

Organization and Representation of Multimedia Information Resources

Organization of Knowledge II

Organization of Materials II

Representation and Organization of Non-textual Information Resources

Seminar in the Organization of Knowledge

Titles of Cataloging-Related Courses

Organization and access to electronic resources was identified as a topic in more specialized archival, digital record management, museum information, and multi-media information courses. The expanded list of courses beyond the text-based collection is noteworthy:

Abstracting and Indexing for Information Retrieval

Access Systems for Archival Materials

Archival Representation

Administration of Archives and Manuscript Collections

Classification for Information Display and Discovery

Digital Image Storage and Retrieval

Digital Libraries

Graphical Information Management

Introduction to Electronic Records Management

Management of Digital Records

Moving Image Cataloging

Museum Informatics

Music and Sound as Information

Principles of Records and Information Management

Serials

Visual Information Retrieval

Full Courses

Full courses dealing with cataloging and access to electronic resources are available. Courses are often offered as seminars or special topics. Seven course titles are listed:

- Cataloging and Classification of Internet Resources (Queens College)
- Metadata Standards and Vocabulary Control (UCLA)
- Meta-data Analysis (North Carolina Central University)
- Metadata Architectures and Applications (University of North Carolina)
- Metadata for Internet Resources (Dominican University)
- Organization of Internet Resources (Catholic University of America)
- Technology and Bibliographic Control (St. John's University)

Major Topics in Cataloging Courses in Electronic Resources

Major topics and subtopics in cataloging and classification of electronic resources were identified by analyzing the online syllabi or description of courses accessible on the schools' Websites. Only the seven separately titled full courses were used in this analysis. Responses to survey questionnaires were added as well.

Among the electronic resources included in cataloging courses, Websites were covered most frequently, while electronic resources on CD-ROM and e-serials were the next most frequently covered. Faculty members expected e-books to be covered by students' projects and presentations. Table 1 shows the result.

For metadata standards and codes, Dublin Core, USMARC, and TEI headers were the most frequently covered codes. They were followed by EAD, SGML (Standard Markup Language), and GILS (Global Information Locator Service). Metadata codes in text, government resources, instructional material, and visual resources were also covered (see Table 2).

Topics in metadata and Web resources include such subtopics as: Resource Selection and Evaluation; Creation, Description, Presentation and Integration of Records; Subject Analysis; Thesaurus; Classification; Access Using Catalogs and Websites; and CORC. Other subtopics listed are: Internet Search Tools and Engines; Interface Design; Data Warehousing; Data Mining; Electronic Commerce; Gateways; and Portals.

TABLE 1. Types of Electronic Resources Cited

Types	No.
Websites (pages, databases, multimedia)	10
CD-ROMs	8
E-serials	6
Images	4
E-books	3
Computer disks	1
Computer tapes	1
Other	2

TABLE 2. Metadata Codes Covered

Metadata Codes	No.
USMARC	10
Dublin Core	11
TEI Header	10
EAD	8
SGML	4
HTML	1
XHTML	1
XML	2
GILS	2
Instructional Management System (IMS)	1
Visual Resources Association Core Categories (VRACC)	1
Resource Description Framework (RDF)	2

Instructions in cataloging electronic courses are provided most often in lecture/seminar and discussion settings with demonstrations by the instructor. Students' hands-on practices, projects, and presentations are also major instructional methods. Guest speakers and field trips are also shown to be part of the instructional effort (see Table 3).

Most often a unit of a course is allocated to cataloging electronic resources in an integrated approach. But less than a unit is also typical coverage in the basic and advanced cataloging courses (see Table 4).

As previously noted, 7 full courses in the cataloging and classification of Internet resources were identified. Faculty members assigned a high rating to the usefulness of the electronic resources instruction, but some instructional challenges in incorporating them were noted. The lack of class time was the most often mentioned challenge in teaching cataloging courses. Lack of knowledgeable faculty and of technical support were also noted. Other problems in the instruction in cataloging area for electronic resources were difficulties in getting good examples, the need to focus on principles, and the lack of clarity in the cataloging rules (see Table 5).

WEB RESOURCES FOR THE INSTRUCTION OF ELECTRONIC RESOURCE CATALOGING

Appendix 1 provides a list of the Web resources most often mentioned in course syllabi for the cataloging and classification of electronic resources available. Web resources in cataloging standards, tools, and reference sources are listed only. Some resources were also provided by respondents to the survey questionnaires.

TABLE 3. Methods of Teaching Cataloging Electronic Resources

Method	No.
Lectures	14
Demonstration	8
Discussions	8
Hands-on	7
Student projects and presentations	7
Guest speaker	3
Workshop	1
Other (field trip, lab use)	3

TABLE 4. Coverage of Electronic Resources

Extent	No. of Responses
Brief	2
Frequent	2
One Unit	5
Several Units	1

TABLE 5. Barriers in Teaching Electronic Resources

Barrier	No. of Responses
Lack of class time	7
Lack of knowledgeable instructor	2
Lack of technological support	1
Other	3

CONCLUSION

Continued changes in information objects and information technology have influenced the cataloging curriculum. The shift from paper-based to electronic-based resources in the library collection also means a shift from ownership to access: libraries purchase access to digital information rather than owning the items. Recent position announcements in library and information science publications reflect a similar trend. Many positions use such titles as "Networked Electronic Resources Librarian," "Electronic Resources Access Specialist," and "Electronic Resources Cataloger," and ask for information technology skills such as knowledge of markup languages and metadata standards, in addition to knowledge of traditional bibliographic tools and standards.

The extent of electronic resources in cataloging instruction in 45 LIS programs in the U.S. was examined. Data were collected by visiting schools' Websites and using survey questionnaires. Fifty-four different course titles in LIS programs were identified as including aspects of organizing and accessing of electronic resources. Many types of electronic resources were covered: Websites (for pages and databases), CD-ROMs, e-serials, images, e-books, computer disks, and computer files. Seven separate, full courses devoted to the cataloging of electronic resources were identified. The major topics in fully developed cataloging courses in electronic resources were identified. The most frequently used methods of teaching were: lectures, demonstrations, discussions, hands-on practice, student projects and presentations, team work, guest speakers, and tours. Some challenges in cataloging instruction in electronic resources were discussed. The most frequently used Web resources and tools available on the Internet in cataloging instruction were identified and listed.

With the future direction of cataloging and catalogers a little uncertain in this rapidly changing environment of information technology, Marcia Bates advises us to get serious about non-text media cataloging as we enter the 21st century.[18] She recommends that schools have a strategic plan for integrating ever-increasing electronic resources into their cataloging instructions. Students will be better prepared during this dynamic transition to digital-based information and services.

NOTES

1. Sherry L. Vellucci, "Cataloging Across the Curriculum: A Syndetic Structure for Teaching Cataloging," *Cataloging & Classification Quarterly* 24, nos. 1-2 (1997): 45.

2. Dru Mogge, "New ARL Directory for E-journals and Discussion List," Feb. 13, 2001, *ARL-EJOURNAL@CNI.ORG*.

3. *Library Journal Academic News Wire*, Jan. 25, 2001, http://www.libraryjournal.com/newswire/newswire.as.

4. Andrew Odlyzko, "The Rapid Evolution of Scholarly Communication," http://www.si.umich.edu/PEAK-2000/odlyzko.pdf (viewed Feb. 21, 2001).

5. Desretta McAllister-Harper, "An Analysis of Courses in Cataloging and Classification and Related Areas Offered in Sixteen Graduate Library Schools and Their Relationship to Present and Future Trends in Cataloging and Classification and to Cognitive Needs of Professional Academic Catalogers," *Cataloging & Classification Quarterly* 16, no. 3 (1993): 99-123.

6. Jerry D. Saye, "The Cataloging Experience in Library and Information Science Education: An Educator's Perspective," *Cataloging & Classification Quarterly* 7, no. 4 (1987): 27-45.

7. Sheila S. Intner, "Cataloging Practice and Theory: What to Teach and Why," *Journal of Education for Library and Information Science* 30, no. 4 (1990): 333-336.

8. Daren Callahan and Judy MacLeod, "Management Issues and the Challenge for Cataloging Education," *Technical Services Quarterly* 13, no. 2 (1996): 15-24.

9. Hope A. Olson, "Thinking Professionals: Teaching Critical Cataloging," *Technical Services Quarterly* 15, no. 1/2 (1997): 51-66.

10. Vellucci, 35-59.

11. Janet Swan Hill and Sheila S. Intner, "Preparing for a Cataloging Career from Cataloging to Knowledge Management," http://www.ala.org/congress/hill-intner_print.html (viewed July 27, 2000).

12. Ingrid Hsieh-Yee, "Organizing Internet Resources: Teaching Cataloging Standards and Beyond," *OCLC System & Services* 16, no. 3 (2000): 130-143.

13. "ALISE Institutional Members," http://www.alise.org/nondiscuss/schools.html (viewed Apr. 10, 2001).

14. Amanda Spink and Colleen Cool, "Education for Digital Libraries," *D-Lib Magazine* 5, no. 5 (1999), http://www.dlib.org/dlib/may99/05spink.html (viewed Aug. 4, 2000).

15. Stephen P. Harter, "An Assessment of Instruction Provided by Library Schools in On-line Searching," *Information Processing & Management* 15 (1979): 71-75.

16. Stephen P. Harter and Carol H. Fenichel, "Online Searching in Library Education," *Journal of Education for Librarianship* 23 (1982): 3-22.

17. Ingrid Hsieh-Yee, "Teaching Online and CD-ROM Resources," *Journal of Education for Library and Information Science* 38, no. 1 (1997): 14-34.

18. Marcia J. Bates, "Information Curriculum for the 21st Century," http://www.ala.org/congress/bates.html (viewed Feb. 10, 2001).

APPENDIX 1

Web Resources for the Instruction of Electronic Resource Cataloging

- ALCTS/CCS/SAC/Subcommittee on Metadata and Classification. *Final Report.* 1999. http://www.ala.org/alcts/organization/ccs/sac/metaclassfinal.pdf (viewed Feb. 26, 2001).

- *Cataloger's Reference Shelf.* http://www.tlcdelivers.com/tlc/crs/ (viewed Feb. 26, 2001).

- *CONSER (Cooperative Online Serials).* http://lcweb.loc.gov/acq/conser/homepage. html (viewed Feb. 21, 2001).

- *Dublin Core Metadata Initiative (DCMI).* http://dublincore.org/ (viewed Apr. 11, 2001)

- *Encoded Archival Description: Official Web Site.* http://lcweb.loc.gov/ead/ (viewed Feb. 25, 2001).

- Getty Research Institute. *Introduction to Metadata: Pathways to Digital Information.* Version 2.0. http://www.getty.edu/gri/standard/intrometadata/ (viewed Feb. 21, 2001).

- *Global Information Locator Service (GILS).* http://www.gils.net/index.html (viewed Feb. 21, 2001).

- Hsieh-Yee, Ingrid. *Organizing Audiovisual and Electronic Resources for Access: A Cataloging Guide.* Englewood, CO: Libraries Unlimited, 2000. Companion site: http://slis.cua.edu/ihy/catmeta.htm (viewed Feb. 25, 2001).

- IFLA. *Digital Libraries: Metadata Resources.* http://www.ifla.org/II/metadata.htm (viewed Feb. 23, 2001).

- *IMS Global Learning Consortium, Inc.* http://www.imsproject.org/index. html (viewed Feb. 26, 2001).

- *Information Runaway: Information Organization and Retrieval.* http:// people.unt.edu/~skh0001/is/abstracts.HTM (viewed Feb. 21, 2001).

- *ISBD(ER): International Standard Bibliographic Description for Electronic Resources.* London: IFLA, 1997. http://www.ifla.org/VII/s13/pubs/isbd.htm (viewed Feb. 26, 2001).

- *Journal of Internet Cataloging: The International Quarterly of Digital Organization, Classification & Access.* 1996- . http://www.haworthpressinc.com:8081/ jic/ (viewed Feb. 21, 2001).

- Library of Congress. *HTML: HyperText Markup Language: A Library of Congress Internet Resource Page.* http://lcweb.loc.gov/global/internet/ html.html (viewed Feb. 21, 2001).

- Library of Congress. Network Development and MARC Standards Office. *MARC 21 Concise Format for Authority Data.* http://lcweb.loc.gov/ marc/authority/ (viewed Feb. 20, 2001).

- Library of Congress. Network Development and MARC Standards Office. *MARC 21 Concise Format for Bibliographic Data.* http://lcweb.loc.gov/ marc/bibliographic/ (viewed Feb. 20, 2001).

- Miller, Eric. "An Introduction to the Resource Description Framework," *D-Lib Magazine*, May 1998. http://www.dlib.org/dlib/may98/miller/ 05miller.html (viewed Feb. 21, 2001).

- OCLC. *Bibliographic Formats and Standards.* http://www.oclc.org/oclc/bib/ toc.htm (viewed Feb. 21, 2001).

- OCLC. *Internet Cataloging Project.* http://www.oclc.org/oclc/man/catproj/ catcall.htm (viewed Feb. 26, 2001).

- Olson, Nancy, ed. *Cataloging Internet Resources: A Manual and Practical Guide.* 2nd ed. 1997. http://www.oclc.org/oclc/man/9256cat/toc.htm (viewed Feb. 26, 2001).

- Pitti, Daniel V. "Encoded Archival Description: An Introduction and Overview," *D-Lib Magazine* 5, no. 11 (Nov. 1999). http://www.dlib.org/ dlib/november99/11pitti.html (viewed Feb. 26, 2001)

- *Resource Description Framework (RDF) Model and Syntax Specification.* http://www.w3.org/TR/PR-rdf-syntax (viewed Feb. 26, 2001).

- Rosenberg, Matt T. *Library of Congress Classification System [outline].* http://geography.miningco.com/science/geography/library/congress/bllc.htm (viewed Feb. 25, 2001).

- *Technical Processing Online Tools.* http://tpot.ucsd.edu/ (viewed Feb. 26, 2001).

- University of Virginia. Electronic Text Center. *The Electronic Text Center Introduction to TEI and Guide to Document Preparation.* http://etext.lib.virginia.edu/tei/uvatei.html (viewed Apr. 11, 2001).

- Visual Resources Association. *VRA Core Categories.* Version 3.0. http://www.gsd.harvard.edu/~staffaw3/vra/vracore3.htm#core (viewed Apr. 11, 2001).

- Vizine-Goetz, Diane. "Using Library Classification Schemes for Internet Resources." http://www.oclc.org/oclc/man/colloq/v-g.htm (viewed Feb. 21, 2001).

- W3C. *XHTML™ 1.0: The Extensible HyperText Markup Language: A Reformulation of HTML 4 in XML 1.0: W3C Recommendation.* Jan. 26, 2000. http://www.w3.org/TR/xhtml1/ (viewed Feb. 21, 2001).

- *The XML Cover Pages.* http://www.oasis-open.org/cover/sgml-xml.html (viewed Feb. 23, 2001).

Teaching Seriality:
A Major Educational Challenge

Arlene G. Taylor

SUMMARY. Teaching the difference between "serial" and "monograph" has plagued cataloging teachers for decades. Seemingly arbitrary differences in treatment of continuing resources based on seemingly arbitrary definitions serve to confuse students and make the cataloging process seem illogical. Models created in the process of trying to reform AACR2 to accommodate electronic continuing resources promise to provide new logic for the teaching of seriality. *[Article copies available for a fee from The Haworth Document Delivery Service: 1-800-HAWORTH. E-mail address: <getinfo@haworthpressinc.com> Website: <http://www.HaworthPress.com> © 2002 by The Haworth Press, Inc. All rights reserved.]*

KEYWORDS. Seriality, continuing resources, cataloging, education, electronic resources

One of the most difficult concepts to explain to new students of library science has always been the difference between "monograph" and "serial." This was true even in the (what now seems straightforward) print world. For example, the *Anglo-American Cataloguing Rules* (AACR2) definition of serial says that "serials include . . . numbered monographic series."[1] Say what? Serials in-

Arlene G. Taylor is Professor in the Department of Library and Information Science, School of Information Sciences, University of Pittsburgh, Pittsburgh, PA.

[Haworth co-indexing entry note]: "Teaching Seriality: A Major Educational Challenge." Taylor, Arlene G. Co-published simultaneously in *The Serials Librarian* (The Haworth Information Press, an imprint of The Haworth Press, Inc.) Vol. 41, No. 3/4, 2002, pp. 73-80; and: *E-Serials Cataloging: Access to Continuing and Integrating Resources via the Catalog and the Web* (ed: Jim Cole, and Wayne Jones) The Haworth Information Press, an imprint of The Haworth Press, Inc., 2002, pp. 73-80. Single or multiple copies of this article are available for a fee from The Haworth Document Delivery Service [1-800-HAWORTH, 9:00 a.m. - 5:00 p.m. (EST). E-mail address: getinfo@haworthpressinc.com].

clude something monographic? "Well . . . ," the teacher tries to explain, "series can be issued successively with numbering, but the individual 'issues' may be monographs. In some libraries," the explanation continues, "series are checked in as serials but are cataloged and shelved as monographs." How could a novice possibly be expected to understand?

AACR2 defines monograph as "a nonserial item."[2] So it really is necessary to understand "serial" in order to understand "monograph." And it is necessary to understand both in order to learn to use AACR2. But "serial" is often dependent upon treatment in a particular setting. Libraries have set up serials management and control systems that require this choice of treatment. Serials need to be subscribed to and checked in. The management systems designed for these processes are ideal for ordering and registering receipt of any publication that is to be received in more than one piece over a period of time. Thus, serials control is given to loose-leaf services, multivolume sets, monographic series that are not numbered, and other such publications that do not fit the AACR2 definition: "A publication in any medium issued in successive parts bearing numeric or chronological designations and intended to be continued indefinitely."[3]

Further complicating the issue is the way the rules call for cataloging serials versus monographic series. A separate chapter is to be followed for cataloging serials; so it is necessary for the new student not only to distinguish serials from monographs but to learn different conventions for their cataloging. If a publication is considered to be a serial, a bibliographic record is created for it according to AACR2, chapter 12. A change in title is noted in one or more linking notes that provide an added entry link to a previous title and/or a following title. On the other hand, a monographic series (which, if numbered, is considered to be a serial) is cataloged as a series added entry named on each bibliographic record for each of the monographs in the series. An entry is prepared for the monographic series title that goes into the name/title authority file. A change in title means that the previous title and/or a following title are given as cross references on the series authority record. The results in a catalog of having some serials represented by bibliographic records (with links as added entries) versus having others represented by series authority records (with links as cross references) can be dramatically different. And in some libraries, some monographic series titles have serial bibliographic records while others have series authority records–the decision often made based upon a decision as to whether to classify the series all with the same classification notation or to provide different classifications based on specific subjects in separate volumes.

Another complication concerns how to catalog a publication that appears on a regular basis with a numeric or chronological designation, but each new issue is meant to replace or supersede all previous issues. Telephone books and directories are examples of this kind of publication. They certainly fit the definition of serial, but if the old volumes are discarded, as they are in many libraries, serial cataloging makes no sense, with its implication that all volumes starting with the first one published years before are available. On the other hand, other reference works are updated with supplements that are not meant to replace earlier volumes, such as the annual yearbooks for encyclopedia sets. Must the encyclopedia set itself be cataloged as a monograph while its yearbooks are cataloged as a serial? Students find this quite bewildering.

Then there are looseleaf publications–monograph or serial? How arbitrary that just because new pages can be inserted between already existing pages (and/or replace existing pages), they are usually cataloged as monographs, while publications like telephone books, in which all pages are replaced by new pages, are supposed to be cataloged as serials.

Besides the choice required in order to use AACR2, one is also required to make the choice in order to use MARC 21 for encoding the bibliographic record. Virtually every cataloging system requires the user to choose among workforms for different physical formats. Included in this choice is a workform for "serial" and one for "monograph." Such workforms are based upon the code in the MARC leader that designates a record as being for either a serial or a monograph.

In the last two decades or so, with the proliferation of many different formats other than text on paper to carry information, the distinction between monographs and serials has become even more difficult to make. Whereas with text on paper a dichotomy between monographs and serials could be (imperfectly) made, with many physical formats a multitude of dichotomous situations can be created: e.g., paper vs. microform, computerized film vs. video, CD-ROM vs. print on paper. Choice of which AACR2 chapter to use as the basis for cataloging an information package is a challenge for even the experienced cataloger. When faced, for example, with manuscript maps issued on CD-ROM serially, but which are expected eventually to cease publication if and when all manuscript maps that can be found in existence have been digitized, what is a rule-conscious cataloger to do? Someone who has not had the privilege of attempting to explain such bibliographic delights to students new not only to cataloging, but to the profession, should not be too quick to complain about what is not taught in library schools these days!

The most recent challenge is that of the World Wide Web with its online publication of "serials" in single databases that are continuously updated by inserting new elements into a searchable database where the new additions are not sequentially added "at the end." In some cases the identical information is also published in sequentially published paper versions. The concept is complicated by all of the Web sites in existence that never become static like a monograph. While there are some Web sites that appear to have become static and/or abandoned by their creators, most are ongoing–the creator adds new information somewhat regularly in order to update and/or improve the site. These seem to resemble looseleaf publications from the print-on-paper world, but they could be considered to be "issued in successive parts bearing numeric or chronological designations and intended to be continued indefinitely." (The "last updated [date]" statements could be considered to be chronological designations.) So, are these serials, the novice asks?

Fortunately, people have been working on the problem and have been making progress in modeling existing publication patterns and in suggesting rule changes toward a solution. The first paper that has been quite helpful from an educational point of view is one written by Jean Hirons and Crystal Graham for the 1997 Conference on the Principles and Future Development of AACR.[4] The authors present in this paper several models of ongoing publications. One of the models illustrates current practice (see Figure 1). Although the terms "determinate" and "indeterminate" in this model are not immediately clear to students, once examples are given and these terms are understood, students begin to understand what AACR2 considers to be a serial, even though they may not see the logic of AACR2's definition. ("Determinate" is used by Hirons and Graham to mean ongoing publications that are intended to be complete eventually, while "indeterminate" is used to mean ongoing publications that are intended to continue indefinitely.)[5]

The concept of "ongoing publication" makes a great deal of sense to new catalogers as they attempt to grapple with the need to describe information packages with enough detail both to identify them and to allow each information package to be distinguished from every other information package, while at the same time limiting the description to only the essential elements. An ongoing publication is not complete and needs to be described to show its incompleteness and to allow for addition and/or change of information as new parts of the ongoing publication are published or added to a Web site. This makes much more sense to students than does the identification of what might be a "serial" that only includes ongoing publications if the publication is intended to go on forever and if the parts are numbered!

Another major issue in cataloging serials has always been how to handle title changes. Through time catalogers have tried various strategies for dealing with these. For many years the theory was that a publication with multiple parts must be cataloged on one bibliographic record. In order to do this if there is a title change between parts, the title on the record must either be the earliest title with later titles identified in notes, or the title on the record must be changed to the latest one with earlier titles identified in notes. Both these methods were tried under earlier cataloging rules, but with AACR it was decided

FIGURE 1. Model Showing "Current Practice" from "Issues Related to Seriality," by Jean Hirons and Crystal Graham, 194.

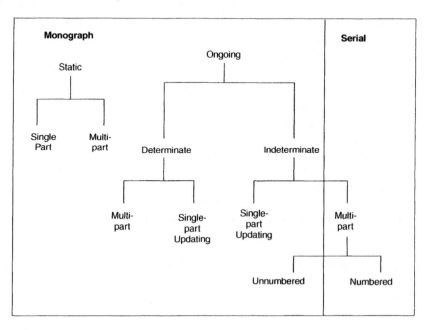

that there could be multiple bibliographic records to reflect title changes, with a new record created each time a title changes.[6] Explaining all this to new students of cataloging is a daunting task. It has been made much more difficult by the existence of electronic resources where there is usually only one "title page," on which the title may change without leaving a trace of the title that was used previously. Again the Hirons/Graham paper comes to the rescue. Following clear explications of the problems involved in cataloging ongoing publications that have title changes, they recommend changes to the rules that would allow successive entry cataloging for changes in successively issued publications (but they recommend a reduction in the number of *meaningless* changes). At the same time they recommend latest entry cataloging for publications that are updated by insertion of new articles into a database that exhibits only one "title page." Again, this makes a lot of sense to students, who, of course, do not have to unlearn previous habits or worry yet about catalogs full of records created under old rules.

In a report to the Joint Steering Committee for Revision of AACR (JSC) that is a follow-up report to the paper for the 1997 conference on AACR, Jean

Hirons and others present a revised model for describing bibliographic resources (see Figure 2).[7] In this model the terms "finite" and "continuing" are used in place of "static" and "ongoing," but "continuing" no longer includes all incomplete resources. The category of "Ongoing Determinate" from the first model becomes "Finite Incomplete" in the second. Whether this makes more or less sense to students is unclear, but what does make a lot of sense in the second model is the inclusion of "Integrating" resources both under "Finite Incomplete" resources and under "Continuing" resources. ("Integrating resources" are defined in the report as "resources that are updated over time for which the updates are integrated into the resource and do not remain discrete."[8] They include e-texts, looseleafs, databases, and Web sites.)

The Hirons report to the JSC also endorses the recommendation made by others that the descriptive chapters of AACR2 be reorganized according to the ISBD area of the record.[9] This would allow emphasis on content in describing all kinds of resources and would not require choices among chapters for describing such things as electronic maps issued serially. It would also allow addition of rules for treating continuing resources of any kind throughout the

FIGURE 2. Model for Defining Types of Publications as Given in "Revising AACR2 to Accommodate Seriality: Report to the Joint Steering Committee for Revision of AACR."

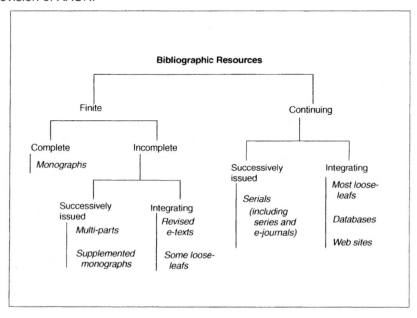

code. Unfortunately (from my point of view), the JSC looked at a prototype of this arrangement and was not convinced of the benefits.[10] JSC did endorse "generalizing" many rules by moving their provisions from Chapters 2-12 into Chapter 1. I believe that the education of new catalogers would be greatly enhanced by not having to distinguish among AACR2 descriptive chapters. A published attempt at integrating the chapters by ISBD areas may be found in Taylor's *Wynar's Introduction to Cataloging and Classification.*[11]

Many more detailed and important rule change recommendations have been made regarding seriality, but, for the most part, they do not strongly affect the education of new catalogers in schools of library and information science. In many schools there is only one half a semester in which to cover all of descriptive cataloging, including description of and access to all kinds of resources, as well as authority control of names and titles. A few other schools allow a whole semester for these topics, but in either case, time for detailed coverage of rules for seriality is limited. What must be gotten across in the short time available is the big picture that identifies what seriality is, what kinds of continuing resources there are, how these resources can be described with enough depth to allow them to be identified and distinguished from each other, and how access points that respond to users' needs can be added to the records. The models shown as Figures 1 and 2 in this paper provide a way of getting across that big picture, and the recommendations for rule changes in the papers that produced these models should be pursued so that there will be a logical implementation of the second model. Logical, easy-to-understand-and-apply rules will go a long way toward enhancing the teaching of seriality.

NOTES

1. *Anglo-American Cataloguing Rules,* 2nd ed., 1988 rev. *(Chicago: American Library Association, 1988), 622.*

2. AACR2, 620.

3. AACR2, 622.

4. Jean Hirons and Crystal Graham, "Issues Related to Seriality," in *The Principles and Future of AACR: Proceedings of the International Conference on the Principles and Future Development of AACR: Toronto, Ontario, Canada, October 23-25, 1997,* Jean Weihs, ed. (Ottawa: Canadian Library Association, 1998), 180-212.

5. Hirons and Graham, "Issues Related," 183.

6. *Anglo-American Cataloging Rules: North American Text* (Chicago: American Library Association, 1967), rule 6D1, 22-23.

7. Jean Hirons, with the assistance of Regina Reynolds and Judy Kuhagen and the CONSER AACR Review Task Force, "Revising AACR2 to Accommodate Seriality:

Report to the Joint Steering Committee for Revision of AACR," http://www.nlc-bnc.ca/jsc/ser-rep0.html.

8. Hirons, "Revising AACR2," http://www.nlc-bnc.ca/jsc/ser-rep2.html.

9. Hirons, "Revising AACR2," http://www.nlc-bnc.ca/jsc/ser-rep3.html.

10. Joint Steering Committee for Revision of AACR, "Outcomes of the Meeting of the Joint Steering Committee Held in San Diego, California, USA, 22-24 March 2000," http://www.nlc-bnc.ca/jsc/0003out.html.

11. Arlene G. Taylor, *Wynar's Introduction to Cataloging and Classification*, 9th ed., with the assistance of David P. Miller (Englewood, Colo.: Libraries Unlimited, 2000), chapter 4.

Serials Cataloging Cooperative Training Program (SCCTP): The Canadian Experience

Elena Romaniuk

SUMMARY. The Serials Cataloging Cooperative Training Program (SCCTP) makes available standardized training materials and provides a pool of experienced trainers to deliver continuing education workshops. The program is authoritative, effective, affordable, and widely available. This paper describes the experiences of a number of trainees and trainers who participated in the Basic Serials Cataloging Workshops given across Canada. *[Article copies available for a fee from The Haworth Document Delivery Service: 1-800-HAWORTH. E-mail address: <getinfo@haworthpressinc.com> Website: <http://www.HaworthPress.com> © 2002 by The Haworth Press, Inc. All rights reserved.]*

KEYWORDS. SCCTP, serials cataloging, continuing education, cooperative training program, Canada

INTRODUCTION

From October 1999 to November 2000, more than 130 Canadian librarians and paraprofessionals attended one of several workshops given under the aus-

---

Elena Romaniuk is Head of Serials Services, University of Victoria Libraries, PO Box 1800, STN CSC, Victoria, BC V8W 3H5, Canada (e-mail: eromaniu@uvic.ca).

[Haworth co-indexing entry note]: "Serials Cataloging Cooperative Training Program (SCCTP): The Canadian Experience." Romaniuk, Elena. Co-published simultaneously in *The Serials Librarian* (The Haworth Information Press, an imprint of The Haworth Press, Inc.) Vol. 41, No. 3/4, 2002, pp. 81-89; and: *E-Serials Cataloging: Access to Continuing and Integrating Resources via the Catalog and the Web* (ed: Jim Cole, and Wayne Jones) The Haworth Information Press, an imprint of The Haworth Press, Inc., 2002, pp. 81-89. Single or multiple copies of this article are available for a fee from The Haworth Document Delivery Service [1-800-HAWORTH, 9:00 a.m. - 5:00 p.m. (EST). E-mail address: getinfo@haworthpressinc.com].

81

pices of a unique CONSER initiative: the Serials Cataloging Cooperative Training Program (SCCTP). In this paper, I will describe the experiences of participants in the Basic Serials Cataloging Workshops given in various Canadian locations.

SCCTP

Inaugurated in 1998, and operational in 1999, SCCTP is the brainchild of Jean Hirons, the CONSER Coordinator.[1] The purpose of SCCTP is to increase the pool of knowledgeable serials catalogers and to raise the quality of serial cataloging records contributed to shared databases.[2] The program uses a distributed, cooperative model to provide standardized training materials and experienced trainers in the field of serials cataloging. In this model, the enormous effort of preparing and delivering serials training programs is distributed among many people. Jean Hirons coordinates the program and takes care of many of its functional details, including the recruitment of experts who develop training materials, and the recruitment of experienced librarians who present them. In addition, she oversees the organization of the Train-the-Trainer sessions and the testing of the documentation in pilot workshops. When finalized, the documentation is available from LC's Cataloging Distribution Service. Regional networks, library associations, universities, and others then sponsor, advertise, and organize the training sessions.

So far, two workshops have been developed by SCCTP: the Basic Serials Cataloging Workshop and the Serial Holdings Workshop. At least two others, including an advanced cataloging concepts workshop, and one dealing exclusively with the cataloging of electronic resources, are now in development.

Since 1999, numerous SCCTP Basic Serials Cataloging Workshops have been held across the United States and Canada. Workshops have also been delivered in Hong Kong, Taiwan, Mexico, and Great Britain. A link to lists of workshops already held, as well as those currently in the planning stages, can be found at the SCCTP Web site.[3] The same Web page also contains a link to the guidelines for workshop sponsors. To facilitate the planning of each session, the guidelines provide a timetable as well as a to-do list for workshop organizers.

The full Basic Serials Cataloging Workshop is designed to be delivered by two trainers over two or three days. The content covers the basics of serials cataloging starting with the definition of a serial, followed by concepts of original and copy cataloging. There are sessions dealing with changes of title, and requirements to be met for the creation of new serial records. Cataloging of electronic serials, subject analysis and classification, and a discussion of new trends in serials cataloging are also covered. A question and answer period can be added. A session on MARC coding is not included, but one can be prepared and incorporated. The course can also be modified to address a particular, specialized subject such as the cataloging of electronic serials.

The workshop is geared to beginning serials catalogers, and to monograph catalogers working with serials, but experienced serials catalogers can also benefit from it: they can use it as a refresher of AACR2 concepts and as a way of learning about the cataloging of electronic serials.

Once registered, each participant is asked to fill out a needs-assessment survey. The trainers then use that information to customize the content of the workshop. Not all sessions are presented in every workshop. At the end of each workshop, the participants are asked to fill out an evaluation form, copies of which are then sent to Jean Hirons and the trainers.

The training is delivered using a combination of instruction, slide presentation, individual and group work, and practice exercises. Exercises make use of both print and electronic serial examples. In addition to those discussed during the workshop, the SCCTP Web site also makes available additional exercises, which the registrants are encouraged to try prior to coming to the sessions. The cost of the workshop is not set by SCCTP but varies depending on the costs incurred by the sponsors. A trainee manual is provided which the participants can annotate and take away with them for future reference.

SCCTP IN CANADA: THE PARTICIPANTS' PERSPECTIVE

Between October 1999 and November 2000, six Basic Serials Cataloging Workshops, and one Train-the-Trainer session, were held in four locations across Canada. The Train-the-Trainer session and two of the Basic Serials Cataloging Workshops were held in Vancouver. The University of British Columbia, School of Library, Archival, and Information Studies sponsored them both. The rest of the sessions were sponsored respectively by McMaster University (Hamilton, Ontario), University of Toronto, Faculty of Information Studies (Toronto), McGill University (Montreal), and the Canadian Library Association, CASLIS-Ottawa Chapter (Hull). In addition to these formal workshops, informal, in-house training sessions were also given at several other institutions, including the University of Ottawa, the Library of Parliament (Ottawa), and at Ryerson University (Toronto). An excellent description of the Train-the-Trainer session in Vancouver can be found in an article by Mary Curran published in a recent issue of *The Serials Librarian*.[4]

I collected information for this paper by contacting most of the workshop organizers, participants, and trainers. I asked each of them to share their impressions of the workshops and to share the most significant aspect of their experience. In the rest of this section, I will summarize what those who responded had to say.

The people attending the Canadian workshops came with varying levels of experience with serials. Some were beginner serials catalogers. Some were monograph catalogers who only occasionally catalog serials. Some were not catalogers at all but worked with serials in acquisitions, or in binding, or in serials check-in. They represented all types and sizes of libraries from all across Canada.

Many common themes emerged from the comments. People came to the workshop for a variety of reasons. Some came because they wanted to learn more about basic serials cataloging concepts or to fill gaps in their knowledge. Some came because the courses they took in school did not include serials cataloging or very little time was spent on the subject. Some came because they had become responsible for cataloging serials but felt that they lacked the knowledge and the expertise to do so. Many came to learn more about the cataloging of electronic serials and to find out about new developments in cataloging.

Overall, the workshops received high praise. They were thought to be well organized, laid out in a logical manner, and easy to follow. They were practical and informative, useful to both beginner and experienced catalogers. For one participant, the workshop helped to clarify the coding and record content of recently migrated and newly converted MARC records. For another, simple statements about serials cataloging (that a cataloger describes the entire run of the serial, instead of the few issues in hand) crystallized existing concepts and made decision-making easier. Prior to the workshop, one library technician, who mostly catalogs monographs, found serials cataloging problematic. It was difficult for her to judge how much editing to provide for incomplete serial copy but she is now confident in making those decisions. Another person said that, prior to the workshop, she considered serials cataloging to be a nightmare but that the knowledge gained from the workshop changed her opinion. In providing a refresher of basic serials cataloging principles, the course was well suited to both her needs and her level of experience. It demystified serials cataloging for her and made her recognize how important some fields are in the description of serials. She found the exercises particularly useful and the atmosphere friendly.

Workshop participants said that the trainers worked well together. They were well prepared, well organized, knowledgeable, and obviously able to draw on a wealth of experience. They explained cataloging concepts clearly and concisely. They created an informal and relaxed atmosphere. Many people specifically mentioned that they appreciated the interactive nature in which the workshops were given. The trainers encouraged participation, answered many practical questions, and made every question seem important. One person said, "it is one thing to attend a course: it is another to listen, to participate, to share and to learn from a workshop." Although most felt that there was adequate time for questions, one person suggested holding a question-and-answer session at the end of the workshop, giving those with less experience an opportunity to talk to the trainers, without detaining those who were ready to leave.

Many workshop participants praised the usefulness and high quality of the course materials and the effectiveness of the visual presentation. The examples and exercises discussed throughout the workshop were helpful in clarifying the concepts being presented and served to improve people's comprehension of the material. One librarian thought that this was one of the better-organized and informative workshops that she has attended. She identified a number of factors that made the workshop work so well. These included following the trainee manual in a step-by-step fashion, doing the exercises together and re-visiting them as a group, having the trainee manual to take away to help with future questions and problems, covering a variety of media, and discussing a number of coding issues. Another librarian observed that, despite the practical nature of the workshop, much philosophical discussion also took place. She found this refreshing because, in her experience, colleagues from other library departments are generally not too eager to get into philosophical discussions about serials cataloging. Other people liked the fact that questions about local policies and practices were answered by trainers working in Canada.

Two people from one small institution found the workshop valuable because they feel isolated from other libraries and have very little time to keep up with new developments. They were concerned about having to start cataloging electronic serials without having enough knowledge to do so. For them, the workshop came along at just the right moment, and was most important for the information it provided on electronic serials. These librarians were reassured by the knowledge that other catalogers are confronting problems similar to their own and that they have, in fact, been cataloging electronic serials correctly. These participants expressed no doubt that SCCTP was meeting a training need in Canada and they would like to attend workshops dealing with other aspects of technical services functions.

Although the cataloging of electronic serials does not constitute a large part of the course, many workshop participants thought that the topic was very well covered. People found these sessions particularly interesting, informative, and useful. Discussions of future trends in serials cataloging were helpful not only in bringing people up-to-date in new developments in cataloging, but also in providing useful background information for future cataloging policy decisions. Many people expressed an interest in attending follow-up, in-depth, workshops focusing exclusively on electronic serials. Others believe that there is a great need in Canada for refresher cataloging courses, as well as for courses dealing with new developments. Some would also like to learn about other topics, in particular the coding and display of holdings statements. One person commented that there are few professional librarians in Canada specializing in serials, yet with the advent of electronic journals, electronic databases, and full-text aggregator databases, the serials field has become much more complex. In her opinion, it would make sense for libraries to hire serials specialists, but in the absence of those, the workshop is also useful because it helps to identify those whose expertise can be drawn upon should the need arise.

Many Canadian participants raised the issue of bilingual content and the need to transcribe bibliographic data in two official languages. This topic is of particular importance to catalogers working in federal government libraries. The workshop held in Hull included many catalogers for whom having to work in both official languages poses the greatest challenge. One participant wanted to know how she should treat bilingual documents to provide satisfactory access for both French and English patrons. She wanted to know whether she should add tracings in both English and French to the same record, or whether she should create separate records. She would have appreciated seeing Canadian examples in the content of the workshop but in spite of their absence she found it to be informative and useful.

There was another important and recurring theme permeating the comments of the Canadian participants. Many people funded their attendance out of their own pockets. Given either limited funding for professional development (or none at all), many would not have been able to attend had the workshop not been offered in a nearby location. Even expenses associated with travel to a more distant Canadian location would have been prohibitive for many. Clearly, the SCCTP system of distributed workshop delivery is key to making it available to Canadians across the country.

SCCTP IN CANADA: THE TRAINERS' PERSPECTIVE

Several trainers answered my call for feedback about their experiences with delivering SCCTP workshops in Canada. The Toronto class was small, with the thirteen participants primarily interested in the basics and keen to do the exercises. The entire morning on the second day was spent on electronic resources. The session generated a lot of questions and the class appreciated extra time spent on this topic.

Most of the McGill workshop's twenty-seven participants were locals, with a few people coming from Alberta, New Brunswick, Boston, New York, and

Ottawa. Many had quite a lot of experience, while others were either new to serials cataloging, or had no cataloging experience at all. Their diverse backgrounds made teaching the class a challenge. Some participants found the pace a bit slow, while others found it a little too fast or just right. In general, though, the participants found the information useful and relevant to their work. The session on cataloging electronic serials was the most popular, while the session on new trends was a little too advanced for the beginners. The group enjoyed the exercises but would have liked to have more time to ask questions and to interact amongst themselves. There was considerable interest in an advanced cataloging course, and the MARC format for holdings was also discussed.

A trainer from the March 2000 Vancouver workshop said that delivering the training was an extremely valuable experience for her. Though her serials cataloging background is strong, preparing for the sessions gave her the incentive to review serials cataloging rules and practices thoroughly. The preparation for the workshop strengthened her own skills and expanded her knowledge. As a result, she feels that she is now providing better cataloging support in her own workplace. She also said that delivery of the sessions by trainers from two diverse institutions worked very well. One trainer from an academic library and one trainer from a public library provided a good balance of different approaches to serials cataloging. The trainees valued hearing how these two libraries actually put some of the theory into practice. This trainer says that there is a real need for an advanced serials cataloging course. The basic workshop gets the trainees started, but when dealing with greater numbers and more complex serials, they will encounter problems that are not addressed in this course.

In the Library of Parliament session, the workshop was given in both official languages. The trainer translated the presentation into French and projected it side by side with the English version. She made adjustments to the presentation with minimal effort and found the well-organized training package easy to deliver and easy for the trainees to follow. This was the first time she used double laptops, double projectors, and double screens, all of which worked very well. Giving the sessions in both official languages ensured that members of both language groups benefited from both the presentation and the discussion. In concluding her comments, this trainer observed that serials cataloging is a specialization in which not many catalogers get an opportunity for in-depth training. She said that there is still a need for both the basic workshop and for the upcoming advanced cataloging workshop.

I close this section with comments from one trainer, who said that SCCTP has provided Canadians with a unique opportunity to improve upon established cataloging skills. She observed that, because cataloging training is generally expensive and in short supply in Canadian libraries, it is unlikely that, without this initiative, such a useful workshop would reach so many Canadians.

CONCLUSION

In working with the feedback I received for this paper, I was struck by the high levels of enthusiasm, excitement, and appreciation permeating the messages about the Canadian workshops. It was evident that many participants came away with increased confidence: ready, willing, and even eager, to catalog serials. I cannot begin to imagine the scope of the effort and the amount of work that bringing SCCTP to fruition created for Jean Hirons and her team of helpers, but what writing this paper has really brought home to me is that many Canadians have had their work lives changed for the better because of their efforts.

Many Canadian respondents said that high travel and accommodation costs, combined with inadequate or non-existent professional development funding, prevent them from attending workshops in the United States. Having the Basic Serials Cataloging Workshop offered in Canada is the main reason they were able to attend. By using this unique, distributed delivery model, authoritative materials, and trained experts in the field, SCCTP has brought effective, affordable, and highly desired serials cataloging training to the Canadian library community.

The issue of bilingual coding in Canadian cataloging records is at the top of the list of concerns for those who catalog in both official languages. It is evident from their comments that continuing education courses on this subject would be welcome by many Canadian catalogers. The cataloging of electronic resources was often mentioned as the most useful part of the Canadian sessions. A chance to attend an in-depth workshop on the same topic was desired by many of the participants, and others also expressed an interest in taking workshops covering advanced serials cataloging concepts as well as serials holdings management.

I became an SCCTP trainer after completing the Train-the-Trainer session in Vancouver in November 1999. A number of reasons motivated me to join the program. I am an experienced serials librarian and cataloger. I enjoy teaching and sharing knowledge. I believe that being an SCCTP trainer provides a unique professional development opportunity and it also makes it easier for me to keep up with new developments in serials cataloging.

In each training session, the program brings together librarians and paraprofessionals with different backgrounds, from a variety of institutions, and from diverse locations. One of its great benefits comes from all of us having an opportunity to learn from each other, by combining our knowledge and experiences, and by sharing solutions to common problems. We are also reassured that no matter how isolated we may feel in our own institutions, our concerns are no different from those of our colleagues.

In closing, I want to share these comments from one of the participants. She said that the course was very beneficial and highly energizing: it was not full of dry information. She liked being in a room full of people who wanted to know the correct way to catalog serials. She liked the fact that the workshop was interactive and that the instructors and the participants were enthusiastic about the subject. She gained a clearer understanding of cataloging concepts and she also enjoyed the hands-on learning. And, at the end, she came away with "an itch to catalog a serial."

NOTES

1. Jean Hirons, "SCCTP–Continuing Education for Continuing Resources" *The Serials Librarian* 37, no. 4 (2000): 113.

2. Serials Cataloging Cooperative Training Program, *About SCCTP*, http://lcweb. loc.gov/acq/conser/scctp/about.html (viewed Jan. 21, 2001).

3. Serials Cataloging Cooperative Training Program, http://lcweb.loc.gov/acq/ conser/scctp/workshops.html (viewed Jan. 26, 2001).

4. Mary Curran, "Serials Cataloging Cooperative Training Program (SCCTP) Train the Trainer Session, Vancouver, B.C., November 17-19, 1999," *The Serials Librarian* 39, no. 2 (2000): 19.

A Question of Access:
The Electronic Journals Tutorial
at the University of Leicester

Danielle Hinton

SUMMARY. Over the past few years, the University of Leicester has seen a massive growth in the number of electronic journals to which the University Library subscribes. The world of e-journal access is complex and oftentimes mysterious to staff and patrons alike. Because of this, the library developed an online Electronic Journals Tutorial. The tutorial, modelled upon the many information retrieval tutorials currently available on the Web, is unique in that it is one of the first of its kind to attempt to support and promote e-journal access. *[Article copies available for a fee from The Haworth Document Delivery Service: 1-800-HAWORTH. E-mail address: <getinfo@haworthpressinc.com> Website: <http://www.HaworthPress.com> © 2002 by The Haworth Press, Inc. All rights reserved.]*

KEYWORDS. University of Leicester, electronic journals tutorial, distance learning

Over the past few years, the University Library has seen a massive growth in the number of electronic journals to which it subscribes. The world of elec-

---

Danielle Hinton is Staff Member of the School of Education, University of Birmingham, Birmingham B15 2TT, United Kingdom.

[Haworth co-indexing entry note]: "A Question of Access: The Electronic Journals Tutorial at the University of Leicester." Hinton, Danielle. Co-published simultaneously in *The Serials Librarian* (The Haworth Information Press, an imprint of The Haworth Press, Inc.) Vol. 41, No. 3/4, 2002, pp. 91-96; and: *E-Serials Cataloging: Access to Continuing and Integrating Resources via the Catalog and the Web* (ed: Jim Cole, and Wayne Jones) The Haworth Information Press, an imprint of The Haworth Press, Inc., 2002, pp. 91-96. Single or multiple copies of this article are available for a fee from The Haworth Document Delivery Service [1-800-HAWORTH, 9:00 a.m. - 5:00 p.m. (EST). E-mail address: getinfo@haworthpressinc.com].

tronic journal access is complex and oftentimes mysterious to university staff and students alike. Because of this, the library developed an online Electronic Journals Tutorial (http://www.le.ac.uk/li/distance/training/ejournals/index.html). The tutorial, modelled upon the many information retrieval tutorials currently available on the Web, is unique in that it is one of the first of its kind to attempt to support and promote e-journal access. Course and section objectives are displayed throughout and combined with a logical navigation system that allows users to work at their own pace and to review or skip over familiar material (see Figure 1). The tutorial also uses a mixture of information and practical exercises with feedback designed to encourage active learning and reinforcement of concepts. This article describes the origins and creation of the tutorial.

THE NEED

The idea for the tutorial arose while investigating the "information skills" guides available to the university's 6,000-7,000 distance learners as part of the ELITE (Electronic Library, IT and staff Education) Project.[1] While students and staff on campus were able to use the paper journals in the library and thus could perhaps function without having to navigate the maze of challenges posed by e-journals, distance learners did not have the same luxury–they had to utilize the online resources and therefore had to learn how to access them. It soon became clear that not only on- and off-campus students but also staff–both library and academic–needed instruction in the use of e-journals. The library therefore developed the tutorial as a first attempt to inform and educate users about the many issues involved. The tutorial helps the user to

- Understand the different types of journals
- Locate an e-journal
- Understand who supplies e-journals
- Know which if any passwords are required
- Understand the issues regarding on- and off-campus access
- Be aware of copyright restrictions
- Know where and how to set up current awareness alerts

STRUCTURE OF THE TUTORIAL

The tutorial begins with an introduction that informs the user of its purpose and objectives and the length of time required to work one's way through it. It then continues on a fairly linear pathway. Throughout the tutorial, users can

FIGURE 1. Electronic Journals Tutorial Home Page

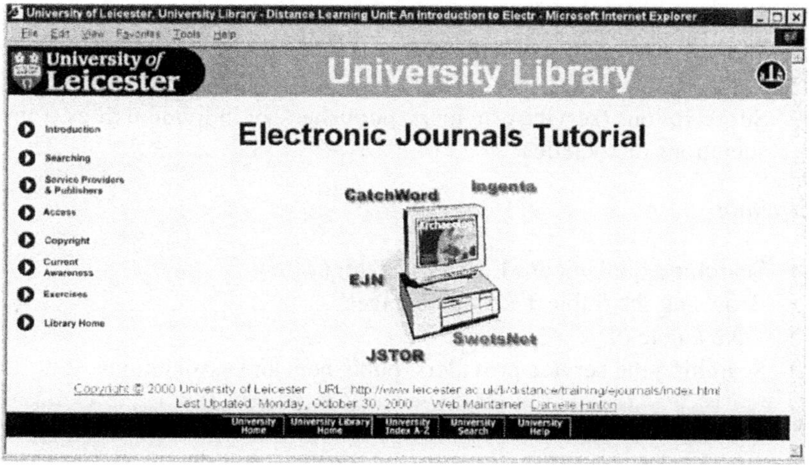

access any of its seven major sections–Introduction, Searching, Service Providers and Publishers, Access, Copyright, Current Awareness, and Exercises–which are found listed on the left-hand of the screen. Since the sections also contain an index of their contents, users are thus able to control their progress through the tutorial. The final section–the exercises–consists of a series of multiple-choice questions that reinforce the concepts taught and test the user's knowledge.

PRESENTATION

The tutorial's layout is designed to follow the University Library's corporate image while keeping the user engaged. Only one exit point (to the library's home page) is given at the bottom of the left-hand navigation. As much as possible, the information provided was kept to a minimum and includes accompanying screen shots, as demonstrated by Figure 2.

TUTORIAL SECTIONS

Clear and separate concepts are grouped together into the tutorial's seven sections. The topics addressed in the various sections are listed below.

Introduction

- The types of journals available
- What is an electronic journal?
- Electronic journals: free or fee?
- Subscriptions (service providers, publishers, or individual titles from associations or societies)

Searching

- Searching the Unicorn Library Catalogue
- Browsing the Subject Resource pages
- Take a note of . . .
- Searching the service providers, publishers and associations

Service Providers and Publishers

This section aims to provide users with background information about each of the service providers and publishers from whom the University Library purchases electronic journal access.

FIGURE 2. An Example of the Use of Screen Shots

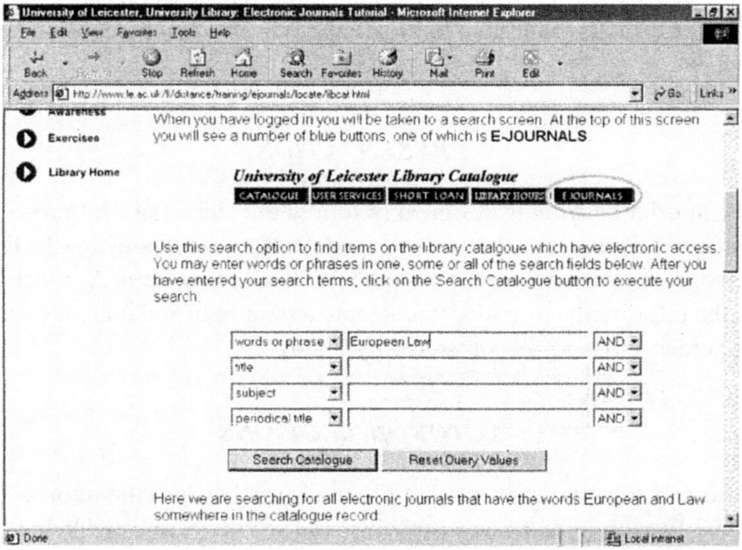

Service Providers

- BioMed
- CatchWord
- Ingenta Journals
- JSTOR
- SwetsNet

Publishers

- Blackwell Science
- Cambridge Journals Online
- Elsevier Science
- IDEAL (Academic Press)
- Oxford University Press
- Springer Link
- Wiley InterScience

Access

- Passwords for on-campus users
- Passwords for distance learners
- ATHENS (Access To Higher Education via NISS Authentication System)
- Access on and off campus (contractual, technical, or embargo restrictions)

Copyright

- Agreements and licenses
- Copyright and Rights in Database Regulations 1997
- Prohibited activities

Current Awareness

- Introduction (details the importance of current awareness services)
- Types of services
- Obtaining articles
- Browsing full-text articles
- Document delivery options

Exercises

This section consists of twelve multiple-choice questions pertaining to the tutorial contents. The exercises are computer marked and provide basic feedback as to whether the questions were answered correctly.

CONCLUSION

The tutorial was an initial attempt to impart basic e-journal information-retrieval skills to the students and staff of the University of Leicester, and especially to distance learners. It is hoped that it will serve as an inspiration and basis for others to develop the concept further. As a community we can not afford to continue to pay increasing monies for e-journals without providing more user training and support.

NOTE

1. Information about the project is available on the World Wide Web at http://www.le.ac.uk/li/distance/eliteproject/index.htm.

POLICIES AND PROCEDURES

Single or Separate OPAC Records for E-Journals: The Glamorgan Perspective

Wayne Morris
Lynda Thomas

SUMMARY. The Learning Resources Centre at the University of Glamorgan creates separate catalogue records for each version of an e-journal that it is licensed to use. This article discusses the considerations taken when determining this approach. *[Article copies available for a fee from The Haworth Document Delivery Service: 1-800-HAWORTH. E-mail address: <getinfo@haworthpressinc.com> Website: <http://www.HaworthPress.com> © 2002 by The Haworth Press, Inc. All rights reserved.]*

KEYWORDS. Electronic journals, cataloguing, single or separate records, user convenience, library management system, house-keeping, consistency

Wayne Morris is Databases Manager, University of Glamorgan, Learning Resources Centre, Pontypridd, CF37 1DL, United Kingdom. Lynda Thomas is Assistant Librarian, University of Glamorgan, Learning Resources Centre, Pontypridd, CF37 1DL, United Kingdom.

[Haworth co-indexing entry note]: "Single or Separate OPAC Records for E-Journals: The Glamorgan Perspective." Morris, Wayne, and Lynda Thomas. Co-published simultaneously in *The Serials Librarian* (The Haworth Information Press, an imprint of The Haworth Press, Inc.) Vol. 41, No. 3/4, 2002, pp. 97-109; and: *E-Serials Cataloging: Access to Continuing and Integrating Resources via the Catalog and the Web* (ed: Jim Cole, and Wayne Jones) The Haworth Information Press, an imprint of The Haworth Press, Inc., 2002, pp. 97-109. Single or multiple copies of this article are available for a fee from The Haworth Document Delivery Service [1-800-HAWORTH, 9:00 a.m. - 5:00 p.m. (EST). E-mail address: getinfo@haworthpressinc.com].

INTRODUCTION

The University of Glamorgan Learning Resources Centre (LRC) currently subscribes to over 3500 e-journal titles, available through a number of different aggregator services.

We have provided access to our e-journals via our WebOPAC since about 1995. Primarily, these were titles available to us through the United Kingdom Pilot Site Licence Initiative[1] (PSLI). This arrangement was tied to continued subscriptions to print titles. Indeed we subscribed to the print version of many of these titles. In recent times, however, particularly with the development of the National Electronic Site Licence Initiative[2] (NESLI), access to the electronic format only has increased markedly. At present, approximately 80% of our e-journals have no print equivalent taken by the LRC.

Nevertheless, we continue to have a significant number of titles that are available to our users in both print and electronic format. Moreover, with the proliferation of aggregator deals available, we find that we often have access to a single title from a number of different aggregators.

Our policy from the outset has been to add records for our e-journals to our catalogue. WebOPAC is a primary means of locating all our resources. We wanted our users to be able to discover all resources available to them in their specific fields of interest regardless of format. We also add records for key Websites to our catalogue. We do, however, offer the ability to interrogate the catalogue by specific sub-catalogues or collections, e.g., new additions, journals. Our users find it useful to have the ability to restrict searches to certain formats on occasions.

The LRC's cataloguing team, Database Services, is responsible for the day-to-day management of the catalogue, which includes provision for materials in all formats. The team consists of a Databases Manager and an Assistant Librarian, both of whom are professionally qualified librarians, and 2.5 Learning Resources Assistants to complete the team. The Assistant Librarian performs most of our cataloguing, with some support from the Databases Manager. Learning Resources Assistants are primarily responsible for managing item data and withdrawing stock from our catalogue. The Databases Manager is also the department's Web Co-ordinator, ensuring that the LRC Website is maintained and developed.

The LRC utilises the *Talis* Library Management System (LMS), produced by Talis Information Ltd.[3] The *Talis* system has evolved from the old *BLCMP* system, which was based on a co-operative cataloguing ideal. Member libraries have access to a large Union Catalogue, and are able to utilise catalogue records created and edited by other member libraries. Records from a number of other databases such as the British Library and Library of Congress are also available.

Cataloguing adheres to AACR2 and *Talis* MARC. The *Talis* MARC format is a standard for the representation of bibliographic information held in a machine-readable form. It is capable of describing all physical forms of library materials. Although differing from other MARC formats in some respects, it is an implementation of the currently relevant British standards.

SINGLE OR SEPARATE RECORDS

We have decided to create a separate catalogue record for every version of a journal we are licensed to use. We concluded that the print and electronic versions are sufficiently different to warrant a record each. We have then created a suitable cross-reference to the alternative version, to alert our users. We currently use the *Talis* MARC 787 Related title tag for this purpose, though we are awaiting the outcome of the harmonisation of MARC 21 and UKMARC.[4] We are also awaiting a decision from the Joint Steering Committee for Revision of AACR[5] for referring to alternative versions of works.

Similarly, we have decided to create separate records where a title is available from a number of alternative aggregators. Along with other factors, we concluded that each version was sufficiently distinct to warrant its own record.

Of course, all of this is a lot of work. We feel, however, that it is worth it in the end. The following text outlines our rationale for opting for this approach.

RATIONALE

Undoubtedly this requires a lot of staff effort. We do, however, invest a lot of money in acquiring these resources so we feel that investing in quality cataloguing ensures that these are effectively exploited.

Considerations

We considered two basic issues regarding the cataloguing of our e-journals:

1. should we include records for all the aggregator services from which access to a title is available, and
2. should we create separate records for all versions including print, or should they be merged into a single record?

There are a number of factors that we considered, many of which are outlined in a CONSER Working Group[6] document outlining the circumstances where single and separate records should be used. The points we considered are described below.

User Convenience

We first addressed this issue from a user's perspective. Would it be clear to users exactly what was available to them in merged or single records? How could we clearly inform users of the various versions available to them? We wanted a way of flagging these alternatives on our WebOPAC. By using the GMD [computer file] we alert users to the availability of an online version in our WebOPAC short title display (see Figure 1).

In this example, our users are immediately alerted to the fact that this particular title is available from five different sources. The first record is for the print copy we subscribe to. The next entries are for the e-journal, which is accessible from four different host sites.

This use of GMDs enables the identification of format, indicating the class of materials to which an item belongs. This is particularly important considering the range of materials now available on WebOPACs. The use of GMDs is optional in AACR2, which should be reviewed given the multiplicity of materials available on WebOPACs. For example, the GMD [text] should be used for printed resources for this reason.

Our intention initially when adding e-journals to our catalogue was to integrate them with the rest of the stock. As indicated earlier, however, we find that users are becoming increasingly aware of the availability of e-journals and use them in preference to the print version. By creating separate records, we are able to create sub-catalogues or collections on WebOPAC where users can search specifically for our e-journals holdings. We also have a sub-catalogue for journals (including e-journals). Sub-catalogue construction is based on certain markers that we associate with various records. E-journals are marked differently from print journals.

Contrary to comments made by the CONSER Working Group[7] and Calhoun et al.,[8] we consider separate records to offer more clarity to users than single records. Users may well be presented with a choice of records, but at least when a record is selected all the information available is clear and concise, including archives and notes to any alternative versions available. In our view, single records can at times overwhelm users with too much detail.

A single record for print and electronic versions is likely to be confusing for users. How would you impart password information and relevant annotation for the electronic version? Bibliographic details, e.g., previous titles, supplements, associated with a print version are not valid for a comparable electronic resource, and are likely to be confusing to users trying to decipher the information.

FIGURE 1. The Short Title Display Resulting from a Keyword Search for the *Journal of Advanced Nursing*

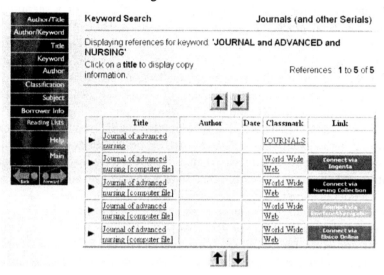

We also considered the self-service objectives of WebOPAC. Users, especially distance learners, increasingly need to be able to search WebOPAC without library staff intervention. Inter-system searching of WebOPACs makes it imperative that international standards are used in the construction of WebOPACs. Users will not expect to understand different standards and approaches to electronic resources on WebOPAC, and it will be inimical to access and exploitation of resources.

Content vs. Carrier

There is discussion about the primacy of carrier over content at present. The International Conference on the Principles and Future Development of AACR[9] discussed content vs. carrier, questioning AACR2 rule 0.24,[10] which instructs us to catalogue from the physical item in hand:

> It is a cardinal principle of the use of part I that the description of the physical item should be based in the first instance on the chapter dealing with the class of materials to which that item belongs.

Descriptive cataloguing is based on the physical format of the material, the carrier rather that the intellectual content of the work. Part II of AACR2[11] deals with the choice and form of access points.

The primacy of intellectual content over carrier has been applied to the single-versus-separate record debate for the cataloguing of electronic resources. A catalogue record for a printed journal has the holdings for a seemingly equivalent e-journal attached to it. It appears, however, that matters of expediency, on occasion, play a part in decisions to append e-journal holdings information to apparently like printed journals, e.g., the need to do something quickly, to be seen to be doing something, the lack of resources.

We have taken the view that the primacy of content over carrier is erroneous. Current standards, MARC and AACR2, have enabled us to integrate electronic resources quickly and effectively with other media into the collection. See Figure 2 for an example of a *Talis* MARC record for an e-journal.

Current cataloguing and authority standards have widespread international recognition and use, and are flexible enough to accommodate and integrate all types of media into WebOPACs.

It has been contested that electronic resources do not exist physically, but they do exist somewhere. Chapter 9 of AACR2[12] provides rules for the cataloguing of computer files available for direct access or by remote access. Taylor[13] has highlighted the shortcomings of AACR2 for the cataloguing of electronic resources, e.g., given their lack of stability, how to determine the chief source of information. As with any other type of media, however, common sense needs to be applied with regard to AACR2. Librarians need to assert their expertise, their ability to bring control to electronic resources.

Library Management System Limitations

We do, of course, have to consider what our current LMS can and cannot offer. Presently, a dedicated Hotlink window within the *Talis* system manages actual links to e-journals. This information is derived from the 856 tag, but the tag itself does not provide the hyperlink. Significantly, it is not possible to have multiple hotlinks on one record. This Hotlink window (see Figure 2) manages the WebOPAC hyperlink, by recording the URL, graphic and alternative text details.

It is true to say that in the UK we have not as yet had a significant debate about the cataloguing of electronic resources. Some initial discussion among *Talis* libraries has taken place, and our initial conclusions were to adopt the separate-record approach. This is by no means a final policy, however, and we expect the *Talis* community to devise a standard approach in the future. We would also hope and expect this topic to take a higher profile within UK cataloguing circles. This is still, very much, a developing area.

FIGURE 2. *Talis* MARC Record for an Electronic Version of the *Journal of Advanced Nursing*. Note the Hotlink Window, Which Controls the WebOPAC Hyperlink

Journal of advanced nursing [computer file]. - Blackwell Science computer file. - S0000133WA

Ctrl no	S0000133WA	Status	Not Contribute	Classif	World Wide Web
Type	Computer media: machine readable			Volumes	0
Info codes	uk q eng			Parent no	

	040 0 00	WA*zWA
	245 0 00	Journal of advanced nursing*zcomputer file
	258 0 00	Computer data and program
	260 0 00	*bBlackwell Science
a	500 0 00	Covers all aspects of nursing care, nursing education, management and research. It is orientated towards intermediate and advanced nursing staff and publishes research papers, news and books reviews. It is essential reading for senior nurses, midwives, health visitors and advanced nursing students.
a	510 0 00	CINAHL; International nursing index; Social sciences citation index; ASSIA; ASSIA plus; MEDLINE; Arts and humanities citation index; Research into higher education abstracts; Studies on women abstracts
a	542 0 00	No password required for on-campus access. For off-campus access use ATHENS username and password
	773 0 00	Ingenta
a	787 0 10	*tJournal of advanced nursing
a	856 0 40	*uhttp://www.ingenta.com/journals/browse/bsc/jan

Hotlink	
URL	http://www.ingenta.com/journals/browse/bsc/jan
Image	ingenta.gif
Text	Connect via Ingenta
Notes	

Archives

We have found that for some reason, the holdings or archives of e-journals can vary between aggregator sites. For example, we currently have access to the *Journal of Advanced Nursing* from four different aggregators. Their archives are as follows:

Ebsco Online	vol. 23 no. 5, 1996 ->
Ingenta	vol. 23 no. 5, 1996 ->
Ovid Nursing Collection	vol. 22 no. 4, 1995 ->
SwetsnetNavigator	vol. 25 no. 1, 1997 ->

It is important that these differences be made clear to users. Notably, e-journal archives seldom go back much further than the early to mid-1990s, often significantly different from a library's print holdings. Archive information is crucial then if we want our users to determine exactly what is available to them. Separate records again perform this task in a clearer manner than single or merged records. See Figure 3 for an example.

Users are made aware of the available archive under our Holdings statement. Notably, as mentioned earlier, this can differ between hosts. We do not at present use *Talis* MARC to record this information. Our *Talis* system also enables us to check in journal issues. As a result we would have concerns that such information could be confusing in a single record. Would users understand that these checked-in issues relate only to a specific version of the title?

Authentication and Access

E-journals aggregator services have a number of mechanisms for authenticating users. Notably IP address is used as a means of authenticating on-campus users. Username and password access governs off-campus access, though this is used for on-campus access by some aggregators too. Moreover, we have found that not all hosts offer the same levels of access. For example, some hosts permit on-campus access only.

We would be concerned that merging details of this nature into one single record could cause possible confusion among WebOPAC users. By creating separate records for each version, it enables us to present our users with these authentication and access details in a much clearer fashion. See Figure 4 for an example.

Users are then able to link directly to the e-journal via the Hotlink at the bottom of the screen. Users familiar with the aggregator service can hotlink to the e-journal directly from the short title display in Figure 1 provided they know the authentication details. In many instances this will be by IP-address authentication.

ISSNs

The ISSN for an e-journal is often distinct from that for the print edition. Though we find ISSNs an unreliable means of identifying suitable bibliographic records on our *Talis* database, they could cause possible confusion for the user where records are merged.

Availability

It is not uncommon for aggregators' servers to be unavailable for a number of reasons, such as busy, maintenance and so on. Notably, there is evidence

FIGURE 3. Serials Holdings Display for One of the E-Journal Versions

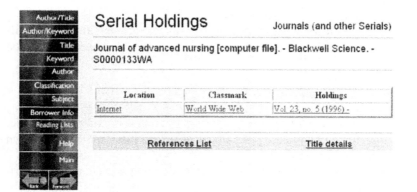

FIGURE 4. Full Title Details. Significant Details are Listed Under Access and URL

Title	Journal of advanced nursing[computer file]
Description	Computer data and program
Publisher	Blackwell Science
Scope	Covers all aspects of nursing care, nursing education, management and research. It is orientated towards intermediate and advanced nursing staff and publishes research papers, news and books reviews. It is essential reading for senior nurses, midwives, health visitors and advanced nursing students.
Access	No password required for on-campus access. For off-campus access use ATHENS username and password
Indexed_in	CINAHL; International nursing index; Social sciences citation index; ASSIA; ASSIA plus; MEDLINE; Arts and humanities citation index; Research into higher education abstracts; Studies on women abstracts
Host	Ingenta
URL	http://www.ingenta.com/journals/browse/bsc/jan
Related_title	Journal of advanced nursing

Hotlink	Connect via Ingenta

that some article files have not been uploaded to the aggregator server, even though they have been advertised as such. A recent JISCmail[14] topic discussed the apparent unevenness in provision.

There is then a clear benefit in creating records for each version that is available. When one version is unavailable, a readily available alternative can be used.

Library Housekeeping Procedures

Experience has shown that the e-journals marketplace is extremely volatile. URLs, authentication and access details change, and titles can be withdrawn and no longer available to users.

With this in mind, we feel that the separate-record approach, although possibly more costly in staff resources in the short-term, affords us savings in subsequent editing in the longer term.

There are other considerations to bear in mind that do not necessarily relate to the primary use of OPAC. For example, the separate-record approach enables us to maintain more accurate statistics of stock additions and withdrawals. It can also help in the accreditation of University courses by showing the full range of materials available in a subject area. We may also want to draw attention to added-value features of e-journals such as e-mail alerts.

In short, e-journals need to be treated the same as any other type of material. We do not catalogue any other type of material that has different versions on the same record. Why should e-journals be catalogued differently?

Consistency

We currently have a mixture of journals. Some titles are available to users in both print and electronic format; others are available in electronic format only. Indeed many of our titles do not exist in print format. The single record approach would lead to an inconsistent approach in this context. Such differences would be confusing for WebOPAC users. CONSER[15] guidelines advise us to use a single record, and sometimes a separate record, which is possibly confusing. Users need access to quality, controlled information. OPAC has to be clear to users. The cataloguing approach to electronic resources needs to be consistent, and their identification needs to be easy.

Staff Time

Catalogue records are created and maintained primarily by our Assistant Librarian, with some support from the Databases Manager. We have not kept statistics of the time it takes to catalogue our e-journals, and the additional effort involved in maintaining multiple records. We have always considered e-journals to be merely another resource that needs to be handled by our team, and have not treated them in any special way. With this in mind we have simply integrated their cataloguing with that for monographs and other resources.

It is true to say, however, that we have on occasions concentrated on adding as many records as possible in a short space of time. This is particularly the case when we have signed an agreement to add many new titles to our collection from a major aggregator.

Although it may be true that creating separate records is more expensive in the short term, we believe that in the long-term we will actually save time, from the benefits of easier editing and uploading records.

The Future

We also have one eye on the future and potential developments in cataloguing and WebOPAC functionality. To date we have created catalogue records for our e-journals from scratch. We do, however, anticipate an increase in the availability of catalogue records for these sources, both on the *Talis* Union Catalogue and via other agencies. NESLI for example can supply MARC records for some of their titles. Clearly, the separate-record approach would enable us to make optimal use of such co-operative or shared ventures.

At present it is not possible to download records from our WebOPAC into personal bibliography manager software. We feel that this will develop in time. Indeed this is already a feature of some systems. The separate-record approach, then, will enable standardised downloading of references from WebOPAC. Other emerging technologies such as CrossRef[16] may also find a place in library WebOPACs.

E-journals are still a developing area, both in terms of provision by aggregators and for libraries and their cataloguers. We need to be able to adapt to the changing demands of this new medium. With this in mind we can perhaps begin to anticipate the emerging standards of the future. Are they likely to recommend using separate records for electronic resources? We need to ensure that what we are doing now will prepare us for the future. Look at electronic resources for the long term.

We should consider the relevance of the ISBD(ER).[17] Moreover, the International Conference on the Principles and Future Development of AACR[18] identified a need to redefine a serial to look at an item's potential for change. Thus, in the future, there is likely to not just be a serial/monograph divide in the cataloguing rules. Electronic sources are likely to belong to a category of integrating resources that will affect library procedures, OPAC displays and retrieval. Electronic resources should not be catalogued on a single record with a comparable print version, as this will not be relevant for possible future cataloguing rules.

We conclude that the separate-record model is best placed to prepare for the future.

CONCLUSION

We have created separate-records for all our e-journals, which has enabled us to quickly and effectively integrate electronic resources into WebOPAC for the benefit of our users. In our view there are a number of compelling arguments in favour of this approach. Significantly, it is our view that separate records actually assist the library user in determining exactly what is available and how to access it.

Why should electronic resources be less well served than any other type of medium in terms of cataloguing and access? Electronic resources are available on WebOPAC through the same access points, and give like descriptive and annotative information as all other media in the collection. Librarians should be about "adding value" to information, in the case of electronic resources through their effective integration with other media on WebOPAC.

If electronic resources are not effectively catalogued and available on WebOPAC with other resources, we will not be effectively exploiting the stock, which we have a responsibility to do for the users of our collections both locally and on the Web.

REFERENCES

1. UK Pilot Site Licence Initiative, http://www.niss.ac.uk/education/hefce/pub97/m3_97.html.

2. National Electronic Site Licence Initiative, http://www.nesli.ac.uk

3. Talis Information Ltd. http://www.talis.com.

4. The British Library Executive Committee. *MARC Harmonisation: British Library to Adopt the MARC21 Format. Survey Results*, http://www.bl.uk/services/bsds/nbs/marc/result1.html, 2001.

5. *Revising AACR2 to Accommodate Seriality, Report to the Joint Steering Committee for Revision of AACR*, prepared by Jean Hirons, CONSER Coordinator, Library of Congress with the assistance of Regina Reynolds and Judy Kuhagen (Library of Congress) and the CONSER AACR Review Task Force, April 1999, http://www.nlcbnc.ca/jsc/ser-rep0.html

6. CONSER Working Group. *Single or Separate Records: Draft Report, 1999,* http://wwwtest.library.ucla.edu/libraries/cataloging/sercat/conserwg/conserwg.draft.html.

7. Ibid.

8. Karen Calhoun (Chair) et al., *Electronic Journals Task Force Report*, http://wwwtest.library.ucla.edu/libraries/cataloguing/sercat/conserwg/Cornell.htm

9. International Conference on the Principles and Future Development of AACR, *The Principles and Future of AACR: Proceedings of the International Conference on the Principles and Future Development of AACR, Toronto, Ontario, Canada, October 23-25, 1997*, ed. by Jean Weihs. Chicago : American Library Association, 1998, p. 148.

10. *Anglo-American Cataloguing Rules*, 2nd ed., 1998 revision, prepared under the direction of the Joint Steering Committee for Revision of AACR2 , a committee of the American Library Association, the Australian Committee on Cataloguing, the British Library, the Canadian Committee on Cataloguing, the Library Association, the Library of Congress (Chicago : American Library Association, 1998), p. 8.

11. Ibid., p. 303.

12. Ibid., p. 220.

13. Arlene G. Taylor, "Where Does ACR2 Fall Short for Internet Resources," *Journal of Internet Cataloging*, 2, no. 2 (1999): 43-50.

14. lis-e-journals. http://www.jiscmail.ac.uk/lists/lis-e-journals.html January 2001.

15. CONSER Working Group, op. cit.

16. CrossRef, http://www.crossref.org.

17. *ISBD(ER):International Standard Bibliographic Description for Electronic Resources, revised from the ISBD(CF): International Standard Bibliographic Description for Computer Files recommended by the ISBD(CF) Review Group* (originally issued by K. G. Saur, Muenchen, 1997 as vol. 17 in the UBCIM Publications, New Series), http://www.ifla.org/VII/s13/pubs/isbd.htm.

18. International Conference on the Principles and Future Development of AACR, op. cit.

Web Resources for Cataloging Electronic Serials and Continuing Resources: An Annotated Bibliography

John Blosser
Tim Hagan
Yvonne W. Zhang

SUMMARY. This is an annotated bibliography intended to gather together selective Web sites that support the cataloging of electronic serials and continuing resources. The Web sites chosen for the reviews cover a range of sophistication and comprehensiveness. All levels of catalogers may find some helpful sites to use in their work. *[Article copies available for a fee from The Haworth Document Delivery Service: 1-800-HAWORTH. E-mail address: <getinfo@haworthpressinc.com> Website: <http://www.HaworthPress. com> © 2002 by The Haworth Press, Inc. All rights reserved.]*

KEYWORDS. Serials cataloging, electronic resources, continuing resources, electronic journals, cataloging

---

John Blosser is Head, Serials Department, and Coordinator of Acquisitions Services, and Tim Hagan is Serials Cataloger Librarian, Northwestern University Library, Serials Department, 1935 Sheridan Road, Evanston, IL 60208-2300. Yvonne W. Zhang is Head, Bibliographic Access Services, University Library, California State Polytechnic University Pomona, 3801 W. Temple Avenue, Pomona, CA 91768.

[Haworth co-indexing entry note]: "Web Resources for Cataloging Electronic Serials and Continuing Resources: An Annotated Bibliography." Blosser, John, Tim Hagan, and Yvonne W. Zhang. Co-published simultaneously in *The Serials Librarian* (The Haworth Information Press, an imprint of The Haworth Press, Inc.) Vol. 41, No. 3/4, 2002, pp. 111-126; and: *E-Serials Cataloging: Access to Continuing and Integrating Resources via the Catalog and the Web* (ed: Jim Cole, and Wayne Jones) The Haworth Information Press, an imprint of The Haworth Press, Inc., 2002, pp. 111-126. Single or multiple copies of this article are available for a fee from The Haworth Document Delivery Service [1-800-HAWORTH, 9:00 a.m. - 5:00 p.m. (EST). E-mail address: getinfo@haworthpressinc.com].

INTRODUCTION

This is an annotated bibliography intended to gather together some helpful Web sites that support the cataloging of electronic serials and continuing resources. They are readily available through hyperlinks that may be bookmarked on the catalogers' browsers. Most of the sites have links within them that lead to local and external sources. It is perhaps fitting that these sites are available on the Internet since they are as fluid as the resources for which they were developed. The Web format allows for easy access to tools for cataloging beyond a library's boundaries, such as guidance for standards and procedures, and explanations of MARC fields with examples that may be static or in real time. The Web sites chosen for the reviews in this article cover the gamut of sophistication and completeness. All levels of catalogers may find some helpful sites to use in their work.

NOT SO LONG AGO

Just when serials catalogers thought they had some control over the cataloging procedures for serials, electronic journals and continuing resources came along and sent many of them back to the proverbial drawing board. One favorite reminiscence of the mid-1990s was the concept of how to describe intangible things one could not hold or collate on one's desk. Catalogers had to retrain themselves in traditional concepts, such as what constitutes the chief source of information, and to embrace new concepts regarding system requirements and user restrictions.

Some courageous serials catalogers pioneered online help. They created local Web sites with library policies and technical services procedures to tackle the challenges of representing access and description of electronic resources in their local OPACs. In addition to local information, links were often provided to outside resources which supported the electronic resource description national initiative. The MARC field tags for electronic resources were evolving during this early period and MARBI discussion papers were being disseminated. These linked documents provided guidance of what to do with electronic resources until official decisions could be confirmed. Electronic journals and continuing resources began to become an integral part of catalogers' lives. There was a good deal of collaboration and sharing (there still is) among catalogers to help each other cope with the new formats. At conferences one might have heard, "What are you doing with your e-journals?" Having the Web as the communication mechanism made the proposed solutions and ideas all the easier to share.

Distribution via the Web is still an important medium of sharing among catalogers. Web browsers store bookmarks for ease of access to cataloging resource materials. Hyperlinking facilitates moving around and between documents as well as linking to the live example of what is being cataloged. Today, the Web remains very important in the professional and moral support of serials catalogers.

METHODOLOGY

One may well assume that searching for almost anything on the Internet will yield a plethora of results through which to sift for the nuggets of desired information. The criteria used in searching for sites for this bibliography were fairly simple since the sites retrieved in both general and more specific searches were too numerous to review. Primarily, review entries were discovered by searching university library sites. Other sites were currently known to the authors. Another approach was to use some commercial search engines available freely on the Internet with terms like "electronic serials cataloging" and "electronic cataloging." A few commercial sites were reaped in the process, but not many public library technical services sites were discovered. To limit the result sets to what would be reviewed in the annotations, the authors chose sites that were primarily comprised of content rather than being lists of links to other sites with content. Not all the sites in the content category were reviewed for various reasons. Some were too brief or too similar to others reviewed. It should be noted that most of the sites were developed for local use and so are tailored to meet those local needs. The intention of this article is to give illustrations of some of the more helpful sites which catalogers may link to, evaluate, and use as an example to develop their own local sites.

REVIEWS

The reviews are divided into three categories: *How to* (broadly applicable reference tools and guidelines); *Support* (local procedures and workflows); and *Editorial* (archives, articles and bibliographies). The annotations attempt to cover five areas of evaluation of the Web sites: authorship/publisher/sponsor; purpose/focus/strengths; navigation/structure/style; content/comprehensiveness; and feedback/revision. The reviews are listed alphabetically within the three categories and are meant to briefly describe the sites to help readers sort the sites for their own use. The authors did not focus on the qualitative aspects of the sites, or try to rank them in any order. The authors encourage the readers to visit all the sites listed, the links for which are maintained online at *http://staffWeb.library.northwestern.edu/serials/iesca/bibliography/index.html*. There are likely many more sites not included in this bibliography, and more that may appear over time, which may be helpful and worthy of viewing.

HOW TO

IFLA

ISBD(ER): International Standard Bibliographic Description for Electronic Resources
http://www.ifla.org/VII/s13/pubs/isbd4.htm

Sponsored by the International Federation of Library Associations and Institutions, this is a site with an international focus on building a catalog record to describe an electronic resource. The table of contents links must be used to navigate through the site. The text layout is clear and easy to read. Links within the text take the user to references or examples, including examples taken from the cataloging of various countries. This is an excellent source of documentation on descriptive cataloging, explanation of electronic resources characteristics, and definitions of terminology used with electronic resources. Seems to be updated and has online feedback to IFLA.

Library of Congress

CONSER Cataloging Manual, Module 31, Remote Access Computer File Serials
http://www.loc.gov/acq/conser/module31.html

CONSER Cataloging Manual, Module 33.18, Electronic Newspapers
http://www.loc.gov/acq/conser/enewsppr.html

CONSER Serials Cataloging Issues
http://lcWeb.loc.gov/acq/conser/issues.html

These Library of Congress Web sites, provided through the CONSER Program, are a wealth of information, a gathering place of national standards for cataloging electronic resources. Module 31 gives detailed, well-written explanations of the description of electronic resources in a catalog record. It begins with a page of linked table of contents, an introduction, and definitions of terms. The rest of the module is divided into two Web pages with various examples and links to live Web sites. Module 33.18 focuses on electronic newspapers. In addition to good examples, Module 33.18 contains gif illustrations of newspaper sections, and links to rules within the *CONSER Cataloging Manual* as well as live online resources. The Serials Cataloging Issues page has many links to current topics in electronic serials cataloging. The information found at these sites is comprehensive and updated. These sites are recommended to be in every serials cataloger's Web browser's bookmarks.

Northwestern University Library

IESCA
http://staffWeb.library.northwestern.edu/serials/iesca/

Created by Yvonne W. Zhang and John Blosser and substantially revised by Tim Hagan, the Interactive Electronic Serials Cataloging Aid (IESCA) is published by Northwestern University Library. Its intent is to help serials catalogers catalog online serial resources by supplying clear examples with links to MARC field descriptions and cataloging guidelines. A strong point is the presentation of multiple examples of notes linked from MARC rules. Good use of Web format to link users within the site and out to cataloging tools. Currently updated with comments invited.

Olson, Nancy B., ed. (OCLC)

Cataloging Internet Resources: A Manual and Practical Guide
http://www.oclc.org/oclc/man/9256cat/toc.htm

Published by OCLC, this well-known and often-cited Web site, edited by Nancy Olson, is recommended to be bookmarked on every serials cataloger's Web browser. The documentation is a rich supplement to the national cataloging standard guidelines. It makes good use of Web page technology in linking from contents provided in a frame to the text. The text is comprehensive and provides clear and easy to read examples. Perhaps the next edition will update some of the minor MARC field changes, such as in the 856 field. Provides a good historical source of cataloging types of online serials resources not encountered as often now, e.g., dial-up and telnet. Feedback is invited by the Project Manager at the end of his foreword.

SUPPORT

Boston University, School of Law

Technical Services Procedures: Cataloging Internet Resources
http://www.bu.edu/lawlibrary/tech/procedures/internetcat.htm

This Web site created by Anne Myers is a selection called "Cataloging Considerations" on the Technical Services Electronic Resources page. The procedures page is a set of simple and straightforward tables containing MARC fields and their tags. The examples cover various situations of supplying electronic access when print or no print version is available at the Law Library. Since the page is fairly succinct, a table of contents with links to the sections is not really needed, but would be a good feature for catalogers visiting the site from other libraries.

Brown University Library

Cataloging Services, Manual of Policies and Procedures, Electronic Resources Cataloging
http://www.brown.edu/Facilities/University_Library/Catalog/ElectRes.html

Created by Gretchen Yealy for Brown University Library Cataloging Services, this site provides guidelines for cataloging remote and direct access files. The information focuses on local processing for remote access electronic files and locally mounted CD-ROM databases. The topic headings are linked to information within the document that is fairly simple to follow. In the examples, though, it would be easier to relate to real data rather than labels of data for what should be there (e.g., "245 00 |a Life |h [computer file]" rather than descriptions of the data "245 00 |a Title of electronic version |h [computer file]"). The browser "back" button takes the user back to the top of the site to select another link. Serves as a good example of a streamlined document to mount for local use. Seems to be updated and has a contact link for feedback.

Cornell University

Cataloging Procedures for Networked Electronic Resources
http://www.library.cornell.edu/voyager/Bibs/ECat/e-catTOC.html

This Web site is sponsored by Cornell University Library Technical Services and is edited by Jim LeBlanc of the Technical Services Support Unit. It is mounted as part of an extensive online manual for their local Voyager Library Management System (LMS). The site is a comprehensive processing guide for cataloging networked electronic resources at Cornell University Library and makes use of links to needed reference materials for field definitions, appropriate tags, and national standards. Excellent use of hyperlinks to manage examples and references within the text. The site consistently provides easy navigation of all page levels. The content covers all networked electronic resources and explains a situation in sufficient detail to allow a cataloger to make a procedural decision. Seems to be updated, but there is no feedback path from this site. One must go to the Technical Services manual site (which is worth a look at *http://www.library.cornell.edu/tsmanual/home.html*) to send a message.

Federal Depository Library Program

GPO Cataloging Guidelines Computer Files
http://www.access.gpo.gov/su_docs/fdlp/cip/cgcomp01.html#quick

Sponsored by the United States Superintendent of Documents, this large Web site begins with a rich Table of Contents that links to the sections of explanations and instructions below. The page numbers listed correspond to the page numbers if printed. Footnotes have links back, and there are "Back to the Table of Contents" links after discrete sections. Where links are not provided, e.g., in a reference to a rule in AACR2, the rule citation is given. The information provided is comprehensive and descriptive of GPO practices. The text covers remote files as well as physical formats of electronic resources. A good source for understanding the GPO MARC record for electronic resources, this site also provides a substantial background for learning about electronic resources processing in general. The site is full of sections one may use as models at a home institution. Seems to be updated and there is a link for feedback.

Harvard University

Cataloging Networked Resources in HOLLIS: Policies and Guidelines
http://elmer.harvard.edu/~robin/catlg_e_stuff.html

There is no publisher or sponsorship stated on this page, but it obviously belongs to Harvard University. Using an abbreviated URL to find parent information seems to be forbidden. The site has a wealth of well-selected examples with very brief explanations of the processing of networked electronic resources at the library. The site would be much improved with the addition of links from a table of contents to the different sections below. As it is, one must scroll down the document. Provides a good source of full record examples for a limited number of cataloging situations. The page has not been updated in some time and there is no feedback link.

Kansas State University Libraries

856 Fields on Bibliographic Records
http://www.lib.ksu.edu/depts/techserv/manual/cataloging/856routines.html

   This excellent site focusing on the MARC 856 field is sponsored by the Kansas State University Libraries Technical Services Department. It is a small section of an elaborate Technical Services Department General Information and Procedures Manual found at *http://www.lib.ksu.edu/depts/techserv/faq.html*. The Web document concentrates specifically on inputting and editing of URLs in local catalog records for both monographs and serials. The style is clear and easy to read, and the illustrations are excellent for Voyager LMS sites. The site is updated for currency, and has an e-mail link for feedback.

Memorial University of Newfoundland Libraries

Cataloging Remote Electronic Resources in Unicorn
http://www.mun.ca/library/cat/remote.htm

   This brief, local procedure site is provided by the Queen Elizabeth II Library of the Memorial University of Newfoundland Libraries. It is easy to navigate from brief contents headings at the top. Despite the brevity of the document, good examples are provided for describing electronic resources in a Unicorn LMS, and there are links to supporting reference material from the "Remote Electronic Resources" selection in the Cataloguer's Toolbox available at the top of this cataloging page. It is currently revised.

Michigan Technological University

Electronic Journals Interim Policies & Procedures
http://www.lib.mtu.edu/jrvp/textonly/aboutjrvp/departments/techservices/tspp.htm

   Sponsored by the J. Robert Van Pelt Library, this local procedural document discusses the issues of cataloging electronic resources and gives examples. The basic format could be improved by having the index at the same address as the full document. The site is currently maintained, but the rules are not completely updated. It does have an e-mail link for feedback.

MIT Libraries

Electronic Resources Documentation
http://macfadden.mit.edu:9500/colserv/cat/erescat/

Supported by the MIT Libraries Collection Services, this clear and concise site covers local policies and procedures for cataloging electronic resources using the GEAC LMS. The procedures make good use of a persistent sidebar to organize the links within the site. Includes a helpful Web page of cataloging examples. Currently updated with a clear invitation for comments.

Penn State University Libraries

Serials Cataloging Team
http://www.libraries.psu.edu/iasWeb/catsWeb/serials/serdocs.htm

This Web site is sponsored by the Cataloging Department of Penn State University Libraries. It focuses on local procedures for cataloging on the SIRSI LMS. One may select a document for computer files processes (covering electronic resources in a physical format), or for electronic journals processes. The site has a simple Web page structure. The Computer File Processes page has a handy link to a "Quick Sheet for Enhancing Copy" which gives an outline of what to change in cataloging copy to meet local practices. Content is adequate, but some rules are out of date. Feedback is readily invited through links.

Princeton University

Cataloging Computer Files
http://libWeb.princeton.edu/katmandu/comp/comtoc.html

Princeton University Library Cataloging Division sponsors this site of cataloging procedures. The material covers direct and remote access serials, providing a good source for learning about computer files cataloging. The pages are clearly organized by MARC fields, but more examples and notes would be a welcome enhancement. The division invites feedback from its main page and lists some categories of responses that would indicate a commitment to revise and expand the documentation for the entire site.

Stanford University

Guidelines for Cataloging Internet Resources
http://www-sul.stanford.edu/depts/catdept/policy/intercat.html

Sponsored by Stanford University Libraries/Academic Information Resources, this site focuses on Internet resources and local procedures. The long page is easily navigated by starting from links in the Table of Contents at the top, and by using the browser "back" button to return to there to select another topic. The layout is clear and pleasing, and the examples given are helpful. The content is comprehensive for local processing of Internet resources and is a good model for establishing local guidelines at other libraries. Of particular interest are the sections with local procedures for the handling of MARCIVE records and instructions for adding URLs for aggregator titles. The site is maintained with revisions as needed.

University of Arizona

Internet Resources Cataloging Procedures
http://dizzy.library.arizona.edu/users/eagleson/catproc.htm

This site, published by the University of Arizona Libraries as part of the CATNET Project, concentrates on local procedures for cataloging Internet resources. The brief Table of Contents for cataloging procedures allows for limited approaches to locate information. A more detailed choice of links would help lead one more quickly to an answer or example. The basic Web page format is functional. Coverage is comprehensive for local practices. Future development of the page is not known, but some maintenance of the site is necessary as several links are not working.

University of California, Los Angeles Charles E. Young Research Library

YRL Serials Cataloging Section
http://wwwtest.library.ucla.edu/libraries/cataloging/sercat/

Sponsored by the Catalog Department of the Young Research Library, this site contains helpful information under the section "Special Situations." The documentation pertaining to electronic resources would seem to be worthy of being listed in a section of its own. There are guidelines for processing CD-ROMs as well as online serials, and a heading link for Internet monographs. One highlight is the document called "Internet: Types of Pages to Use as Chief Source." In table format, this document presents definitions and examples for the different choices of chief source of information on the Web. The pages of the different sections are clear, and reflect the effort and thought that must have gone into their design. The individual documents seem to be revised, but there is no communication link.

University of California, San Diego

TPOT: Cataloging–Electronic Resources Cataloging
http://tpot.ucsd.edu/Cataloging/Electronic/

Published by the University of California, San Diego, this site is a selection from the Technical Processing Online Tools page. It concentrates on remote access resources, but has links to procedures for direct access electronic resources as well as guidelines to cataloging electronic resources in general. The comprehensive documentation of local procedures is clearly formatted. Since separate sections are created by individuals at UCSD, they lack uniformity, but are clearly identified with creation and revision dates. Incorporating a linked contents would aid in the navigation of some pages. There is readily available access to feedback.

University of Florida, George A. Smathers Libraries

Serials Handbook
http://www.uflib.ufl.edu/serials/serhandserhand.htm

Published by the University of Florida and maintained by the Serials Unit of the George A. Smathers Libraries, this is a creative approach to organizing local procedures for serials processing, including a selection for electronic resources. The site uses tables and forms for good database management. The section on electronic resources deals mostly with the ordering process, but there are two links currently to information on the MARC 856 field. It is obvious from parenthetical notes that some parts are still in the making. A recommended site for viewing, with a clear invitation for feedback.

University of Michigan

Serials Cataloging Documentation
http://www.lib.umich.edu/libhome/acqser/sercat/scptoc.htm

This is a wonderful example of managing procedural documentation on the Web, published by the University of Michigan Library, Acquisitions/Serials

Division, Serials Cataloging Unit. One needs to hunt for the links relating to electronic resources cataloging, but scrolling down the screen gives one an idea of the magnitude of effort behind mounting the site. For the electronic references, look at "Aggregator Services Cataloging," "Multiple Versions Procedures: Electronic Serials and Online Versions of Print Serials," and "Cataloging Original Electronic Serials." Each document is comprehensive for local procedures and the format is clear and easy to read. The site is updated and has a clearly marked contact for comments.

University of North Dakota, Chester Fritz Library

Electronic Resources Acquisitions and Access Guidelines
http://www.und.nodak.edu/dept/library/Departments/abc/Edocgid.htm#Cataloging24

Published by the University of North Dakota Chester Fritz Library, Acquisitions/Bibliographic Control department, this is a basic and straightforward site for documenting local procedures for cataloging electronic resources. The section "Cataloging Web Sites: Chester Fritz Library Guidelines" uses a table with text box menus to explain and give examples of the MARC fields used in describing online resources. Headings also link to pages with information and references to works relating to the issues of electronic resources. The site is updated and there is a clear path for communication of feedback.

University of Oregon

Guidelines for Cataloging Electronic Resources
http://libWeb.uoregon.edu/orbis/staffhome/cataloging_elec_resources.html

Established as a report of the Orbis Library Consortium Task Force on Cataloging, Display and Access for Electronic Resources, this document, revised July 1999, provides guidelines for cataloging standards among the cataloging units of the consortium libraries. The brief and easy to follow text would be enhanced by the incorporation of a contents section with links to the different topics covered. The style is pleasant and serves as an example for a clean and fresh Web page design.

University of Rochester Libraries

Cataloging Guidelines for Internet Resources
http://www.lib.rochester.edu/cat/catguide.htm

Guidelines for Coding Internet Resources in Voyager
http://www.lib.rochester.edu/cat/marc.htm

"Cataloging Guidelines for Internet Resources," published by the University of Rochester Libraries in 1997, has well-organized documentation for local procedures regarding the cataloging of electronic resources in the Voyager LMS. "Guidelines for Coding Internet Resources in Voyager" seems to be an updated version at a higher level of Web design. The whole linked site for cataloging at the University of Rochester Libraries is very professional in look, and entertaining as well, especially if you are of the feline persuasion. Please view *http://www.lib.rochester.edu/cat/*. Both sites complement each other, the older site perhaps being easier for a visitor to follow in the contents outline provided, but the newer version being highly linked within and outside the document in a way that may make more sense for a local cataloger while cataloging. A creative site that looks as though it may have been fun to build in spite of the concentrated effort it no doubt required. The newer site is updated and comments are invited.

University of Virginia Library, Cataloging Services Department

Cataloging Procedures Manual, Chapter XII, Part D
http://www.lib.virginia.edu/cataloging/manual/chapters/chapxiid.html

This comprehensive section of a much larger work of local cataloging procedures (see *http://etext.lib.virginia.edu/cataloging/manual/home.html*) is published by the University of Virginia Library, Cataloging Services Department. This section focuses on serials remote access computer files cataloging. A companion site dealing mostly with workflow management may be found at *http://www.lib.virginia.edu/cataloging/local/*. The cataloging of remote resources page is clear and easy to read, but could be improved with a more detailed selection of links from the contents at the top of the page to the text. Links from the few examples of titles listed would be useful. No feedback mechanism or update information is readily available.

VIVA, The Virtual Library of Virginia

Guidelines for Cataloging VIVA Electronic Collections
http://viva.lib.virginia.edu/~ejs7y/vivacat/guidelines.html#secIV

This is an excellent site on cataloging for consortium sharing of electronic collections, sponsored by the VIVA Users Services Committee, Subcommittee on Cataloging and Intellectual Access. Designed to guide member libraries of VIVA, the comprehensive documentation makes effective use of hyperlinks to examples of MARC records, to MARC field references, and to canned and live samples used as illustrations. The sections where one title is linked to either a canned or live example of the catalogs of seven other institutions are excellent comparison tools. More advanced topics in cataloging electronic resources, such as multiple URLs, uniform title and aggregator access, are clearly addressed. This Web site has a professional look and is well organized. Last modified in early 1999, but there are three named contacts which would indicate comments are welcome.

Willamette University

Procedures for Cataloging Internet Resources
http://dewey.willamette.edu/home/org/techserv/catinter.htm

This brief cataloging Web site is sponsored by the Mark O. Hatfield Library Technical Services division of Willamette University. It is a good example of what can be done to fill the need for succinct documentation of local procedures on the Web. It is a handy reference tool for the novice or experienced cataloger of electronic resources. Minimal use of links is justifiable in this short version of cataloging procedures. It is currently updated, and comments are welcome on the Technical Services Home Page.

EDITORIAL

Occasionally overlooked are sites which are, or contain, online articles, presentations, bibliographies and discussion list archives. These sites can be an enormous aid to catalogers. While the degree of content and formats may vary widely, they are definitely an asset to electronic resources cataloging. Included here are several examples.

Hawkins, Les

Serials Published on the World Wide Web: Cataloging Problems and Decisions
http://web.mit.edu/waynej/www/hawkins.htm

This article, authored by Les Hawkins of the U.S. ISSN Center, National Serials Data Program, provides some background information on the nature of online serials that has affected decision-making in the cataloging of remote electronic resources. The article is an excellent source of examples of online resources linked to the resource and a copy of the OCLC record. Some of the cataloging rules may have changed since this article was published by The Haworth Press in 1997, but the content is helpful reading.

Library of Congress

Draft Interim Guidelines for Cataloging Electronic Resources
http://lcWeb.loc.gov/catdir/cpso/dcmb19_4.html

This mostly static document supplied by the Library of Congress Cataloging Policy and Support Office provides a background and rationale for cataloging access to electronic resources along with an extensive set of interim guidelines for cataloging. Though the guidelines are considered interim due to the dynamic nature of the resources and systems available to describe and link to them, they have been adopted by many institutions. These guidelines are an excellent source for learning about the concepts and types of resources to be cataloged, the issues and definitions of electronic resources, and a place to go for examples of bibliographic records. The document is comprehensive for the time when it was written.

Tyler, Tom

URLs, PURLs & TRULs: Link Maintenance in the Web-Accessible OPAC
http://www.du.edu/~ttyler/ci199/proceedings.htm

This paper authored by Tom Tyler, Associate Director for Budget and Planning, University of Denver, was presented at the 1999 "Computers in Libraries" conference. It concentrates on issues of the MARC 856 field for display of the URL for an online resource. The comprehensiveness of scope makes it more suitable for the experienced cataloger, but gives good background information on working with the URL. Contains two tables showing information on displays of the URL in selected OPACs. Good use of the Web format to link to parts of the paper from the table of contents, and to examples from a selection of headings along the side frame. Includes good supporting material.

University of California, Davis

Cataloging Electronic Resources: Strategies for Coping with Change
http://neuheim.ucdavis.edu/staff/serWeb/clanov99/index.htm

Authored by Pat French and published by the University of California, Davis General Library, this creative use of a PowerPoint presentation from November 1999 is an excellent overview of acquisitions and cataloging issues relating to electronic resources. It provides a clear and succinct picture of the parameters of electronic resources and would be a great way for novice acquisitions and cataloging staff to enter the world of electronic resources processing. There are hyperlinks available to supporting information, and a Table of Contents from which to choose topics of interest. This is a valuable resource that would benefit many in the library community if updated from time to time to capture recent decisions and new issues regarding electronic resources processing.

Yale University Library

Report of the Task Force on Cataloging Remote Access Electronic Serials
http://www.library.yale.edu/cataloging/netinfo/ejtfrpt3.htm

Published by Yale University Library, this task force report includes discussion of local practices plus many general issues relating to cataloging electronic serials. It is a good document to refer to for inspiration on planning procedures to handle electronic resources, and to compare the issues to some real recommendations. The information gives a solid foundation to the "why" and "how" of devising procedures, but in broad enough terms to be applicable to other library settings. The page, though long, is formatted for clear organization and navigation with links. Sample records are included. Recommended reading for those in the planning stages of electronic resources cataloging processes.

Internet Resources Cataloging in ARL Libraries: Staffing and Access Issues

Jeanne M. K. Boydston
Joan M. Leysen

SUMMARY. Many academic libraries have made the decision to catalog Internet resources. There are many factors included in this decision. Based on a survey, this article examines the types of Internet resources that are being cataloged in ARL institutions, the level of staff performing the cataloging and the impact this has made on these cataloging departments. Access issues are also examined. The results contained in this article will illustrate the current situation in libraries and provide data for comparison with future studies. *[Article copies available for a fee from The Haworth Document Delivery Service: 1-800-HAWORTH. E-mail address: <getinfo@haworthpressinc.com> Website: <http://www.HaworthPress.com> © 2002 by The Haworth Press, Inc. All rights reserved.]*

KEYWORDS. Internet, catalogers, cataloging staff, support staff, professional staff

Jeanne M. K. Boydston is Associate Professor and serials, humanities monographs and electronic resources cataloger, and Joan M. Leysen is Associate Professor and social science monographs and electronic resources cataloger at Iowa State University at Ames, IA 50014-2140.

[Haworth co-indexing entry note]: "Internet Resources Cataloging in ARL Libraries: Staffing and Access Issues." Boydston, Jeanne M. K., and Joan M. Leysen. Co-published simultaneously in *The Serials Librarian* (The Haworth Information Press, an imprint of The Haworth Press, Inc.) Vol. 41, No. 3/4, 2002, pp. 127-145; and: *E-Serials Cataloging: Access to Continuing and Integrating Resources via the Catalog and the Web* (ed: Jim Cole, and Wayne Jones) The Haworth Information Press, an imprint of The Haworth Press, Inc., 2002, pp. 127-145. Single or multiple copies of this article are available for a fee from The Haworth Document Delivery Service [1-800-HAWORTH, 9:00 a.m. - 5:00 p.m. (EST). E-mail address: getinfo@haworthpressinc.com].

INTRODUCTION AND BACKGROUND

Despite the ongoing debate over whether libraries should catalog the Internet, many academic libraries have made the decision to catalog selected Internet titles. Included in a library's decision to catalog these resources are factors such as what type of resources to catalog, what access to provide and what level of staff will be needed to provide that access. For purposes of this study, Internet resources include: e-journals, databases and free Web pages.

Academic cataloging departments traditionally employ a combination of professional and support staff, but the numbers and responsibilities of these staff positions have changed over time.[1] Researchers have highlighted the 1960s especially as a time of significant change in library staffing.[2] The rapid growth of library collections, supported by federal funding, resulted in a need not only for additional staff to maintain these collections but also different levels of staff. Libraries began creating new non-MLS positions with titles such as library associate and paraprofessional, and a number of library technician programs emerged. A formal acknowledgement of these new positions was made in 1970 with the publication of *Library Education and Manpower*.[3] The creation of the American Library Association Council on Library/Media Technicians to provide assistance to this new level of staff affords further evidence of this trend.

As these positions became more established, libraries began examining the responsibilities of the professional and support staff, and cataloging functions were no exception. Budget cuts forced administrators to identify more economical ways to accomplish cataloging activities. In 1985, Veaner projected there would be fewer catalogers, more contract cataloging and "off loading" all production-type work including cataloging to support staff.[4] Eskoz also reported a "modest trend toward and involving paraprofessional staff in higher levels of cataloging."[5] Studies conducted since 1977 confirm the increased involvement of support staff in original cataloging.[6]

Although this shifting of original cataloging may be viewed by some as an indication of the deprofessionalization of cataloging, there is evidence of reprofessionalization as well. Technological innovations, especially the rapid growth of the Internet as an information resource, have created a new need for the skills of the MLS cataloger.[7] Changes in position responsibilities to include Internet cataloging have already taken place. Buttlar and Garcha reported that the number of librarians who cataloged Internet resources grew from 1.2% in 1987 to 31.4% in 1997, reflecting the growth of the Internet. In 1997, MLS catalogers were performing duties associated with automated systems, such as managing networks, interfaces and workflows; authority control; database maintenance; and supervision.[8] Broader roles for the MLS cataloger have been suggested, such as evaluating bibliographic access systems and their impact on patrons, seeking closer contacts with patrons where local input can be gathered and conducting research to investigate local problems.[9] MLS catalogers are becoming workflow managers and trainers of support staff.[10] In addition, MLS librarians are facing increased pressure to publish and participate in professional activities, particularly at institutions where librarians hold faculty status.

The roles of MLS and support staff have continued to become more blurred with overlap in responsibilities common.[11] Accelerated by recent technological advances in cooperative cataloging, new vendor services such as PromptCat, outsourcing, improved integrated library systems, and increased patron expectations, technical services departments have been reevaluating cataloging priorities, organizational structures, workflows and staff responsibilities. As reported in the literature, this focus has been on print and other non-electronic materials. Until recently, little information has been published on priorities, staffing and workflows associated with electronic resources cataloging.[12]

The purpose of this article is to examine the type of Internet resources being cataloged in Association of Research Libraries (ARL) member institutions, the level of staff performing the cataloging and the impact this has made on these cataloging departments. Where appropriate, comparisons will be made with similar studies of print materials. Selected access issues will also be examined. The results will illustrate the current situation in libraries and provide data for comparison with future studies.

METHODOLOGY

A survey instrument was formulated to gather information on the staffing and access issues of Internet cataloging. In November 2000, this survey was mailed to the technical services department heads at 106 ARL member institutions in the United States. ARL institutions were selected because they represent a fairly homogenous group of similar-sized research libraries. The number of member libraries is large enough for a representative sample, but easily manageable within the constraints of this study. The heads of technical services were instructed either to answer the survey themselves or were given the option to forward it to a staff member more directly responsible for cataloging Internet resources. The types of Internet resources studied were: e-journals, databases and free Web pages. A cover letter accompanying the survey explained the purpose of the survey, supplied instructions for completing it, and provided assurances that all data would be reported in the aggregate. Those individuals who failed to respond by the initial deadline were sent reminders.

The survey was designed to gather several types of information about the participant libraries. These included general and demographic questions, such as the number of volumes in the library, student enrollment, bibliographic utility and integrated library system utilized. Participants were also asked to indicate which of the above-mentioned Internet resources they cataloged, the level of cataloging provided, when they began cataloging these resources, the number of Internet resources they catalog per year and to date, and whether they participate in the CORC project. Information was also requested on the type of access the library provides for Internet resources. Questions also covered the type of staff and training venues used for Internet cataloging. The cataloging responsibilities of various types of staff and the reasons behind these decisions were also examined. Queries also addressed staff and organizational changes that have occurred since the advent of Internet cataloging. For a complete copy of the survey, see Appendix I.

FINDINGS

Seventy-two libraries responded to the survey for a return rate of 68%. Only two respondents indicated they did not catalog Internet resources at the present time, so the analysis is based on the responses from the 70 libraries that catalog Internet resources. Not all respondents answered every question, and a few questions yielded insufficient information from which to draw conclusions. In addition, where questions allowed multiple responses, findings are reported as numbers rather than percentages. Some total responses do not equal 100% due to rounding.

Several survey questions were designed to collect general or demographic information about the sample libraries. The majority, 43% (n = 69) of libraries responding to the survey, had a student enrollment of 20,001-40,000. Thirty-three percent of the institutions have an enrollment of 10,001-20,000. The remaining 23% were divided, with 12% reporting a student population of 40,001 or more and 11% with a student enrollment of less than 10,000. Eighty percent of the libraries surveyed reported volume holdings of 2,000,000 or more. Sixteen percent had holdings in the 1,000,000-2,000,000 range while only 4% indicated library volume holdings of 999,999 or fewer. These answers reflect, no doubt, the criteria for membership in the ARL.

Libraries have evolved greatly since the days of handwritten catalog cards. Today there is a greater reliance on cooperative cataloging and a dependence on the various bibliographic utilities. OCLC started operations in 1967 with a membership of 54 Ohio libraries. Since its inception, that membership has grown to 30,000 libraries worldwide.[13] RLIN was founded in 1974 by four libraries and now has over 160 member libraries.[14] So, it would be expected that OCLC and RLIN would be the bibliographic utilities most used by the majority of libraries. OCLC is the utility of choice for 81% (n = 69) of the respondents to the current survey, while 6% of the libraries use only RLIN. Thirteen percent use both OCLC and RLIN.

Most libraries have some type of integrated library system to manage bibliographic control activities, circulation and other functions. The integrated library system chosen by 27% of the libraries in the current study is an Innovative Interfaces, Inc. product. Twenty-six percent, however, selected an Endeavor product such as Voyager or Alph Exlibris. The epixtech products, Dynix, Notis and Horizon, are found in 17% of the libraries, and Sirsi Unicorn in 10%. Three percent used either a Geac product or a locally developed system. More than one integrated library system was used in 3% of the surveyed libraries.

The last ten years have witnessed an explosion of information available on the Internet. During the spring semester 1999, Lubans found that Duke University students used the Internet for 50% of their information-seeking needs.[15] Responding to patron acceptance of the new technology, librarians struggled to bring some order to this largely uncontrolled mass of information. The results from the current survey indicated that most libraries began to catalog Internet resources in the last ten years. From 1990 through 1994, 17% (n = 65) of the libraries began to catalog the Internet. The majority, however, began in the next five years, with 15% in 1995, 20% in 1996, 18% in 1997 and 15% in 1998. Fourteen percent of the libraries began cataloging Internet resources in 1999 or 2000. The average number of Internet resources cataloged per year tended to be lower than one might expect. Of the 47 libraries that listed a specific number, 60% cataloged fewer than 1,000 Internet resources a year. Another 19% cataloged 1,001-2,000 Internet resources during the year. Twenty percent of the libraries cataloged over 2,500 Internet resources in a given year.

Sixty percent (n = 57) of the libraries reported 5,000 or fewer Internet records in their library catalog. Nine percent of the libraries have 5,001 or more such records contained in their catalogs and 25% report over 10,001 records. These numbers may be misleading, however, as the criteria for what constitutes an Internet catalog record were not specified in the survey. The totals may or may not include e-books and tape loads of Marcive records for Internet government documents.

As cooperative cataloging projects have grown for traditional materials, similar projects were launched to meet this need for electronic resources. In 1994-1996, OCLC sponsored the Intercat Project, whose objective was to create a cooperative database of bibliographic records for Internet resources.[16] Later, in 1999, OCLC began the Cooperative Online Resource Catalog (CORC).

CORC is a set of Web-based cataloging tools and services. Among these services, it allows librarians to create cataloging records for Internet resources by utilizing the MARC and Dublin Core formats.[17] A slight majority of the respondents, 55% (n = 69), participate in the CORC project, while 45% do not.

STAFFING ISSUES

The distribution of cataloging responsibilities among various levels of staff has been based on type of cataloging copy (Library of Congress, member or original), physical or publication format, language or subject content. The current study focuses on type of copy and format of materials as criteria for the distribution of these responsibilities. In 1990, a study found that 92% of ARL libraries assigned paraprofessionals LC copy and 91% assigned them member copy.[18] The current study found a similar distribution of work occurs with Internet resources. As indicated in Table 1, support staff are most often assigned copy cataloging of Internet resources. MLS catalogers, however, are still heavily involved in some type of copy cataloging. Sixty-eight percent of the libraries assigned original cataloging to MLS catalogers only. Twenty-nine percent of ARL libraries use MLS and support staff for original Internet resources cataloging. This number will most likely increase as standards for Internet cataloging become more established. Local decisions on the level of cataloging for the various types of Internet resources will also be a factor.

Another past method of distributing work among catalogers is by the type or format of material. Survey participants were asked whether the three types of Internet resources (e-journals, databases, or free Web pages) were assigned to different levels of cataloging staff. As illustrated in Figure 1, support staff are most often assigned e-journals followed by databases and then free Web pages. This is also true of MLS catalogers; however, more of them were involved in cataloging these resources, especially databases and free Web pages.

Cataloging responsibilities are often separated into three categories: descriptive cataloging, subject cataloging and classification. Studies of print resource cataloging show that support staff are more likely to be involved in original descriptive cataloging, followed by subject analysis and, to a lesser extent, classification.[19] As noted in Table 1, approximately 50% of the ARL libraries use support staff and MLS catalogers to do descriptive cataloging and subject analysis. An almost equal percentage of libraries use MLS and support staff for classifying Internet resources as do the number who use MLS catalogers only, 31% and 32%, respectively. As with print resources, the percentages for classification are generally lower, but this may reflect local policies not to classify Internet resources.

TABLE 1. Staff Responsibilities

Responsibilities	n	MLS Staff	Support Staff	MLS and Support Staff	NA
Type of Record					
Library of Congress Copy	69	25%	36%	35%	4%
Member Copy	68	32%	21%	47%	0%
Original	69	68%	3%	29%	0%
Cataloging Function					
Descriptive Cataloging	68	43%	10%	46%	1%
Assigning Subject Headings	69	52%	6%	42%	0%
Assigning Call Numbers	65	32%	8%	31%	29%

n = number of respondents

Looking historically at cataloging tasks, these findings fit a general scheme for new processes and formats. When new, the process or format is the exclusive domain of MLS catalogers. As its occurrence becomes more commonplace, documentation and standards are developed. Eventually, the process moves from MLS to support-staff catalogers.[20]

The use of support staff to catalog Internet resources can be based on a number of factors. Oberg studied the changing responsibilities of support staff in 1990 and suggested that, among other reasons, the shortage of qualified librarians and declining or static library budgets led to the increased responsibilities of support staff.[21] Many library managers also cite career development as a reason for the increased use of support staff for complex cataloging tasks.[22] In the current study, 48 respondents included information on why support staff are used to catalog Internet resources. The reason given the most often was the increased number of Internet resources to be cataloged, followed by concern for the growth and development of support staff. A lesser number of responses attributed the use of support staff to lower costs at this level, MLS cataloger vacancies and recruitment difficulties, and the need to free MLS catalogers' time for professional activities.

FIGURE 1. Types of Internet Resources

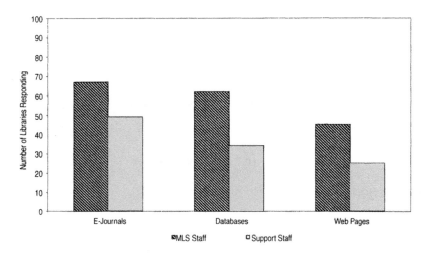

Nineteen libraries provided reasons for which support staff were not used. The major reason given was that there was enough other work for support staff to do and that there were sufficient MLS catalogers to complete the Internet cataloging. Other reasons stated were the well-established local division of workflow and that the work was not appropriate for the classification level.

Support staff cataloging is revised in 40% (n = 53) of the institutions in the current study. Many libraries qualified their response by indicating that revision was performed only during the training period. MLS catalogers do the revision in 75% of the cases and in 25% of the libraries this revision is a shared activity with support staff.

IMPACT OF INTERNET RESOURCES CATALOGING

The impact of Internet resources cataloging can be determined by examining numbers of catalogers, their cataloging assignments and changes to the organizational structure of the cataloging department. Without knowing the total FTE cataloging staff, conclusions based on exact numbers of staff are difficult. The number of staff cataloging Internet resources varied among libraries, but generally a small portion of the total staff is involved in cataloging this format. Sixty-five percent (n = 69) of the libraries indicated that 25% or less of the total cataloging staff are involved in Internet cataloging. An additional 22% reported 26 to 50% of their cataloging staff are assigned this activity. Only 13%

of the libraries have more than half of their cataloging staff performing Internet resources cataloging. There was no significant difference in these percentages when numbers of MLS and support staff catalogers were compared. These numbers may also reflect the library's local criteria on what should be cataloged and the emphasis placed on this format with respect to print and other non-electronic formats. The term "cataloging staff" may also have been interpreted to include all staff in the cataloging department instead of all staff involved in cataloging activities.

Changing cataloging assignments to include Internet cataloging is another indicator of the importance placed on the cataloging of the Internet. Since beginning Internet cataloging, the numbers of MLS and support staff catalogers involved in this cataloging increased in 34% and 48% (n = 65) of the libraries respectively. These percentages are higher for support staff perhaps because the proportion of support staff to MLS catalogers is generally higher. Yet, in the last five years, only 14% of the libraries hired additional new staff to catalog Internet resources and 7% (n = 69) have upwardly reclassified support staff for this purpose. MLS catalogers were reassigned in 17% of the libraries and about half that percentage of libraries reported reassigning support staff. Decreases in MLS and support staff involved in Internet cataloging occurred in 7% and 2% (n = 65) of the libraries respectively. Less than one-third of the libraries reported no change in MLS or support staff numbers as a result of Internet cataloging (n = 70 and n = 65, respectively).

The degree of change in the cataloging department's organizational structure can provide evidence of the impact of cataloging Internet resources. Calhoun finds that most technical service departments are still organized with print resources in mind, and that electronic resources call for a different organizational structure due to their uniqueness.[23] An almost equal number of libraries reported the cataloging of Internet resources had changed the organization of the cataloging department "somewhat" as reported no change, 49% and 43% respectively. Nine percent of the libraries felt this change had "greatly" affected their organization. Some of the effects noted by the group included the development of a backlog of non-electronic materials, the creation of separate units or departments for the cataloging of Internet resources and more flexibility and crossing of lines between monographs and serials.[24]

Training is necessary in order to catalog any new format. Training for the cataloging of Internet resources may be obtained through workshops conducted at national, state or local levels. The training may also be provided by network associations and bibliographic utilities, or it may be conducted in house. Recently, the OCLC Institute announced the availability of a Web-based course on cataloging Internet resources.[25] Fifty (n = 67) of the libraries in this survey reported using more than one venue for training, such as in-house training in conjunction with workshops at the national, state, or network level. Seventeen libraries, however, used only in-house training.

Training can be an ongoing process, however, 47% (n = 67) of the libraries indicated that they spent more time in training initially than they now spend for on-going training. Sixteen percent indicate they spent less time initially, and 21% indicating the amount of training time has remained about the same. Thirteen percent were uncertain about the amount of time spent in training initially versus currently.

ACCESS ISSUES

The type of access given to Internet resources also varied with each library. The majority of libraries, 40 (n = 65), provide their patrons with a Web-based clickable list by both title and subject. One library provides both a Web-based subject list coupled with other local access, while two offered only locally defined access. Twelve libraries have only a title list and four provide their patrons with only a subject list. Six libraries indicated that they use a combination of title, subject and local access. Several libraries commented that the type of access provided varied depending upon the type of material or the presence of a print copy in the library's holdings.

One of the hotly debated issues in cataloging Internet resources revolves around the use of one or multiple cataloging records for serial titles. Briefly stated, should there be one record that contains information for both the print and electronic formats of a resource, or should there be separate records for each format? Each approach can have its own positive and negative impact on the organization structure and workflow.[26] Out of 68 respondents, 40 followed the multiple-record model and provided individual MARC bibliographic records for each Internet resource and recorded information about the Internet version on the print record. Twenty-two libraries utilized the single-record approach by adding notes and access points related to the Internet version to the print record. Six libraries created MARC bibliographic records for the Internet version, but did not indicate whether they also modified the corresponding print record.

It is interesting to note that 64 libraries provide both some type of catalog record and Web-clickable access. Twenty-eight of these libraries use a multiple-record approach and provide the patrons with Web-clickable list by both title and subject. Calhoun's opinion is that multiple access methods created by "different functional groups tend to be uncoordinated and poorly integrated." She suggests, "We must redesign and integrate the functionality of our libraries' catalogs and Web sites so they can function as a coherent information system."[27]

There are many factors that can influence the level of cataloging given to a particular Internet resource. As with print resources, priority is usually given to titles that support the curriculum or research of the institution. In addition, serial subscriptions or purchased monographs are given precedence over gift or otherwise free acquisitions. Fifty-six libraries in the current survey gave only full-level cataloging to e-journals, probably reflecting the paid subscription status and potential long-range stability of these titles. Fifty-eight gave this treatment to databases and 32 cataloged free Web pages using full-level cataloging. Less than full-level cataloging was utilized for e-journals by 3 libraries, for databases by 2 libraries and for free Web pages by 5 libraries. In addition, many libraries reported that they used a combination of full, less-than-full and local cataloging depending upon the individual resource. Of special interest was the finding that 22 libraries do not catalog free Web pages at all. Undoubtedly, the instability and lack of control over the content of these resources are factors in the reluctance of many libraries to catalog them.

CONCLUSION

By cataloging Internet resources, many academic libraries are providing improved bibliographic control and access to these resources. Their approach to this new format has been cautious and continues to evolve as the Internet grows and patron demands change. The majority of these libraries catalog fewer than 1,000 resources per year. They offer patrons a Web-clickable list by both title and subject, in addition to creating MARC bibliographic records. Most of the libraries utilize the multiple-record approach by providing records for both Internet and corresponding print formats. Less than a quarter of the cataloging staff is assigned to catalog these resources. Yet, approximately one-third of the libraries reported an increase in MLS staff since beginning the cataloging of electronic resources and almost one-half reported an increase in support staff. Forty percent of the libraries reported no change, and a few hired new staff. Only a small percentage of libraries felt the organization of the cataloging department was greatly affected by the cataloging of Internet resources. The majority felt there was some effect.

The cataloging responsibilities of the MLS and support staff cataloger continue to be blurred as they have been with print materials. The division of Internet cataloging responsibilities between MLS and support staff mirrors the distribution used with print and non-electronic materials. Support staff are more likely to catalog electronic items with copy. They also perform some original descriptive cataloging and subject analysis and, to a lesser extent, classification. The distribution of cataloging by type of Internet resource, like the level of cataloging, follows locally defined priorities, usually giving preference to paid resources, such as e-journals and databases. Support staff are assigned Internet cataloging due to the overwhelming amount of electronic resources to be cataloged and a desire on the library's part to enhance their career growth. Reasons not to utilize support staff for the cataloging of Internet resources were the volume of work already being assigned to them, and the existence of enough MLS catalogers to handle the Internet resources.

Future staffing and access issues will be determined by a number of factors, such as numbers of catalogers, growth of the Internet, improved cataloging standards and knowledge of patrons' information-seeking behaviors. MLS professionals are aging and the current workforce is thinning as the baby boomers enter retirement age. In addition, the numbers of positions available are outnumbering the job seekers.[28] In 1998, 30% of the catalogers in ARL libraries were aged 55 or older and there were 302 fewer catalogers than in 1990. Additionally, younger colleagues are not replacing these aging catalogers on a one-on-one basis.[29] What will happen when the older catalogers retire? With fewer numbers of MLS librarians in technical services departments, cataloging responsibility, supervision and training are likely to shift more toward support staff positions. The role of the MLS cataloger may include reduced direct cataloging responsibilities and include more administration, management and systems activities. Further studies building on the work of Mohr and Schuneman will help to track this trend.[30]

The standards for cataloging Internet resources[31] are, like the resources themselves, in a state of flux. As more libraries begin to contribute Internet resource cataloging to the bibliographic utilities, a body of model or example records will start to accumulate. In addition to traditional records, the local library catalog might contain records created by vendors, consortia members, and perhaps authors themselves. These records may follow different standards (MARC, Dublin Core, or other metadata standards) and levels of cataloging (full, minimal, core). Integrated library systems must be able to massage the various records together in a seamless interface. Still, there is a need for a unified body of acceptable standards, such as LC practice for print materials, to guide the cataloger of Internet resources. Once standards for Internet cataloging become further defined, training and cataloging will be more efficient. With models to follow, there will be less training and more opportunities for support staff involvement. The development of standards will also reduce the need of each local library to respond independently to the same cataloging issues. Advances in automated cataloging activity and cooperative cataloging efforts, such as CORC, will also have an effect.

There are numerous resources on the Internet that support the institutional curriculum and research needs of the library patron. Further study is necessary to determine how patrons access Internet materials to assist libraries in developing or revising their policies of providing access to Internet resources. With knowledge of patron access strategies, the scope and purpose of the library catalog and its collections can be refined. Libraries need to assess the practice of providing and maintaining multiple access to Internet resources. Integration of access, such as cataloging records and Web-clickable lists, needs to be examined. Decisions need to be made on what level of cataloging is acceptable for the various types of Internet resources.

The growth rate of the Internet and electronic technology in general, plus the changing nature of scholarly communication, will have a strong effect on the future of cataloging Internet resources. Aggregators and serials publishers are providing numerous full-text electronic versions of print serial titles with links to multiple related resources, and the future of e-books is yet to be determined. The electronic environment allows the patron's informational needs to be met with a convenience and speed unprecedented in library history. Technological improvements will only increase these expectations. Given the rapid growth of the Internet and patrons' enamored interest in Internet resources, can libraries afford to maintain this cautious approach to cataloging these materials?

NOTES

1. For the purposes of this study, a professional is defined as an individual holding the MLS or similar degree. The terms *support staff* and *paraprofessional* are often used interchangeably. In the current study, the term *support staff* is used to indicate library workers without an MLS degree. For an historical review of support staff see: Jennifer A. Younger, "Support Staff and Librarians in Cataloging," *Cataloging & Classification Quarterly* 23, no.1 (1996): 27-47.

2. Ibid., p. 30-1; Robert E. Molyneux, "Staffing Patterns and Library Growth at ARL Libraries, 1962/63 to 1983/84," *Journal of Academic Librarianship* 12, no. 5 (Nov. 1986): 292-97; Terry Rodgers, *The Library Professional: Notes from the Underground* (Jefferson, N.C. : McFarland & Company, 1997), 146-155.

3. *Library Education and Manpower* (Chicago, Ill.: American Library Association, Office for Library Personnel Resources, 1970). This document identified two categories of library personnel–professional and supportive–and defined the training and requirements for each. The supportive classification included the job titles of library associate and library technical assistant positions with requirements ranging from post-secondary school training in relevant skills to a bachelor's degree. The document was revised in 1976.

4. Allen B. Veaner, "1985 to 1995: The Next Decade in Academic Librarianship, Part I," *College & Research Libraries* 46, no. 3 (May 1985): 209-229.

5. Patricia A. Eskoz, "The Catalog Librarian–Change or Status Quo? Results of a Survey of Academic Libraries," *Library Resources & Technical Services* 34, no. 3 (July 1990): 380-92.

6. Sally Braden, John D. Hall, and Helen H. Britton, "Utilization of Personnel and Bibliographic Resources for Cataloging by OCLC Participating Libraries," *Library Resources & Technical Services* 24 , no. 2 (spring 1980): 135-154; Eskoz, "The Catalog Librarian," 388; Larry R. Oberg et al., "The Role, Status, and Working Conditions of Paraprofessionals: A National Survey of Academic Libraries," *College & Research Libraries* 53, no. 3 (May 1992): 215-38; Deborah A. Mohr and Anita Schuneman, "Changing Roles: Original Cataloging by Paraprofessionals in ARL Libraries," *Library Resources & Technical Services* 41, no. 3 (July 1997): 205-18; Sever Bordeianu and Virginia Seiser, "Paraprofessional Catalogers in ARL Libraries," *College & Research Libraries* 60, no. 6 (Nov. 1999): 532-40. The number of paraprofessional or support staff performing original cataloging varied depending on the survey population and whether total original cataloging tasks or only original descriptive cataloging were reported. Braden et al. (1977) reported between 12% and 15% of OCLC member libraries used both professional and support staff for original cataloging. Eskoz's (1983-84 and 1986-87) findings were higher, 30%-35%, in her two studies of academic libraries. Oberg reported 51% of ARL institutions assigned original descriptive cataloging to paraprofessionals. Five years later, Mohr and Schuneman reported 74.7% for ARL institutions. Considering original cataloging in general, Bordeianu and Seiser stated 67% of ARL libraries used paraprofessionals for original cataloging.

7. Some selected articles examining this view include: Vinh-The Lam, "Cataloging Internet Resources: Why, What, How," *Cataloging & Classification Quarterly* 29, no. 3 (2000): 49-61; Dilys E. Morris and Gregory Wool, "Cataloging: Librarianship's Best Bargain," *Library Journal* 124, no. 11 (June 15, 1999): and 44-6. Norman Oder, "Cataloging the Net: Can We Do It?" *Library Journal* 123, no. 16 (Oct. 1, 1998): 47-51; William E. Studwell, "Are Catalogers Ready for the 'Information Superhighway'?" *Technicalities* 14, no. 7 (July 1994): 2-3; Arlene G. Taylor, "The Information Universe: Will We Have Chaos or Control?" *American Libraries* 25 (July/Aug., 1994): 629-32.

8. Lois Buttlar and Rajinder Garcha, "Catalogers in Academic Libraries: Their Evolving and Expanding Roles," *College & Research Libraries* 59, no. 4 (July 1998): 311-21.

9. Jennifer A. Younger, "The Role of Librarians in Bibliographic Access Services in the 1990's," *Journal of Library Administration* 15, no. 1-2 (1991): 125-50.

10. James S. Chervinko, "The Changing State of Original Cataloging: Who's Going to Do It Now?" *Illinois Libraries* 74, no. 5 (Nov. 1992): 493-5; Magda El-Sherbini and George Klim, "Changes in Technical Services and Their Effect on the Role of Catalogers and Staff Education: An Overview," *Cataloging & Classification Quarterly* 24, no. 1-2 (1997): 23-33.

11. Larry R. Oberg, "The Emergence of the Paraprofessional in Academic Libraries: Perceptions and Realities," *College & Research Libraries* 53, no. 2 (Mar. 1992): 99-112.

12. Some of these include: Ruth C. Carter, ed., "Managing Cataloging and the Organization of Information: Philosophies, Practices and Challenges at the Onset of the 21st Century. Part II: Specialized and Academic Libraries in the United States," *Cata-*

loging & Classification Quarterly 30, nos. 2/3 (2000); Karen Calhoun, "Redesign of Library Workflows: Experimental Models for Electronic Resource Description-Final Version December 2000" http://lcweb.loc.gov/catdir/bibcontrol/calhoun_paper.htm (viewed March 28, 2001). Mary Grenci, "The Impact of Web Publishing on the Organization of Cataloging Functions," *Library Collections, Acquisitions & Technical Services* 24 (2000): 153-170.

13. Additional information about OCLC can be found at: *http://www.oclc.org/about/* (viewed Mar. 28, 2001).

14. Additional information about RLIN can be found at: *http://www.rlg.org/rlg.html* (viewed Mar. 28, 2001).

15. John Lubans, "Students & the Internet, Spring 1999 Survey," May 13, 1999: http://www.lib.duke.edu/lubans/docs/study3.html (viewed Mar. 28, 2001).

16. "Intercat Cataloging Project Call for Participants," http://www.oclc.org/oclc/man/catproj/catcall.htm (viewed Mar. 28, 2001).

17. "Integration of the OCLC Cataloging Service and CORC," *Technical Bulletin* 239 (last updated: June 20, 2000), http://www.oclc.org/oclc/tb/tb239/index.htm (viewed Mar. 28, 2001).

18. Oberg et al., "The Role, Status, and Working Conditions of Paraprofessionals," 224.

19. Mohr and Schuneman, "Changing Roles," 208-210.

20. Jane Padham Ouderkirk, "Staff Assignments and Workflow Distribution at the End of the 20th Century: Where We Were, Where We Are and What We'll Need to Be," *Cataloging & Classification Quarterly* 30, no. 2/3 (2000): 343-355.

21. Oberg, "The Emergence of the Paraprofessional in Academic Libraries," 99.

22. Mohr and Schuneman, "Changing Roles," 212.

23. Calhoun, "Redesign of Library Workflows."

24. For further discussion of this flexibility see: Grenci, "The Impact of Web Publishing," 166-7.

25. Information on this course is available at the OCLC Institute Web site: *http://www.oclc.org/institute/oll/index.htm* (viewed Mar. 28, 2001).

26. Grenci, "Impact of Web Publishing," 165-166.

27. Calhoun, "Redesign of Library Workflows."

28. Evan St. Lifer, "The Boomer Brain Drain: The Last of a Generation?" *Library Journal* 125, no. 8 (May 1, 2000): 38-42.

29. Stanley Wilder, "The Changing Profile of Research Library Professional Staff," *A Bimonthly Report on Research Library Issues and Actions from ARL, CNI and SPARC* 208/209 (Feb./Apr. 2000): *http://www.arl.org/newsltr/208_209/chgprofile.html* (viewed Mar. 28, 2001).

30. Mohr and Schuneman, "Changing Roles," 205-218.

31. These standards include: *Anglo-American Cataloguing Rules*. 2nd ed., 1998 rev. (Ottawa: Canadian Library Association, 1998); *ISBD(ER): International Standard Bibliographic Description for Electronic Resources*, http://www.ifla.org/VII/s13/pubs/isbd.htm; Library of Congress, Cataloging Policy and Support Office. *Draft Interim Guidelines for Cataloging Electronic Resources*, http://www.loc.gov/catdir/cpso/dcmb19_4.html (viewed Mar. 28, 2001); Melissa Beck, *CONSER Cataloging Manual, Module 31*, Remote Access to Computer File Serials," http://lcweb.loc-gov/acq/conser/module31.html, Update Fall 2000. Nancy B. Olson, ed., *Cataloging Internet Resources, A Manual and Practice Guide*, 2nd ed. http://www.purl.org/oclc/cataloging-internet. Initially, the Intercat Project provided examples of Internet cataloging.

APPENDIX I. Staffing for Internet Resources Cataloging Survey

Instructions: Please answer the following questions concerning your library by circling the appropriate letter or filling in the answers as necessary. If your library is not cataloging Internet resources at the present time, answer only the first question below and return the survey. If your library is cataloging Internet resources, please answer all the survey questions. All information which you provide will be considered confidential. Thank you for your participation in our survey. **Please return your questionnaire by November 27, 2000.**

1.) Does your library catalog Internet resources (e-journals, databases, Web pages)?

a.) Yes   b.) No   c.) Not at the present time, but plan to in the future

If yes, please continue.

If no or not at the present time, please return the survey. A brief comment about why you are not cataloging Internet resources would be appreciated. _____

I. Institutional Information

2.) Student enrollment:

a.) 0-5000   b.) 5001-10,000   c.) 10,001-20,000   d.) 20,001-40,000   e.) 40,001 and up

3.) How many volumes are in your library's holdings?

a.) Fewer than 100,000   b.) 100,000-499,999   c.) 500,000-999,999
d.) 1,000,000-2,000,000   e.) More than 2,000,000

4.) What integrated library system or OPAC does your library use? _____

5.) What bibliographic utility does your library use to create or contribute Internet resource catalog records?

a.) OCLC   b.) RLIN   c.) Don't use bibliographic utility
d.) Other, please specify _____

6.) Does your library participate in the OCLC CORC Project?

a.) Yes   b.) No

II. Cataloging Internet Resources Information

7.) In what year did your library begin cataloging Internet resources? _____

8.) Per year, how many Internet resources are cataloged by your library? _____

9.) How many records for Internet resources are in your library's catalog? _____

10.) What type of access does your library provide for Internet resources? Please circle all that apply.

a.) Each Internet resource has an individual MARC bibliographical record in our catalog
b.) We add notes and access points regarding the Internet version to the MARC record for the paper version
c.) We provide a Web-based clickable list by subject
d.) We provide a Web-based clickable list by title
e.) Other, please specify _____

11.) How much has the cataloging of Internet resources changed the organization of the cataloging department (or similarly named entity with the same function)?

a.) Greatly   b.) Somewhat   c.) Not at all
Please elaborate. _____

12.) How many of your library's cataloging staff catalog Internet resources? _____

Please approximate what percentage this is of the entire cataloging staff.

a.) 0-25%   b.) 26%-50%   c.) 51%-75%   d.) 76%-100%

13.) How many people who catalog Internet resources have an MLS (or similar graduate level degree in library/information science)? _____

Please approximate what percentage this is of the entire cataloging staff.

a.) 0-25%   b.) 26%-50%   c.) 51%-75%   d.) 76%-100%

14.) How many people who catalog Internet resources do not have an MLS? _____

Please approximate what percentage this is of the entire cataloging staff.

a.) 0-25%   b.) 26%-50%   c.) 51%-75%   d.) 76%-100%

15.) How has the number of **MLS degreed catalogers** directly involved in Internet cataloging changed since your library began cataloging Internet resources?

a.) Increased   b.) Decreased   c.) Stayed the same by reassigning existing staff
d.) Stayed the same

16.) How has the number of **support staff catalogers** directly involved in Internet cataloging changed since your library began cataloging Internet resources?

a.) Increased   b.) Decreased   c.) Stayed the same by reassigning existing staff
d.) Stayed the same

17.) In the last five years has your library hired additional new staff specifically to catalog Internet resources?

a.) Yes   b.) No

If yes, how many MLS FTE? _____   How many support FTE? _____

18.) Has your library reclassified MLS degreed positions to catalog Internet resources?

a.) Yes-upward classification b.) Yes-downward classification c.) No
If yes, how many FTE? _____

19.) Has your library reclassified support staff positions to catalog Internet resources?

a.) Yes-upward classification b.) Yes-downward classification c.) No
If yes, how many FTE? _____

20.) If support staff catalog Internet resources in your library, why was this decision made? Please circle all that apply.

a.) Concern for growth and development of support staff
b.) Increased number of Internet items to be cataloged
c.) High cost of cataloging by MLS degreed staff
d.) Freed MLS catalogers to spend more time on other activities outside cataloging, such as national and state committee work, administration, publishing
e.) Difficulty in recruiting MLS catalogers
f.) Administrative decision not to fill vacant MLS cataloger positions
g.) Other, please specify _____

21.) If support staff in your library do not catalog Internet resources, why was this decision made? Please circle all that apply.

a.) Union or civil service restrictions
b.) Sufficient MLS catalogers to keep up with the work
c.) Inappropriate work for classification level
d.) No one available to train them
e.) Sufficient amount of other work already exists for support staff
f.) Locally established division of workflow
g.) Other, please specify _____

22.) What percent of your library's Internet resource cataloging is performed in a team approach (i.e., both MLS degreed librarians and support staff are involved in cataloging the same item)?

a.) Less than 25% b.) 26%-50% c.) 51%-75% d.) 76%-100% e.) Don't know
f.) No team approach used

In cataloging Internet resources what level of staff is responsible for the following? Check all that apply.

	a.) MLS degreed	b.) Support	c.) Not applicable
23.) Descriptive cataloging	____	____	____
24.) Assigning call numbers	____	____	____
25.) Assigning subject headings	____	____	____
26.) Adapting member input cataloging (non-Library of Congress)	____	____	____
27.) Copy cataloging (Library of Congress)	____	____	____
28.) Original cataloging	____	____	____

29.) If support staff is cataloging Internet resources, is their work revised or reviewed?

a.) Yes b.) No

30.) If yes, by whom?

a.) Support staff b.) MLS degreed staff c.) Support and MLS degreed staff

31.) Which of the following venues for training have you found the most useful? Circle all that apply.

a.) Workshops presented by national-level professional associations
b.) Workshops presented by state-level associations
c.) Workshops presented by network associations
d.) Workshops presented by local-level associations or groups
e.) In-house training
f.) Other, please specify _____

Can you briefly describe why?_____

32.) How would you describe the amount of time your library spent initially in training staff versus the amount of time now spent for on-going training?

a.) More   b.) Somewhat more   c.) About the same   d.) Somewhat less   e.) Less
f.) Don't know

III. Specific types of Internet resources

33.) At what level of cataloging does your library catalog e-journals?

a.) Full-level   b.) Less-than-full-level   c.) In-house standards   d.) Don't catalog

34.) At what level of cataloging does your library catalog databases (online indexes)?

a.) Full-level   b.) Less-than-full-level   c.) In-house standards   d.) Don't catalog

35.) At what level of cataloging does your library catalog free Web pages (such as home pages, organization Web pages, etc.)?

a.) Full-level   b.) Less-than-full-level   c.) In-house standards   d.) Don't catalog

36.) What type of Internet resources are cataloged by support staff ? Circle all that apply.

a.) E-journals   b.) Databases   c.) Free Web pages   d.) Support staff don't catalog Internet resources

37.) What type of Internet resources are cataloged by MLS degreed staff? Circle all that apply.

a.) E-journals   b.) Databases   c.) Free Web pages   d.) MLS degreed staff don't catalog Internet resources

Thank you for your time and participation in our survey. **Please return the survey in the enclosed envelope by November 27, 2000.**

Jeanne Boydston
Serials and Electronic
Resources Cataloger
515-294-3456
jboydsto@iastate.edu

Joan M. Leysen
Monographs and Electronic
Resources Cataloger
515/294-0428
jleysen@iastate.edu

Notes for Remote Access
Computer File Serials

Beatrice L. Caraway

SUMMARY. The notes in a catalog record convey information about various aspects of the publication described, including publishing and issuing information, indexing and supplementary material, numbering, sources of information, and so on. For serials in electronic format, in addition to all of this information, they also provide clarification of the item's location and means of access, its file structure and system requirements, its relationship to other publications, and more. This compilation presents common examples and variations of notes presently found in records for remote access computer file serials. *[Article copies available for a fee from The Haworth Document Delivery Service: 1-800-HAWORTH. E-mail address: <getinfo@haworthpressinc.com> Website: <http://www.HaworthPress.com> © 2002 by The Haworth Press, Inc. All rights reserved.]*

KEYWORDS. Electronic serials, e-journals, remote access computer file serials, cataloging

Notes in the serial catalog record have, in recent years, taken on an increasingly important role. Notes have always been the workhorse of the serial rec-

Beatrice L. Caraway is Interim Bibliographic Support Librarian at Trinity University, 715 Stadium Drive, San Antonio, TX 78212-7200 (E-mail: bcaraway@trinity.edu).

[Haworth co-indexing entry note]: "Notes for Remote Access Computer File Serials." Caraway, Beatrice L. Co-published simultaneously in *The Serials Librarian* (The Haworth Information Press, an imprint of The Haworth Press, Inc.) Vol. 41, No. 3/4, 2002, pp. 147-168; and: *E-Serials Cataloging: Access to Continuing and Integrating Resources via the Catalog and the Web* (ed: Jim Cole, and Wayne Jones) The Haworth Information Press, an imprint of The Haworth Press, Inc., 2002, pp. 147-168. Single or multiple copies of this article are available for a fee from The Haworth Document Delivery Service [1-800-HAWORTH, 9:00 a.m. - 5:00 p.m. (EST). E-mail address: getinfo@haworthpressinc.com].

ord, hauling along the load of information that these records accumulate year after year. Now, however, because we rely on them to explain the many and varied characteristics and requirements of electronic publications and the often-confusing relationships they have with other publications and formats, they are ever more crucial to catalogers and users alike. In this article, we will look at the kinds of notes that catalogers are constructing today to explain, amplify or clarify characteristics of electronic serials.

For the purpose of this piece, which is to show the kinds of notes being composed for remote access computer file serials, let us agree upon what constitutes a note.[1] Those who learned and performed cataloging before the advent of MARC might say that a note is anything that is not part of the record from the title and statement of responsibility area through the series area, and that is not an added entry.[2] They might add that the cataloger composes a note for the sake of explanation or amplification, drawing information from the publication itself or from other sources.

In contrast, those who have cut their cataloging teeth on the MARC format might immediately and more succinctly answer, "5XX," which is correct. However, the *CONSER Editing Guide*[3] expands the category of "note" to include "notes generated on output from other fields in the record (e.g., 246, 310, etc.)." The guide's list of other fields that may generate notes mentions the 022, 037, 074, 086, 222, 321, 362 (indicator value "1," or unformatted note), and the 760-787. Of these, however, all but the 310/321 and unformatted 362 have display constants that identify the kind of information that is given in the "note," and the "note" itself is usually a simple transcription of prescribed information.[4] In contrast, the 310/321 and the unformatted 362 do allow the cataloger some license in wording, so we will include some pertinent examples from records for electronic serial publications. Finally, even though the 856 field is not mentioned in the section on notes in the *CONSER Editing Guide*, the z subfield of the 856 is later referred to as a "public note" and is described as "relating to the electronic location of the serial, written in a form that is intended for public display." Like the other fields we have already mentioned, it, too, affords the cataloger the freedom to describe the electronic location of the serial or specify the nature of the relationship of the electronic resource to the bibliographic item described by the record.

To sum up, then, if we agree to think of the note as that part of the record which the cataloger composes rather than transcribes (as, for example, the title) or structures in a prescribed way (as, for example, added entries or the physical description), we should also consider such bits of the record as the i subfield in the 246, the 310/321, the unformatted 362, and the z and 3 subfields in the 856 as fitting the notion of "note." Even though we may not be used to thinking of these as notes, in all these cases the cataloger composes a phrase to explain or clarify or describe something about the publication–and that sounds a lot like a note!

Our purpose here is not to debate the finer points of what constitutes a note, strictly speaking, but to justify including in this compilation the kinds of phrases that catalogers are using in the subfield *i* of the 246, in the 310/321 and unformatted 362, and in the subfields *z* and *3* of the 856.

As we try to create useful catalog records for electronic serials, we often encounter unfamiliar situations and then struggle to describe them clearly and briefly. This compilation includes examples from all the fields discussed above and is intended to inspire and encourage serials catalogers as they create notes to describe and explain electronic serials.

Many working catalogers have generously shared their files of notes. Thanks go to: Everett Allgood (New York University), Valerie Bross (UCLA), David Burke (Villanova), Jim Cole (Iowa State University), Renette Davis and Merle Steeves (University of Chicago), Ryan Finnerty and Renee Chin (UCSD), June Garner and Amy Murphy (Mississippi State University), Beth Guay (University of Maryland), Tim Hagan (Northwestern University), Fred Hamilton (Louisiana Tech University), Frieda Rosenberg (University of North Carolina), and Lida Sak (Rutgers).

Note that all these examples address the situation in which separate records are made for the electronic serial. They are not appropriate for the "single-record" approach.

246 VARYING FORM OF TITLE

The print constants available for the second indicators 2-8 in the 246 can generate notes that specify any one of several common sources of variant titles (e.g., 7 for "running title" or 8 for "spine title"). When these print constants cannot generate an accurate note, the *i* subfield expresses the source of the varying form of title. As you would expect, electronic serials provide sources of variant titles that do not fit any of the sources described by indicators 0-8.

1. $i Title on journal main page: $a Information notes
2. $i Title on journal home page: $a American journal of physiology. $p Advances in physiology education
3. $i Title from home page: $a Grant award database, FY . . .
4. $i Title on "what's new" screen, viewed Apr. 1999: Jane's international . . .
5. $i Title on ARS news & information screen: $a ARS magazine
6. $i Title on Windows icon: $a E-guide
7. $i Title on database selection menu: $a Newsbank newsfile

8. $i Running title on .pdf files: $a Fujitsu sci. tech. j
9. $i Journal home page also has title: $a FJ online
10. $i Title also in French in cover ill. on opening screen: $a Nouvelle revue d'optique
11. $i Also on index page: $a AgExporter magazine
12. $i "About MR" screen contains the title: $a Mississippi review Web
13. $i Logon screen: $a ABSEARCH databases, ASHA American Speech-Language-Hearing Association
14. $i WWW issues for Oct. 15, 1995- have added title: $a University Press electronic news
15. $i Also known as: $a Sociofile database
16. $i Also referred to as: $a Annual reviews in genomics and human genetics
17. $i Also cited erroneously as: $a Chemical automation design news
18. $i Listserv name: $a Cites
19. $i Listserv title: $a Prices
20. $i File name: $a EFFON

The following notes in the 246 $i represent different ways of saying that the varying form of title is drawn from the HTML document title tag. This title is reflected in the title bar that displays at the top of the window. It tends to be very unstable, changing each time the Web designer modifies the HTML document title. Several of the following have changed since they were cataloged.

20. $i Title bar title: $a WordVirtual.com
21. $a Title in title bar: $a IFPP
22. $i Title on HTML header: $a Hitachi review index
23. $i Source code title for hypertext version: $a Hyperpsycoloquy
24. $i HTML source title: $a CIS Congressional universe
25. $i Journal home page document source title: $a AJP: Advances in physiology education
26. $i Issue-selection page source title: $a PNI. $p News from the journal
27. $i Issue document source title: $a PNS

310/321 FREQUENCY

From the *CONSER Editing Guide*, 1994 ed.: Fields 310 and 321 contain, respectively, the current and former frequencies.

1. Monthly, with weekly additions
2. Annual volumes, to which articles are added following the review process
3. Quarterly issues, with articles added to issues until their close

362 DATES OF PUBLICATION, COVERAGE, OR DURATION

From the *CONSER Editing Guide*, 1994 ed.: Field 362 contains beginning and/or ending numeric, alphabetic, and/or chronological designations of an item . . . The unformatted note is used when the first and/or last piece is not in hand, but the information is known.

1. Coverage as of Oct. 13, 1999: Vol. 10, no. 3 (summer 1999)-
2. Electronic coverage as of July 16, 1997: Vol. 30, no. 1 (May 1989)-
3. Electronic coverage in full text as of Mar. 23, 1999: Vol. 12, no. 1 (Jan. 1998)-
4. Full-text electronic coverage as of Dec. 1, 1998: Working paper no. 4935-
5. Full text as of Apr. 11, 2000: Vol. 9, no. 1 (Mar. 1997)-
6. Coverage as of Jan. 11, 2001: abstracts: Vol. 27, issue 7 (Jan. 1996)- ; full text: Vol. 28, issue 1 (Jan. 1997)-
7. "Launched on May 10, 1995"–Welcome screen.
8. Began online version with: Vol. 44, no. 1 (Feb. 1995).

500 GENERAL NOTE

From the *CONSER Editing Guide*, 1994 ed.: Field 500 is used for unformatted notes whenever the other 5XX note fields are not applicable.

Notes about Titles

1. Title from home page (viewed June 15, 2000).
2. Title from journal homepage (viewed Dec. 31, 1999).
3. Title from opening screen.
4. Title from title screen (viewed Apr. 3, 1999).
5. Title from caption (viewed May 12, 2000).
6. Title from table of contents page (viewed Feb. 10, 1999).
7. Title from table of contents caption of ftp version.
8. Title from contents frame (viewed Dec. 1, 1998).
9. Title from vol. contents page (viewed Sept. 30, 1997).
10. Title from back issues table of contents screen.
11. Title from masthead on Ethnic newswatch Web page (viewed Feb. 26, 2000).
12. Title from publisher's statement page (viewed Oct. 31, 1997).
13. Title from program index file.

Publishing Statements

1. Published: University of Alberta, 1998; Sheffield Hallam University, Dept. of English, 1999-
2. Publisher varies: Stone Mountain, GA: ATLA Center for Electronic Resources in Theology and Religion, <v. 5 (2000)- >.

Physical Description and Accompanying Material

1. Some issues accompanied by .gif files.

General Contents and Coverage Information and "Includes" Statements

1. Online version contains full text of each issue beginning with Jan. 1999, including all figures and tables; abstracts from Jan. 1998 on; and tables of contents from Jan. 1997 on. All contents are searchable.
2. Web site includes some numbers issued under earlier name of body.
3. Online version also includes issues from earlier titles: . . .
4. Includes the complete text of the earlier title plus its predecessor: European political cooperation documentation bulletin.
5. Web site includes all issues with the journal's earlier title.
6. Web site also includes issues with the journal's earlier title: San Diego metropolitan magazine.
7. Current year only available online.
8. Website contains current week only.
9. Holdings vary, recent years only.
10. Online version containing only the text of AgExporter; tables and graphics not included and some articles not available; only tables of contents available online for Jan.-Nov. 1996 issues.
11. Inclusive coverage: 1974 to the present.
12. Database coverage: 1969-
13. Dates of coverage: 1993 to the present.

Miscellaneous General Notes

1. Blackstone Press publishes the main articles from the journal in print form.
2. Consists of two sections, MERIA journal, a refereed journal, usually issued quarterly; and MERIA news, which is updated frequently.
3. Continuously updated.
4. Updated monthly.
5. Each title is updated periodically.
6. Vol. 1 (1914)-v. 7 (1920) are digital reproductions of the reprint ed. published: New York : Johnson Reprint Corp., 1960.

Issuing Information/Available From
(See field 550 for notes relating to issuing bodies that are traced.)

1. Made available by Emerald, the service of MCB University Press, which provides electronic delivery of its journals.
2. Made available through: OCLC FirstSearch Electronic Collections Online.

Description Based on Notes

1. Description based on: Vol. 2, no. 1 (Dec. 1999); title from title screen (viewed on Jan. 15, 2000).
2. Description based on: Vol. 13, no. 2 (June 1999 release); title from welcome screen.
3. Description based on: Vol. 44, no. 5 (May 1996); title from contents screen (viewed May 4, 1999).
4. Description based on online display of content as of Jan. 1999; title from title screen.
5. Description based on JSTOR World Wide Web homepage; title from title screen (viewed on July 8, 1999).
6. Description based on content as of Sept. 1998.
7. Description based on: Working paper no. 4935, published 1994; title from analytical t.p. (viewed Dec. 1, 1998).
8. Description based on: Vol. 2, no. 1 (Dec. 1999); title from available issues screen (viewed on Jan. 15, 2000).
9. Description based on: Vol. 1, no. 2 (Nov. 1, 1999); title from general information screen (viewed Dec. 9, 1999).
10. Description based on: Vol. 8, issue 1 (1997); title from journal information screen (viewed Sept. 1, 2000).
11. Description based on: Vol. 70, no. 52 (Sept. 24, 1999); title from caption of online issue (viewed Sept. 29, 1999).
12. Description and title from journal information screens as viewed Apr. 11, 2000.
13. Examined for cataloging on Feb. 12, 1998.

506 RESTRICTIONS ON ACCESS NOTE

From the *CONSER Cataloging Manual*: When a publication is not freely available and the electronic location is given in field 856, catalogers may note the restriction using field 506.

1. Tables of contents and abstracts are freely available; full-text access is restricted to current subscribers.

2. Access to the Blue Ribbon Services area restricted to subscribers; username and password required.
3. Access restricted to subscribers.
4. Access restricted to institutions with paid online subscription.
5. Access restricted to registered users connecting from an approved IP address.
6. Full text restricted to institutions and individuals with a subscription or membership in the society; table of contents and article abstracts accessible to all users.
7. Access to full text restricted to institutions with a print subscription and requires a site/user ID and password. Tables of contents, announcements, etc., available without restriction.
8. Access restricted to institutions with a subscription to the Proquest Direct Online Service.
9. Access restricted to subscribing institutions.
10. Access restricted to LINK subscribers.
11. Restricted to subscribers with a site license.
12. Restricted to institutions with a site license to the JSTOR collection.
13. Access restricted by licensing agreement.
14. Access limited to individual subscribers and institutions with site license agreements.
15. Access limited to subscribers/license holders.
16. Subscription and registration required for access.
17. Subscription required for access to abstracts and full text.
18. OhioLINK membership required for access.
19. Licensing required.
20. Full contents available only to subscribers.
21. Electronic holdings available only to subscribing institutions.
22. Subscription based access.

Local Restrictions

1. Electronic access restricted to Villanova University patrons.
2. Access restricted to members of the Iowa State University community.
3. Internet version restricted to affiliated MSU patrons with a valid user ID.
4. Access restricted to the Northwestern University community and other subscribers.
5. Access to full text journals limited to authorized Pitt and UPMC affiliated users.

515 NUMBERING PECULIARITIES NOTE

From the *CONSER Cataloging Manual*: Make notes on any numbering or issuing peculiarities. Electronic serials may have unusual numbering patterns.

Numbering or Issuing Peculiarities

1. Some issues published out of chronological sequence.
2. The current issue also has vol. numbering; older issues identified only by date.
3. Published in one vol. per calendar year; articles are numbered sequentially in each vol., and added to the current year's vol. as they are received.
4. Published on an article-by-article basis, with articles added to the latest, "open" monthly issue.
5. Numbered articles are added continuously to topical categories.
6. Consecutively paged articles are added continuously to periodically cumulated vols.
7. Articles posted individually as processed, cumulated into annual vols. (one per year, 1997-)
8. Articles are continuously added to the current annual vol.
9. Articles are posted as they are available into monthly issues.
10. Published in one vol. per calendar year; each article issued is a number of a vol.
11. The current issue consists of the most recent articles; older articles are stored in the searchable EIoP archive.
12. Began with the simultaneous release in summer 1989 of annual cumulations for the years 1986 through 1988 and the 2nd quarter cumulation for Jan.-June 1989; quarterly issues thereafter are cumulative, with the fourth issue each year comprising the final archival cumulation; cumulative issues for 1981-1985 and 1986-1990 also published.
13. Articles are published continuously on the Internet in an "Issue in Progress," which is declared, every 6 mos., as a "New Issue."
14. As additional issues of both sections of MERIA are published, old issues will be listed under the link, "Back issues."
15. Latest issue revised after initial publication with new articles, corrections, or interactive letters to the editor.
16. Numbering in preliminary table of contents is abbreviated (e.g., 1/1, 1/2, etc.).
17. Successive articles are uniquely identified by a manuscript number and date.
18. Articles are published immediately after acceptance and submission of the final manuscript to the publisher rather than when an issue is completed.
19. Publication updated daily; monthly issues only are retained.
20. Each issue is cumulative, superseding the previous issue.
21. Each issue includes correspondence collected on e-mail over the past six months.

Preliminary Issues

1. Vol. 1, no. 1 also called Prototype issue.
2. Vol. 1, issue 1 also called debut issue.
3. Issue for Jan. to June 1996 is a demonstration issue containing selected articles from the print edition of that issue.

Items Not Published

1. Issues consisting of abstracts, typically of the Experimental Biology (EB) and ASBMB annual meetings, are not included.

516 TYPE OF COMPUTER FILE OR DATA NOTE

From the *CONSER Editing Guide*, 1994 ed.: Record information that characterizes computer file aspects of a serial in field 516. More specific information, such as the format or genre of the serial files (e.g., ASCII, hypertext, electronic journal), may be included along with a general description (e.g., text and graphic files).

From the *CONSER Cataloging Manual*: Make a brief note as to the type of remote access computer file serial if it is not otherwise clear in the record. Terms such as "electronic journal" may be given in the note, either in a formatted style (e.g., Text (electronic journal)) or in a free text note (e.g., Electronic journal available in ASCII and RichText). The availability of multiple file formats is also described in this field.

1. Numeric (summary statistics)
2. Text (HTML)
3. Text (citations)
4. Text (electronic journal)
5. Text (electronic newspaper)
6. Text and graphics (electronic journal)
7. Hypertext (electronic journal), with links to related publications and databases
8. HTML-encoded text and graphic files (electronic serial)
9. Electronic journal
10. Electronic journal with video and audio files
11. Electronic journal; some articles available in PDF
12. Electronic newspaper in hypertext
13. Electronic journal with articles in PDF
14. Electronic serial in PDF format
15. Electronic serial in ASCII text

16. Text and JPEG graphics formats
17. Electronic journal with full texts of articles in PDF and, Oct. 1997-HTML formats.
18. Electronic journal with full-text articles available in PDF and gzipped PostScript file formats; tables of contents and abstracts HTML encoded
19. Electronic journal with full-text articles in PDF format; tables of contents and abstracts HTML encoded. Includes multimedia files in various formats
20. Electronic journal with articles in PDF and HTML formats; abstracts and/or tables of contents HTML encoded
21. Electronic journal; tables of contents, abstracts, and article information HTML encoded; articles from 1992-1994 in TeX format; those from 1995- in TeX, DVI, and PostScript formats, and also, 1996- , PDF format
22. Electronic journal issued in formatted-text files: TeX, DVI, PostScript, and PDF
23. Most issues in PDF format; some html
24. Abstracts, tables of contents, and citation information are HTML encoded; articles are available in portable document format (PDF) and as Postscript Level 2 files
25. Articles are in PDF, DVI, and PS file format, abstracts are HTML encoded
26. Electronic serial in ASCII text, Dec. 1991-Jan. 1995; HTML-encoded text, fall 1996/winter 1997-
27. Hypertext, with links to text and non-text files; some articles in Acrobat PDF
28. Hypertext, with search capabilities
29. Chiefly text (HTML) with search software and image data
30. Tables of contents and citation information are HTML encoded
31. In HTML and/or PDF formats
32. Available in HTML, zipped-ASCII, and PDF formats
33. Electronic journal in TeX, PostScript, and Acrobat file formats
34. Files in HTML, text, pdf, and PowerPoint formats
35. Bit-mapped images; PDF, PostScript, and TIFF formats available for printing
36. Available in ASCII, Acrobat, and PostScript file formats

520 SUMMARY, ETC., NOTE

From the *CONSER Editing Guide*, 1994 ed.: Field 520 contains unformatted notes describing the scope and contents of the work.

1. The science magazine of the U.S. Dept. of Agriculture.
2. A service from the editors of Successful farming that provides access to current weather conditions, diverse business and production news, ideas and advice, and the latest information on precision farming and agricultural computing as well as discussion groups devoted to machinery, weather, livestock, and technology.
3. A broad-based journal covering both the empirical and theoretical approaches to behavior ecology; includes studies on the whole range of behaving organisms–plants, invertebrates, vertebrates, and humans.
4. " . . . access to Dept. of the Navy policy, procedures, information, data, and tools of interest to the Navy Acquisition/Procurement Work Force."
5. Contains cumulative bibliographic citations to statistical books and articles in more than 1,000 journals, with coverage generally extending back to 1974, earlier in some instances.
6. Publishes research announcements of significant advances in all branches of mathematics.
7. Serves as the Institute of Physics Publishing's Web-based online research service. It features the Institution of Electrical Engineers' INSPEC Database, with the possibility of additional databases being added in the future.
8. Contains full text and abstracts, 1999- ; abstracts and PDF, Nov. 1998; abstracts only, <1996>-Sept. 1998.
9. Provides image and full-text online access to back issues. Consult the online table of contents for specific holdings.
10. Online edition provides also abstracts of articles from print ed. v. 1 (1997)-11 (1997).

TARGET AUDIENCE NOTE

From the *CONSER Editing Guide*, 1994 ed.: Field 521 contains information about the users or the intended audience of the material described. In CONSER records, this field is limited to quoted notes describing the intended audience of the publication.

1. "The audience is U.S. agricultural producers, exporters, trade organizations, state departments of agriculture and any other export-oriented organization."
2. "Aimed particularly at teachers of the 16-19 age range, including first year undergraduates, but contains teaching advice relevant to any physics teacher."

525 SUPPLEMENT NOTE

From the *CONSER Editing Guide*, 1994 ed.: Field 525 records the issuance of supplements or special issues not input as separate records . . . , Field 525 is used primarily for unnamed supplements and/or special issues, but named supplements that are not cataloged on a separate record may also be mentioned.

1. Electronic supplementary materials to articles published in the print journal published on Springer-Verlag's server accessible via the World Wide Web.
2. Has supplement: Leonardo electronic almanac gallery. [Corresponding 856 $3 is: Leonardo electronic almanac gallery $u http://mitpress.mit.edu/e-journals/LEA/GALLERY/gallery.html]
3. Supplements accompany some volumes.
4. Electronic supplementary material also available.

530 ADDITIONAL PHYSICAL FORM AVAILABLE NOTE

From the *CONSER Editing Guide*, 1994 ed.: Field 530 is used to note the existence of one or more reproductions or versions in different physical formats.

1. Online version of the print publication.
2. Online version of the print title.
3. Online version of the print publication; also available on microfilm.
4. Online version of the print publication or reprints thereof.
5. Online version of the reprint of the original, which was published quarterly: Washington, D.C.: Population Association of America.
6. Full-text, online version of the print publication: Working paper series (National Bureau of Economic Research), with abstracts and/or bibliographic information for earlier papers.
7. Full-text, online version of the print publication, with abstracts of articles from earlier issues.
8. Online version of the print publication's news section.
9. Early issues are an online version of the print publication, which was discontinued after the 1996 issue.
10. Online version of the print publication. Beginning in 1999, includes a separate page, Nucleic acids research methods (also called NAR methods online), for methods papers that are published only online, as well as papers on novel methods that are published both in the print edition and online.
11. Online version of: Agricultural research (Washington, D.C.).
12. Electronic version of: Metabolic engineering.

13. Online version of the print: Neighborhood networks newslines.
14. Issued also on microfiche and CD-ROM.
15. Issued also in print, 1999-
16. Also available in a print ed.
17. Also available in a print ed. with title: Fleece on paper.
18. Also issued in a print version.
19. Also issued in a print edition.
20. Print version available.
21. Also issued in paper format.
22. Published 1976-1996 in print form.
23. Print version: Mississippi review.
24. Issued also in a monthly print version with title: Slate on paper, which contains highlights from the online version.
25. Content also available serially in printed version, with title: California Legislature, State Senate Publications Office catalogue, list of titles by stock number.
26. Contains articles from the print publication: Pacific discovery.
27. No. -106 issued also in print, with title: Newsletter (Kokuritsu Kokkai Toshokan (Japan)).
28. Also available in print with title: Chemicals in our community.
29. Available in a print edition, with title: Bibliography and index of geology.

538 SYSTEM DETAILS NOTE

From the *CONSER Cataloging Manual*: A "mode of access" note . . . must be given in all records for remote access serials to explain the means by which the serial can be accessed. . . . The mode of access note is considered one of the "system details" for remote access computer files and is given following the system requirements note, if present.

1. System requirements: Web browser.
2. System requirements: World Wide Web browser, Internet access, and RealPage viewer.
3. System requirements: World Wide Web browser and Adobe Acrobat Reader.
4. System requirements: Acrobat reader for full text of PDF documents.
5. System requirements: Adobe Acrobat Reader to view articles; Web browser which supports forms to subscribe to Table of Contents service.
6. System requirements: TeX or PostScript required to view and print 1994 and 1995 issues; Acrobat reader required for 1996- issues; Netscape 1.1 or higher recommended.

7. System requirements for sound files: Sun audio files (also known as "basic" audio) using mu-law data format. Files are monaural and can be played on most PC, Mac, or UNIX systems with audio hardware and software. All musical examples are digitized at 44,100 samples/second (standard for commercial CD recording). Spoken examples are digitized at 8,000 samples/second. Size of audio files (in KB or MB) indicated parenthetically in the text.

8. System requirements for graphic files: GIF graphical image format representing musical examples, facsimiles of original documents and other visual materials.

9. System requirements: World Wide Web browser software capable of displaying frames and graphics and playing audio and MIDI files.

10. System requirements: File decompression utility for zipped files; Acrobat reader for full text of PDF documents.

11. System requirements: Ability to view and print articles in the format desired.

12. System requirements: Browser plug-ins required to view some articles in their totality.

13. System requirements: Acrobat reader for full text of articles; ability to play multimedia files in various formats.

14. System requirements: WWW browser such as Netscape, and/or SilverPlatter WinSPIRS, MacSPIRS, or UNIX client software.

15. System requirements: RealAudio player required to listen to digital audio recordings.

Mode of Access

1. Mode of access: World Wide Web.
2. Mode of access: Online access via Internet.
3. Mode of access: World Wide Web via Internet at the NSF web site.
4. Mode of access: Internet, World Wide Web and e-mail (e-mail subscriptions are available via a form at the World Wide Web site).
5. Mode of access: Electronic mail or via the Internet. For email subscription, send message to: E-Poetry@ubvm.cc.buffalo.edu. To access via the Internet, connect to: http://wings.buffalo.edu/epc/rift/
6. Mode of access: Titles and abstracts by e-mail subscription, etna@mcs.kent.edu with the subject: ETNA registration. Articles by anonymous FTP or netlib-type mailer; World Wide Web.
7. Mode of access: Electronic mail, FTP, gopher, and World Wide Web.
8. Mode of access: Electronic mail, FTP, gopher, telnet, and World Wide Web. For e-mail subscription, send to: listserv@library.berkeley.edu, the message: sub cites [first name last name]. For telnet access, telnet to MELVYL.UCOP.EDU and enter the command: SHOW CURRENT CITES. Also distributed on the PACS-L and PACS-P lists.

546 LANGUAGE NOTE

From the *CONSER Editing Guide*, 1994 ed.: Field 546 provides information concerning the language or languages of the text, summaries, etc.

1. Issues for Mar. 1995-June 1997 also available in French; Oct. 1997- also available in French and Spanish.
2. User interface and guide in English, French, and German.
3. Includes some text in French.
4. English, with some Hebrew text $b (Hebrew alphabet).
5. Articles in Spanish and English.

550 ISSUING BODY NOTE

(See 500 for notes relating to issuing bodies that are not traced.)

From the *CONSER Editing Guide*, 1994 ed.: Field 550 refers to current and former issuing bodies.

1. Digitized and made available by Project Muse.
2. Digitized and made available by CatchWord Ltd.
3. Digitized and made available by: Stanford University Libraries' High-Wire Press.
4. Online version published with the assistance of HighWire Press, Internet imprint of the Stanford University Libraries.
5. Digitized and made available by MCB University Press.
6. Issued in its electronic form by the American Institute of Physics.
7. HTML version for v. 1- made available by Project Muse.
8. Issued by: Association of Research Libraries, Office of Scholarly Communication, <1996>
9. Issued by: Instituto Laboral de Educación Sindical; distributed by the Catherwood Library as part of WorkNet@ILR.
10. Issued on behalf of: American Studies Association; digitized and made available by: Project Muse.
11. Published by: MIT Press for Leonardo/ISAST.
12. Sponsored by the Emily Dickinson Society.
13. Hosted by: University of Maryland, Baltimore County.
14. Published in cooperation with the Blanton-Peale Institute.

Official Organ, Publication, etc.

1. Official organ of the Section of Analytical Chemistry of the International Union of Pure and Applied Chemistry.

2. Official publication of the Henry James Society; digitized and made available by: Project Muse.

555 CUMULATIVE INDEX/FINDING AIDS NOTE

From the *CONSER Editing Guide*, 1994 ed.: Field 555 contains a statement of volumes and/or dates covered by cumulative indexes for a serial and a statement of location of these indexes, whether issued as part of the serial or issued separately.

Informal Notes

1. Includes a cumulative list of titles, scientists and keywords for all issues published 1978- .
2. Includes an index of descriptions, covering all issues published since the serial first began in 1964 under an earlier title.
3. Includes various subject indexes (e.g., Crop production, Plant diseases), both cumulative and by individual year.

556 INFORMATION ABOUT DOCUMENTATION NOTES

From the *CONSER Editing Guide*, 1994 ed.: Use field 556 to record information about the documentation for serials that explains their contents and use. Documentation for computer files may be published in print accompanying the computer file, or may be available by remote access.

1. User's guide available online via World Wide Web.
2. User's guide available online via World Wide Web. Service guide also available via World Wide Web.

580 LINKING ENTRY COMPLEXITY NOTE

From the *CONSER Editing Guide*, 1994 ed.: Field 580 is used to express complex relationships that cannot be accurately generated by using the display constants associated with the linking entry fields (765-787).

Supplement/Special Issue

1. Issued as a supplement to and contains computer programs previously published in the print journal: Computer physics communications.

Other Edition Available

1. Related edition also available in print.
2. Also available in archival version: Experimental biology online. Annual.

Preceding Title

1. Continues a print publication of the same title.
2. Continues a print version with the same title.
3. Continues print version which ceased with v. 47, no. 1 (Jan. 1998).
4. Continues the journal in paper format of the same title; v. 33-35 issued in both paper and electronic formats; beginning with v. 36 (1994) issued in electronic format only.
5. Continues the print publication: European foreign policy bulletin.
6. Continues the print publication: Discussion paper (University of Michigan. Research Forum on International Economics).
7. Continues the print ed.: General/flag officer worldwide roster.
8. Continues the print serial: Child development disorders.
9. Continues a paper format publication with the title: Bulletin (National Science Foundation (U.S.)).

Nonspecific Relationship

1. Duplicates in part the supporting information available on microfiche. Beginning with 1999, issued in online format only.
2. Updates: Moody's bank & finance manual.
3. Cumulated monthly in print as: Mergent corporate news reports.
4. Annual archival volumes available in print with title: Molecular modeling annual, and on CD-ROM with title: Journal of molecular modeling.
5. The database combines Sociological abstracts with Social planning policy and development abstracts (SOPODA).
6. Issue announcements and a discussion list are available. Send message to Listserv@jse.stat.ncsu.edu with command subscribe jse-announce <yourfirstname yourlastname> for issue announcements or with command subscribe jse-talk <yourfirstname yourlastname> for the discussion list.

590 LOCAL ACCESSIBILITY

1. Item accessible through library's Web page.
2. Item accessible through Iowa State University Library's Web page.

3. Item accessible in Parks Library only.
4. Also available on the University's INFO system.

856 ELECTRONIC LOCATION AND ACCESS

From the *CONSER Cataloging Manual*: Field 856 identifies the electronic location of the item from which it is available as well as the information needed to access the item. Information in the field should be sufficient to connect to a service, transfer files electronically, subscribe, or access issues of an electronic journal or newsletter.

Ed. note: We are concerned only with subfield $z, which provides a note for public display to amplify the information that relates to the electronic location or identifier in $u; and with $3, which supplies information about the item specified in $u, when that item does not have a one-to-one correspondence to the item described in the bibliographic record.

1. $z Address for accessing the journal from an authorized IP address through OCLC FirstSearch Electronic Collections Online. $u . . .
2. $u http://firstsearch.oclc.org $z Address for accessing the journal using authorization number and password through OCLC FirstSearch Electronic Collections Online
3. $u http://www.idealibrary.com $z Logon procedure and access to this title is available via the I.D.E.A.L. (service provider) homepage
4. $u http://webspirs.silverplatter.com/cgi-bin/er17.cgi $z Requires login and password
5. $z Connect to this internet resource. (Requires username and password. Contact Reference Dept. for password.) $u http://www.moscowtimes.ru
6. $z Access from campus or login via Rutgers account. The username is: rutgers; the password is: rutgers. $u . . .
7. $z Click on DIRECT LOGIN button to bypass username/password. $u . . .
8. $u http://www.usda.gov/news/pubs/index.htm $z Select the desired issue of the fact book from the list of available publications.
9. $u http://www.state.ia.us/educate/law/index.html $z (Includes hypertext links to the Code of Iowa)
10. $z URL accesses index of newsletters and news releases, from which a link may be made to the issue desired. $u . . .
11. $z Enter search terms "san AND diego AND table [or column]" and click on submit button to get list of tables or (columns) each with date of coverage; then make choice from list and click on it to view the data (or the issue in text or pdf format)
12. $z E-mail notification about new issue through distribution of table of contents and article retrieval instructions: $u mailto:info.curtin.edu.au $f libres $h listproc $i subscribe

13. $3 Leonardo electronic almanac gallery $u http://mitpress.mit.edu/e-journals/ LEA/GALLERY/gallery.html [Corresponding 525 is: Has supplement: Leonardo electronic almanac gallery.]
14. $3 Partial archive: $u gopher://info.lib.uh.edu:70/11/articles/e-journals/uhlibrary/pacsreview $2 gopher
15. $3 Hitachi review, 1995- $u http://www.hitachi.co.jp/Sp/TJ-e/index.html

The following examples of 530, 555, and 856 notes address the situation in which the single-record approach is used to note (in the record for the print version) the existence of the electronic version of the serial. Each belongs to a record describing the print version of the work.

530 OTHER PHYSICAL FORMATS

1. Also available via World Wide Web; $b OCLC FirstSearch Electronic Collections Online; $c Subscription required for access to abstracts and full text.
2. Available also online via the World Wide Web to institutions with a site license to the JSTOR Project and/or Project Muse.
3. Available also in Ebsco Online [JSTOR/Project Muse, etc., depending on the collection]; fulltext articles available in PDF [and/or HTML] to affiliated MSU patrons with a valid user ID.
4. Available also on the Internet; restricted to institutions with a site/user ID and password.
5. Online version available on the World Wide Web.
6. Also available in an online ed.
7. Also available via the World Wide Web.
8. Issued also in electronic format under title: Copyright and new media legal news.
9. Also available on the World Wide Web, with title: School law index. Includes hyperlinks to the text of the Code of Iowa.
10. Also available as an online database, with title: Biological and agricultural index; access restricted to members of the Iowa State University community.
11. Also available on the World Wide Web as part of the collection: International agriculture and trade (WRS).
12. Also available on the U.S. Dept. of Agriculture Web site.
13. Also available as an online database in the Reference Area at Parks Library.
14. Data herefrom also available in the online database: Current contents connect.
15. Also available in an online version, by which it was later absorbed: Chemistry of materials. ACS electronic supporting information.

16. Latest edition also available online via the World Wide Web; access restricted by password.
17. Recent issues are also available on the Internet via WWW.
18. Selected issues also available via the World Wide Web.
19. Tables of contents and selected articles also available online.
20. Contents pages available on WWW.
21. Backfile also issued online via JSTOR.
22. Some issues, including those published under an earlier title, also available via the World Wide Web.
23. Later issues also available on the World Wide Web.
24. Later issues also available on the World Wide Web. Beginning in 1999, short, as well as some full, methods papers are available online only, under title Nucleic acids research methods (also called NAR methods online); papers containing novel methods submitted in non-methods categories of the journal are printed in the journal and also published online.
25. Later issues also available in PDF format on the World Wide Web.
26. Later issues (excluding those consisting of annual meeting abstracts) also available on the World Wide Web.
27. Text of most articles from later issues also available on the World Wide Web.
28. Issues for <1994>-1996 also available on the World Wide Web.
29. Issued 1994-1996 also in an online version, by which it was later absorbed.

RELATED WEB SITES

1. (530) Has related Web site, with title: Science news online.
2. (530) News reports also available on the World Wide Web.
3. (555) Indexed on the publication's Web site.
4. (555) Indexed on the Web site for: IMI descriptions of fungi and bacteria.

856 ELECTRONIC LOCATION AND ACCESS

1. $z Online version available through Web of Science at: $u . . .
2. $z Online version: $u ttp://www.library.northwestern.edu/journal/matcorr/
3. $z Full text: check e-journal site for available issues. $u http://www.journals.cup.org/owadba/owa/ISSUESINJOURNAL?JID=DPP
4. $z Link to the electronic version of this title: $u http://ojps.aip.org/dok/
5. $z Available online, 1999- $u http://link.springer-ny.com/link/service/journals/10111/index.html

6. $u http://www.sciam.com/ $z (Related Web site, with the full text of selected articles and abstracts of others, as well as other sections from the journal, together with additional online features)
7. $3 Selected articles available at: $u . . .
8. $3 Tables of contents and abstracts: $u http://www.edpsciences.com/ jcp/
9. $3 News reports: $u http://www.fisonline.com/top%5Fb5.htm $z Click, as desired, on the Index or Report under "Industrial Manual"
10. $z Continued online at: $u http://www.gov.on.ca/OMAFRA/english/ infores.html $z Select the report from among the "Other information, programs and services"
11. $z Related material available on the World Wide Web at: $u . . .

NOTES

1. First, let us agree on the type of electronic publication under discussion in this article. The focus of this article is the remote access computer file serial, defined in module 31.1 of the *CONSER Cataloging Manual* as "a work issued in designated parts for an indefinite period of time, in computer file format, and accessed 'via input/output devices connected electronically to a computer' (*AACR2*). This is in contrast to a direct access computer file serial which is issued in a physical carrier, for example, a CD-ROM or floppy disk. The terms 'electronic serial,' 'online serial,' and 'remote access serial' are also used here for 'remote access computer file serial'" ("Module 31, Remote Access Computer File Serials," in *CONSER Cataloging Manual* [Washington, D.C.: Serial Record Division, Library of Congress, updated 01/02/2001], http:// www.loc.gov/acq/conser/mod31pt1.html#what (10 Apr. 2001)). Subsequent excerpts in this article taken from Module 31 are drawn from this same source.

2. One classic delineation of the note is set out by Arlene G. Taylor: "Many works require description beyond that presented formally in the title and statement of responsibility area through the series area. Notes qualify or amplify the formal description. Some notes contribute to identification of a work (e.g., a note giving the original title of a translated work). Some contribute to the intelligibility of the record (e.g., a note explaining the relationship to the work of a person who has been given an added entry). Other notes aid the reader who does not have in hand an exact citation (e.g., a summary or contents notes). Still other notes characterize an item (e.g., a thesis note), or give its bibliographic history (e.g., notes giving previous titles)" (Bohdan S. Wynar, *Introduction to Cataloging and Classification*, ed. Arlene G. Taylor, 7th ed. [Littleton, Colorado, 1985], 85).

3. *CONSER Editing Guide*, 1994 ed. (Washington, D.C.: Serial Record Division, Library of Congress, 1994). Subsequent excerpts in this article taken from the *CONSER Editing Guide* are drawn from this same edition.

4. It is important to point out that in principle this is true, but in practice, display constants are driven by the system in use. Some systems may not provide for print constants or may have print constants that are inconsistent with what OCLC uses.

On Pins and Needles:
Using Structured Metadata
for Collocation and Browsing Capability

Gregory Wool

SUMMARY. Structured metadata–metadata based on organizing principles–can facilitate the task of information retrieval by providing context and meaningful differentiation in search results as well as collocating items with similar characteristics and highlighting semantic relationships among index terms. Types of metadata structure include rule basis, authority control, categorization, and relationship control. Most information found in library catalog records is structured metadata, but online catalog systems often suppress structural features (especially those providing relationship control) through simplified machine sorting of search results. Catalog displays that respect and highlight metadata structures are needed to improve collocation and browsing capability. *[Article copies available for a fee from The Haworth Document Delivery Service: 1-800-HAWORTH. E-mail address: <getinfo@haworthpressinc.com> Website: <http://www.HaworthPress.com> © 2002 by The Haworth Press, Inc. All rights reserved.]*

KEYWORDS. Metadata, structured metadata, online information access, information organization, machine sorting, collocation, browsing

Gregory Wool, MA, MLS, is Associate Professor, Monographs Cataloger, and Authorities Unit Supervisor at the Iowa State University Library, 204 Parks Library, Ames, IA 50011-2140 USA (e-mail: gwool@iastate.edu).

[Haworth co-indexing entry note]: "On Pins and Needles: Using Structured Metadata for Collocation and Browsing Capability." Wool, Gregory. Co-published simultaneously in *The Serials Librarian* (The Haworth Information Press, an imprint of The Haworth Press, Inc.) Vol. 41, No. 3/4, 2002, pp. 169-176; and: *E-Serials Cataloging: Access to Continuing and Integrating Resources via the Catalog and the Web* (ed: Jim Cole, and Wayne Jones) The Haworth Information Press, an imprint of The Haworth Press, Inc., 2002, pp. 169-176. Single or multiple copies of this article are available for a fee from The Haworth Document Delivery Service [1-800-HAWORTH, 9:00 a.m. - 5:00 p.m. (EST). E-mail address: getinfo@haworthpressinc.com].

Seeking out the right journal, journal article, book or other information package in a catalog or index can often seem like finding a needle in a haystack. Even if despite certain similarities, a single needle is easy to distinguish from a single wisp of hay, the multitude of unwanted hay easily overwhelms and obscures the wanted needle. Thank goodness for metal detectors, which in this day and age make such a proverbial task manageable (even if it is still necessary to tear apart–ahem, deconstruct–the haystack)!

Metadata–the descriptions and index terms assigned by catalogers and indexers to documents of all sorts–are what make "metal detecting" (meta-detecting?) for information possible. But just as some instruments are more precise in their detecting power than others, metadata are the more helpful to the searcher the more meaningfully they represent documents. Meaningful representation consists of showing (1) how a document is different from all others and (2) how it is like some others, in ways important to the searcher.

At one end of the meaningfulness spectrum, a keyword search for "needle" in the Library of Congress online catalog recently brought up 744 records, the first dozen of which included:

- the Woody Guthrie sound recording *Work Songs for Nursery Days*, including the song "Needle Sing"
- *Learn Needle Tatting Step-by-Step* by Barbara Foster
- *The Connecticut Syringe Exchange Programs*, an annual report assigned the subject heading "Needle exchange programs–Connecticut–Periodicals"
- *The Wicked Trade*, a maritime adventure novel by Jan Needle
- Charles Andrews' *From Capitalism to Equality*, published by Needle Press

What these items and the other 739 have in common, of course (and what distinguishes them from the other several million in the catalog), is that their bibliographic records include the discrete character string "needle" in a keyword-indexed field. While someone looking for a Guthrie recording of "Needle Sing" would have had good luck with this search, most catalog users would find the haphazardly arranged results (on 30 screens) inefficient and frustrating.

Of course, keyword searches can be more precisely targeted through such devices as phrase searching (e.g., "sewing needle"), truncation ("needle*"), and Boolean logic ("needle AND thread"). Relevance ranking, the algorithm-based assessment of frequency and placement of search terms, is available in many search environments and can make results easier to comprehend. Still, in most cases keyword searching is based on a flawed premise: that the presence of a certain word or words in either the metadata or the full text makes all the difference in finding what one needs. The fact that a single word can have multiple meanings, and that several words can be used interchangeably to express a single concept, serves to limit the precision (retrieving only what is sought) and recall (retrieving everything sought for) of almost any keyword search.

STRUCTURED METADATA

Keywords (whether couched in full text or assigned as "descriptors" by authors or publishers) are simple metadata. Efficient information retrieval depends on the presence of *structured* metadata. The term "structured metadata" refers to metadata based on an organizing principle; examples include terms from a thesaurus or subject-heading list, classification numbers, uniform titles, established name headings. Structured metadata bring together documents with common characteristics (a process called "collocation") and facilitate browsing of categories and other relationships among documents. By providing a context for documents as well as a framework for identification and collocation, structured metadata can provide the meaningful representation needed to zero in on a searching target and effectively evaluate the results.

There are at least four kinds of structure that give metadata leverage:

- Rule basis
- Authority control
- Categorization
- Relationship control

These are listed roughly in descending order of widespread use and ascending order of power.

Rule basis is what is usually meant by the term "standardization." Standards for bibliographic description such as *AACR2* not only define the types of data to be recorded, but specify where each type of data may come from and, in some instances, what form it may take. Standards based on the International Standard Bibliographic Description (ISBD) also specify a sequence of data within a record. By presenting a familiar pattern across records, such standards aid interpretation of a record, even for those unfamiliar with the rules. In a different sphere, policies of the Library of Congress such as "specific entry" and the "20% rule" set boundaries to the assignment of its subject headings that help make those subject term choices meaningful to catalog users.

Authority control standardizes human-designated index terms ("access points" in *AACR2*-speak) by establishing a preferred form for the term and setting up cross-references from other forms searchers might use. This type of metadata structure makes collocation possible, as it ensures that all of a particular author's works can display together, or all works on a given subject, or all editions of a work published under a number of different titles. It also lowers (at least somewhat) the barrier separating the user from a structured index terminology.

Categorization, to put it simplistically, divides the world into meaningful groups. The works of a particular author may form a category, as may the editions of a classic work. The special power of categorization, though, is found in subject indexing, where a thesaurus or a subject-heading list defines scopes and establishes boundaries of topics. While the resulting categories may seem arbitrary, they wield the force of standardization and widespread agreement, thus strengthening collocation and making intelligent browsing possible.

One form of *relationship control* is a special kind of authority control. But instead of harmonizing search vocabulary by linking multiple synonyms to an established term, it links related categories and again, facilitates browsing. This type of structure can be discerned in subject vocabularies (for which it is referred to as "syndetic structure"), as well as the control of serial publications with title changes, mergers, and splits. For subject access, it can help overcome the problems of arbitrary categorization and present options to the researcher with a "fuzzy" information need.

Relationship control is also achieved by arranging the parts of an index term so that the general concept is expressed at the beginning, followed by one or more qualifiers, each further specifying what comes before. This enables related categories to appear together in a linear display. Examples include the display of names with the "family" name preceding given names (e.g., "Smith, John J." and "Syracuse University. College of Medicine"); use of phrase inversion, qualifying terms, and subdivisions in Library of Congress subject headings; and the enumerative coding in classification schemes.

PUTTING STRUCTURED METADATA TO WORK

From the examples given above, it is apparent that structured metadata account for nearly all the information found in library catalogs. If we keep in mind that other information environments make use of metadata structurings as well, a brief look at how online catalogs use–and could use–structured metadata will be instructive.

Enriched Keyword Forage

The prevailing use of structured metadata in online catalogs is to enhance the effectiveness of keyword searching. With rules governing the recording of titles and other source information, and subject vocabulary control limiting and focusing the expression of "aboutness," search terms with even a modicum of literary warrant stand a better chance of retrieving relevant information than they would in a database with little or no control. The odds would be even better if more variants of terms in the database were linked as cross-references to those terms (as has been proposed by Bates and others).[1]

Record Structure and Interpretation

As noted above, rule-based catalog information enables records to be read and interpreted in a predictable manner, a virtue of perhaps greater importance in printed and filmed catalogs than online. In the print formats, the sequencing and punctuation requirements of ISBD served to signal the various categories of information in a familiar citation style, a task handled much more crudely online by locally configured "labels."

Search Enhancement or Redirection

When author names and subject terms in a bibliographic record are under authority control, they can serve as the gateway to complete, noise-free sets of search results. A common strategy of catalog users is to start with keyword searching (e.g., "find *needle*"), then examine the most relevant records for terms to either click on or use for a better-targeted search (e.g., "*Pins and needles*").

Browsing and Discovery

A well-organized list of search results at the term level can reveal aspects of an information need the searcher had not thought to express, whether couched in a phrase ("Needle biopsy"), a related word ("Needlework"), a qualifier ("Needles, Hypodermic"), or a subheading ("Needlepoint lace–Armenia"). The collocation of related records also makes browsing easier and discovery more likely in author and title searches. As Allyson Carlyle notes: "The use of relationship-based organization of records in catalog displays has the potential to increase a user's understanding of the nature of the items retrieved in an author or work search and to shorten long displays."[2] Another significant aid to browsing is the display of subjects that are broader than, narrower than, or otherwise related to a retrieved subject term; this has become a common feature in online catalogs in just the last few years.

It is important to note that "well-organized" does not mean "strictly alphabetical," especially for long lists. Discussing filing in *Introduction to Cataloging and Classification*, Wynar and Taylor distinguish between "alphabetical" and "categorical" filing. Categorical filing, which by defining "filing elements" takes the formal aspects of index terms into account along with the alphabetical sequence of words and letters, was used especially in the card catalogs of large research libraries, where separation of related entries in a file was a serious issue. For subject headings beginning with the same word (as an example), straight phrases, inverted phrases, terms with parenthetical qualifiers, and subdivision strings were filed in separate sequences. Alphabetical filing, by contrast, arranges all index strings in a single alphabetical sequence, either word-by-word ("Needle sharing" ahead of "Needlepoint") or letter-by-letter (the reverse).[3] In the online environment, alphabetical filing is the norm for index-term displays, on the premise that anything more sophisticated would place unwarranted demands on system memory.

Under the influence of computerized filing practices, the 1980 *ALA Filing Rules* abandoned most vestiges of categorical filing in favor of strict word-by-word alphabetization, even as the Library of Congress (LC), in a new edition of its own rules, reaffirmed the categorical approach, especially for its highly structured subject headings. John Rather explained the LC policy this way: "If the arrangement of the file violates the form or meaning of the headings, users will be hampered in their efforts to use the catalog successfully."[4] But while the LC filing rules were successfully implemented in the online catalog system developed at LC, the Voyager system LC adopted in 1999 uses letter-by-letter filing for its online displays.

Alphabetical filing represents much of what is wrong with online information retrieval. It works beautifully when the searcher knows exactly what she wants, with the exact wording and spelling that has been entered into the database. Otherwise—if the correct name is not entered in full, if the information need is not quite focused—the searcher is left to pick through many screens of search results to find a few items of interest. Strict alphabetical filing of search results either breaks up or hides categories, and renders relationships invisible. In so doing it makes all structured metadata—whether LC subject headings or uniform titles for serials—appear unsuited to the online environment and thus out of date, feeding calls for the simplification (de-structuring) of all metadata.

But while structured subject headings are almost universally treated as simple character strings for filing and display, the same can no longer be said for classification numbers. Not long ago, these were routinely sorted on a character-by-character, "nothing before something" basis, producing numerous variations from shelflist order and making classification browsing nearly impossible. Many automation systems now have rectified this situation, using filing elements within the numbers to produce a sequence suitable for online shelf-listing, and as a side benefit, making relationship-based online "shelf browsing" possible.

CONCLUSION

Finding a needle (as opposed to "just something short, thin, and pointed") in a bibliographic haystack is seldom simply a matter of choosing the right keyword or combination of keywords. The right keyword is likely to bring up a long list of results to comb through, a task made easier and more efficient when categories and relationships among the items are visible. That these categories and relationships are not always (or even often) expressed precisely in the user's search terminology is not important here. As Yee and Layne note in their *Improving Online Public Access Catalogs*, "It is important for all catalog designers to realize that users often cannot specify in advance the terms that will be used in the catalog to describe the author, work, or subject they seek. One job of the catalog is to facilitate *recognition* on the part of the user, rather than to demand exact *specification*."[5]

The various kinds of structured metadata used in library catalogs, through such devices as name standardization and filing-element specification, serve to bring similar items together and make meaningful distinctions apparent. When the structural integrity of such metadata is preserved in displays, browsing and recognition both become easier. But when structured index terms are treated as simple character strings in sorting, closely related names, titles, or subjects become widely scattered (often across several screens), discouraging exploration and discovery. To a considerable extent, making online bibliographic resources easier to use and more effective means respecting metadata structures and displaying them to best advantage.

Metadata structures distill the knowledge and judgment of professional organizers of information, thus offering valuable guidance to the searcher. When properly deployed, they give shape, definition, and color to the information-searching environment, making it seem much less like an endless mass of hay.

NOTES

1. Marcia J. Bates, "Subject Access in Online Catalogs: A Design Model," *Journal of the American Society for Information Science* 37 (1986): 365.

2. Allyson Carlyle, "Fulfilling the Second Objective in the Online Catalog: Schemes for Organizing Author and Work Records into Usable Displays," *Library Resources and Technical Services* 41 (1997): 80.

3. Bohdan S. Wynar and Arlene G. Taylor, *Introduction to Cataloging and Classification*, 8th ed. (Englewood, Colo.: Libraries Unlimited, 1992), 531.

4. John C. Rather, "Filing Arrangement in the Library of Congress Catalogs," *Library Resources & Technical Services* 16 (1972): 240.

5. Martha M. Yee and Sara Shatford Layne, *Improving Online Public Access Catalogs* (Chicago: American Library Association, 1998): 6.

BIBLIOGRAPHY

American Library Association. Resources and Technical Services Division. Filing Committee. *ALA Filing Rules*. Chicago: American Library Association, 1980.

Association for Library Collections and Technical Services. Cataloging and Classification Section. Subject Access Committee. Subcommittee on the Display of Subject Headings in Subject Indexes in Online Public Access Catalogs. *Headings for Tomorrow: Public Access Display of Subject Headings*. Chicago: American Library Association, 1992.

Bates, Marcia J. "Subject Access in Online Catalogs: A Design Model." *Journal of the American Society for Information Science* 37 (1986): 357-376.

Carlyle, Allyson. "Fulfilling the Second Objective in the Online Catalog: Schemes for Organizing Author and Work Records into Usable Displays." *Library Resources and Technical Services* 41 (1997): 79-100.

Hagler, Ronald M. *The Bibliographic Record and Information Technology*. 3rd ed. Chicago: American Library Association, 1997.

Hearn, Stephen. "Machine-Assisted Validation of *LC Subject Headings*: Implications for Authority File Structure." *Cataloging & Classification Quarterly* 29, no. 1/2 (2000): 107-115.

Mann, Thomas. "Teaching *Library of Congress Subject Headings*." *Cataloging & Classification Quarterly* 29, no. 1/2 (2000): 117-126.

Rather, John C. "Filing Arrangement in the Library of Congress Catalogs." *Library Resources & Technical Services* 16 (1972): 240-261.

Rather, John C., and Susan C. Bibel. *Library of Congress Filing Rules*. Washington, D.C.: Library of Congress, 1980.

Taylor, Arlene. *The Organization of Information*. Englewood, Colo.: Libraries Unlimited, 1999.

Wool, Gregory. "Filing and Precoordination: How Subject Headings Are Displayed in Online Catalogs and Why It Matters." *Cataloging & Classification Quarterly* 29, no. 1/2 (2000): 91-106.

Wynar, Bohdan S., and Arlene G. Taylor. "Filing." Chap. 28 in *Introduction to Cataloging and Classification*. 8th ed. Englewood, Colo.: Libraries Unlimited, 1992.

Yee, Martha M., and Sarah Shatford Layne. *Improving Online Public Access Catalogs*. Chicago: American Library Association, 1998.

OCLC's CORC Service:
A User's Perspective

Michael Wright

SUMMARY. OCLC's CORC service consists of two Web-based utilities: the CORC Resource Catalog (RC) and the Pathfinder utility. The RC consists of a generator for creating MARC or Dublin Core bibliographic records for Internet resources as well as a database of such records. The Pathfinder utility features a database of research guides in a Web format and offers a straightforward method to create original research guides. Both elements of the CORC service are well wrought and should be of interest to libraries. *[Article copies available for a fee from The Haworth Document Delivery Service: 1-800-HAWORTH. E-mail address: <getinfo@haworthpressinc.com> Website: <http://www.HaworthPress.com> © 2002 by The Haworth Press, Inc. All rights reserved.]*

KEYWORDS. OCLC, CORC, cataloging, electronic resource, Pathfinder, MARC, Dublin Core, Internet

CORC (the Cooperative Online Resource Catalog), OCLC's service designed to speed cataloging and discovery of electronic resources, received an amazing amount of attention and interest, both within and without the OCLC community, when it was unveiled as a research initiative in 1998. Now a con-

---

Michael Wright is affiliated with the Bibliographical Center for Research, 14394 E. Evans Avenue, Aurora, CO 80014-1478 (E-mail: mwright@bcr.org).

[Haworth co-indexing entry note]: "OCLC's CORC Service: A User's Perspective." Wright, Michael. Co-published simultaneously in *The Serials Librarian* (The Haworth Information Press, an imprint of The Haworth Press, Inc.) Vol. 41, No. 3/4, 2002, pp. 177-182; and: *E-Serials Cataloging: Access to Continuing and Integrating Resources via the Catalog and the Web* (ed: Jim Cole, and Wayne Jones) The Haworth Information Press, an imprint of The Haworth Press, Inc., 2002, pp. 177-182. Single or multiple copies of this article are available for a fee from The Haworth Document Delivery Service [1-800-HAWORTH, 9:00 a.m. - 5:00 p.m. (EST). E-mail address: getinfo@haworthpressinc.com].

tinuing OCLC service with over 855 participating libraries and a growing database of over 425,000 records, interest in CORC remains high. CORC participation is limited to OCLC cataloging users with a full or partial cataloging authorization.

CORC is not an attempt to get libraries to comprehensively catalog the World-Wide-Web–a task nearly all agree is impossible due to its sheer size–but rather an attempt to cooperatively build a database of and guide to some of the Web's most useful resources, making them more easily accessible to libraries and their users.

Unlike OCLC's familiar Passport and Cataloging MicroEnhancer (CatME) products, CORC is a fully Web-based interface, using a browser, either Netscape or Internet Explorer, to interact with the CORC software on OCLC's server.

As one might expect, the interface is point-and-click, rather than command driven, and makes extensive use of drop-down menus and so-called radio buttons.

In a nutshell, CORC actually consists of two services: the Resource Catalog (RC) and the Pathfinders service, which are basically independent of each other. The Resource Catalog includes a cataloging utility and database, while the Pathfinder service includes a database of subject-specific research guides which may or may not contain items from the RC.

CORC RESOURCE CATALOG

The Resource Catalog consists of bibliographic records, in MARC or Dublin Core formats, representing electronic resources including online versions of serials, digitized archival images, Web pages, etc. The RC also contains a record generator, which can create AACR2 minimal-level (OCLC's Encoding Level K for MARC or 3 for Dublin Core) bibliographic records by extracting data from Web pages, a process known as harvesting. These records can be edited and upgraded or left as they are, and can then be exported to a local system or Web page. CORC's RC is synchronized with OCLC's WorldCat bibliographic database; all CORC records appear in WorldCat within 24 hours of creation.

In addition, CORC offers full access to the OCLC online authority file (including interactive access from individual Resource Catalog records) and to WebDewey, an optional, subscription-based version of Dewey Decimal Classification.

Probably most interest in CORC has been directed toward the cataloging utility, the Resource Catalog, from which users can search both the RC and

OCLC's WorldCat bibliographic databases, create records, and import records created elsewhere.

Using a natural language interface, CORC draws upon standard Boolean searching, much like other databases. Not surprisingly it is reminiscent of OCLC's FirstSearch service. Search elements can be drawn from a number of sources: typical elements such as subject, title, and name are of course there, but searches can also include URL phrases, cataloging source, and language, among others. Up to four terms can be linked using the standard Boolean operators (and, or, not). The database is fast and relevance ranking applies (or can be turned off at the user's discretion). Search results can vary dramatically depending on how the search is constructed. Unlike most Web search engines, however, exactly reproducing a search will achieve the same results consistently, due to the controlled nature of the database. Unfortunately, the database is still relatively small in relation to the Internet and many items aren't yet represented. In addition, a fair number of the records in RC aren't for Web resources as such; there are many for photographs and archival collections, records which include MARC 856 fields. Some of these came in when OCLC seeded the initial database with records from its NetFirst service, although institutions are still encouraged to add them. This is fine, but it is a bit frustrating when searching for Web resources on a given subject to have records for digitized photographs pop up instead.

A strength, at least in concept, of the RC is that the records are selected by librarians; presumably this means "no junk." By and large this appears to be true, although the old maxim, "one person's junk is another's treasure" comes to mind on occasion. Certainly the usual odd hits for pornographic and other spurious sites don't occur in CORC as they seem to with regular Web browsers.

There are no standards for inclusion of resources in CORC; OCLC assumes that librarians will police their own choices. If a library deems a resource useful and wishes to catalog it, a record can be created and entered in the Resource Catalog. In this respect CORC is really no different than the main OCLC database, WorldCat. Indeed, as previously noted, the two databases are synchronized.

When creating records in CORC, users can elect to build records using a blank template or have CORC extract data ("harvest") from an existing Web resource and automatically generate a K-level (less from full cataloging which meets minimum AACR2 requirements for a bibliographic record) MARC record or a 3-level Dublin Core record.

A truly useful CORC feature is the ability, when cataloging from an existing Web page, to actually open a live link to the page, either as part of a split CORC display or in a separate browser screen.

When harvesting to create a MARC record, CORC will automatically attempt to generate the MARC 008 or Fixed Field, tags 245 and 260, as well as summary notes and subject terms which may or may not be similar to Library of Congress subject headings. All harvested records include an 856 field. In addition CORC includes a drop-down menu which can create a completed 006 tag for any format.

As mentioned, the resulting record qualifies as Minimal-level cataloging; most libraries will want to add additional MARC tags to bring the record up to the Full standard.

Libraries subscribing to WebDewey may, if desired, choose to have CORC prepare Dewey Decimal Classification numbers as well. However, the software which constructs the numbers works by matching terms found in the Web page against the Dewey index, and in the process CORC may pick up terms which are tangential to the subject of the Web document. Because of this, the numbers created by CORC deserve scrutiny. For instance, if a library is using CORC to harvest data from a Web resource on the Denver ACRL meeting, and the site includes restaurant information, the software might build a Dewey number for restaurants.

Similar to OCLC's Passport and Cataloging MicroEnhancer software, CORC also allows users to create a new bibliographic record by cloning an existing record. CORC extracts data from the existing record and the user can then edit it to suit, entering the "new" record into the database.

Unlike other OCLC services, CORC's Resource Catalog now features URL checking and notification on data in 856 fields, a major enhancement. URL-checking software is constantly scrambling through the CORC Resource Catalog records looking for broken or otherwise inactive links in MARC 856 fields. When one is found, CORC can automatically notify the inputting library of the bad link. The library can then correct the URL. This is clearly a boon for libraries which have cataloged remote-access electronic resources.

In addition to MARC records, CORC can be used to create records in Dublin Core (DC) format, and can display these in either Dublin Core HTML or RDF. CORC-produced DC records are very similar to those created in the other major DC record generator, DC Dot (http://www.ukoln.ac.uk/metadata/dcdot/).

PATHFINDERS

In addition to the CORC Resource Catalog and record creation, there's another piece to CORC: the Pathfinders database.

Pathfinders are simply bibliographies in a Web format. Contents of CORC pathfinders usually include Web resources, but aren't limited to them. Pathfinders can be built using any resource a library wishes to include (books, articles, databases, etc.) using a straightforward point-and-click format which is similar in look to the Resource Catalog.

Once a Pathfinder is assembled and added to the Pathfinders database, it can be exported in its entirety in HTML format for use in the library's Web page, or the Pathfinder can be left on OCLC's server and only an HTML link to it exported. By selecting the latter option, OCLC will maintain any URL appearing in the Pathfinder.

Pathfinders can be very simple affairs or they can be dressed up using cascading style sheets and images. Even the most complex-looking Pathfinder is still very easy to create. Indeed, ease of use is a strong point of the utility. A series of Pathfinders on whatever subject can be assembled in a matter of minutes.

DOCUMENTATION AND SUPPORT

All CORC documentation is available in PDF from the CORC Website (http://www2.oclc.org/corc/documentation/)–OCLC is not distributing printed documentation for CORC. From rather spotty beginnings, the CORC manuals have improved quickly and now are up to OCLC's usual high documentation standards, although their look is very different from that of other OCLC manuals. CORC documentation is updated frequently.

CORC's first-line support is offered by OCLC-affiliated regional library networks and by OCLC itself, which offers 24/7 help availability. In addition, there is a busy CORC listserv as well as an active and enthusiastic CORC Users Group, complete with special interest groups.

TO PARTICIPATE, OR NOT TO PARTICIPATE?

So, the ultimate question: Why should a library use CORC?

If a library catalogs a lot of Web-based resources, the CORC's ability to build a quick bibliographic record via harvesting is a big convenience, more so with the link to the OCLC Authority File. The records as generated are basic, but the editing features are easy to use and the records are thus easy to upgrade. Along the same line, these features also make producing records from scratch very straightforward. While some expert Passport or CatME users may find CORC's interface awkward at first, it is easy to adapt to.

OCLC plans, within the next two years, to roll out a new cataloging utility which will be based upon the CORC service. This Web-based utility will then replace the venerable Passport software for cataloging, although an enhanced version of the Cataloging MicroEnhancer will remain. If libraries wonder what the future of OCLC cataloging looks like, CORC will be its springboard. Those institutions that are using CORC regularly will likely have a smoother transition when the old software is discontinued.

Ultimately, the most powerful reason to use CORC for cataloging electronic resources is the URL-checking feature, which satisfies a long-standing need in part of the library community. Indeed, perhaps the biggest roadblock for cataloging electronic resources has been how to best keep up with 856 fields. CORC eliminates this problem.

As for CORC's Pathfinder database, public services staff in particular should be giving it a serious look. Pathfinders take an existing product that many skilled public services departments have been offering right along–the research guide–and updates it to a straightforward Web format. It's a simple way to gather resources on a given subject, and the export features allow staff to whisk the pathfinders to a local Web page for quick use by the library's clientele.

Overall, CORC is a well thought-out product that has created a small but growing niche for itself. For libraries that are cataloging electronic resources or are considering doing so, or that want to explore the creation of Web-based resource guides, the CORC service deserves a serious look.

NATIONAL PROJECTS
AND LOCAL APPLICATIONS

NESLI MARC Records:
An Experiment in Creating MARC Records for E-Journals

Ross MacIntyre

SUMMARY. This article concerns an experiment in producing US-MARC records for e-journals within the UK's National Electronic Site Licence Initiative (NESLI). This involved working with an aggregator, Swets Blackwell, to produce sample records that were made available for comment. Some other related developments are also mentioned. *[Article copies available for a fee from The Haworth Document Delivery Service: 1-800-HAWORTH. E-mail address: <getinfo@haworthpressinc. com> Website: <http://www.HaworthPress.com> © 2002 by The Haworth Press, Inc. All rights reserved.]*

Ross MacIntyre, MSc, is Senior Project Manager, MIMAS, Manchester Computing, University of Manchester, Oxford Road, Manchester, M13 9PL, UK (E-mail: ross.macintyre@man.ac.uk).

The author thanks Robert Bley, of Swets Blackwell, for consolidating the feedback responses included herein.

[Haworth co-indexing entry note]: "NESLI MARC Records: An Experiment in Creating MARC Records for E-Journals." MacIntyre, Ross. Co-published simultaneously in *The Serials Librarian* (The Haworth Information Press, an imprint of The Haworth Press, Inc.) Vol. 41, No. 3/4, 2002, pp. 183-192; and: *E-Serials Cataloging: Access to Continuing and Integrating Resources via the Catalog and the Web* (ed: Jim Cole, and Wayne Jones) The Haworth Information Press, an imprint of The Haworth Press, Inc., 2002, pp. 183-192. Single or multiple copies of this article are available for a fee from The Haworth Document Delivery Service [1-800-HAWORTH, 9:00 a.m. - 5:00 p.m. (EST). E-mail address: getinfo@haworthpressinc.com].

KEYWORDS. NESLI, electronic journals, e-journals, cataloguing, MARC

INTRODUCTION

The National Electronic Site Licence Initiative (NESLI)[1] was established in 1998 by the UK Higher Education Funding Council's Joint Information Systems Committee (JISC). The overall aim of NESLI is to facilitate and promote the use of e-journals in UK Higher Education Institutions (HEIs). NESLI might be described as being a (voluntary) virtual consortium of UK HEIs and specifically the only one approved by JISC to negotiate for full-text e-journal content on its behalf.

Following a formal tendering process, a consortium of Swets & Zeitlinger (now Swets Blackwell) and the University of Manchester was appointed to act as the Managing Agent (MA) for the initiative. The MA reports to a Steering Committee composed mainly of senior UK academic librarians. The MA performs the day-to-day service operations: publisher negotiation, communicating offers, taking orders, service delivery (where orders have been placed with Swets Blackwell), support, and a small amount of service development in related areas–and it is this later aspect that is the focus of this paper. It must be noted that the funding for any development activity was reduced to zero in the third year of the initiative. A summary of the initiative by Woodward[2] was included in *The Serials Librarian* recently.

The Manchester component of the MA is Manchester InforMation and Associated Services (MIMAS), a section within Manchester Computing at the University of Manchester, home to one of the UK's three National Data Centres. MIMAS hosts data and applications principally for the UK Higher Education community, though users also include the Research Councils, Further Education and other European academic institutions. The technical developments for NESLI were undertaken principally by MIMAS, with the support of Swets development staff.

TECHNICAL DEVELOPMENTS

As part of the technical development of the service, a number of research areas were proposed. A summary of results in each area follows:

1. The implementation of UK education's standard authentication mechanism (ATHENS) for access via *SwetsnetNavigator* (SN).

Result: The mechanism implemented is best explained as consisting of three elements: authentication, conversion and connection. The user enters his or her ATHENS username and password on the login screen and these are authenticated against the ATHENS system for the resource type of "NESLI." The call to ATHENS is made by the server hosted at Manchester. Once authenticated, the ATHENS identifier and resource type are converted to SN account data, again on the Manchester server. These data are then passed to the SN server, based in the Netherlands, and a user session is initiated. The user is now interacting directly with the SN NESLI delivery system.

2. Negotiating with publishers to allow "trusted" access. There seemed little need to perform a third authentication check, typically IP-based, once both ATHENS and the Swets subscription record had okayed the access, as described above.

Result: Comparatively little progress has been made. However, three publishers were willing to take the matter forward and discuss it at a technical level. Interestingly, one publisher still wanted the IP address of the access passed as a parameter, as this was used for compiling usage statistics.

3. Creation of journal title "link lists" for all journals on offer, i.e., the URLs of the material in SN.

Result: Alphabetic lists of the journals available from each publisher making a NESLI offer are freely available on the Web site. They include links to each journal's home page on the publisher's Web site and also to the journal's issue list page within SN. They are provided in a variety of formats.

4. Preparation of aggregated usage statistics for the NESLI Steering Group.

Result: The main SN log file contains data relating to the company's global user base. Once a month Swets Blackwell in the UK creates an extract of usage data relating solely to NESLI customers and passes this to MIMAS, who produces the spreadsheets requested by the NESLI Steering Committee. This is described in more detail in an article by MacIntyre.[3]

5. Off-site authentication for IP-authenticated linking to SN.

Result: The direct links to SN are IP-authenticated. This can mean that users browsing their library's OPAC from home, for instance, can be refused access to licensed material. A mechanism has been implemented that prompts for an ATHENS username and password when a NESLI title is requested, but refused, as a result of an IP check.

6. Creation of MARC records for each NESLI subscriber.

Result: The project started using existing data files from Swets, as this was the most pragmatic approach. MIMAS undertook an initial mapping to USMARC (now MARC 21) format, and code was developed based on this. It was planned also to offer UKMARC assuming there was a demand and that the data proved acceptable. Feedback was sought from USMARC user sites. (This feedback is summarised in detail in the following section of this paper.)

Though there were many comments about the precise contents of each field, the most significant additional data element requested was "local data" detailing the individual site's subscription. This would have required an extract from the subscription database on a per-customer basis by Swets. This was done for a sample site, but, unfortunately, no funding remained to take the development further.

FURTHER DETAIL–MARC RECORD

The file from Swets had one record for each title with the following fields:

1. Title
2. Paper ISSN
3. Electronic ISSN
4. Publisher
5. Country of Publication
6. Language
7. Subject 1
8. Subject 2
9. Frequency (issues/year)
10. Earliest Year in Swets

There were also 5 fields internal to Swets. From the above is generated a USMARC file containing the fields listed in Figure 1.

Figure 2 lists 5 additional (sub)fields that had been requested when an initial trawl for opinions was made, but could not be derived from the existing data supplied.

FIGURE 1. USMARC File Description

001 Control number. Use 'NESLI-' followed by the ISSN.
005 Date and time of creation of record (YYYYMMDDhhmmss.s)
008 Bytes:

0-5	Creation Date of record (YYMMDD)
· 6	Publication status = 'c' (Current)
7-10	Start year of journal. Use field (10).
11-14	End date of journal = 9999, which means continuing
15-17	3 letter code for country of publication. Use field (5).
18	Frequency - one letter code. Derived from (9).
19	Regularity = 'r' if regular, 'x' if not. Derived from (9).
20	ISDS center = blank
21	Type of serial = 'p' (Periodical)
22	Form of original item = blank
23	Form of item = blank
24	Nature of entire work = blank (Unspecified)
25-27	Nature of contents = blanks (Unspecified)
28	Government publication = 'u' (Unknown, could say blank => isn't)
29	Conference publication = '0' (isn't)
30	Title page availability = 'u' Unknown
31	Index availability = 'u' Unknown
32	Cumulative Index availability = 'u' Unknown
33	Script (i.e. alphabet) = blank (Unspecified, could say 'a' or 'b' => Roman)
34	successive/latest entry = '1' (latest)
35-37	3 letter code for Language. Use field (6).
38	Modify status = space (not modified).
39	Cataloguing source = 'd' (Other)

022	$a	ISSN (usually there are 2 '022' fields). Use fields (2) & (3).
040	$a	"NESLI"
	$b	"eng"
	$c	"NESLI"
041	$a	Language turned into code. Use field (6).
245	$a	Title up to " - " string. Use field (1).
	$b	Rest of title. Use field (1).
	$h	"PDF"
260	$a	Publisher Address (Only country is available)
	$b	Publisher Name. Use field (4).
310	$a	Frequency (translated to English text). Use field (9).
650	$a	Subject (in separate fields). Use fields (7) & (8).
856	$a	"swets2.nesli.ac.uk"
	$u	href to journal in Swets (calculated from ISSN)

FIGURE 2. Additional USMARC Fields Requested

082	$a	Dewey Decimal Number
210	$a	Abbreviated title
260	$c	First date of publication (print and electronic)
710	$a	Any relevant/appropriate Corporate Body mentioned elsewhere in the record (e.g. Learned Society)
780	$a	Previous title of journal (if any)

For example a record from Swets that contains:

1. Acta Physiologica Scandinavica–Internet
2. 0001-6772
3. 1365-201X
4. Blackwell Science Ltd
5. ENGLAND
6. English
7. Anatomy and Physiology
8.
9. 12
10. 1998

becomes the USMARC record found in Figure 3.

FEEDBACK RECEIVED

Some initial views and suggestions were sought at the time of the data mapping to USMARC. The following is a consolidated list of the feedback received from the sites after the production of sample data.

PRICING

One response suggested a price could be charged, though it should be in the same region as charged by OCLC.

USMARC STANDARD CONFORMANCE

Field 001

One respondent said that they would want to change the 001 field to be ISSN.

Field 245 Caused Some Controversy

One respondent said there must be punctuation between the title and the format description, e.g., "Acta Zoologica Internet" should be "Acta Zoologica–Internet version."

FIGURE 3. Example USMARC File

```
001    'NESLI-0001-6772'
005    '19991018145732.0'
008    '991018c19989999enkmr p     u0uuu 1eng d'
022    '0 '
       $a    '0001-6772'
022    '0 '
       $a    '1365-201X'
040    ' '
       $a    'NESLI'
       $b    'eng'
       $c    'NESLI'
041    '0 '
       $a    'eng'
245    '00'
       $a    'Acta Physiologica Scandinavica'
       $b    'Internet'
       $h    '[computer file]'
260    '0 '
       $a    'ENGLAND'
       $b    'Blackwell Science Ltd'
310    ' '
       $a    'Monthly'
650    ' 4'
       $a    'Anatomy and Physiology'
856    '40'
       $a    'swets2.nesli.ac.uk'
       $u    'http://swets2.nesli.ac.uk/link/access_db?issn=0001-6772'
```

Another respondent preferred "Acta zoologica–electronic serial," as the title should all be in lower case except for the first word and proper nouns. Another said "Internet" should not be included in the title, but $h[computer file] should be used instead, and also pointed out that this was soon to change to $h[electronic resource], to conform to ISBD. Thus the correct present format would be, for example, $aActa zoologica$h[computer file].

Field 260

Comments included the following:

- "Get rid of 'Ltd.' after each publisher name"
- "Should have country publisher is located in, not country of origin of journal"
- "Both indicators should be blank"
- "The correct format is, e.g., $aOxford (England) :$bBlackwell Science; n.b. USMARC requires punctuations."

Field 650

Three respondents said this should contain true Library of Congress subject headings, e.g., $aPhysiology$vPeriodicals and that they couldn't load records with this field as it was. Another, however, said that this was "OK as is."

Field 856

One respondent would prefer to have all possible URLs included here if there are options, e.g., direct to publisher's site, and not just access via NESLI/SN. "It is easier to delete URLs we do not want than to add new ones."

There was general agreement that it is a good idea to have the URL. One respondent wanted to add a subfield 'z,' explaining "accessible via XXXX service."

"Would be useful to have a subfield to say which ISSN is paper, and which electronic, but this is not in the MARC standard."

One respondent said that they would not want this field to be filled if they only had subscriptions at a Table of Contents level. They wanted it only if they had subscriptions at full-text level.

One respondent would also prefer subfields 'd' and 'f' to be included in the 856 field, containing file path and file name respectively, for instance,

'$aswets2.nesli.ac.uk$dlink$faccess_db?issn=0001-6772

$uhttp://swets2.nesli.ac.uk/link/access_db?issn=0001-6772' - using the URL in the "Acta

Physiologica Scandinavica" example.

One respondent was concerned about how the URLs in the 856 field would work for off-campus users. They stated they would try to add local cache authentication or some other local scripted link to ensure access for off-site users

ADDITIONAL USMARC FIELDS WANTED

Additional fields had already been requested (see Figure 2), but were not available. Moreover, the following were requested after the test data had been circulated:

- Field 256 (corresponding to UKMARC field 258) containing 'Computer journal' in subfield 'a,' taken from ISBD(ER)–International Standard Bibliographic Description (Electronic Resources)–although not yet incorporated into AACR2

- A field 538 (corresponding to UKMARC field 542) with preferably 'Mode of access: World Wide Web' in subfield 'a'
- Another field 538 (this one corresponding to UKMARC field 537) detailing any system requirements, if applicable
- Field 785 (succeeding title) when applicable

Two customers asked for a "first issue date" field. The Managing Agent could supply this on a per-journal basis, but not easily on a per-customer subscription basis. It was unclear if it would not be better to add these "local" data locally in any event.

One customer asked for a "previous title of journal" field. This was to be supplied.

One customer said that inclusion of the "dates of coverage" would be very useful although they realised that this is somewhat difficult when some publishers are adding older volumes retrospectively and libraries' ability to access back/current volumes could change dependent on their subscription status. They gave the following example from OCLC which they thought might be helpful:

362 1 $aCoverage as of June 7, 1999: Vol. 4, no.1 (1997)-

Here the field's first indicator must be 1 to generate an unformatted note.

OVERALL

The sites were asked whether, after having seen this initial example, they would be interested in receiving MARC records as part of a NESLI deal. Sixteen libraries responded. Of these, thirteen said yes, they would like MARC records from the Managing Agent. Their comments are found in Table 1.

The other three libraries responded in the negative. Their comments are found in Table 2.

CONCLUSION

As was noted above, some of the additional data requested could have been provided, but this unfortunately remained an experiment.

Many libraries are now cataloguing their e-journals separately and wrestling with implementation issues, such as which ISSN to quote (and note that UKMARC does not allow the repetition of field 022 (ISSN)). Although there may be differences of opinion regarding adherence to MARC standards and local preferences, it was clear that these records would be valuable to the institutions.

TABLE 1. "Yes" Respondents

# of respondents	Their comments
3	Interested if their suggested changes (see Additional USMARC Fields Wanted above) can be incorporated.
1	If records can be delivered by FTP, or by use of a Z39.50 client for downloading
1	No comment
1	A high priority, but will only take it up if the price is right, and the format is USMARC
3	Will use if format is USMARC
1	So important that they will not subscribe to any NESLI deals without it
3	Will use if UKMARC is used (1 of these "depending on cost")

TABLE 2. "No" Respondents

1	Because too much editing would be required to get it into their library system
2	Because they already have access to free MARC records from the union database provided by their library system vendor

There was nothing particularly groundbreaking here. Certainly there are many suppliers providing cataloguing records (it may be interesting to see a list compiled, if one does not exist already, with cost included, naturally). It is notable that the provision of cataloguing records for electronic serials is now being taken into account when purchasing decisions are made, although subscription price is much more of an issue.

Understandably, institutions want to move closer towards an ideal of "auto-cataloguing," that is, being able easily to add e-journal records to, or delete them from, the catalogue upon subscription or cancellation, to lessen some of the administrative pain currently associated with managing electronic journal access provision.

NOTES

1. The NESLI Web site: http://www.nesli.ac.uk
2. Hazel Woodward, "NESLI–Gathering Momentum," *The Serials Librarian* 41, no. 1 (2000): 79-84.
3. Ross MacIntyre, "Electronic Journal Usage Data within NESLI," *Serials* 13, 3 (2000): 161.

Linking Articles and Bibliographic Records with Uniform Resource Names

Juha Hakala

SUMMARY. The article describes how Uniform Resource Names based on Serial Item and Contribution Identifiers can be resolved using the ISSN register as a way station pointing to the article databases. The European Union-funded DIEPER project and the ISSN International Centre are building a demonstrator service based on the principles described in the text. *[Article copies available for a fee from The Haworth Document Delivery Service: 1-800-HAWORTH. E-mail address: <getinfo@haworthpressinc. com> Website: <http://www.HaworthPress.com> © 2002 by The Haworth Press, Inc. All rights reserved.]*

KEYWORDS. Uniform Resource Names, Serial Item and Contribution Identifier, International Standard Serial Number, resolution services, DIEPER project

INTRODUCTION

There are many techniques for linking related information entities in the Internet. By far the oldest and most common one is HTTP and URLs. Alas, this

Juha Hakala is Director of Information Technology at Helsinki University Library–the National Library of Finland, P.O. Box 26, Fin-00014 Helsinki University, Finland.

[Haworth co-indexing entry note]: "Linking Articles and Bibliographic Records with Uniform Resource Names." Hakala, Juha. Co-published simultaneously in *The Serials Librarian* (The Haworth Information Press, an imprint of The Haworth Press, Inc.) Vol. 41, No. 3/4, 2002, pp. 193-199; and: *E-Serials Cataloging: Access to Continuing and Integrating Resources via the Catalog and the Web* (ed: Jim Cole, and Wayne Jones) The Haworth Information Press, an imprint of The Haworth Press, Inc., 2002, pp. 193-199. Single or multiple copies of this article are available for a fee from The Haworth Document Delivery Service [1-800-HAWORTH, 9:00 a.m. - 5:00 p.m. (EST). E-mail address: getinfo@haworthpressinc.com].

method has well-known deficiencies; the average lifetime of a URL is very short–although just how short nobody really knows for sure.

In order to bypass the problems related to URLs the Internet community has specified Uniform Resource Names and a set of resolution services based on them. Leslie Daigle, Ron Daniel Jr., and Cecilia Preston have written about the status of the URN development effort as of 1998.[1] A comparison of this article and an updated one on the same theme[2] shows that a lot has happened since then.

All key documents specifying the URN system are Internet standards, while most other resolution services have not been standardised at all, or have been standardised only partially, and not necessarily by the Internet community. URN system architecture fits very well into the Internet infrastructure, although it is independent of any current Internet protocol such as HTTP or Domain Name Service (DNS). This guarantees that the system will have a very long lifetime, and will scale up with the rest of the Internet. It does not mean that the URN system will be easy to implement, or that it will eventually cover every Internet document.

Although the URN infrastructure is not yet widely implemented, pilot studies have examined how well the URN system can accommodate the existing identifier systems. As Françoise Pellé reports in her article in this volume, a URN namespace ID "ISSN" has already been registered for the ISSN system, and a pilot service for resolving ISSN-based URNs has been built. The registration process for a namespace for the ISBN system has also been completed, and the Internet standard, which registers the namespace ID "ISBN" for ISBNs, will be published in March 2001.

USING SICI'S WITHIN THE URN FRAMEWORK

In a highly distributed and scaleable system such as the URN framework each traditional identifier system is "a different case"; the fact that ISSN fits well into the URN system does not mean that ISBNs will. In the Internet standard RFC 2288[3] only a generic analysis of whether ISSN, ISBN, and the Serial Item and Contribution Identifier (SICI) can be used as URNs has been made. A more concrete analysis is needed in order to make sure that resolving URNs based, for instance, on SICI is truly feasible in the global Internet.

Generally, the technical difficulty of designing a URN resolution service for an identifier system is dependent on two factors:

- Is the identifier dumb, or does it provide a hint on where to find a resolution service?

- How many potential resolution services are there?

ISBN is a good example of an intelligent identifier, although this intelligence can sometimes be a bit erratic. Analysis of the ISBN will reveal not only the geographic region where the ISBN has been assigned, but also the publisher who is responsible for the book. Resolution of ISBN-based URNs can and in practice must be decentralised to national bibliography databases, maintained by the national libraries. If ISBN were a dumb identifier, such decentralisation would be impossible since there would be no way of knowing where the correct resolution service is to be found.

ISSN is a dumb identifier. It does not have a publisher identifier; serials published by a certain company get seemingly random ISSNs. Although ISSNs are in fact allocated to national and regional agencies in blocks, which yields the system some "intelligence," a resolution service should not rely on these blocks, but should use the global ISSN database. It contains bibliographic descriptions of every serial that has received an ISSN. Thus, it is easy to resolve ISSN-based URNs even though the identifier itself does not help in locating the resolution service.

The ISSN database can deliver the bibliographic record of the serial, and the URL(s), or the URN resolution service might forward the user directly to the serial's home page. The default service is the bibliographic record, since it is always available.

Like ISSN, SICI is a dumb identifier. But there is not, and will never be, a global SICI database, a resource which would contain bibliographic information about each serial issue and article. Instead, this information will be dispersed into a large number of databases maintained by publishers, libraries, and other information intermediaries. As a dumb identifier with a large number of potential resolution services, SICI poses interesting challenges to the design of the URN-resolution process.

Generally, a combination of dumb identifier and multiple potential resolution services is a problem, since there is no simple way of finding out which resolution service is the correct one. If there are just a few candidates, each one can be polled in a pre-determined order. But this method does not scale to a very large number of resolution services, when some kind of gateway service is needed for providing information about the correct service or services.

An efficient and global resolution service for SICI can be accomplished by using the global ISSN register as a way station. No other database contains bibliographic data about the vast majority of serials, although the largest union catalogues may get quite close. In the future, if the ISSN register is mirrored to other servers, it will be possible to use all database copies in parallel for URN resolution purposes. On the Internet, all services should be decentralised since otherwise the system will not scale up to the level required. Having the ISSN database as the only gateway service is a risk, but on the other hand the present incarnation of the Digital Object Identifier (DOI) is centralised in the same way.

The first step in resolving a SICI-based URN is to deliver the query to the URN resolver in the ISSN database. The resolver will parse the SICI string in order to extract the ISSN from it. The ISSN will then be used as a search key for retrieving the bibliographic record of the serial from the ISSN register.

The ISSN register already contains quite a few records describing electronic serials. These records as a rule contain a URL for the serial home page. This URL is appropriate for resolving a URN based on the ISSN of the serial. However, in order to resolve SICI-based URNs, this URL is definitely not valid. The user resolving a SICI-based URN is interested in getting the article to which the SICI refers, not in finding the home page of the serial itself. The serial may be published in a totally different location than the resolution service indicates, or it may never have had an electronic version at all during its lifetime.

How is one to differentiate between the two kinds of URL links? Probably the easiest solution is to add a new data element into the MARC record, for specifying the addresses of databases or services which hold full text of. the journal's articles and/or bibliographic information about them. The linking information could also be stored elsewhere in the global ISSN register, but for the sake of simplicity we will describe only the MARC-record-based solution.

Different volumes of the journal may be available from different services. Therefore it must be possible to qualify the linking information by specifying volumes and, if necessary, even issues, which are available in the service.

At least in theory it is also possible to make the link information context specific. For instance, if the link points to the legal deposit collection maintained by the National Library of Finland, the appropriate IP addresses–those of the Finnish legal deposit libraries–could be specified as qualifiers to the resolver link. Then the display of the linking information could be suppressed if the user's IP address does not match the ones listed.

Maintaining this kind of volatile information in the global ISSN register may pose some technical challenges. Another problem is that access lists for popular services such as JSTOR might be very extensive.

For the time being the new MARC tag or subfield(s) for the required additional data elements have not been included in the MARC format used in the global ISSN register. For testing purposes, 9XX tags can be utilised.

The SICI resolution service of the ISSN register will verify the existence of a link or links to SICI resolution services. If there are many services, a further check is done to verify which services have the volume and/or issue needed.

Once a service matching the request has been found, the application will either forward the query to the resolution service, or make the query, receive the result, and pass it on to the user.

An Internet draft registering namespace ID "SICI" for the SICI system and outlining the above resolution architecture is under construction. We believe that the draft can be delivered to the Internet Engineering Task Force (IETF) during spring 2001. Like other informational RFCs the URN namespace ID registrations are usually approved quite quickly.

CHALLENGES AND SOLUTIONS

The resolution service for ISSN-based URNs built by the ISSN International Centre relies on a plug-in that needs to be installed on a Web browser, and a custom-built resolver module, which has been integrated into the ISSN register.

A user who has installed the plug-in will be able to type ISSN-based URNs into the location window of the browser, and as a response get the bibliographic record describing the journal. The user does not need prior knowledge about the location or even the existence of the ISSN register.

Modifying these existing tools so that they fit for SICI resolution purposes as well should not be too complicated. The main programming challenge is to support URN resolution also in the article databases built by the DIEPER (Digitised European Periodicals)[4] project and eventually in other document delivery services.

Once the URN namespace for an existing identifier has been specified, it is trivial to expand these identifiers into URNs. For instance, every ISSN will become a URN if the string *urn:issn:* is added in front of the ISSN. Actually there is no need to add anything into the database, since any URN query can be modified into a traditional identifier query simply by removing the namespace identifier and the letters *urn:* from the beginning of the query string.

The URN system, just like other systems such as DOI and OpenURL, faces the challenge that any resource to be incorporated into the resolution service must be identified first. Sometimes this is a non-issue: by definition everything in the ISSN register has been identified with an ISSN already. But, for instance, when the DIEPER project digitised a number of key mathematical periodicals from the 19th century, neither serials nor the articles were identified in advance. The first step was to acquire ISSNs for the processed journals.

Once ISSNs had been acquired, it was necessary to build SICIs. Anyone familiar with the standard knows that in a large-scale project this can't be done manually, unless the aim is to solve the unemployment problems in the country. A SICI generator has been available for a few years, but even this tool, although it makes the burden of creating SICIs a lot easier, was not efficient enough for DIEPER purposes.

In the course of the DIEPER project it was possible to build a generator, which creates SICI automatically from article metadata saved in Extensible Markup Language (XML). However, this SICI generator can be used only with XML files following the RDF standard.

The DIEPER project has in any case proven in practice that automatic generation of SICIs is possible. While doing this we on the other hand did find some areas in which SICI functionality was not quite what we needed. For instance, an article may be digitised for printing and display purposes with very different resolutions. Both versions will however get the same SICI.

CONCLUSION

Co-operation between the ISSN International Centre and the DIEPER project has produced some interesting insights into how to build global resolution services for articles available on the Internet. The feasibility of these ideas is being tested in a pilot project. Extending pilot services into production systems will require financial and political support.

National libraries have committed themselves to investigating and developing URN-based resolution services. There are many reasons for this. The URN framework is technically reliable, because it is not dependent on any current Internet protocol. Because of this, and since all parts of the URN infrastructure have been standardised by the Internet community, it is quite likely that the URN framework will still be in use when some other resolution services have been forgotten. But URN services will not be possible without effort: libraries and other service builders need to invest in the system.

Although URNs as such are free of charge, building the URN resolution services–and using them–may not be. URN infrastructure as defined by the Internet community is rather simple, and does not directly support creation of commercial services. But it should be possible to build such services on top of the URN framework, or to link URNs into an existing commercial resolution service.

NOTES

1. Leslie Daigle, Ron Daniel Jr., and Cecilia Preston, "Uniform Resource Identifiers and Online Serials," *The Serials Librarian* 33, no. 3/4 (1998): 325-341.
2. See the updated article in *E-Serials*, 2nd ed., edited by Wayne Jones (The Haworth Press, Inc., forthcoming 2003).

3. Clifford Lynch, Cecilia Preston, and Ron Daniel Jr., "Using Existing Bibliographic Identifiers as Uniform Resource Names," RFC 2288, Feb. 1998, http://www.ietf.org/rfc/rfc2288.txt (viewed Mar. 18, 2001).

4. DIEPER, Digitised European Periodicals, http://www.sub.uni-goettingen.de/gdz/dieper/ (viewed Mar. 18, 2001).

Bibliographic Protocol:
Fine-Grained Integration of Library Services with the Web

Robert D. Cameron

SUMMARY. Bibliographic protocol (bibp) is a new web-based protocol designed to provide library-based services for bibliographic links on the web. Links to books and journals may be easily created using bibp:ISBN and bibp:ISSN hyperreferences. A decentralized service model ensures that local bibliographic servers take precedence over publisher and global servers. The required resolution technology is widely deployed on the Internet and bibp-Z39.50 gateway software is available for implementation of library-based services. Future developments include additional support for article-based linking and server-to-server protocols for metadata sharing. *[Article copies available for a fee from The Haworth Document Delivery Service: 1-800-HAWORTH. E-mail address: <getinfo@haworthpressinc. com> Website: <http://www.HaworthPress.com> © 2002 by The Haworth Press, Inc. All rights reserved.]*

KEYWORDS. Bibliographic protocol, bibp, bibliographic links

Robert D. Cameron is Associate Dean of Applied Sciences and Professor of Computing Science at Simon Fraser University, 8888 University Drive, Burnaby, BC, Canada V5A 1S6.

[Haworth co-indexing entry note]: "Bibliographic Protocol: Fine-Grained Integration of Library Services with the Web." Cameron, Robert D. Co-published simultaneously in *The Serials Librarian* (The Haworth Information Press, an imprint of The Haworth Press, Inc.) Vol. 41, No. 3/4, 2002, pp. 201-215; and: *E-Serials Cataloging: Access to Continuing and Integrating Resources via the Catalog and the Web* (ed: Jim Cole, and Wayne Jones) The Haworth Information Press, an imprint of The Haworth Press, Inc., 2002, pp. 201-215. Single or multiple copies of this article are available for a fee from The Haworth Document Delivery Service [1-800-HAWORTH, 9:00 a.m. - 5:00 p.m. (EST). E-mail address: getinfo@haworthpressinc.com].

INTRODUCTION

Imagine that, as a librarian at State University, your job is to provide web-based access to published literature for patrons in the stateu.edu domain. Ideally, whenever a patron accesses a bibliographic reference on the web, you could capture that access and direct it to a local server at, say, bibhost.stateu.edu. In this way, the local server would be able to highlight local holdings, interlibrary loan and document delivery options in addition to providing access to global service options through the web. This is fine-grained integration of library services with the web: as users explore the web and navigate sites describing ongoing research and current developments, accessing references to published works automatically brings up library-based service for the works in question.

This fine-grained integration is precisely the goal and capability of a new web protocol called bibliographic protocol (bibp). It is still a goal because libraries still must deploy bibp servers and authors must start creating bibp links. But the capability is real: all the technology pieces are in place to make server deployment and bibp linking quite straightforward. For libraries, bibp-Z39.50 gateway software is available that makes server deployment as simple as installing a PHP script into a properly configured web server. For authors, simple instructions describe how to create bibp:ISBN and bibp:ISSN links and to enable them with a JavaScript client-side resolver. Even without local library support, the bibp links so created are supported by the prototype global server at usin.org. But the premise here is that, if libraries take the initiative to offer bibp service, web authors will find the utility of bibp linking extremely attractive.

Consider, for example, bibp:ISSN/0361-526X as a Uniform Resource Identifier (URI)[1] for *The Serials Librarian* and bibp:ISBN/0-262-02473-X as a URI for *From Gutenberg to the Global Information Infrastructure* by Christine L. Borgman. These URIs denote the bibliographic items in question, but do not specify any particular bibliographic service for them. It is the job of bibliographic protocol to direct access requests for these items to an appropriate bibliographic service. By default, these requests will be directed to a service at bibhost.stateu.edu (if that service exists) for users in the stateu.edu domain. Using the bibp-Z39.50 gateway software described herein, such a service could report on local holdings as well as provide gateways to related services through partner libraries and global services.

From the author perspective, a highly desirable goal is achieved: the author can link to a published item without determining and specifying a URL to service it. Even without local library support, services will initially be provided by a global service such as our prototype server at usin.org. As library-based services are deployed, the information accessible through a link will improve in quality and relevance to the user context. As these services begin to network and share data, further service improvements will be made. With contributions by publishers and information intermediaries, yet more information becomes available. Contrasted with the decaying service phenomenon of URL-based linking, there should be considerable interest by authors in creating bibp links.

In essence, bibliographic protocol is an implementation of the Uniform Resource Name (URN)[2,3] concept for the limited domain of published bibliographic items. By focusing on the specific needs of bibliographic identification and bibliographic service, the concerns of authors, publishers, libraries and users have been brought into focus in the creation of a decentralized bibliographic support model as described in the next section of this paper. Keeping simplicity and the need for deployability paramount, technology to realize this model has been developed; this is the topic of the third section of the paper.

In contrast, the longstanding promise of URN-based linking has yet to be realized. There are other concerns as well. The Dynamic Delegation and Discovery Service (DDDS) currently proposed for URN implementation is based on a concept of centrally controlled, authoritative resolution. Even if it eventually becomes implemented and deployed, the centralized approach seems inherently unscalable and unsuitable for day-to-day resolution of bibliographic service requests. Furthermore, bibliographic identification is confused with other forms of identification under the URN scheme and managed through a top-down process of namespace allocation under the control of the Internet Assigned Names Authority (IANA).[4] Cybersquatting is a known outcome of top-down allocation under DNS, and there is some evidence that this may be repeated under the URN. In contrast, the bibp URI scheme provides a single cohesive namespace in which systematic principles of bibliographic identification consistent with longstanding practice can be applied.[5,6] Management of this namespace has yet to be resolved, but ought to be vested in an appropriate international institution primarily responsible to scholars and librarians.

Moving from analysis and design considerations underlying bibliographic protocol to actual implementation work, the fourth and fifth sections of this paper are organized as how-to documents for authors and libraries. The fourth section provides instructions for authors for bibp linking to books and journals. The fifth provides instructions for libraries to capture and service bibp requests using PHP-based bibp-Z39.50 gateway software. By adhering to the instructions and the protocol, authors and libraries at various sites should be able to develop bibp links and services independently but with full confidence that they may interoperate through the protocol.

The extension of bibp linking to the article level is the topic of the sixth section. Although libraries may not generally be in a position to provide article-based service at the current time, the gateway software allows serial holdings information to be highlighted in conjunction with article-level access through publisher and global services.

The paper concludes with remarks about the current state of bibliographic protocol work as well as future directions.

A DECENTRALIZED BIBLIOGRAPHIC SUPPORT MODEL

Bibliographic protocol is designed based on a decentralized, hierarchical model of a bibliographic service network. The hierarchy involves bibliographic service definitions at four levels:

1. Global services;
2. Publisher-specified services;
3. Library-specified services;
4. User-specified services.

Each successive level in the hierarchy overrides services that may exist at preceding levels.

Global services provide default bibliographic service if none of the other options is available. Current implementations of bibliographic protocol use the prototype server at usin.org. However, preferences for different default global services may be set within bibp client software. It is anticipated that there may be competing providers of default global services over time. Alternatively, an internationally chartered institution may be given responsibility to operate a preferred global server at some point.

Document publishers may override global services though the citehost mechanism. In essence, a citehost is the name of a bibp server that specifically provides bibliographic service for the bibp links contained in a particular document. The inclusion of the citehost mechanism within bibliographic protocol recognizes the important contribution that publishers make and the strong interest on the part of many publishers to provide added value to electronic journals through reference linking.[7]

The citehost mechanism allows a distinct citehost to be designated within each published document. In other words, the citehost is a document-specified server. In fact, the mechanism is available for any web document, including those written by authors who self-publish. However, an individual author is not likely to want to undertake the task of maintaining an operating citehost.

Local library services take precedence over publisher and global services using the bibhost mechanism. In essence, this allows libraries to highlight the "appropriate copy"[8] of the cited resource as it is available to users in a particular domain. This may be particularly relevant to users in academic domains. For example, as soon as the State University Library installs a bibp server at bibhost.stateu.edu, that server takes precedence over global or publisher-specified services for users in the stateu.edu domain. Whenever a bibp link is accessed by a user with the domain, the university library has the chance to highlight local holdings and services with respect to the referenced item. The net result is that fine-grained integration between the web and the library can be achieved.

When both a citehost and a bibhost exist, the protocol is designed to communicate the citehost setting to the bibhost. Thus the local library service can also highlight the availability of information from the publisher as well as providing local context. In general, the expectation is that library-operated bibhosts will evolve towards the notion of bibliographic gateways or metaservices with respect to cited items. For any given item, the goal will be to present a selection of available services that exist and to allow the user to choose from various service options.

Finally, users may choose to override global, publisher, and/or library-specified services. The expectation is that most users will not take the necessary steps to configure personal preferences, but will simply rely on the default service when documents containing bibp links come their way. However, if users are outside of an academic domain, they may wish to identify a commercial bibliographic service provider (BSP) that can provide access and document delivery options to them. Of course, even academic users may override the use of the local library if they find that another BSP provides better service. Ideally, the possibility of open competition between BSPs and libraries should provide for the evolution of high-quality services. Libraries will retain the inside track by providing default service for their local domains, while BSPs may pick up business where commercial users are willing to pay for quality, speed and coverage.

As perhaps the ultimate exercise of user control, users may also choose to install personal bibliographic servers on their own computers. For example, a user who has an extensive collection of annotated references as well as a considerable personal library may want the annotations and holdings highlighted whenever a bibp link is accessed. Of course, the personal bibliographic server would not operate in a vacuum, but would also provide gateway service to libraries, publishers and global services.

Overall the resolution hierarchy described above provides a flexible array of options for bibliographic service through a natural hierarchy reflecting the concerns of authors, publishers, libraries and users. Implementation of this model has been a key challenge in our work and is the subject of the next section.

MAKING IT WORK

Given the concept of the bibp link, the overriding question has been how to make it work, bearing in mind the requirements of simplicity, deployability and scalability. From the simplicity perspective, it should be easy for authors to create bibp links and easy for libraries to install bibp servers. From the deployability perspective, the ideal is to work with the installed base of web clients and network services as they currently exist. Although the technology-inclined can have great fun developing new browser software and/or network services, relying on their deployment by disinterested users and/or network administrators is a recipe for long delay if not outright failure. Finally, the scalability perspective is critical as well. If bibp links are ever to become widely used in everyday web browsing, the bottleneck of funneling all bibp requests through one or a few global services must be avoided.

The relative domain name, a core feature of the Domain Name System (DNS),[9] is the key network technology that provides for both simplicity and deployability of bibliographic protocol. Simply stated, the protocol relies on the relative domain name bibhost to locate different bibp servers in different local environments. For users in the stateu.edu domain, service from bibhost.stateu.edu may be expected, while users in the provincialu.ca domain may be served by bibhost.provincialu.ca. There is the possibility of an accidental pre-existing use of bibhost in some domains, so the protocol does define a confirmation step to ensure that a server responding to the bibhost name does indeed implement bibliographic protocol.

Fixing the name bibhost as the standard name for bibp servers imposes some constraints. A domain may have only one default bibp server and that server must be known as bibhost if it is indeed to be the local default. Other uses of bibhost should be avoided–a constraint on domain administration. Nevertheless, this association of particular relative names with particular services is a recommended practice in domain administration.[10] Furthermore, the relative importance of bibliographic service as an application area and the simplicity of having a standard name for it are both strong arguments in favor of reserving the name bibhost in this way.

The second key technology that provides for the immediate deployability of bibliographic protocol with the installed base of existing web browsers is JavaScript. Authors of documents containing bibp links can enable the protocol by incorporating a JavaScript client-side resolver in their documents. This eliminates the need for any user action to install new web browsers or plug-ins for the purpose of bibp implementation. The JavaScript has been carefully written to be very short and hence easy to incorporate into web documents with a copy-and-paste operation (see Figure 1).

FIGURE 1. JavaScript Client-Side Server

```
<script type="text/javascript">
<!--    // bibres js  version 1.1
        // (c) Robert D. Cameron and Serban Tatu, November 2000.
        // GNU General Public License, Version 2 applies.
var BibP_BaseURL;
var BibP_nocitehost = typeof(BibP_citehost) == "undefined";
function BibP_SetBaseURL (server) {
        BibP_BaseURL = server + "bibp1.0/resolve?" +
        (BibP_nocitehost ? "usin=" : "citehost="+ BibP_citehost+ "&usin=")}
BibP_SetBaseURL(BibP_nocitehost ? "http://usin.org/" :BibP_citehost);
function BibP_onMouseOver () {
        window status = "bibp:" + this.href.substring(BibP_BaseURL.length);
        return true}
function BibP_onMouseOut () {window.status = "";  return true}
function BibP_ProcessLink(L, srchKey) {
        var spot = L.href.indexOf(srchKey);
        if (spot != -1) {
                L.href = BibP_BaseURL + L.href.substring(spot + srchKey.length);
                L.onmouseover = BibP_onMouseOver;
                L.onmouseout = BibP_onMouseOut}}
var BibP_Icon = new Image ();      // To test for local bibhost icon.
function BibP_onIcon () {
        if (BibP_Icon.height!=0) {
                var oldBase = BibP_BaseURL;
                BibP_SetBaseURL("http://bibhost/");
                for (var i = 0; i < document.links.length; i++)
                        BibP_ProcessLink(document.links[i], oldBase)}}
function BibP_onLoad () {
        for (var i = 0; i < document.links.length; i++)
                BibP_ProcessLink(document.links[i], "bibp:");
        BibP_Icon.onload = BibP_onIcon;  // Now test for bibhost.
        BibP_Icon.src = "http://bibhost/bibp1.0/bibpicon.jpg"}
if (typeof(navigator.bibpSupport) == "undefined") {
        window.onload = BibP_onLoad}
// -->
</script>
```

The detailed program documentation for the JavaScript resolver is contained in the bibliographic protocol specification document.[11] A few points are worth noting. In the case that a citehost is undefined, global service defaults to http://usin.org/ and bibp links are dynamically rewritten to use this server. A publisher-specified citehost may override this. The test to determine whether a local bibp server exists is carried out by checking for the presence of the Bibp Identification Icon at http://bibhost/bibp1.0/bibpicon.jpg. Note that this URL uses bibhost as a relative domain name. If a local server is found, links are rewritten to use that server in preference to either the global server or citehost.

One small wrinkle is that, in the absence of a local bibhost, some web browsers guess that service may be available at http://www.bibhost.com/. This is a poor practice on the part of the browser, but a service has been registered at that site to ensure correct protocol implementation.

The JavaScript resolver has been carefully written to enable bibp service with most current and anticipated future web browsers. The resolver is known to enable bibp service with Netscape 3 through 6, Internet Explorer 4 through 5.5 and Opera 4 and 5 (although service is limited in some browser/operating system combinations). Cross-platform operation has been attained by carefully restricting the JavaScript coding to those features which are standard. This also helps future-proof the resolver, in notable contrast to commonplace use of ad hoc version testing to attain cross-platform support. The final two lines of the resolver represent another aspect of future planning: if and when future web browsers provide (presumably better) bibp support, they may disable the JavaScript resolver by appropriate definition of the property navigator.bibpSupport.

Although JavaScript enables bibliographic protocol for the vast majority of web users, bibliographic protocol itself does not rely upon it. For example, bibp support has been directly incorporated into recent versions of the Lynx web browser (2.8.4dev17 and above). It is also possible to implement server-side capture of misdirected bibp links. This may occur when JavaScript is disabled and the browser interprets the bibp link as a relative URL. Together with the JavaScript resolver, these and other support mechanisms provide a reasonably advanced state of deployability for the protocol.

Scalability is the final design issue that has been of overriding importance in bibliographic protocol development. The protocol and recommended practice have been carefully defined to ensure that the portion of bibliographic service handled by global servers is gradually reduced as local bibliographic services come online. One aspect of this is ensuring that bibhost and citehost service can be completely implemented without consulting the global server. A second aspect is that the recommended practice for incorporation of the JavaScript resolver is through the copy-and-paste operation rather than by reference to a source file stored at any global server.

INSTRUCTIONS TO AUTHORS

For concreteness, now may be a good time to create a web document with your first bibp link. For the time being, let us assume that we are only linking books or journals via ISBN or ISSN. Here are the instructions:

1. Determine the ISBN or ISSN of the book or journal of interest. For example, 0361-526X for *The Serials Librarian*. Ideally, the ISN

should be used in proper canonical form, with correct hyphenation and a check digit X capitalized if present. The analysis tools at http://usin.org/bibp/utilities/ISBN-analyzer.php and http://usin.org/bibp/utilities/ISSN-analyzer.php may be helpful.

2. Form the full identifier by prepending either the string ISBN/ or ISSN/ to the ISN, as appropriate.
3. Create the URI by prepending the scheme prefix bibp:.
4. Use this URI to create a standard HTML hyperreference, as illustrated by the following example:

```
<a href="bibp:ISSN/0361-526X">The Serials Librarian</a>
```

5. Copy and paste the JavaScript client-side resolver into the head element of the HTML document, that is, between the <head> and </head> tags. Do not modify the JavaScript in any way. Note: this step needs to be done only once for a given document.

Check it out! With no local bibhost available, you should get some kind of reasonable response from usin.org for any bibp link you try. Of course, if bibhost service is available, that service will be used instead.

For completeness, we also include here the instructions for defining a citehost as a document specified server:

1. Determine the URL prefix of the citehost service. This may be the URL of the citehost server itself or of a server subdirectory which provides citehost service. For example, the server may be available at http://pubhost.com/bibpserver/.
2. Copy and paste the following lines into the head of the HTML document immediately before the JavaScript resolver, replacing the two occurrences of the example URL with the actual URL. Make sure to include the trailing slash character with the URL in each case:

```
<link rel="citehost" href="http://www.pubhost.com/bibpserver/" />

<script type="text/javascript">

        BibP_citehost = "http://www.pubhost.com/bibpserver/"

</script>
```

The link element is used to communicate the citehost information to web browsers that provide native bibp support, such as bibp-aware Lynx. The JavaScript communicates the citehost information for use by the JavaScript resolver.

These instructions should be relatively easy to follow. As one method of introducing bibp linking on a university campus, course reading lists with bibp links for journals and books may be created.

A BIBP-Z39.50 GATEWAY

This section presents instructions for installation of a local bibhost that automatically captures bibp accesses in a local domain and uses a local Z39.50 service to provide bibliographic and holdings information. The assumption is that a local Z39.50 server is available for accessing catalogued materials. If not, it is possible to adapt the gateway software to use other methods for retrieval and reporting of ISN-based data.

The first task is to build an Apache web server with integrated support for Z39.50 client-side access through the PHP/YAZ combination. PHP is a server-side scripting language widely used with Apache and other web servers. PHP/YAZ is an open-source PHP extension providing access to the YAZ toolkit for Z39.50 client-side access. YAZ and PHP/YAZ are both products of IndexData which have been contributed to the open source community. For this we are grateful. We also acknowledge the fine work of the open-source PHP and Apache projects.

The task of building the web server is typically a job for a system administrator. For experienced Linux/Unix administrators, the job goes reasonably smoothly following the standard download and install instructions for YAZ, PHP, and Apache. YAZ should be installed first and PHP should be built with YAZ as a static extension. PHP 4.01p11 or later is required. If the installation task is an upgrade of an existing web server with Apache and perhaps PHP already available, then the config.status files from previous installations should be used as templates for subsequent installation.

Once the web server is available, installation and configuration of the bibp-Z39.50 gateway is reasonably straightforward, involving the following steps:

1. Create the directory bibp1.0 as a top-level directory within the server data area.
2. Download the following files from the server software area at USIN.org and install them in the bibp1.0 directory:

- ISBN-ISSN.php–ISN analysis functions;
- USIN.php–USIN parsing functions;
- MARC.php–MARC processing functions;

- bibp-z3950.php–bibp-Z39.50 gateway script.

3. Modify the settings within the configuration section of bibp-z3950.php as follows:

- replace the title, banner, and icon settings with ones appropriate to your institution;
- modify the Z39.50 server information to use server addresses, port numbers and database names of the appropriate local servers, as well as to specify the identifying codes that are displayed to the user.

4. Configure the Apache web server with the following rewrite rule (httpd.conf):

```
RewriteEngine On

RewriteRule ^/bibp1.0/resolve$ /bibp1.0/bibp-z3950.php?%{QUERY_STRING}
```

This step is necessary to ensure that bibp-z3950.php is used to respond to resolve requests issued under bibliographic protocol.
5. Install the Bibp Identification Icon in bibp1.0/bibpicon.jpg. This directory and filename cannot be changed and are required to ensure that your server will be recognized as implementing bibliographic protocol.
6. Have your network administrator create the appropriate DNS records so that your server is accessible via http://bibhost/ in your local domain.

This completes the installation process. All bibp requests from your local domain should now be redirected through your server. This applies for documents containing bibp links that originate at your site or at any other site on the web.

ARTICLE-LEVEL LINKING AND BEYOND

From the outset, the work with bibliographic protocol has contemplated article-level linking as a fundamental concern and objective. Building on the initial ISBN and ISSN domains, the identifiers used with bibliographic protocol follow the scholar-friendly identification principles of the Universal Serial Item Name (USIN) scheme.[12] Detailed syntactic specifications that provide for coverage of the vast bulk of the referenced literature are published with the bibliographic protocol specification.[13] However, widespread use of the protocol for article-level linking is not encouraged at this time, because server-side support needs considerable development. Nevertheless, the framework is sufficiently well-defined so that article-level links may be created for demonstration and prototyping purposes.

For articles in print-based journals, the USIN scheme defines a set of simple syntactic conventions based on volume, issue and page numbering. The following USINs are illustrative:

- ISSN/0361-526X:36–the USIN for volume 36 of *The Serials Librarian* (1999);
- ISSN/0361-526X:36(1/2)–the USIN for issue 1/2 of this volume;
- ISSN/0361-526X:36(1/2)@175 and ISSN/0361-526X:36@175–two equivalent USINs for the article starting at page 175 of this issue, namely the article entitled "STM X-REF: A Link Service for Publishers and Readers" by Gerry Grenier. The issue may be omitted because *The Serials Librarian* is paginated by volume.

The case of multiple articles starting on the same page number is handled by appending lower case "alphabetic" numerals to identify the particular article in question. For example, ISSN/0001-0782:38(1)@43a and ISSN/0001-0782:38(1)@43b respectively denote the two short articles "Women and Computing in the UK" by Alison Adam and "Announcing a New Resource: The WCAR List" by Laura L. Downey, both appearing on page 43 of *Communications of the ACM*, volume 38, number 1 (January 1995).

As these examples illustrate, it should be relatively straightforward to teach users to create bibp:USIN links. The simplicity of citation for journal articles in print publications is particularly important to encourage linking through the protocol. This is a key concept: use simple notations for the normal case when simple notations suffice. Notational complexity need be added only when additional information is required for unambiguous article identification.

Turning now to the case of articles in unpaginated e-journals, the USIN convention is to use an article label syntax in place of the page number syntax. Article labels may be numeric or symbolic and are introduced with the $ operator in the conventional USIN syntax. The following examples are typical:

- ISSN/1201-2459:2(3)$4–the USIN for "Reflections on Milton and Ariosto" by Roy Flannagan, published as article 4 in *Early Modern Literary Studies*, volume 2, number 3
- ISSN/1073-0486:1999$11–the USIN for "Satisfiability Coding Lemma" by Ramamohan Paturi, Pavel Pudlak, and Francis Zane, published as article 11 in volume 1999 of *Chicago Journal of Theoretical Computer Science*

- ISSN/1368-7506:1(3)$Cameron–the USIN for the article "Towards Universal Serial Item Names" published in the *Journal of Digital Information*, volume 1, issue 2. Here the symbolic label "Cameron" uniquely distinguishes this article from others in the same issue.

The following rules are used to precisely determine the article label to be used in each instance:

1. First, explicit article labels (numeric or symbolic) issued at the time of publication take precedence. These labels may have issue scope or volume scope as illustrated in the first two examples above.
2. In the absence of explicit labeling, labels are derived from article URLs if possible. More precisely, a label-determination algorithm is applied to the set of article URLs that are created at the time of publication. Subsequent changes to the URLs by the publisher will not change the assigned labels. The label determination algorithm essentially identifies the smallest URL symbol that uniquely identifies an article in the context of a volume or issue. A definitive reference algorithm for label determination is under development.
3. Finally, if no clear article label may be determined through the first two rules, an authoritative USIN database must be consulted. Establishment of such a database and an appropriate registration process is future work.

Beyond article-level linking, the USIN syntactic framework provides a generic, hierarchical syntax designed for scalability and extensibility. The concept of publication domains is used to organize the identification space; the two initial domains emphasized in this paper are ISSN and ISBN. The parameterized publication domain RDNS allows namespaces for institutional publications based on a restricted set of well-established DNS names. For example, RDNS(IETF.org) is the publication domain for publications of the Internet Engineering Task Force and RDNS(SFU.CA) is the publication domain for institutional publications of Simon Fraser University (theses, technical reports, and so on). The NBN publication domain, parameterized by ISO country code, has been set aside for identification of documents by national bibliography number. For example, NBN(AU) is reserved for identification of documents registered by the National Library of Australia. Of course, all this presupposes considerable further work to establish the identification standards and develop the necessary metadata repositories and exchange protocols.

In application to article identification, USINs may be contrasted with Serial Item and Contribution Identifiers (SICIs) and Digital Object Identifiers (DOIs). Philosophically, USINs are similar to SICIs in that they are compound or "intelligent" identifiers in the parlance of Paskin.[14] However, SICIs suffer from a number of drawbacks that make their use in bibp linking problematic. They are complex and difficult to construct. They cannot be directly used in web URIs without escape encoding.[15] They also suffer from an ambiguity problem that ought never to be allowed in an identifier syntax; distinct articles may have the same SICI when they occur on the same page of a serial with similarly abbreviated titles.[16]

If SICIs ever become widely used for article identification, it may make sense to provide support for them through bibliographic protocol. One method would be to define SICI as a new top-level publication domain within the USIN syntax. A better method may be to provide a USIN-to-SICI transformation module as a standard facility in bibp server software. An entirely automatic transformation to a minimal SICI is possible and would insulate users from the need to work with the complex SICI syntax.

The Digital Object Identifier is founded on the "dumb identifier" model, philosophically distinct from USINs and SICIs. In essence, a DOI is simply a database key that has been registered by the document rightsholder to uniquely denote it. The DOI initiative has considerable support by a significant group of publishers and is likely to become increasingly important over time. However, DOIs exist for particular articles only when they have been registered. Thus the space of denotable items under the DOI initiative is and will remain far smaller than that under the USIN structure. Most importantly, the DOI has no support for legacy items, whereas an underlying principle of the USIN system is to organize legacy identification artifacts and concepts into a scalable hierarchical syntax. Furthermore, because DOIs cannot be constructed from available metadata, they also make it difficult for libraries and other information intermediaries to implement independent document services.

The application of the bibp:USIN framework to reference linking in e-journals is only in its initial stages with a project in collaboration with the *Canadian Journal of Communication*. The DOI will retain a considerable lead in this area for quite some time, perhaps indefinitely, and it may be necessary to find some appropriate way to accommodate DOI-based identification within the bibp:USIN framework.

CONCLUDING REMARKS

Bibliographic protocol is designed to provide fine-grained integration of library services with the web. Using bibp-Z39.50 gateway software, libraries may immediately begin offering support for bibp:ISBN and bibp:ISSN links for books and journals.

NOTES

1. T. Berners-Lee, R. Fielding and L. Masinter, "Uniform Resource Identifiers (URI): Generic Syntax," Request for Comments 2396 (Internet Engineering Task Force, August 1998). bibp:RDNS(ietf.org)/RFC:2396

2. K. Sollins and L. Masinter, "Functional Requirements for Uniform Resource Names," Request for Comments 1737 (Internet Engineering Task Force, December 1994). bibp:RDNS(ietf.org)/RFC:1737

3. Leslie Daigle, Ron Daniel, Jr., and Cecilia Preston, "Uniform Resource Identifiers and Online Serials," *The Serials Librarian* 33, no. 3/4 (1998): 325-341. bibp:ISSN/0361-526X:33@325

4. L. Daigle, D. van Gulik, R. Iannella, and P. Faltstrom, "URN Namespace Definition Mechanisms," Request for Comments 2611 (Internet Engineering Task Force, June 1999). bibp:RDNS(ietf.org)/RFC:2611

5. Robert D. Cameron, "Towards Universal Serial Item Names," *Journal of Digital Information* 1, no. 3 (October 1998). bibp:ISSN/1368-7506:1(3)$Cameron

6. Robert D. Cameron and Serban G. Tatu, "Bibliographic Protocol Level 1: Link Resolution and Metapage Retrieval," http://www.cs.sfu.ca/~cameron/bibp-revised.html.

7. Karen Hunter, "Adding Value by Adding Links," *Journal of Electronic Publishing* 3, no. 3 (March 1998). bibp:ISSN/1080-2711:3(3)$hunter

8. Herbert Van de Sompel and Patrick Hochstenbach, "Reference Linking in a Hybrid Library Environment Part 3: Generalizing the SFX Solution in the 'SFX@Ghent & SFX@LANL' Experiment," *D-Lib Magazine* 5, no. 10 (October 1999). bibp:ISSN/1082-9873:5(10)$van_de_sompel

9. P. Mockapetris, "Domain Names–Concepts and Facilities," Request for Comments 1034 (Internet Engineering Task Force, November 1987). USIN:bibp:RDNS (ietf.org)/RFC:1034

10. M. Hamilton and R. Wright "Use of DNS Aliases for Network Services," Request for Comments 2219 (Internet Engineering Task Force, October 1997). bibp: RDNS(ietf.org)/RFC:2219

11. Robert D. Cameron and Serban G. Tatu, "Bibliographic Protocol."

12. Robert D. Cameron, "Towards Universal Serial Item Names."

13. Robert D. Cameron and Serban G. Tatu, "Bibliographic Protocol."

14. Norman Paskin "Information Identifiers," *Learned Publishing* 10, no. 2 (April 1997): 135-156. bibp:ISSN/0953-1513:10@135

15. C. Lynch, C. Preston and R. Daniel, "Using Existing Bibliographic Identifiers as Uniform Resource Names," Request for Comments 2288 (Internet Engineering Task Force, February 1998). bibp:RDNS(ietf.org)/RFC:2288

16. F. Schwarz and C. Hepfer, "Changes to the Serial Item and Contribution Identifier and the Effects of Those on Publishers and Libraries," *The Serials Librarian* 28, no. 3/4 (1996): 367-70. bibp:ISSN/0361-526X:28@367

Marrying Bibliographic
and Fulltext Resources:
An A&I Publisher's View

Michael H. Miyazaki

SUMMARY. Today's researchers have access to amazing information resources, especially in their ability to quickly identify and retrieve published information pertinent to their research. Partly responsible is the partnership between Internet-based bibliographic and fulltext resources. CSA, as a bibliographic publisher, has been in the forefront of linking bibliographic and fulltext resources, as shown through its Internet Database Service. CSA has also developed market-driven products to take advantage of other emerging information sources. *[Article copies available for a fee from The Haworth Document Delivery Service: 1-800-HAWORTH. E-mail address: <getinfo@haworthpressinc.com> Website: <http://www.HaworthPress. com>* © 2002 by The Haworth Press, Inc. All rights reserved.]

KEYWORDS. Fulltext searching, information services, online databases, abstracting services, information providers, online information retrieval, electronic publishing

To most of us older than thirty, the research resources that average college students can access from their computers are astounding. Imagine Stephanie, a

Michael H. Miyazaki is Marketing Manager of CSA, 7200 Wisconsin Avenue, Bethesda, MD 20814 USA.

[Haworth co-indexing entry note]: "Marrying Bibliographic and Fulltext Resources: An A&I Publisher's View." Miyazaki, Michael H. Co-published simultaneously in *The Serials Librarian* (The Haworth Information Press, an imprint of The Haworth Press, Inc.) Vol. 41, No. 3/4, 2002, pp. 217-225; and: *E-Serials Cataloging: Access to Continuing and Integrating Resources via the Catalog and the Web* (ed: Jim Cole, and Wayne Jones) The Haworth Information Press, an imprint of The Haworth Press, Inc., 2002, pp. 217-225. Single or multiple copies of this article are available for a fee from The Haworth Document Delivery Service [1-800-HAWORTH, 9:00 a.m. - 5:00 p.m. (EST). E-mail address: getinfo@haworthpressinc.com].

college junior taking Intermediate Genetics, who starts a research paper on genetically modified corn at two in the morning. From her dorm-room computer she electronically connects to her university library, searches bibliographic databases (like the *CSA Biological Sciences Database*), scans article abstracts, selects relevant references for which she retrieves the electronic fulltext of articles and books, and copies charts, quotes, and relevant data. She accesses pertinent Web sites, finding current statistical information and late-breaking news stories; and she copies some illustrations. A bibliographic manager helps her format her references. The paper, replete with illustrations and current data, gets printed on her color printer, and Stephanie still has time for a nap before her 9:00 a.m. class.

Fifteen years ago this situation would have seemed like a rosy vision of a fairly distant future. Today a number of factors have made the above scenario almost standard. These include innovations with the Internet, the wide distribution of powerful, easy-to-use, affordable technology, and the availability of a multitude of information resources. Most importantly, academic libraries have re-shaped themselves from information warehouses to proactive information providers. Thus instead of the researcher having to be in the library, through campus networks, the library is in the classroom, in the laboratory, in the professor's home office, and in the dorm room.

PARTNERING BIBLIOGRAPHIC AND FULLTEXT RESOURCES

One of the primary components enabling the scenario just described is the marriage of bibliographic databases with fulltext resources. Bibliographic databases allow the researcher to pinpoint the best reference sources with maximum efficiency. However, students still need access to fulltext resources–articles, monographs, Web sites–to do an effective job of research. It is very important to facilitate this kind of access. Currently CSA's Link-to-Fulltext feature and *Web Resources Database*, both available through the Internet Database Service, are two of the tools that provide powerful integration between bibliographic and fulltext resources.

CSA–BACKGROUND AND PHILOSOPHY

An established publisher of Abstracting and Indexing (A&I) publications, CSA has also published bibliographic journals for nearly forty years, has more than twenty years experience as an online provider, and was among the pioneers in publishing bibliographic databases on CD-ROM. CSA's Internet Database Service, launched in 1994, was the first site to offer subscriptions to bibliographic databases.

The CSA mission is "providing information assistance to researchers" rather than strictly "bibliographic publishing." What's the difference? CSA's chairman, Robert Snyder, is fond of pointing out that in the late 1800s, buggy-whip manufacturing was a thriving business with nothing but growth on the anticipated horizon. However, with the advent of other forms of transportation, firms who saw themselves strictly as "buggy-whip manufacturers," rather than "transportation service providers," and who did not adapt accordingly, were eventually out of business. With this type of situation in mind, CSA strives to extend the limited definitions of publishing and to maximize the rapidly increasing possibilities of technology–all to meet the needs of the information researcher.

LINKING TO FULLTEXT RESOURCES FROM CSA

One of the many ways CSA has done so is by using Internet technology to facilitate access to fulltext resources via its Internet-based search service. The Link-to-Holdings module links bibliographic search results to library holdings, thus allowing the researcher to determine if a reference is in her institution's serials collection. The Link-to-ILL module allows the researcher to request a document from her institution's Interlibrary Loan department. The Link-to-Document Delivery module allows the researcher to request fulltext from a commercial document delivery service. So, once academic journals in electronic format began to proliferate, it was logical for CSA to develop a Link-to-Fulltext module.

The goal has been to make the Link-to-Fulltext module as seamless, efficient, and intuitive for the end-user as possible. Once the researcher has entered a search, an initial list of search results appears (see Figure 1).

From this list, the researcher can either click "View Record" or "Locate Document" for citations of interest. View Record will take researchers to an abstract of the document, from which the researcher can also access the Locate Document option. Once the researcher clicks on Locate Document, the system provides the researcher with Document Acquisition choices (see Figure 2).

The easiest, of course, is Retrieve Electronic Fulltext. If the electronic fulltext is available to the researcher from her institution's collection, there is a link to the fulltext service provider next to "Retrieve Electronic Fulltext." In steps that vary from one electronic fulltext provider to another, the researcher is led to the electronic fulltext version of the article (see Figure 3).

FIGURE 1.The Results of a Search for "Genetically Modified Food*"–Displaying Citation Information for 4 of 22 Records Found

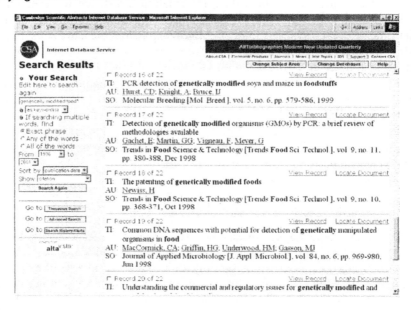

If the electronic fulltext is not available to the researcher, she can still determine if it is in her library's serials collection (Link-to-Holdings) or obtainable through Interlibrary Loan (Link-to-ILL).

At present, CSA offers links to fulltext for electronic journals provided by the following services:

- CatchWord
- EBSCO Online
- HighWire Press
- IDEAL (Academic Press)
- Information Quest (RoweCom)
- Kluwer Online
- LINK (Springer)
- OCLC FirstSearch Electronic Collections Online (ECO)
- ScienceDirect
- Swetsnet*Navigator*

FIGURE 2. The Document Acquisition Screen Brought Up by Clicking "Locate Document" for Record 16, "PCR Detection of Genetically Modified Soya and Maize in Foodstuffs," from the Journal *Molecular Breeding*.

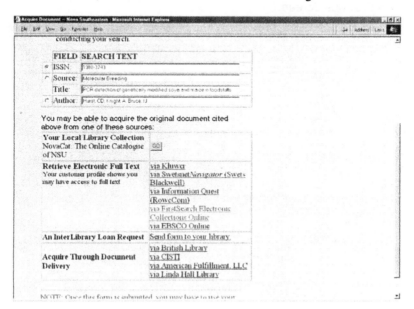

And the list is growing.

In all, researchers can presently link from CSA databases to more than 5,500 electronic journals. However, for a researcher to access the electronic journal article from our database, the researcher's library must subscribe to the electronic journal in question.

For these features to work, the library that subscribes to our bibliographic databases needs to integrate its electronic fulltext subscription information with our system. Initial set-up is easily done through the Site Administration portion of our service (see Figure 4).

The Site Administration page also allows institutions to update information about their link feature preferences and electronic journal subscriptions.

PAST AND FUTURE CHALLENGES

As you might expect, one of the biggest challenges faced by CSA so far has been trying to standardize the offerings from disparate electronic journal suppliers. Access routes to the articles vary. Some offer PDF files of the fulltext

FIGURE 3. A PDF File of the Fulltext of the Article, "PCR Detection of Genetically Modified Soya and Maize in Foodstuffs," from the Journal *Molecular Breeding*, Retrieved by Clicking "Via Firstsearch Electronic Collections Online" on the Previous Screen.

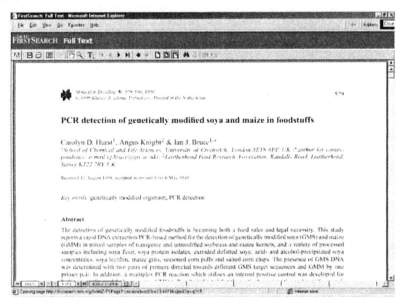

article; others use HTML pages. Integrating each new electronic journal provider remains a challenge. However, the experience of integrating each successive provider makes the next one smoother. Furthermore, we are working with library systems integrators who are making available new integration solutions. One such is Ex Libris, whose recently-introduced SFX service provides a reference linking system that supports a hybrid library environment and further facilitates linking for the subscribing library's users.

The issue of "pay-per-view" access also presents a challenge. Generally, the end-user can access fulltext only from electronic journals for which his library has subscriptions. CSA has the technology to offer such "pay-per-view" access when the end user tries to obtain the fulltext for a journal available electronically, but not subscribed to by his library. Currently, at least one fulltext provider, CatchWord, is offering "pay-per-view" access which our customers can choose to activate or avoid. However, we are still trying to find a way to offer these services in a framework that most libraries find helpful rather than distracting or possibly economically burdensome.

FIGURE 4. The Site Administration Area of the CSA Web Site Allows Subscribers to Initiate and Update Links to Holdings, Fulltext, Interlibrary Loan, and Document Delivery.

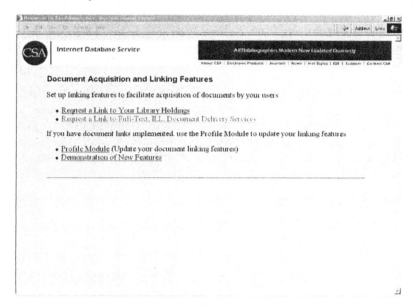

MAXIMIZING RESOURCES

As stated earlier, the academic library is undergoing a metamorphosis from being an information warehouse, located in a fixed geographic space with fixed hours, to being a campus-wide 24-hour-a-day, 7-day-a-week information distributor. Electronic subscriptions to databases and journals put a copy of each publication at every computer across campus. And with these subscriptions, one doesn't have to worry that the publications become aged, damaged or missing. Similarly, CSA has found that its policy of providing unlimited access and unlimited use for a fixed annual subscription fee encourages usage and drastically lowers the database's cost-per-search. Fulltext linking also encourages access to the electronic journals involved. Not only is there a result of reducing the cost-per-access of these resources, but the overall library mission of information dissemination is also effectively and efficiently served.

LINKING TO WEB-BASED RESOURCES

In the opening example, Web sites were necessary resources for students' research. However, conventional Web search engines can make finding pertinent research information very time consuming. Recognizing this, CSA developed the *Web Resources Database* of Web sites indexed by its editors using the same criteria followed for selecting coverage of academic journals. Thus, when the researcher clicks on the results listed under "Web Resources Related to Your Search," germane Web sites are listed (see Figure 5).

By clicking on the site address, she is hyperlinked to the Web site, at the pertinent page level. The frame interface structure also allows her to immediately access other Web sites that her search retrieved without having to return to the search results list (see Figure 6).

Currently, the *Web Resources Database* provides links to more than 130,000 Internet-based resources.

FIGURE 5. The Results After Clicking on "Web Resources Related to Your Search."

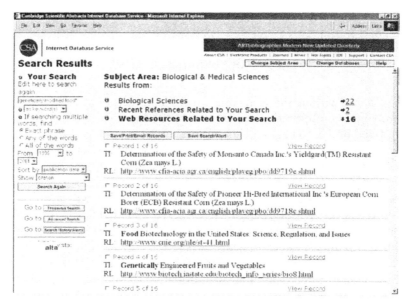

FIGURE 6. The Display After Selecting the First URL from the List of Web Resource Results. Notice that the Original Result List Is Preserved in the Frame at the Upper-Right to Facilitate Review of the Sites Retrieved.

CONCLUSION

Bibliographic databases continue to serve as vital resource identification tools that facilitate access to complete fulltext documents. A&I publishers provide a necessary added value that enhances research and makes it more efficient, and recognize the need to enhance services in order to accommodate the needs of researchers. It is the needs of researchers that have inspired CSA to provide delivery of publications via the Internet, to find the most seamless way to link from citation to fulltext, and to develop new products such as the *Web Resources Database* that take advantage of new information sources. Failing to do so, bibliographic publishing may indeed experience the fate of buggy-whip manufacturing.

Improving Access to E-Journals
and Databases at the MIT Libraries:
Building a Database-Backed Web Site
Called "Vera"

Nicole Hennig

SUMMARY. The MIT Libraries provide access to databases and electronic journals via the online catalog and the Web. The Vera database was created in order to improve public access to a growing number of resources listed on Web pages and also to help the staff more easily maintain these pages. Details of the database, called "Vera" (Virtual Electronic Resource Access), are described, including field definitions and how the database is used by both staff and public. The development of the database helped to improve access and made it easier to maintain a growing number of resources. It has also led to many further questions and discussions among the staff of the MIT Libraries about the scope of the OPAC and how tools like Vera should be related to it. *[Article copies available for a fee from The Haworth Document Delivery Service: 1-800-HAWORTH. E-mail address: <getinfo@ haworthpressinc.com> Website: <http://www.HaworthPress.com>]*

Nicole Hennig is Web Manager at the MIT Libraries, Building 10-500, 77 Massachusetts Avenue, Cambridge, MA 02139-4307 (E-mail: hennig@mit.edu).

The author would like to thank Wayne Jones for providing information about serials cataloging practices and for reading drafts of this article.

[Haworth co-indexing entry note]: "Improving Access to E-Journals and Databases at the MIT Libraries: Building a Database-Backed Web Site Called 'Vera'." Hennig, Nicole. Co-published simultaneously in *The Serials Librarian* (The Haworth Information Press, an imprint of The Haworth Press, Inc.) Vol. 41, No. 3/4, 2002, pp. 227-254; and: *E-Serials Cataloging: Access to Continuing and Integrating Resources via the Catalog and the Web* (ed: Jim Cole, and Wayne Jones) The Haworth Information Press, an imprint of The Haworth Press, Inc., 2002, pp. 227-254. Single or multiple copies of this article are available for a fee from The Haworth Document Delivery Service [1-800-HAWORTH, 9:00 a.m. - 5:00 p.m. (EST). E-mail address: getinfo@haworthpressinc.com].

KEYWORDS. Database, electronic journals, Web interface

INTRODUCTION

Like so many academic libraries, the MIT Libraries provide access to both licensed and freely available e-journals and databases via an online catalog and via pages on a Web site. The catalog access is part of a well-established practice whereby cataloging departments create bibliographic records for items which the library owns or licenses, and adds those records to an integrated library system whose design and search mechanisms have been purchased from a commercial vendor. The Web access is something much newer: a way of providing quick access to full-text content of thousands of titles, by listing them on Web pages, backed by a home-grown database.

The MIT Libraries' Web access to its e-journals and databases did not always have the look and functionality which it does now. The current system, which we call Vera,[1] is the product of nine months of work by the Libraries' Web Manager and the Web Advisory Group in consultation with a wide range of staff throughout the Libraries.[2] Before Vera, the Libraries' lists of electronic resources were simple Web pages generated by Perl scripts. Our staff called this tool the "list-builder." For a sample from a Web listing of e-journals, see Figure 1.

The pages themselves were simple alphabetical lists. E-journals were listed by title only and databases were listed by subject and title on separate pages. The program used to build these pages (accessed through a Web form) was slow and frustrating to use because every time a staff member made a single change to any one title, he or she would have to first remember which pages contained that title, and then make the program rebuild all the pages that contained it. In some cases it could take ten minutes or more to change one URL. In addition, the program would fail to build the pages completely from time to time, and no one on our staff was able to completely solve this problem, so we had to run the program again to get a complete set of updated pages.

In March of 1999 we conducted some usability tests[3] of our Web site, including some of these pages. In addition to giving users specific tasks and asking them to think out loud while navigating the site, we included a brief survey. One of our main findings from the survey was that many of our users considered our lists of databases and e-journals to be the most valuable and useful content on our web site. At the same time, our usability test findings showed us that these pages were difficult to find and difficult to use.

In order to find a solution to both the public interface problems and our staff maintenance problems, we decided that this system of generating pages needed

FIGURE 1. Web Page Produced by the "List-Builder"

D Dalton Transactions
Data and Knowledge Engineering
Demography (JSTOR)
Development
Development Genes and Evolution (Springer LINK) (free trial for 1998)
Developmental Biology
Developmental Review
Diacritics (Project Muse)
Differentiation : Research in Biological Diversity (Springer LINK) (free trial for 1998)
Digital Signal Processing: A Review Journal
Discrete & Computational Geometry
Distributed Computing

E Earth surface processes and landforms
Earthquake engineering and structural dynamics
Ecological Applications (JSTOR)
Ecological Monographs (JSTOR)
Ecology (JSTOR)
Econometric Theory (Must register at logon screen)
Econometrica: Journal of the Econometric Society (JSTOR)
Economic Journal (JSTOR)
Economic Theory (Springer LINK) (free trial for 1998)
Ecotoxicology and Environmental Safety
Eighteenth-Century Life (Project Muse)
Eighteenth-Century Studies (Project Muse)
Electronic Journal of Communication
Electronic Research Announcements of the American Mathematical Society
Electronics & Communication Engineering Journal (IEEE/IEE Electronic Library Online)
Electronics Letters (IEEE/IEE Electronic Library Online)
ELH (English Literary History) (Project Muse)

to be replaced, and that a database-backed Web site was the way to go. After exploring various options, we chose FileMaker Pro as the database software. We did this for several reasons: MIT has a site license for the software and there is expertise and experience on the staff in using it. FileMaker also has built-in Web capability and it is easy for non-programming staff to maintain in the long run. We did not want to end up with a system that only a chosen few understood, as had happened previously.

From both the public view and the staff view, Vera has developed into something much more than the simple improvement to the public interface which we originally envisioned. Our staff now use it to track licenses, to manage URLs, and to interact with our proxy server–among many other functions, which are discussed below–but the main focus has always been on designing a better interface and access for our users.

Vera is not meant as a substitute for our online catalog, but rather as a complement to it. All of our e-journals and most of our databases are also cataloged in the OPAC. There are some things Vera does better than our current catalog (called Barton), and vice versa (see Table 1).

TABLE 1. Comparison of Vera and Barton

Vera: Web Database	Barton: OPAC (a GEAC Advance System)
broad subject access to e-resources (approximately 65 subjects)	specific subject access (Library of Congress Subject Headings)
highly configurable screen design (allowing us to create simple, user-friendly layouts)	screen design configurable within certain limits, based on our OPAC software
brief descriptions of each database	brief descriptions available for some databases (in the full record view)
simple lists of titles with their coverage dates, making it easier to scan the list and select the appropriate title	must view the full record to see dates and publishers
icons showing off-campus availability, classes offered, donors, additional licensing information, and help screens	no indication of whether the resource is available off-campus
dynamic URLs; easy to update groups of URLs automatically, depending on various conditions in the database	usually only one URL, sometimes two; must view the full record to see it; each URL must be updated one at a time
license management fields	no license management information
lacks integration with print versions of journals	print and electronic versions are well integrated and often are found next to each other in the same search results set
includes a small number of cross-references	many more cross-references and access points for each title
lacks authority control[4]	authority control

In the sections below, there are more details about how Vera works, how it looks, and how and why we made certain decisions about its design. We will demonstrate not so much how to build a FileMaker Pro database, but the rationale and logic which could go into using *any* database program to build a Web-based e-resource listing.

VERA ON THE WEB: THE PUBLIC INTERFACE

The Vera database is used to create the public Web pages where users access the more than 200 databases and 2,800 e-journals (as of May 2001) to which the MIT Libraries have access. Strictly speaking, the letters of the name stand for *Virtual Electronic Resource Access*, but that is really just a convenient retro-fitted expansion. Giving the database a name (just as we named our OPAC) has proven very useful both for publicizing it and for instructing our users on what it is. "Vera" is often the way users refer to it at the reference desk when they have questions.

The process of inventing a new system gave us the opportunity to include features that we wish were included in our OPAC. We began with the users' needs, added our staff's needs (for maintaining licensing information), and worked up to designing a system, rather than trying to make an existing system more user-friendly. See Figure 2 for the home page of Vera.

This page illustrates some of the organizational and design decisions we made. After looking at examples of how other libraries designed their Web listings of electronic resources, we noticed that some provided access to databases and e-journals on entirely different sets of pages. We decided, instead, to

FIGURE 2. Vera's Home Page

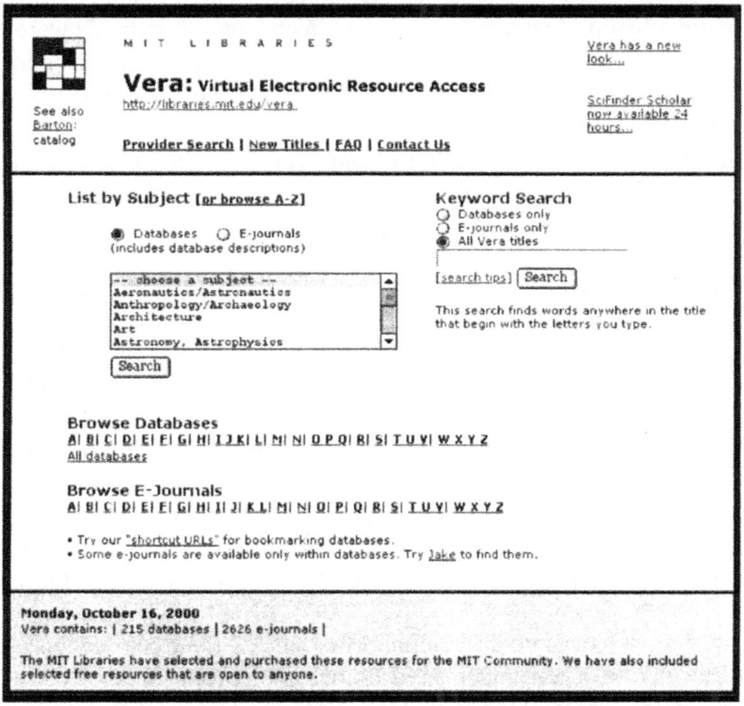

provide users with "one-stop shopping" for both databases and e-journals. This is partly because we feel that in many cases the distinction between the two is irrelevant and unknown to users, and partly because the distinction between the two is shifting in the publishing world.[5] The fact that users don't understand what is meant by "databases" or "e-journals" was confirmed in some usability tests we did.[6] This screen gives users the option to limit their search to databases or to e-journals, but the default is to search both, since most users will use the default settings.

Titles in Vera can be found by the following methods:

- selecting a subject from a menu (broad subjects)
- alphabetical browsing of titles
- keywords searching of titles
- selecting the name of the provider (such as JSTOR) from a menu (on a separate screen, because it's a lesser-used feature)

The categorization of e-journals by subject is a major change from our former simple listing. In our previous set of Web pages, e-journals were accessible only by a very long alphabetical list–only databases were categorized by subject. A question often asked by users was, "what e-journals are available for computer science (or any broad subject)?" That's not an easy question to answer using the OPAC, which uses only very specific LC subject headings. Vera solves this by adding broad subject categories for listing e-journals and databases.

Browsing by Subject

To create our list of subjects we started with a list of about forty topics that we were using for databases. We analyzed them, reworded some, and ended up with about sixty-five subjects which are used in the current version of Vera. This was done by reference and collection librarians who had a good sense of what our users were looking for. Our goal was to keep them broad (e.g., Physics) but to have fairly specific subjects when the needs of the MIT users demanded them (e.g., Chemical Engineering, Civil Engineering, Electrical Engineering, Mechanical Engineering, Nuclear Engineering, Ocean Engineering).

The Vera subjects are a flat alphabetical list, with no hierarchies. Any title in Vera may be listed under any number of appropriate subjects. Figure 3 shows the first screen of the result set for the search of databases under the subject "Aeronautics/Astronautics."

FIGURE 3. Subject Results Screen for Databases

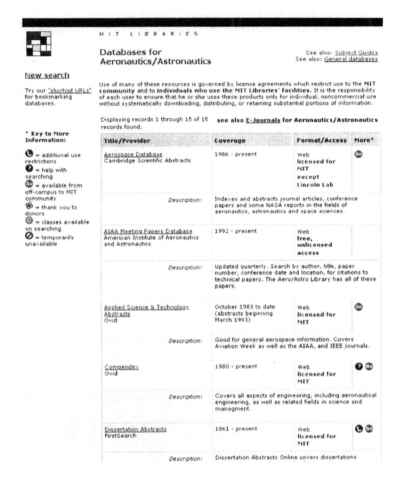

The results screen (see Figure 4) includes:

- title (hyperlinked to the entrance of the product)
- coverage dates
- format: "Web," "CD-ROM," "local software," or "client software needed"
- restrictions: "licensed for MIT" or "free, unlicensed access"
- icons indicating which titles are available from off-campus (the "Go" button)

- icons for some other hyperlinked bits of information (explained later in this article)
- statement about the user's responsibilities and licensing restrictions

In addition to the specific results, there are also cross-reference links to e-journals on the same subject, a link to "General databases," and a link to the Libraries' list of Web pages called "subject guides" compiled by our subject selectors. The subject guides, for example, often contain links to additional resources which are not listed in Vera.[7]

The subject results screen for e-journals is the same, except without the descriptions. We use a different color stripe across the top of the results table for e-journals as a visual cue to users that they are viewing a different type of results set.

Browsing by Title

Browsing by title yields the same form of results as does searching by subject, except that the description is omitted. This is because we wanted to provide the quickest way in to a title for users who already know what they are looking for. We are assuming that if a user is familiar with a particular resource

FIGURE 4. E-Journal Subject Results Screen

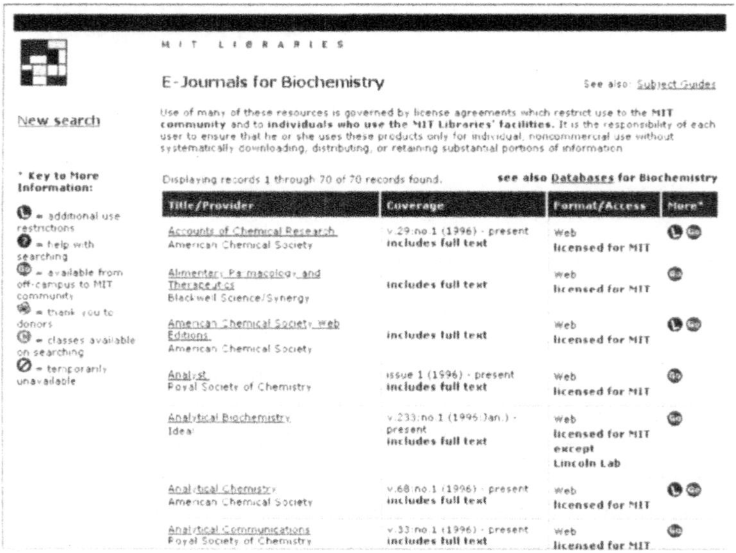

enough to search for a specific title, then he or she doesn't need to see the description every time. (For typical results from a title search of databases, see Figure 5.)

Other General Features

Following are some of the other main features of the Vera Web interface:

- *Access.* We use three categories: licensed for MIT, on-site access only, and free, unlicensed access.[8]
- *Coverage dates.* Coverage dates are provided for both databases and e-journals in Vera. Those for databases are input manually (since they often require a sentence or two to explain),[9] but those for e-journals are imported once a month from the summary holdings information in the serial records from our OPAC. Each Vera record has a unique ID number. At the beginning of the project we decided to add these to a MARC 035 field in the local serials catalog records, and they are used as the match point between those records and the records in the FileMaker Pro database. Catalogers now routinely add this "Vera ID number" to the MARC record whenever they catalog a new e-journal.
- *Feedback form.* Users may send comments to our Web Advisory Group using this form. The comments tend to fall into three categories: access problems and technical difficulties, comments or suggestions about the interface, and suggestions for purchases of new titles (we've added a link to our general "suggested purchases" form for these).
- *Shortcut URLs.* These are a kind of persistent URL which we have created for all of the databases in Vera. They are of the form http://libraries. mit.edu/get/, followed by an abbreviation of the particular database (for example, http://libraries.mit.edu/get/webofsci for *Web of Science*). The purposes are: (1) to give users an easy-to-remember URL which will always be functional; (2) to have a short and unchanging URL to use on printed brochures and publications; and (3) to have a URL that can be used on the other pages of our Web site when a database is cited and linked to (saving us the work of updating these URLs in multiple locations). This is controlled by an ".htaccess" file on the Libraries' main Web server. We use the Vera database to generate this file for uploading to the main server. Figure 6 is a sample of what the users see on our "shortcut URLs" screen.
- *Icons for further information.* There are icon links leading the user to: information about restrictions on use; help with searching (usually pages created by MIT librarians); to indicate which titles are available from off-campus access via our proxy server; information about a donor who

paid for the resource; information about classes which we offer on searching the resource; and an indication that the resource is temporarily unavailable. Each icon is a hyperlink to that additional bit of information (See Figure 7).

Other features in Vera include a "Frequently Asked Questions" page, a dynamically updated counter displaying the number of titles Vera contains, a "new titles" link to resources added in several time periods from the past two weeks to the past six months, and a "new" icon which automatically appears next to each title for two weeks after its creation date. We have also included a link to information about the "Jake" project in order to help our users find titles that are "hidden" within database packages.[10]

VERA: THE STAFF INTERFACE

For maintaining the database, the staff access Vera via one of two methods: through FileMaker Pro on the network, or through Web screens de-

FIGURE 5. Title Browse Screen for Databases

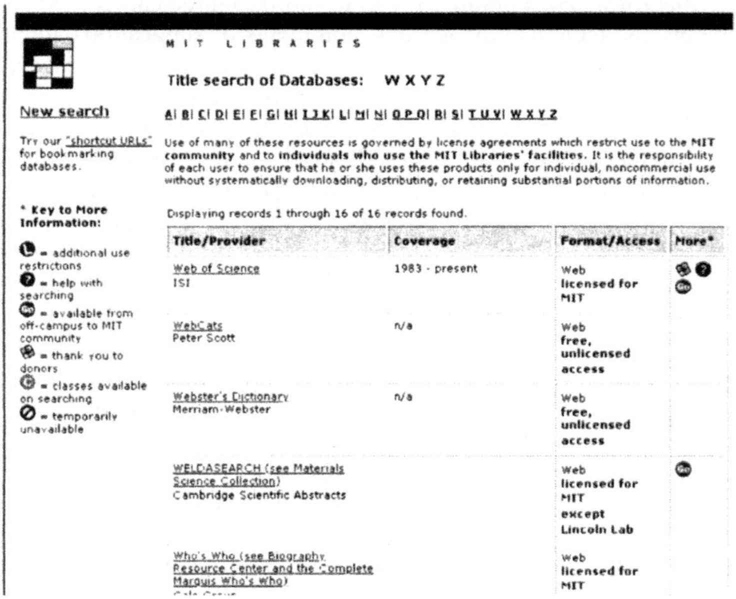

FIGURE 6. Shortcut URLs

Books24x7.com

http://libraries.mit.edu/get/books24x7 [Go]

Boston Library Consortium Web Gateway

http://libraries.mit.edu/get/blc-web

Britannica Online

http://libraries.mit.edu/get/britannica

Brown University Women Writers Project

http://libraries.mit.edu/get/wwp

Burndy Library

http://libraries.mit.edu/get/burndy

Business and Industry

http://libraries.mit.edu/get/bus-ind [Go]

CenStats

http://libraries.mit.edu/get/censtats

FIGURE 7. Key to Icons

* Key to More Information:

🔵 = additional use restrictions

❓ = help with searching

🟢 = available from off-campus to MIT community

🎁 = thank you to donors

🔵 = classes available on searching

🚫 = temporarily unavailable

signed for administrative purposes. Since we have one staff person who handles most of the data entry (our Digital Resources Acquisitions Librarian), we use FileMaker on the network for the majority of the staff work. This allows us to take full advantage of all the database features, such as global find and replace, without having to program it all into a Web interface.

We have another small group of staff, called "Vera Contacts," who do some additional data entry. This group is made up of six people who represent our larger group of about thirty subject selectors. For this group we've created a Web interface for data entry. Through their "Vera contact" the subject selectors may add and remove existing Vera titles from their subject lists, change or enhance the database descriptions written by our Digital Resources Acquisitions Librarian, and enter new titles that are "free & unlicensed." We chose six people to represent the selectors so that there would be fewer people to train in consistent methods of data entry.

See Figure 8 for an example of the staff Web interface used by our Vera Contacts for adding and removing titles from subject lists in Vera. Figure 9 is an example of the main screen used by our Digital Resources Acquisitions Librarian for data entry within FileMaker Pro.

FIGURE 8. Vera Staff Web Interface–Adding and Removing Subjects

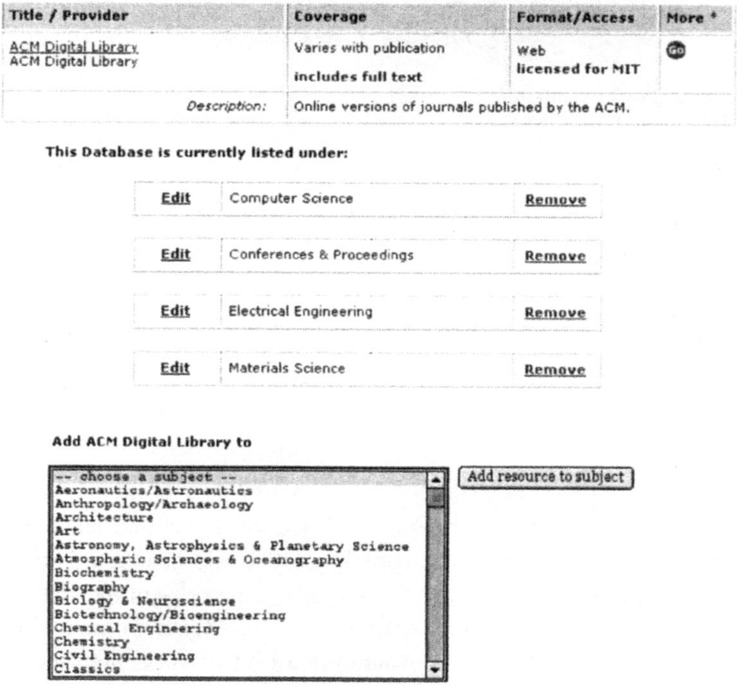

FIGURE 9. Vera Staff Interface in FileMaker Pro

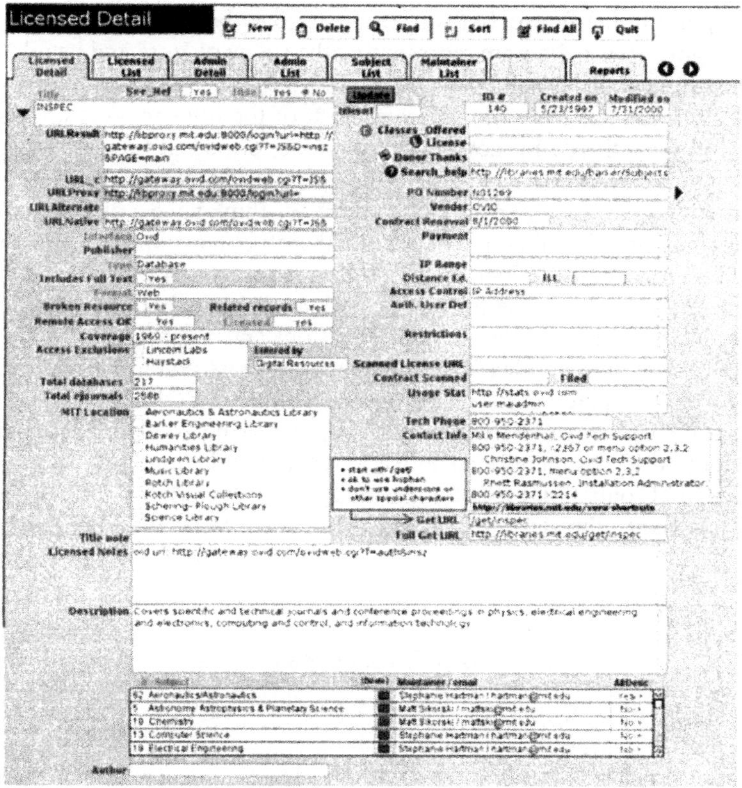

The Scope of Vera

We had many discussions on what the scope of the Vera database should be and finally agreed that free and unlicensed titles should be included (rather than segregating them on other pages just because they are free), but also agreed that we would be very selective and include only the most important free titles for each subject (decisions are left up to each subject selector). We did this to avoid making it hard to find our licensed resources in the middle of extremely long lists of free titles.[11]

We also continue to maintain a set of Web pages we call "subject guides" (http://libraries.mit.edu/subjects/). These are the usual bibliographies or "pathfinders" of Web sites and other materials that most libraries offer. They are a place where selectors can list many additional free, unlicensed resources that we don't list in Vera. This is a "working decision" that we will revisit at some point in the future, but so far our sense is that the decision was a good one. Figure 10 is a diagram representing the scope of Vera and its relationship to the "subject pages" and our OPAC (Barton).

As you can see from the diagram, most of the titles in Vera are also cataloged in our OPAC. In fact, every individual e-journal (in a non-aggregator package) is cataloged in our OPAC under its individual title, but there are catalog records for only those packages which we think have a distinctive enough name that might be known to a user and therefore a means by which he or she might search for titles. For example, there are records for *JSTOR* and the *ACM Digital Library*, but none for the "American Chemical Society Publications" (Vera includes records for all individual titles and all packages).

Individual journal titles from aggregator databases such as *ProQuest Direct* and *Lexis-Nexis* are not listed separately in either our OPAC or in Vera, since their content changes so frequently. (We point to the Jake project to help users find these titles, as mentioned above.) Free and unlicensed titles are cataloged in the OPAC only if the selector has made a specific request for the cataloging. Like so many libraries, we are struggling with what the true scope of our

FIGURE 10. Scope of Vera

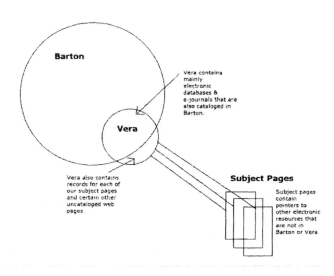

OPAC should be, especially now that we have another tool (Vera) that serves as a primary entry point for our users of electronic resources.

A question that we are considering is, why are we doing double entry into two databases (Vera and our OPAC) for most of our electronic resources? The current situation is the result of migrating from simple lists of our titles on Web pages, to a complex database for handling them. We are still looking at ways to save work and one step we have taken is to import the e-journal coverage dates from our OPAC into Vera monthly. However, it's not easy to do this for all the information, because we have different rules for when and how we list a title in the OPAC versus Vera. For example, sometimes the cataloging rules and CONSER standards demand two or more records for titles which are more conveniently listed under just one title (and one ID number) in Vera. And sometimes the opposite is true: there are two records in Vera for a single, authoritative record in the OPAC. In either of these cases, it is not possible to import the coverage dates from the e-journal record into Vera because there is no one-to-one match on the Vera ID numbers. Instead, we add the coverage dates manually, just as we do for all the databases.

So far, the advantages of having a custom database that integrates licensing information with titles and the Web display have made it worthwhile to enter items in two databases. The extreme flexibility of Vera allows us to do things not possible in our catalog records, such as allowing us to respond quickly to our users' need for which information is displayed and how it should be displayed. It is also very useful to have the data entry of the item happen at the time of ordering it, so that as soon as the license is settled, we can give our users access (since there is no physical item to be received). We are in the process of migrating to a new system for our OPAC (GEAC to Ex Libris) and we hope that our new implementation will be much more flexible than the old. So the future of Vera and its relationship to our OPAC remains under discussion.

Database Fields: Detailed Descriptions

The Web interface of Vera for the public looks simple, but it is backed by a relational database containing a wealth of additional information which is used and managed by several Libraries' staff members. The database contains four files:

- *maintainers:* This file contains the names of the six Vera Contacts who each maintain several subjects, doing the data entry for selectors. The maintainer file contains his/her name, e-mail, and the subjects he/she manages.
- *resources:* This is the main file, containing a record for each title; see below for descriptions of the various fields for each resource.

- *subjects:* The subject file contains the name of the subject, a unique ID number, and the maintainer's name.
- *rs items:* This file brings together resources and subjects. A record is created for each instance of a title associated with a subject. A resource can be listed under as many subjects as apply.

Figure 11 illustrates the various relationships among the files.

In order to come up with the fields we use in Vera, we began by looking at the Dublin Core metadata elements (http://dublincore.org/documents/dces/). This was useful especially for the concepts of "format" and "type." There were many more specific things we wanted to track, and so we added many additional fields.

Each of the fields used in the Vera records for e-resources is described below:

Title: Text field. Used for entering the title of the resource. We generally use the form of the title that users know, which is sometimes a little different than the title that gets entered in our OPAC according to strict cataloging rules.

Title note: Text field. A place to enter additional title information that we would like to appear on the public Web screens after the title. For example: "Be sure to log off by pressing the 'exit' button on the bar at the top left of the screen. Our license allows only a few simultaneous users."

FIGURE 11. Database Structure

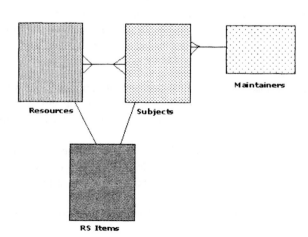

Resources   Subjects   Maintainers

RS Items

"Dynamic URL management": This is a phrase we use to describe the interaction of the next few fields described below.

> *URL native:* Text field. The original URL given to us by the vendor. Does not display on public Web screens, but is used in calculations described below.

> *URL alternate:* Text field. An alternate URL that we use in some cases instead of the native URL. This is used for items that are password-protected and go through a special script on our end. Does not display on public Web screens, but is used in calculations described below. For example: http://libsys.mit.edu/dbs/linkit?econlit.

> *URL proxy:* Global field. This is a string that we must put in front of the URL in order to send the user through our proxy server (for off-campus access).[12] It looks like this: http://libproxy.mit.edu:8000/login?url=. It does not display on public Web screens, but is used in calculations described below.

> *URL calculated:* Calculation field. Checks to see if the URL alternate field mentioned above has something in it. If so, it gets entered here for use by another calculation (see URL result). If the URL alternate field is empty, the URL native field contents get entered here for use by the next calculation (URL result). Does not display on public Web screens, but is used in calculations described below.

> *URL result:* Calculation field. This field checks five other fields described below. If conditions are right, then it appends the contents of the URL proxy field to the front of the URL in the URL calculated field.

The logic is this (fields mentioned here are fully described later in this article):

if

SystemOK = "yes" and ProxyUp = "yes" and Access_Remote = "yes" and

Licensed = "yes" and Access_Control = "IP Address"

then

append the contents of the "URL proxy" field to the front of the URL in

"URL calculated."

Otherwise, it copies the contents of the "URL calculated" field. This is an example of a URL result:

http://libproxy.mit.edu:8000/login?url=http://gateway.ovid.com/ovidweb.cgi?T=J

S&D=wast&PAGE=main

In plain English, that means that if our system is OK (meaning our systems person has configured it for that title), and our proxy server is up and running normally, and remote access is allowed in our contract with the vendor, and it's a licensed title (rather than a free, unlicensed title), and access is controlled by IP address rather than by password, then we want our proxy server URL string to be appended to the beginning of the URL.

This is the only field of the five URL fields that displays to the user, and even then we don't show the actual long, complex URL. Instead we hyperlink the title to go to that URL when clicked.

We call this set of five URL fields and the five additional fields involved in the logic behind them "dynamic URL management." The great thing about it is that it allows us to easily change the URL or a whole group of URLs as needed. For example, if our proxy server is malfunctioning, we can set the global "proxy up" field to "no" and then instantly all the URLs that previously had the proxy string appended to them will no longer have it, thereby allowing us not to interrupt access for our users who are on campus, while we troubleshoot the proxy problem.

Or, for another example, if we have recently negotiated with a vendor to allow off-campus access, but haven't configured the proxy server for it yet, our Digital Resources Acquisitions Librarian can set the "remote access OK" field to yes. The "system OK" will remain on "no" by default until our Systems Librarian has had a chance to configure it. Then he sets "system OK" to "yes" and the URL changes automatically.

Publisher, interface, and vendor: "Publisher" describes the publisher of the information, "Interface" describes the name of the interface, and "Vendor" describes who we purchase it from. In some cases one, two, or all three of these are the same, and in some cases they are different.

For example, for *Journal of Health Politics, Policy and Law,* Duke University Press is the publisher, Project Muse is the interface, and Johns Hopkins University Press is the vendor. Vendor is for our internal use and does not display on the public Web screens.

The public Web screens are set up so that the contents of the interface field displays, unless there is no named interface, in which case the publisher displays. Interface is a selection menu, and we add an "interface" name to this menu each time we get a new group of records from one provider that use the same Web search interface.

In designing this, we wanted to be able to decide on a case-by-case basis whether to show the publisher or the interface to the public–this allows us to do that, while still keeping all the detailed information in the database behind the scenes for our own use.

On the public Web screens, we call this concept "Provider." It appears under each title on all the results screens, and also the contents of the Interface field is used to make a menu for the user to select from on our "provider" search screen (see Figure 12).

Format: Text menu containing four choices: Web, CD-ROM, client software needed (*SciFinder Scholar*, for example, requires users to download and install software on their PC or Mac), local software (*Datastream*, for example, is available only on certain PCs in one of our libraries).

Type: Text menu containing four choices: database, e-journal, e-book, other. Only database and e-journal are used currently. When we built the database we had several discussions about which types we should include and considered long lists of types, such as "indexes & abstracts," "directories," "e-books." We then realized that we would need to spend time deciding which category some things belong to, since the boundaries are changing. We also realized from our usability testing that users don't make these kinds of distinctions. If they do make distinctions, they are not the same ones we as librarians think of. So we decided to keep it simple and just use the broadest division, "databases" and "e-journals."

Even with just those two categories, we will from time to time list an item as both a database and an e-journal, when a subject selector feels it is very important for users to see it in both lists. Usually this happens when for a large pack-

FIGURE 12. Provider Search Selection Menu

Search by Selected Provider

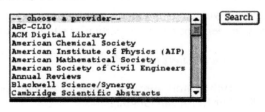

age of e-journals, such as *"ScienceDirect (Elsevier),"* we are listing each e-journal individually (under e-journals) and also making a listing for the package as a whole (once under databases and once under e-journals). We do this only if we have access to all or almost all of the titles in the package and if the product provides a search across issues.

For packages of e-books, we list only the package as a whole in Vera (such as *Books24x7*), not each book title in it. A package of e-books is listed as a database. We don't use the e-books designation in this menu at this time, since we aren't listing them as individual titles.

Access control: Text menu containing three choices: IP address, password, or none. This is used to indicate how the vendor controls access to the title. Free and unlicensed titles are listed, of course, as "none." The choice in this field is used by the URL calculation fields mentioned above.

Includes full text: A check box. If checked, the phrase, "includes full text" appears on the Web screens. We've consciously chosen the word "includes" so as to accurately describe those resources in which parts but not all are full text.

Broken resource: A check box. If checked, an icon ⊘ appears after the title. This helps users see that this is a known problem with the title. Clicking on the icon links to a page where we describe the status of these problems (http://nic.mit.edu/3down/; scroll down to the "library services" section).

Coverage dates: A free-text field (not a date field). For e-journals we import the dates from our catalog, using a script that adds the word "present" to open date ranges, such as:

> v.29:no.1 (1996)-present

We added the word "present" to open date ranges, since we've had many reports from our reference staff that when users are looking at a record from our OPAC, they don't understand that a hyphen with nothing after it (e.g., "1990-") means "to the present."

For databases, we manually enter a range of years (e.g., "1990-present") or a more complete description of the particular situation, such as:

> *Anthropological Literature Index:*

> > late 19th century–present; articles 2 or more pages long in English & other European languages

Access exclusions: Checkboxes with two choices: Lincoln Lab, and Haystack Observatory. In some cases, our negotiated licenses prohibit access for these two off-site MIT departments. If checked, the phrase "except Lincoln Lab" or "except Haystack" will appear after "licensed for MIT" on the Web screens. This helps users from those departments see at a glance which titles are not available to them (a feature we never had in our old system).

Total databases and *Total e-journals:* Calculation fields. Calculates the total number of databases and e-journals, excluding "see-references" and "hide = yes" records. Appears on the Vera home page so users can see the latest count of how many titles are in the database.

Monday, October 16, 2000
Vera contains: | 215 databases | 2626 e-journals |

See-reference: Text field, a checkbox. If checked, indicates that this record is a duplicate of another record using an alternative form of the title. Allows us to display an item under alternate titles. This is sometimes used also to display an item as both a database and an e-journal.

Hide: Text field, radio buttons, "yes" or "no." If "yes," hides record from public view. By default, new records have this checked until our staff person finishes entering all the information.

Who supports: Text field, a menu. Resources are supported centrally by our Digital Resources unit, or supported locally by individual library units (in the case of some freely available titles). The menu allows selection of one of these choices.

MIT Location: Text field, checkboxes. This is used when a product requires the user to be on campus in one or more of our libraries (CD-ROMs and local software). It's a list of libraries with a checkbox in front of each. This is an example of what appears on the Web:

CD-ROM
Dewey Library
on-site access only

Author: Text field. This field is not yet used. At the time of creating Vera we defined it with the idea that in the future we might want to list items that have a personal author, such as an electronic book.

Licensed notes: Text field. This field is used by our Digital Resources Acquisitions Librarian. It does not display publicly. It's a text field for general notes.

Description: Text field. A brief description for each database (we don't write them for e-journals) is written by our Digital Resources Acquisitions Librarian. This can be modified later by a subject selector, through the staff Web interface.

Subject: Text selection menu. A menu containing our list of about sixty-five broad subjects. This is a FileMaker "portal" to the RS-items file which contains a record for each instance of a title being assigned to a subject. We assign as many subjects as apply.

Alt description: Text field. A subject selector may choose to have an alternate description, different from the standard one, associated with the title as it is listed under his or her subject. For example, *Lexis-Nexis* has a slightly different description when it's listed under Law than when it's listed under Business & Management.

Vera ID number: Number field. Automatically generated unique ID number.

Created on: Date field. Auto-generated creation date of the record.

Date modified: Date field. Auto-generated modification date of the record.

Classes offered: Text field. A URL for information about classes offered by our library staff on how to use the resource. The icon ● will appear on the Web and link to this URL.

License: Text field. A URL for additional licensing information. The icon ● will appear on the Web and link to this URL. For example, the fact that *SciFinder Scholar* limits downloads to 5,000 records appears in this field.

Donor thanks: Text field. A URL for a page thanking the donor of a particular title. The icon ● will appear on the Web and link to this URL.

Search help: Text field. A URL for help pages created by our staff, or sometimes by a vendor. The icon ● will appear on the Web and link to this URL.

PO number: Alpha-numeric field. The purchase order number and a link to another FileMaker database we use to manage purchase information.

Contract renewal: Date field. The date the contract comes up for renewal.

Payment: Text field. Used by the Digital Resources Acquisitions Librarian to record additional information about payments.

IP range: Text field. The range of IP addresses on our campus to which the resource is available. Many vendors use this method to control access to the products.

Distance ed: Menu selection: yes or no. Does the vendor allow the resource to be used for distance-education purposes? Used to generate reports for our staff on the Web.

ILL: Menu selection: yes or no. Does the vendor allow the resource to be used to supply interlibrary loans? Used to generate reports for our staff on the Web.

Authorized user definition: Text field. Used for special descriptions of authorized users if we have not been able to negotiate our standard MIT definition.

Restrictions: Text field. Used to describe restrictions on interlibrary loan and other restrictions, such as simultaneous user limits.

Scanned license URL: Text field. A URL for a link to the PDF version of the license contract. Used by our Digital Resources Acquisitions Librarian (not for public use).

Contract scanned: Date field. Date the contract was scanned into a PDF file.

Contract filed: Date field. Date the contract was filed in our paper files.

Usage statistics: Text field. Information on how to obtain the usage statistics for the resource. Used in a report for staff.

Tech phone: Text field. Vendor phone numbers to call for technical help. Used to generate reports for our staff on the Web.

Contact info: Text field. Used for additional contact information, such as names of tech support staff at the vendor site, alternate phone numbers, etc. Used to generate reports for our staff on the Web.

Get URL: A "shortcut" URL that we've created for each database (described above). For example: http://libraries.mit.edu/get/ulrichs. This field is used to generate a report that contains the ".htaccess" file for uploading to our main Web server (not the FileMaker server). It lists all the shortcut URLs and which full URLs they should point to.

REPORTS IN VERA

A big advantage of using a database to track all of this information is that we can easily create many different reports for staff use. Our Digital Resources Acquisitions Librarian, Systems Librarian, and Web Manager use the following reports available within the FileMaker database (not on the Web):

- *access exceptions:* shows which titles are not allowed for Lincoln Lab and Haystack Observatory
- *export "get URLs":* used by the Web Manager to generate the ".htaccess" file for shortcut URLs described above
- *titles entered since . . . :* by date
- *no subjects:* shows titles that don't have subjects attached (if any); used for quality control
- *system OK (not):* shows which titles are not yet configured for the proxy server, or don't work with our proxy server
- *titles added locally:* shows which titles have been added by staff members other than our Digital Resources Acquisitions Librarian

We also provide several reports through the Web for our staff. A few are listed below:

- vendor contact info for tech support
- list of resources that allow interlibrary loan
- titles sorted by expiration and renewal dates of their contracts
- Vera ID numbers for catalogers (for adding to catalog records so coverage dates of e-journals can later be imported to Vera from the OPAC)

Of course, with FileMaker it is very easy to generate any other kind of custom reports as needed.

SERVER MANAGEMENT

We use two Windows NT servers to run the Vera database. Since FileMaker Pro is a database, a Web server, and a CGI all rolled into one, we need no additional server software. We use FileMaker Pro version 4.1. Vera was built before version 5 was available.

One server runs the live copy and one the "working copy" of the database. Our staff connect to the working copy to make changes and updates, while the public connects to the live copy. Every night we run a script to copy the working copy over the live copy and make additional backups to another server. The advantage to this is that we can use the working copy as a testing ground for new Web screens, and also that public use won't be interrupted if there are any technical problems due to staff errors. This means that any changes we make during the day don't show up until the next day. For those few changes we want to make to the live copy (such as indicating a "broken" resource), we will from time-to-time also connect to the live copy.

CONCLUSION

The original idea was that Vera would simply be an improved public Web interface for the MIT Libraries' electronic journals and databases, but it has grown into something much more than that. It is also a working database which members of the staff use to track license agreements and to easily manage changes to large groups of titles. Vera has a flexibility which our catalog does not have, and its ease of use and simplicity are characteristics which we might want to implement in our catalogs in the future. For example, our users appreciate the broad subject access which Vera provides, and staff appreciate the time which is saved by such features as the global find and replace.

The process of creating our own database for managing our e-resources led to a number of larger discussions and learning processes.

- *User-centered design helped make the development of Vera a priority.* Conducting usability testing of our Web site helped us to understand that creating Vera should be our first priority, before working on a redesign of the rest of our Web site. It also helped us to understand what users want and need and how they view our e-resources and the use of them.
- *User-centered design also means including our staff as users.* It was very useful to consult with a broad range of our staff during the planning process. Involving our Digital Resources Acquisitions Librarian led us to include all of the license management capability. Another staff member came up with the idea of "dynamic URL management." Involving some reference staff helped us to understand what would be useful for users (since they are so familiar with how users find and use these resources).[13]

- *FileMaker Pro has the advantage of being very easy for staff to use.* FileMaker alone running on one server may not be the most speedy back end as the database grows (which it is doing very quickly!), so if we decide to keep Vera in its current form we will look into options for improving performance. However, we are very happy with our choice of FileMaker from the point of view of staff maintenance and ease of further development.
- *Vera is very popular with our users.* There is something about the simplicity of Vera from the users' point of view that has made it very popular and useful. It gives them access in a way that our OPAC doesn't. The combination of being able to scan through lists of resources by broad subject, and to see the vital information at a glance is so much easier than finding and using these titles in our OPAC. We have received many positive comments from users of Vera, both for the design of Vera and the wealth of resources it contains.
- *Vera is a complementary tool to our OPAC.* The relationships between the details of licensing information and the information that is displayed to the public is a key aspect that would make it difficult to replace Vera by providing access only through the OPAC.
- *Developing Vera has sparked many new (and old) questions about the best ways to provide access to our electronic resources.* Having such a useful complementary mode of access has led to many discussions among our staff about how we should provide access to electronic resources in the future. Some of our questions are: what is the scope of the catalog? What is the scope of Vera? What should be included in one or the other–or both? There are many difficult short-term and long-term decisions to be made and we are following with interest similar discussions throughout the library community.[14]

NOTES

1. "Vera: Virtual Electronic Resource Access," http://libraries.mit.edu/vera.

2. The Web Advisory Group of the MIT Libraries is made of up four members of the library staff and chaired by the Web Manager. The group is responsible for developing and recommending policies and standards and for coordinating the overall organization and presentation of networked resources and services. For more information, see http://macfadden.mit.edu:9500/webgroup/.

The Web Advisory Group at the time Vera was being planned was made up of Pat Flanagan, Stephanie Hartman, Wayne Jones, Marlene Manoff, and Nicole Hennig. The original Vera planning team was made up of Ellen Duranceau, Pat Flanagan, Nicole Hennig, and Joan Kolias.

3. For complete results of these usability tests, see: http://macfadden.mit.edu:9500/webgroup/usability/results/index.html.

4. For a full discussion of the value of authority control for Web resources generally, see: Barbara Tillett, "Authority Control on the Web," in *Bicentennial Conference on Bibliographic Control for the New Millennium: Confronting the Challenges of Networked Information and the Web*, http://lcweb.loc.gov/catdir/bibcontrol/tillett.html.

5. We use the term "e-journal" to mean an electronic version of a printed journal as well as a journal available only on the Web, where the primary search interface is by specific volume, issue, and table of contents. We use the term "database" to mean searchable collections of "e-journals" and monographic e-resources, such as *Lexis-Nexis* or *Dow Jones Interactive*, where the primary search interface is a search across many hundreds or thousands of different titles. We also use the "database" category in Vera as a place to put anything that is not an "e-journal": simple Web pages, links to other library catalogs, etc.

This perspective is similar to what is happening in the cataloging world, in which databases and other e-resources do not fit into the traditional *monograph* or *serial* categories, and so will be better accommodated in the proposed *integrating* category, all under the broad rubric of *continuing resources*. For more information, see: Jean Hirons, *Revising AACR2 to Accommodate Seriality: Report to the Joint Steering Committee for Revision of AACR*, http://www.nlc-bnc.ca/jsc/ser-rep0.html.

6. In addition to the usability tests mentioned in note 3, we did some informal tests of the Vera Web screens before we rolled them out. More than one user, when asked to find a specific e-journal, clicked on "databases" instead of "e-journals."

7. We use the subject guides as a place to list many additional free resources. These guides contain links back to their appropriate subject list in Vera as well. For a sample subject guide, see: http://libraries.mit.edu/guides/subjects/eecs/.

8. There are a few exceptions, which we also note on the screens. Some of our licensed resources do not allow access for certain related MIT labs or centers: Lincoln Labs, the Haystack Observatory, and the Woods Hole Oceanographic Institute.

9. Many databases require a few sentences to explain the coverage dates. For example:
Morningstar Principia Pro Plus for Mutual Funds
For data, generally 1970 (or fund inception date)–present; for commentary, 1993-present

10. Jake is a project hosted by the Cushing/Whitney Medical Library at the Yale University School of Medicine. It helps the user determine which research database indexes or contains the full text of a particular journal. For more information about Jake see: http://jake.med.yale.edu/docs/about.html and http://www.openly.com/jake/.

11. For Vera's scope statement, see: http://macfadden.mit.edu:9500/webgroup/vera/scope.html.

12. Our proxy server is called "Ezproxy" and is available from Useful Utilities at http://www.UsefulUtilities.com/.

13. In particular, several staff members contributed in the following ways: Joan Kolias (Information Technology Librarian for Collection Services) urged us to begin with Dublin Core. Ellen Duranceau (Digital Resources Acquisitions Librarian) came up with ideas for most of the licensing information fields (and more). Pat Flanagan (Reference Coordinator) contributed much of the users' point of view in the early stages. Wayne Jones (Head, Serials Cataloging Section) and Christine Moulen (Library Systems Manager) contributed in coordinating the importing of e-journal cover-

age dates from our OPAC. The idea for how we are managing URLs came from Eric Celeste, our Assistant Director for Technology Planning and Administration. And the members of our Web Advisory Group (Darcy Duke, Pat Flanagan, Stephanie Hartman, Nicole Hennig, Wayne Jones, and Marlene Manoff) contributed much in the way of user interface decisions.

14. See the Web site of the *Bicentennial Conference on Bibliographic Control for the New Millennium* for many interesting papers on these and related issues: http://lcweb.loc.gov/catdir/bibcontrol/.

The Elektronische Zeitschriftenbibliothek: A Successful Library Service for Electronic Journals in Germany

Evelinde Hutzler
Gerald Schupfner

SUMMARY. The University Library of Regensburg, Germany, has developed a special service for the use of electronic journals, called the Elektronische Zeitschriftenbibliothek (EZB). This Electronic Journals Library has been online since 1997 and is now used by 138 libraries. The participating libraries are cooperating in order to offer their users a constantly updated service of high quality. The EZB offers user-friendly access to a large number of titles. Free titles and licensed e-journals are presented within a single user interface. Each title entry offers information regarding the accessibility of full-text articles. This service is steadily growing due to the increasing number of electronic journals. Usage statistics demonstrate the service's popularity. *[Article copies available for a fee from The Haworth Document Delivery Service: 1-800-HAWORTH. E-mail address: <getinfo@haworthpressinc.com> Website: <http://www.HaworthPress.com> © 2002 by The Haworth Press, Inc. All rights reserved.]*

Dr. Evelinde Hutzler (e-mail: evelinde.hutzler@bibliothek.uni-regensburg.de) and Gerald Schupfner (e-mail: gerald.schupfner@bibliothek.uni-regensburg.de) are affiliated with the University Library of Regensburg, 93042 Regensburg, Germany.

The authors want to thank Mrs. Claudia Reisinger for her valuable help in translating the manuscript of this article.

[Haworth co-indexing entry note]: "The Elektronische Zeitschriftenbibliothek: A Successful Library Service for Electronic Journals in Germany." Hutzler, Evelinde, and Gerald Schupfner. Co-published simultaneously in *The Serials Librarian* (The Haworth Information Press, an imprint of The Haworth Press, Inc.) Vol. 41, No. 3/4, 2002, pp. 255-270; and: *E-Serials Cataloging: Access to Continuing and Integrating Resources via the Catalog and the Web* (ed: Jim Cole, and Wayne Jones) The Haworth Information Press, an imprint of The Haworth Press, Inc., 2002, pp. 255-270. Single or multiple copies of this article are available for a fee from The Haworth Document Delivery Service [1-800-HAWORTH, 9:00 a.m. - 5:00 p.m. (EST). E-mail address: getinfo@haworthpressinc.com].

KEYWORDS. Elektronische Zeitschriftenbibliothek, electronic journals, access, usage statistics, library cooperation

THE BEGINNINGS OF A SUCCESSFUL SERVICE

In 1996 the University Library of Regensburg[1] was one of the first German libraries to confront the opportunities and problems presented by electronic journals. At that time, the number of electronic journals was still quite small, amounting to some hundred titles in the fields of science and research. However, one could expect their number to grow quickly, as more and more universities and academic institutions were starting to issue journals via their Web servers and an increasing number of publishers were beginning to offer electronic editions of their print journals on the Internet.

The general conditions for a simple and effective use of this new type of publication were still unsatisfying. First of all, there was no standardized or structured access to electronic journals. Furthermore, there were no suitable models for making these publications accessible in or via libraries.

Therefore, the University Library of Regensburg took upon itself the task of filling this gap by developing a special service for electronic journals. Thus, the Electronic Journals Library, in German called the Elektronische Zeitschriftenbibliothek (EZB), came into being. From the very beginning, the main objective for creating the EZB was to facilitate the usage of electronic journals. Therefore, the focus was not on cataloguing rules but on a user-friendly presentation along with the development of user-oriented tools.

We wanted to offer a simple, standardized access platform to as many electronic scholarly journals as possible. Another important goal was to give detailed information on subscription and access conditions for each title. Free e-journals should be presented together with licensed ones under one interface. In order to achieve these goals, the EZB was designed as a database-driven service offering user-friendly browsing and search facilities, while at the same time allowing libraries to manage information about licensed titles.

The EZB has been online since 1997. Initially it was a local offering of the University Library of Regensburg. A few months later, however, it was extended to a cooperatively run service so other libraries could use it as well. During 1998, other Bavarian libraries started to join. The number of participating institutions has now grown considerably: at the time of this writing, the EZB is used by 138 libraries,[2] mostly within the German-speaking countries. All participating libraries jointly collect information on journal titles and administer the data stored in a central database maintained in Regensburg. Because of its cooperative organization, the EZB is able to keep pace with the rapid increase in electronic journals and to present a large and constantly updated collection of titles. The large number of titles and the short refresh period of data are essential for the quality of the EZB; they contribute to the popularity of this service.

WHAT DOES THE ELEKTRONISCHE ZEITSCHRIFTENBIBLIOTHEK OFFER USERS?

Our aim is to provide users of the EZB with fast, structured, and demand-specific access to electronic journals. For this reason, the titles are listed within a standardized user interface, spanning all publishers and vendors. EZB users do not need to know who publishes a certain title; rather, they use a single entry point for accessing electronic journals.

Standardized Access to Scientific and Academic Full-Text Journals

The EZB itself does not store any electronic journal content; instead, participating institutions collect bibliographic data pertaining to the journals and record them in the central database in Regensburg. The journals must be scientific or academic in nature, and their articles must be available in full-text on the Internet. Journals on the popular-science level or journals offering only tables of contents or abstracts are not included. This quite narrow selection of academic/scientific full-text journals can be considered a mark of quality of the EZB because it guarantees a quite high degree of consistency in EZB content for the user.

As of February 2001, the EZB contained approximately 8800 titles covering all subjects. The majority of these titles were electronic parallel editions of the printed product. About 900 titles were published in electronic form only. Almost 1800 journals provided free access to their full-text articles.

Table 1 shows the distribution of the EZB titles by the various subjects. Regarding the numbers, one has to bear in mind that some titles are recorded in more than one subject.

As expected, most titles are in the fields of medicine, technology and science. In the fields of social sciences and the arts, the number of e-journals is considerably lower. But some subjects, such as economics with 714 titles and psychology with 454 titles, nevertheless show a remarkable collection. Other subjects, though, are much more poorly represented.

Access Information

A traffic light symbol shows the accessibility of each title so that users always know which titles actually offer full-text access to them:

- A green light marks free e-journals.
- A yellow light denotes titles which are licensed at the respective member library; full texts can be accessed by the institutional users. An additional "readme" page shows further information concerning access and use.
- A red light stands for journals without a subscription. In these cases, full-text access is not possible. Usually, however, tables of contents and sometimes even abstracts are freely available.

TABLE 1. EZB Title Content (02-28-2001)

Subject	Number of titles
Medicine	2333
Technology	1675
Biology	1159
Chemistry and Pharmaceutics	819
Economics	749
Physics	632
Computer Science	555
Mathematics	507
Psychology	461
Sociology	428
Education Science	361
Political Science	334
Agriculture, Forestry, etc.	281
Law	279
Geology and Paleontology	266
Linguistics and Literary Studies	226
History	201
Geography	169
Philosophy	167
Ethnology	106
General Science	99
English, American Studies	90
Theology and Religious Studies	78
Sports Science	66
Art History	38
Archaeology	37
Classical Studies	30
Musicology	28
Romance Studies	24
German Studies	23
Slavonic Studies	5

The distribution of yellow and red lights depends on the institution, as each member library has a different collection of journals to which it subscribes. What users see is determined in various ways. For example, a library may pass a parameter within a link to the EZB which leads to the display of its own collection, or an institution's collection may be selected based on the IP-address of the requesting client. Additionally, users can always choose for themselves which institution's collection they want displayed.

Besides selecting a participating institution one can also opt, for instance, to have only free and licensed titles displayed for the browse and search functions (see Figure 1).

Until recently this method of marking access rights was sufficient because the number of articles available on the Internet was relatively small and a license in most cases covered access to all of them. Over the years, however, the access possibilities have become more complex. For example, some online licenses, just as print subscriptions, are canceled, or the subscription allows access only to a certain part of the electronic articles. The marking of free titles must also become more subtle, as an increasing number of journals offer only a certain portion of articles at no cost (for instance, just the current issue or, on

FIGURE 1. Display Options

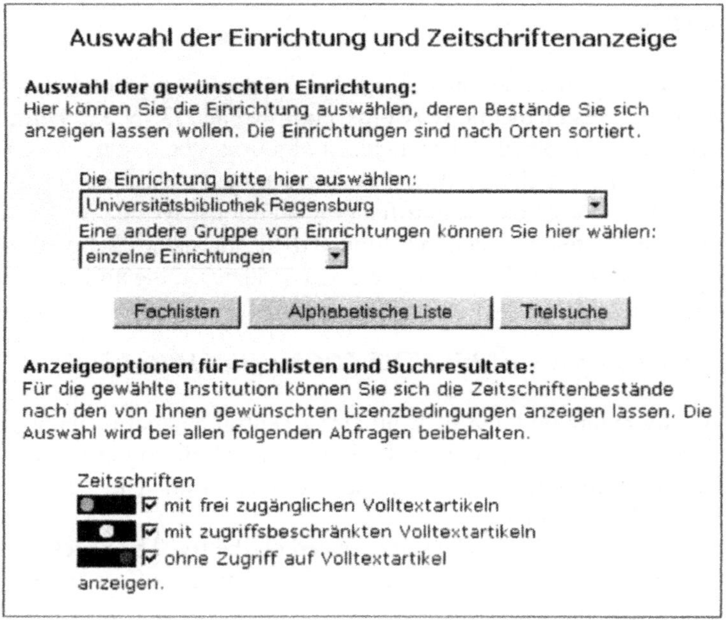

Auswahl der Einrichtung und Zeitschriftenanzeige

Auswahl der gewünschten Einrichtung:
Hier können Sie die Einrichtung auswählen, deren Bestände Sie sich anzeigen lassen wollen. Die Einrichtungen sind nach Orten sortiert.

Die Einrichtung bitte hier auswählen:
Universitätsbibliothek Regensburg
Eine andere Gruppe von Einrichtungen können Sie hier wählen:
einzelne Einrichtungen

Fachlisten   Alphabetische Liste   Titelsuche

Anzeigeoptionen für Fachlisten und Suchresultate:
Für die gewählte Institution können Sie sich die Zeitschriftenbestände nach den von Ihnen gewünschten Lizenzbedingungen anzeigen lassen. Die Auswahl wird bei allen folgenden Abfragen beibehalten.

Zeitschriften
☑ mit frei zugänglichen Volltextartikeln
☑ mit zugriffsbeschränkten Volltextartikeln
☑ ohne Zugriff auf Volltextartikel
anzeigen.

the contrary, just older volumes). In order to keep up with these trends, the University Library of Regensburg is currently extending the data format of the EZB so that one can, if necessary, split the respective titles according to the different publication periods and provide the proper access information for each. We plan to introduce multicolored traffic lights in order to mark the access rights accordingly.

At the same time, these newly developed functions can also solve the problems caused by title changes, which is most important in cases where the full texts of a journal are kept on different servers before and after a title change, with different URLs therefore leading to the articles.

Browsing Functions

The titles entered in the EZB can be displayed in alphabetical order or in subject lists. A list of all subjects gives the basic information on all e-journals, showing how many titles are available in each category. The individual subject lists show the journal titles in alphabetical order (see Figure 2).

A click on the journal title leads directly to the journal homepage, and if it is on subscription, one can access the full-text articles. A little information symbol "i" leads to the bibliographic data of each title. The licensed titles have an additional "readme" link, where the user can find library-specific access information.

Search Functions

In addition to browsing, one can also search for a particular journal title. The EZB allows users to search by title keywords, publisher and ISSN. Furthermore, the user can create a combined alphabetical list of journals belonging to various selected subjects. The search can, if desired, be restricted to just free and/or licensed titles, and the user can search for new additions by means of a date search. At present, the search function is limited to the journal level, but we plan to extend it to the article level; this will be discussed later in the article.

THE EZB AS AN EFFICIENT TOOL FOR LIBRARIES

As previously mentioned, the EZB utilizes a central database[3] maintained in Regensburg. This database contains both the general bibliographic journal data and the license information of each member institution. The data are administered via WWW forms.

For each request, EZB Web pages are created on the fly. The pages sent in reply reflect the current status of the database. This concept offers significant advantages for the member institutions.

FIGURE 2. Part of the Subject List Psychology

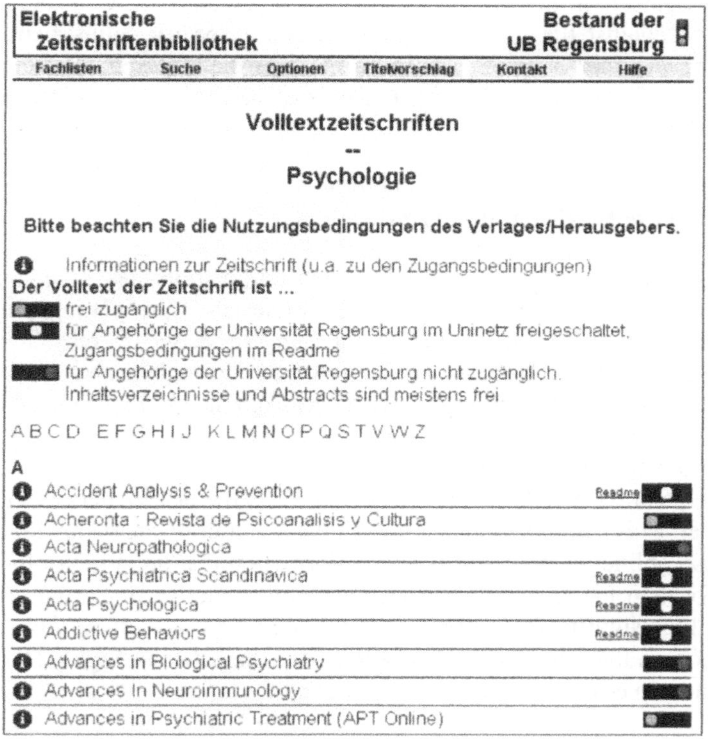

Cooperative Maintenance of Bibliographic Data

The content of the EZB is built and maintained collaboratively by all 138 participating libraries. For this purpose, all partners appoint local administrators who are given permission to enter and update bibliographic data in the central database. This cooperative structure minimizes local efforts and facilitates a constant enlargement and updating of the service.

Data maintenance is particularly labor-intensive. For example, the Internet addresses of the e-journals have to be updated at regular intervals to guarantee the quality of the data. To do this, an automatic link-checker reviews the addresses of the catalogued journals. The resulting error list is handled cooperatively. The number of inactive links is thus kept to a minimum in a very efficient manner. It is also quite tedious to update access information concerning free e-journals. Contrary to link changes, access modifications cannot be verified automatically. The fact that a formerly freely available journal has become subject to license may be brought to our attention by users, but it must be checked against the journal homepage, and a specific adjustment must be made to the access status. The more libraries that participate in the maintenance of this information, the better we can verify the access information of free titles in the long term.

Administration of License Information
Through the Participating Libraries

The EZB allows a decentralized license administration and the inclusion of individual access information for licensed journals. Each participating library can enter its own license information for each journal title, thereby changing the color of the title's traffic light. The data entered may include an optional, special URL that allows full-text access if it differs from the journal's homepage. Consortia of several libraries can administer their shared licenses in a central place. All these administrative tasks are performed via Web-based forms.

The local EZB displays are created based on the license data of a particular member. This means that all users in a given institution are being directed only to those online journals and license information that are accessible and relevant for their locality. The displays created for other participating institutions might look significantly different even though they are derived from the same data pool in the same database system. Thus the EZB is a highly flexible system and can easily be adapted to local conditions.

Statistical Functions

All accesses to the EZB site and all clicks on journal titles are logged into the database. They allow detailed library-specific access statistics and provide useful information for further license agreements. Moreover, we can analyze user behavior in detail and thus obtain valuable ideas concerning further developments of the EZB. Usage statistics will be discussed later in this article.

INTEGRATION
OF THE ELEKTRONISCHE ZEITSCHRIFTENBIBLIOTHEK
INTO THE SERVICE SPECTRUM OF LIBRARIES

The EZB is linked to library catalogues and bibliographic databases and is thereby integrated into the library service spectrum in various ways. This link permits the user to search for electronic journals just as for traditional library media, and access them from within OPACs and databases.

Link Between the EZB and Library Catalogues

Some German libraries record electronic journals in their OPACs and make them accessible by means of the EZB. But how do they accomplish this link between the catalogue and the EZB?

They indicate in the catalogue entry the journal's EZB URL instead of that of the journal's own homepage. Thus, this Internet address does not link directly to the journal homepage but to a so-called "frontdoor" page in the EZB. This frontdoor shows which EZB member libraries offer full-text access to this title and contains a link to the actual journal.

This method of linking the EZB and library catalogues avoids double input because URL and license changes need to be made only in the EZB and not in the catalogue as well. The particular user and access information is maintained in the EZB.

It is to the users' advantage that they can search simultaneously for electronic and printed media and always receive the currently valid access information. For example, they can search for a journal title in the University Library of Regensburg OPAC and retrieve entries for the print and the electronic edition, if both exist. The entry for the electronic edition contains an Internet address which leads to the EZB frontdoor (see Figure 3).

This frontdoor shows whether the University of Regensburg has access rights to the full-text articles of the respective journal. If a yellow light is dis-

FIGURE 3. Example of a Link Between the EZB and Catalogue

played, the user can jump directly to the journal and retrieve the desired articles.

This frontdoor concept results from cooperation between the EZB and the Zeitschriftendatenbank (ZDB), the national union catalogue for serials in Germany. The electronic journals are catalogued in the ZDB. The title entries are then transferred to the regional and local German library OPACs. In the course of this data exchange, the EZB frontdoor URL is transmitted to the catalogue as well, if requested. The frontdoor URL consists of the EZB Internet address and the unique ID of the respective title in the ZDB. One thus gets an unambiguous and stable URL which makes the electronic journal permanently accessible. In the EZB, each title simply has to be connected to the respective ZDB number. As soon as this number has been entered, a frontdoor is automatically generated for the journal.

Link to Bibliographic Databases

We have also achieved a link between the EZB and bibliographic databases.[4] While browsing the result list of a database search, one can switch to the EZB and access full-text articles if possible.

In practice this means that buttons with the inscription "Full Text via EZB?" are displayed next to the articles in the result list. A click on such a button starts a search for the respective journal in the EZB, guided via the ISSN of the title. The result is an EZB page that shows if the title is available electronically. In case of sufficient access rights, the user can download the requested article (see Figure 4).

This link between literature search and full-text articles is currently achieved at quite a simple level technically. One is guided only to the journal title and not directly to the article. But it still is another quite practicable and expandable method of offering access to electronic journals.

USAGE OF ELECTRONIC JOURNALS

The EZB is popular not only with libraries but also with users. High access figures, where library staff have been excluded, prove that. We log all accesses to the EZB, paying special attention to accesses to journals via the EZB pages.

Accesses to Journal Titles

The numbers show an obvious increase in EZB use. Whereas in 1998 more than 106,000 hits on journal titles were registered, we had more than 560,000 title hits in 1999. In 2000, we counted 2,486,311.

FIGURE 4. Example of a Link Between the EZB and a Database

Figure 5 shows how the usage of the EZB has evolved since January 1999.

The number of total daily title accesses has grown constantly and significantly, from 657 a day in January 1999 to 12,614 a day in February 2001. The main reason for this is the continually increasing number of member libraries.

Many member libraries have also observed a considerably growing use of the electronic journals on their EZB pages. At the University of Regensburg, we have witnessed a growth in daily hits from 63 at the beginning of 1999 to 543 in February 2001 (see Figure 6).

An analysis of the statistical data shows that users are particularly interested in journals offering full-text access. Electronic journals that allow full-text access from within the University of Regensburg campus account for the majority of title hits. During the year 2000, for instance, the most frequent use by far–that is, 55%–resulted from licensed journals (see Figure 7).

This is quite a high percentage, since Regensburg had fewer than 1500 licensed journals in 2000. The most requested electronic titles were major journals whose print editions were also heavily used.

Requests for the free titles and licensed journals providing full-text access accounted for 79% of the hits. This indicates that our users do appreciate the fact that we restrict the EZB to full-text journals and that we display the access restrictions in a clear and simple way. On the other hand, 21% of the hits led to

FIGURE 5. Usage Statistics Showing the Average Daily EZB Title Accesses

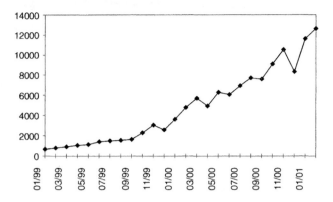

journals known not to be on subscription and that offered users only tables of contents or abstracts. This shows that this level of information is also requested.

Accesses to Search Result Lists, the Alphabetical Title List, and Subject Lists Within the EZB

It is also interesting to see how often the different EZB pages, especially search result lists, the alphabetical list of all titles, and the subject lists, are requested.

The statistics show that all three types of title access are used (see Figure 8).

Most EZB users prefer the subject lists, whereas accesses via either the overall alphabetical list or the search result lists are less frequent. As one can see from Figure 8, the alphabetical listing and the subject lists accounted for 71% of the accesses. This indicates how important the EZB's browsing functions are. The fact that users can not only search the EZB but also browse its subject and alphabetical lists seems to be one of the biggest advantages compared to catalogues offering search functions only.

The users of the University Library of Regensburg take advantage of the browsing functions even more frequently, especially the subject lists, as shown in Figure 9.

Whereas only 20% of the accesses involved the search result lists, the browsing of subject lists–accounting for 67% of the accesses–had much more importance in Regensburg. One of the reasons for this intensive use could be

FIGURE 6. Usage Statistics Showing the Average Daily Title Accesses to the EZB Pages of the University Library of Regensberg

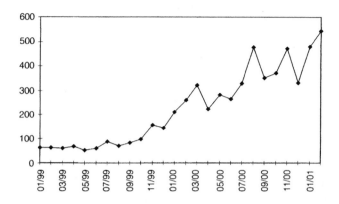

the fact that the link leading to the EZB from our library homepage is directed to the subject lists overview, whereas other member libraries guide their users to the general EZB homepage or to the alphabetical list. One can presume that the user behavior is influenced by the respective default.

PROJECTED DEVELOPMENTS OF THE EZB

The continually growing number of accesses to the EZB shows that the concept of presenting electronic journals in a dedicated system besides the traditional library catalogue has proven its worth. According to the analysis of their behavior, users seem to appreciate especially the browsing capabilities, the transparent collection profile, and the method of displaying access information. This user-oriented nature of the EZB will be further strengthened through the implementation of an article search tool. However, as the link to catalogues and databases proves, the EZB is not thought to be an isolated application. The EZB is already integrated into some digital libraries in Germany. This integration into digital libraries will become more and more important in the future.

The EZB is currently being developed and expanded at the University Library of Regensburg within the framework of a project sponsored by the Deutsche Forschungsgemeinschaft (the German Research Society), the central public funding organization for academic research in the country. On a medium-term basis, three enhancements are planned.

FIGURE 7. Title Accesses to the EZB Pages of the University Library of Regensberg During the Year 2000, Segmented According to Accessibility

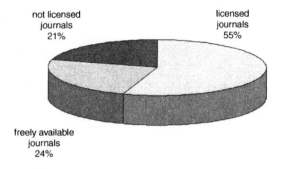

FIGURE 8. EZB Accesses to the Search Result Lists, the Complete Alphabetical List, and Subject Lists During the Period from March to December 2000

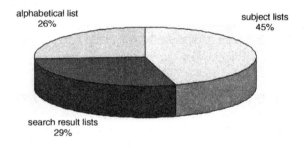

Development of an English-Language Interface

The University Library of Regensburg is currently creating an English-language EZB user interface. We plan to make this service internationally accessible and will accept libraries in non-German-speaking countries as new members.

Integration of a Search Tool for Electronic Articles

We are planning to develop an article search tool within the EZB. This will considerably enhance the EZB search functions, which are currently limited to the journal level. Using bibliographic article data provided by the publishers, we hope to integrate a publisher-independent article search tool into the EZB and to indicate the access rights for articles by the customary traffic lights.

FIGURE 9. Accesses to the Search Result Lists, the Complete Alphabetical List, and Subject Lists During the Period from March to December 2000 on the EZB Pages of the University Library of Regensburg

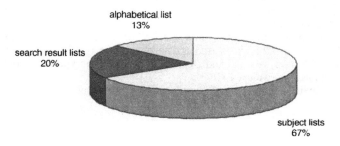

alphabetical list
13%

search result lists
20%

subject lists
67%

Integration of Alerting Services

We are also planning to integrate alerting services into the EZB. Our goal is to quickly inform our users whenever new titles or new articles are published that fit their interest profiles. While some publishers are already offering such alerting services for their own journals, these services are of limited value because the user must register for each service separately. The only way of offering real added value is through a publisher-independent alerting service with a standardized user interface and a large spectrum of titles, for which the user has to register only once. We plan to integrate such an alerting service into the EZB.

A first step will be an alerting service for journal titles. Here EZB users can be informed about new journals in the various subject areas. Furthermore, they can be notified whenever a new title on a given subject is on subscription. In a second step, the alerting service will be extended to the article level.

As these new user services increase the attractiveness of the EZB still more, the level of its use, which is already intense, will continue to grow.

You can find the EZB (presumably with an English user interface in the spring of 2001) on the Internet for free at:

http://www.bibliothek.uni-regensburg.de/ezeit/

NOTES

1. The University Library of Regensburg (http://www.bibliothek.uni-regensburg.de) was founded in 1964 as a modern integrated library and comprises at present approximately 3 million items and approximately 10,000 printed periodicals. It is a service organ of the University of Regensburg, which is divided into 12 faculties and offers a large range of subjects. About 15,000 students can use the traditional media and also

access electronic media by means of networked PCs in the reading rooms of the branch libraries or in the centralised information-processing pools of the university. Additionally. the approximately 4000 employees of the university can access the currently licensed e-journals (currently about 2500 titles) via networked workstations. In 2000, we had roughly 1500 e-journals on subscription.

2. You can find a list of the EZB member libraries at: http://www.bibliothek.uni-regensburg.de/ezeit/about.phtml.

3. The EZB utilizes different "public domain" or "Open Source" software packages. MySQL, version 3.22.20a, is used as database server; as WWW server we use an Apache 1.3.4 with mod_ssl 2.2.5 and OpenSSL/0.9.2b for encrypted communication. As database connection we use PHP/3.0.7

4. This link exists currently for Silverplatter ERL databases.

Access to E-Serials
and Other Continuing Electronic Resources
at Kansas City Public Library

David King

SUMMARY. This article discusses e-serials and other continuing electronic resources at Kansas City Public Library. An overview of electronic resources available at the library is given, and includes a discussion of magazines and newspapers, reference materials, periodical databases, government documents, and Web site links. Access methods for each type of resource are given. Problems with using the 856 field in a consortium setting is discussed. Future growth of e-serials at Kansas City Public Library is also mentioned. *[Article copies available for a fee from The Haworth Document Delivery Service: 1-800-HAWORTH. E-mail address: <getinfo@haworthpressinc.com> Website: <http://www.HaworthPress.com> © 2002 by The Haworth Press, Inc. All rights reserved.]*

KEYWORDS. Electronic serials, continuing resources, 856 field, Web-based access, subject Web links, consortium, Kansas City Public Library

INTRODUCTION

E-serials and access to them at public libraries are many things. Access may, for instance, be through a simple Web link on a reference page or through

---

David King is Information Technology Librarian, Kansas City Public Library, 311 E. 12th Street, Kansas City, MO 64106 (E-mail: david@kclibrary.org).

[Haworth co-indexing entry note]: "Access to E-Serials and Other Continuing Electronic Resources at Kansas City Public Library." King, David. Co-published simultaneously in *The Serials Librarian* (The Haworth Information Press, an imprint of The Haworth Press, Inc.) Vol. 41, No. 3/4, 2002, pp. 271-279; and: *E-Serials Cataloging: Access to Continuing and Integrating Resources via the Catalog and the Web* (ed: Jim Cole, and Wayne Jones) The Haworth Information Press, an imprint of The Haworth Press, Inc., 2002, pp. 271-279. Single or multiple copies of this article are available for a fee from The Haworth Document Delivery Service [1-800-HAWORTH, 9:00 a.m. - 5:00 p.m. (EST). E-mail address: getinfo@haworthpressinc.com].

a MARC 856 field in a bibliographic record in the library's Web-accessible catalog. This article will focus on e-serials and other continuing electronic resources at Kansas City Public Library. A description of the electronic resources available at the library will be given, as well as a discussion of access to them, and future plans regarding e-serials at the library.

The Kansas City Public Library, established in 1873, consists of a main library and nine branch libraries. The library serves over a million and a half people in Kansas City, Missouri, and the surrounding metropolitan area. The library's collection consists of over 2,500,000 items, including more than 2,000 serials. Kansas City Public Library also administers the Kansas City Library Consortium (KCLC) comprising of 24 area libraries. Together, KCLC libraries share a 3.5 million-item collection.

CONTINUING ELECTRONIC RESOURCES AT KCPL

E-serials are but one type of a broader category that today has come to be called "continuing resources." Examples of continuing resources include "serials, monographic series, electronic journals, loose-leaf for updating publications, databases, and Web sites." [1] When one looks at this list, one sees that Kansas City Public Library subscribes to and provides access to a large body of continuing electronic resources, all accessible through the library's public Web site.

This section will discuss each type of electronic resource found at Kansas City Public Library:

- Magazines and Newspapers
- Reference Materials
- Periodical Databases
- Government Documents
- Web Sites

Magazines and Newspapers

Online magazine and newspaper access is primarily provided through the library's *Magazines and Newspapers* page (located at http://kclibrary.org/docdel/). A link to this page is found on the library's home page. The *Magazine and Newspapers* page has five main links: *Search for Articles* (links to the periodical database list); *Document Delivery Services* (interlibrary loan forms can be found here); *Library Holdings* (search for periodicals using title and/or ISSN number); *Newspaper and News Web Sites*; and *Magazine Web Sites*. The bulk of this area of the Web site is accessed through these last two links.

The *Newspaper and News Web Sites* page includes five sections: Local and Regional Newspapers; United States Newspapers; International Newspapers; News Web Sites, and Directories of News Web Sites. Altogether, there are 63 links to news sites, both the online versions of "traditional" paper-based news sources and the newer electronic-only news sites. For example, in the News Web Sites section, *CNN* and *ABC* are linked with the *Drudge Report*.

The *Magazine Web Sites* page is arranged in 12 broad categories such as Local and Regional, Art and Literature, and Health and Fitness. Under each of these headings are four to eight links leading to online magazines related to each category. There are a total of 71 links to magazines. Also found on the *Magazine Web Sites* page is a listing of 16 magazine directories, with summaries included after the link.

Kansas City Public Library also subscribes to some newspapers online, through *ProQuest* and through *NewsBank*. In this way, the library provides access to the *Chicago Sun-Times*, the *Kansas City Star*, and the *St. Louis Post-Dispatch*. The Document Delivery department at KCPL updates these pages regularly.

Reference Materials

Kansas City Public Library subscribes to and provides online access to a number of "traditional" reference resources. The *Library Databases* page provides links to five encyclopedias, including the *Encyclopaedia Britannica* and *Funk and Wagnalls New World Encyclopedia*. That page also has a link to the *World Almanac* and the *Information Please Almanac*, and to *xrefer*, which provides access to over 50 continuing reference resources, including titles like *Who's Who in the Twentieth Century* and *The Concise Dictionary of Linguistics*.

Some of these reference resources, like *xrefer* and the *Encyclopaedia Britannica*, are free Web resources, while others, like the *World Almanac*, are resources the library subscribes to through *FirstSearch*.

Periodical Databases

As mentioned above, the *Library Databases* page links to 56 periodical databases, encyclopedias, almanacs, and business databases. One of the larger databases to which the library subscribes is *ProQuest*. Through *ProQuest*, the library provides access to almost 3,000 periodicals and over 34 newspapers, most of which are in full-text format. The library also provides access to

EBSCOHost, which allows access to over 2,000 periodicals, pamphlets and reference books, many of which are full-text. The library also provides access to a number of non-periodical online databases, including *Books in Print*, *FactSearch*, and *Standard and Poor's NetAdvantage* databases.

Access to each of these online databases is provided primarily through the *Library Databases* Web page, linked to from the main library Web page. Links can also be found on the *Magazines and Newspapers* page and some of the subject-specific reference link pages. Most of these can be accessed both within the library system and remotely, using a valid library card number and PIN.

Sources in the *Reference Materials* and the *Periodical Databases* sections are selected through a collection development task force subcommittee that focuses on electronic material. This task force makes sure that each database/reference work selected for online access is Web accessible and can be accessed remotely using the library's proxy server.

Government Documents

Many traditional government documents are considered serials, and the same is true in the electronic world. Kansas City Public Library has two ways to access online government serials–through online databases and through the library's government documents Web site.

KCPL subscribes and provides access to three online government databases. *CenStats* provides access to familiar government document statistics such as county business patterns, ZIP-code business patterns, and international trade data. *Stat-USA* provides access to the *National Trade Data Bank* (NTDB). *GPO Monthly Catalog*, through *FirstSearch*, provides access to GPO publications.

The government documents Web site is a subsection of the reference and Internet subject links section of the library's Web site. It provides access to federal, state, local, and international government information. Links on these pages include a wide variety of subjects, including a link to the British Royal Family, access to Missouri's state government Web page, and a link to current job openings in the Kansas City, Missouri, city government.

Web Sites

Reference subject links can also be considered a type of continuing electronic resource. Kansas City Public Library has an extensive subject links section (located at http://kclibrary.org/ref/). The links area has nine broad subject areas, with 48 subcategory links. Each of these subcategories links to a page devoted to a specific subject. Summaries of most links are included.

The library's reference department manages this section of the Web site. Subject specialists in the reference department continually explore and critique possible Web links for inclusion in the reference links Web pages. These specialists also update the pages on a monthly basis, removing dead links and adding new ones.

ACCESS TO E-SERIALS AND CONTINUING ELECTRONIC RESOURCES

All access to Kansas City Public Library's electronic resource collection is accomplished through the library's Web site, in a number of ways. One can access the resources through the Web site–clicking, surfing, and searching until an item of interest is found.

Access to many full-text newspapers and journals is provided through the library's *Library Databases* page (http://kclibrary.org/databases/). Using a proxy server with *EZProxy* software, the library is able to provide access both within the library and remotely, by use of a valid library card number and PIN.

The library also uses the 856 field in bibliographic records in its OPAC to link to some items–primarily for *netLibrary*, a collection of e-books. The link to the e-book is accomplished by using the 856 field to house the electronic pointer to the e-book, which is on a server at *netLibrary*.

Members of the Kansas City Library Consortium, administered by Kansas City Public Library, have experimented with direct linking to online journals through the catalog record. For example, the *Japanese Journal of Religious Studies* has a record in the library catalog (shown in Figure 1). The general material designation "[computer file]" is added after the title proper. The notes section mentions that the title was taken from the journal's home page, last viewed on April 27, 2000. The 856 field–shown in the OPAC as "Related URL"–provides a clickable URL that leads to the journal.

A second example comes from another consortium site. Baker University (Baldwin City, Kansas) adds online access points to its library's government document records. For example, the record for *Compilation, Privacy Act Issuances* (shown in Figure 2) includes the GMD "[computer file]" following the title proper and the Related URL field points users to the Web site of the document (in this case at http://purl.access.gpo.gov/GPO/LPS4279).

FIGURE 1. Record for the *Japanese Journal of Religious Studies*

 ## Japanese journal of religious studies

No holdings at this branch; click **HERE** for holdings at other locations.

Details for this record

Title:	Japanese journal of religious studies [computer file]
Publisher :	Nagoya : Nanzan Institute for Religion and Culture, [19uu]
Subject Heading(s) :	Religions--Periodicals. Japan--Religion--Periodicals.
Description :	QuarterlyElectronic coverage as of Apr. 27, 2000: Vol. 13, no. 2-3 (June-Sept. 1986)-v.15, no. 2-3 (June-Sept. 1988), v. 20, no. 1 (Mar. 1993)-
Note :	• Description based on: Vol. 13, no. 2-3 (June-Sept. 1986); title from journal home page (viewed Apr. 27, 2000).
Finding Aids :	Online cumulative index.
Corporate author :	Kokusai Shukyo Kenkyujo (Japan) Nanzan Shukyo Bunka Kenkyujo.
Related URL :	http://www.nanzan-u.ac.jp/SHUBUNKEN/books-frame.html
DBCN :	ART-7135

PROBLEMS WITH THE 856 FIELD

We have encountered a few problems when using the 856 field to link to the actual journal and/or book through the library catalog, most relating to sharing the catalog in a consortium setting. The biggest problem is: Who may view the electronic version of the item? In a traditional setting, a serial's MARC record is included in the library's catalog for the entire consortium to see–but to use the material, one needs to actually visit the library that physically owns the item.

FIGURE 2. Record for *Compilation, Privacy Act Issuances*

Details for this record

Title:	Compilation, Privacy Act issuances [computer file].
Alternate title :	Privacy Act issuances ... compilation :
Publisher :	[Washington, D.C. : Office of the Federal Register], National Archives and Records Administration : [For sale by the U.S. G.P.O., Supt. of Docs, 1994?-
Subject Heading(s) :	Public records--Law and legislation--United States--Periodicals. Public records--United States--Periodicals.
Description :	computer optical discs ; 4 3/4 in.Biennial1993-
Note :	• Title from title screen. • "This compilation of Privacy Act Issuances is published by the Office of the Federal Register in compliance with the requirements of the Privacy Act of 1974 (5 U.S.C. 552a)"-- CD-ROM insert card.
Summary :	• This compilation contains: "descriptions of systems of records maintained on individuals by Federal agencies which were published in the Federal Register as required by the Privacy Act of 1974 [and] rules of each agency which set out the procedures that agencies will follow in helping individuals who request information about their records."
Corporate author :	United States.
Related URL :	Searchable database
DBCN :	ASM-6502

Now, with electronic resources, one doesn't need to travel anymore. Consortium members can simply click the URL in the 856 field and instantly get to the item, right? Wrong! Since an individual library is paying for the item, rather than the whole consortium, only the paying institution has the legal right to access it. The problem arises when a user from one consortium library clicks on the URL of an item purchased by another consortium member, and can't access the item. How does one word the 856 field link so everyone knows that one institution's users/students can access an item, but others can't?

Also, it has yet to be determined who can claim ownership of an item in the catalog, and how that ownership will be displayed, both to the library user and through the catalog's back-end database. For example, the catalog record for the *Journal of Religion and Society* shows that only one of the consortium sites owns the item (shown in Figure 3). However, anyone in the world with Internet access can get to the journal and read the articles, because the publisher is currently providing free access to everyone. It makes sense that the consortium member would claim ownership, since it is providing access. However, the online journal isn't a physical item in anyone's collection–possibly confusing to someone searching from another consortium site.

FIGURE 3. Record for the *Journal of Religion and Society*

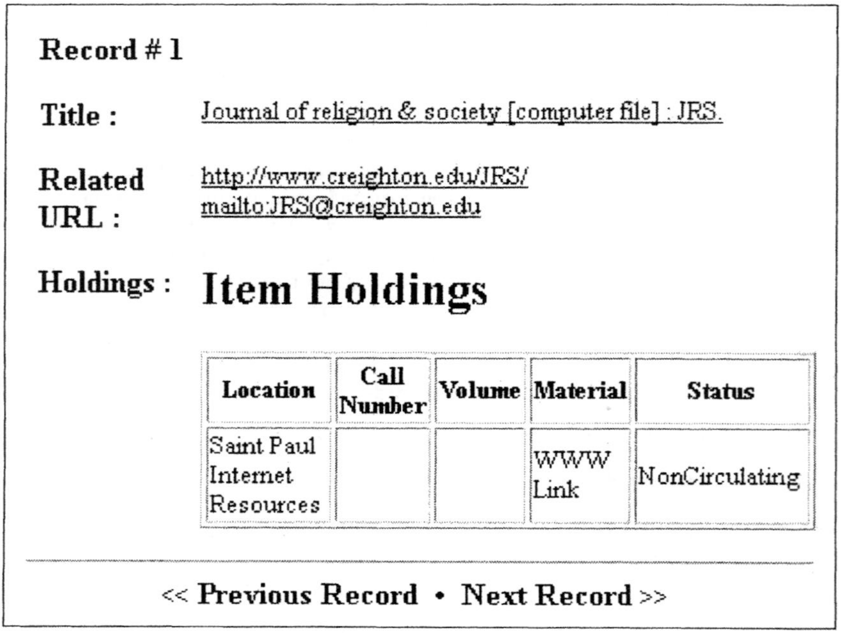

Record # 1

Title :   Journal of religion & society [computer file] : JRS.

Related URL :   http://www.creighton.edu/JRS/
mailto:JRS@creighton.edu

Holdings :   Item Holdings

Location	Call Number	Volume	Material	Status
Saint Paul Internet Resources			WWW Link	NonCirculating

<< **Previous Record** • **Next Record** >>

FUTURE GROWTH OF ELECTRONIC RESOURCES
AT KANSAS CITY PUBLIC LIBRARY

There are a number of impending projects planned in regard to electronic resources at Kansas City Public Library. For instance, the library's Document Delivery department now has a line for e-serial purchases in the library's yearly budget. This will cover the more "traditional" types of electronic journal and magazine subscriptions. Purchasing will probably be done through some type of electronic journal access and management software, like the EBSCO Online service.

Another project in our long-term development plan is to investigate the feasibility of linking to online journals directly through the library's catalog. This project would include purchased electronic journals and possibly journals that are accessed through periodical databases. Another possibility is to create a Microsoft Access database that lists all serials holdings information for electronic serials, separate from the library catalog. If this route was taken, the resulting Access database would be accessible through the library's Web site.

Kansas City Public Library has been quick to begin implementing access to electronic resources. With ongoing development, both within the library system and in the consortium, Kansas City Public Library will continue to strengthen its e-resource presence, providing simpler, quicker access to these publications.

NOTE

1. Jean Hirons, *Revising AACR2 to Accommodate Seriality: Report to the Joint Steering Committee for Revision of AACR,* April 1999, http://www.nlc-bnc.ca/jsc/ser-rep4.html (14 February 2001).

BOOKS, SERIALS, AND THE FUTURE

E-Books: Should We Be Afraid?

Susan Cleyle

SUMMARY. The e-book revolution is finally here. E-books are the last area of a library to leave the paper frontier and venture into the virtual world. Libraries are staring down a future filled with non-paper resources and the role of safe-keeping the archival paper resources of the past. Is this something that should be feared by libraries or embraced like the world embraced the horseless carriage a century ago? This paper will review the current e-book players and the state of the technology with a look at how libraries can be involved in this revolution and in so doing ensure their place in the e-book future. *[Article copies available for a fee from The Haworth Document Delivery Service: 1-800-HAWORTH. E-mail address: <getinfo@haworthpressinc.com> Website: <http://www.HaworthPress.com> © 2002 by The Haworth Press, Inc. All rights reserved.]*

KEYWORDS. E-books, electronic access, Gemstar, NetLibrary, library future

Susan Cleyle is Systems Librarian at the Queen Elizabeth II Library, Memorial University of Newfoundland, St. John's, NF, A1B 3Y1 (e-mail: scleyle@mun.ca).

[Haworth co-indexing entry note]: "E-Books: Should We Be Afraid?" Cleyle, Susan. Co-published simultaneously in *The Serials Librarian* (The Haworth Information Press, an imprint of The Haworth Press, Inc.) Vol. 41, No. 3/4, 2002, pp. 281-292; and: *E-Serials Cataloging: Access to Continuing and Integrating Resources via the Catalog and the Web* (ed: Jim Cole, and Wayne Jones) The Haworth Information Press, an imprint of The Haworth Press, Inc., 2002, pp. 281-292. Single or multiple copies of this article are available for a fee from The Haworth Document Delivery Service [1-800-HAWORTH, 9:00 a.m. - 5:00 p.m. (EST). E-mail address: getinfo@haworthpressinc.com].

INTRODUCTION

Electronic serials, the Internet and now e-books have found their way into today's library. The Internet has certainly revolutionized how libraries collect and deliver material. Libraries have embraced the Internet and worked diligently to get their users interested in this new medium. Librarians were on the front line and we were proud. But gradually we have slipped out of first and the library is no longer where people come to learn about the Web. Electronic resources may help us reclaim our first-place status. Electronic resources like e-journals can enhance our ability to get resources to the desktops of our patrons and e-books are going to be part of this trend. Libraries need to embrace this technology. This is not the time to focus our energies on traditional services. Electronic resources are the resources of the future and we must turn our attention to them if we are to remain a viable service in today's society.

The new and fresh e-book industry is a rapidly changing model. Publishers, writers, hardware vendors and librarians are all jostling for a position in the e-book marketplace. Each sector has its own agenda and its own goals as to what they want e-books to deliver.

E-BOOKS–WHY WOULDN'T THEY BE POPULAR

David Dorman says: "What we now call e-books are actually electronic versions of printed books."[1] This simple statement is one that libraries need to keep in mind. Books are printed text–whether they were written on parchment, typeset by hand or written electronically. Moving books to a different medium still leaves us with a book. It will only be how we read it that has changed.

Publishers are confident that people will want to read books in this new format. Certainly for them, the transition to e-books has not really been a transition at all. The industry already digitizes books before they are printed on paper and now with e-books the final printing step can be removed. The cost can be lowered and the distribution widened. It is also a medium that has caught many authors' attention. We are all familiar with the now famous e-book dabbling by Stephen King. But many other less famous authors are looking to e-books as an opportunity to get their works published. Authors can convert their works themselves and offer them over the Web without having to deal with publishers. Finally, libraries are interested in e-books as an opportunity to push content to the desktops of the user, lessen collection size and offer patrons a new exciting way to read. No wonder there is such an interest from all facets of the book world.

One can get dizzy when looking at the status of the e-book industry today. There are many players all looking for a piece of the e-book pie and trying to find their niche for the future development of this technology. To that end, many companies are forming partnerships and marrying themselves to complementary services in an attempt to secure a piece of the market. Many of the players involved in this industry seem committed to avoiding another battle like the VCR industry saw with VHS and Beta and are supporting the Open eBook Initiative.

OPEN eBOOK INITIATIVE

As library professionals we understand all too well the importance of standards. It is essential that standards be in place to secure the future of e-books yet this has only partially taken hold. The Open eBook Initiative is a body that came together in 1998 to develop an e-book standard. "The purpose of the Open eBook Forum (OEBF) is to create and maintain standards and promote the successful adoption of electronic books."[2] Members come from all walks of e-book life, from publishers and authors, to e-book reader and online e-book vendors. A complete list of who belongs to this forum is available on the OEBF site.[3]

In September 1999, the Open e-book Publication Structure Specification (v. 1) was approved. It is based on HTML and XML. The idea is to have one format that all authors and publishers can use and all readers will interpret. The National Institute of Standards and Technology (NIST) is a neutral member of the OeB and provides technical support as needed.

While the standard has been adopted by many organizations, in practice vendors are still promoting their own proprietary reading platforms first and adherence to the standard second. Their energies are focused on securing a section of the market. One of the highest profiled sections of this industry is the battle of the portable e-book readers.

PORTABLE E-BOOK READERS

There are two types of portable e-book readers: dedicated and multi-purpose. Two companies, Nuvomedia and Softbook, monopolized the dedicated reader market until 2000, when they were both bought by Gemstar (http://ebook-gemstar.com/), who then licensed its e-book technology to Thomson Multimedia in March 2000. Thomson makes products under many labels including RCA. The intention is to mass-market portable dedicated e-book readers. The Nuvomedia Rocket e-book and the reader from

Softbook have been revamped under the RCA label. The new models were distributed for Christmas 2000 under new names: the REB1100 (formally the Rocket e-book reader) and the REB1200 (formally the Softbook reader but now in colour). These readers are not cheap by any means. The REB1100 costs $299USD and the REB1200 is $699USD (see Figures 1 and 2).

The former Rocket e-book REB1100 is a single-screen display and weighs in at 17 ounces with 8MB of RAM. This memory can be upgraded to a maximum of 128MB. The battery can last up to 15 hours if using the backlight and 35 hours if not. The touch screen (4.75" × 3") is monochrome. The REB1200 can handle the same amount of RAM but weighs in at a heftier 33 ounces. The battery does not last as long (6-12 hours, depending on if the reader uses the back light or not) but the touch screen on this unit is larger (8.2" diagonal) and is available in colour.

By partnering with Thomson, Gemstar is the first company to get its dedicated readers to the mass market. Whether they have mass appeal has yet to be shown. This may change as bookstores like Barnes and Noble (http://www.barnesandnoble.com) and Powells (http://www.powells.com) now offer e-books for the Gemstar e-book readers.

Another dedicated e-book reader is EveryBook (http://www.everybook.net). At the time of writing it was licensing its EB Journal product to N-Vision Technologies (http://www.nvisiontek.com) but the product was not yet commercially available. This e-book reader is set up to read like a book in that the screen displays on two pages instead of the pallet format of the Gemstar readers. N-Vision is going to market this colour device as a two-screen laptop computer for business applications instead of a portable e-book reader.

A new reader is also making an appearance. The goReader (http://www.goreader.com) was to be available in the summer of 2001. This product is aimed at university students and those needing access to a lot of textbooks. The goReader can have up to 500 titles loaded. It weighs about 5 pounds and will have a 7.3" × 9.7" full-colour SVGA screen. Its touch screen will also allow highlighting, note-taking and magnification of images. It will also have a calculator, calendar and electronic notepad. Although the price has not been finalized, the device will sell for between $400 and $600USD (see Figure 3).

MULTI-PURPOSE READERS

The above readers are designed primarily for one task–to download and read e-books. Other devices can do more. The Franklin e-bookMan (http://www. franklin. com) reader is one such device. Franklin began shipping its product in February 2001. Its arrival marks more cheaply priced readers (ranging from $129USD to

FIGURE 1. An RCA REB1100. Photo courtesy of RCA

$229USD). These devices will hold not only e-books but also MP3s and allow for the synching of Outlook2000. They also come with a date, address and to-do book. The lower priced models come with 8MB RAM and the higher priced with 16MB RAM. They run on AAA batteries, which can last from 12 to 20 hours. At the time of writing, the e-bookMan shipped without the Operating System loaded. Buyers have to install the OS themselves, which takes 5MB of space.

Palm Pilots can also read e-books. The Palm m100 (http://www.palm.com/products/palmm100/), the new entry-level Palm Pilot, has 2MB of memory and can use the peanutpress (a division of netLibrary) Peanut Reader software to read e-books or any other reader software designed to work with the Palm OS (http://www.peanutpress.com). The cost is about $149USD. The Palm size is small (6″ × 3.12″ × 0.72″) but weighs only 4.4 ounces, and provides a personal organizer as well as the ability to store several e-books.

Public libraries have used this new medium successfully. Loaning out readers with preloaded titles has proven to be a popular service. A search of the

FIGURE 2. An RCA REB1200. Photo Courtesy of RCA

Web for e-books and public libraries produces a huge result set. Popularity may be due to the newness of the technology or the portability of one reader with many titles. Maybe in a work or research environment, portable e-book readers have a better chance of being more widely accepted. Several books can be loaded and carried around at once. Think of the benefits for service personnel who are on the road or out of the office who could benefit from an e-book loaded with manuals and reference guides. Students with many textbooks could also benefit from a portable e-book reader.

Yet despite a positive start, portable e-book readers do not seem to have kept the interest in the consumer market as this author originally thought they would. Portability is important and has enticed many, but e-book readers are still expensive and require high maintenance. The title has to be downloaded and maintained in a library (database) separate from the portable reader. The reader has to be recharged. And these readers do not lend themselves to the "comfort" that can be obtained when reading a paper book.

COMPUTER-BASED E-BOOK READERS

Although it was initially the portable e-book readers that caught everyone's interest and excitement, the main activity and focus in early 2001 seemed to be moving towards a more commercial use for e-books–delivering and reading e-books over the Web. The infrastructure for many organizations is already there. In libraries, offices and homes, the Internet has found a permanent place.

FIGURE 3. The goReader. Photo courtesy of goReader

If e-books are available over the Web, the user does not require additional hardware. What is needed, though, is software that makes reading from a screen a more pleasant experience and of course the willingness on the part of the reader to sit in front of a computer screen to read a book.

Reader software allows an e-book to be read on a computer or in the case of some readers on a personal digital assistant (PDA). There are several players involved in this area including the Peanut Reader mentioned above. It shouldn't surprise the reader to learn that Microsoft also produces reader software. Microsoft Reader (http://www.microsoft.com/reader/) is a free download that attempts to make screen print read more like paper print. It also allows for highlighting and marking. It runs on all Windows platforms and prospective authors can write in Microsoft Word and use an add-on to convert to Reader format. Barnes and Noble offer e-books for Microsoft Reader. Franklin's eBookman will also read books in Microsoft Reader format.

Other computer e-book readers include Adobe's Acrobat PDF format. Another reader product, Glassbook, allowed for two-page display and display rotation. It was acquired by Adobe in August 2000 and has been integrated into the Adobe Acrobat e-book reader v.2. Barnes and Noble offers e-books written in Adobe (http://www.adobe.com/products/ebookreader/main.html).

Many writers who until recently could not get their material published may now do it themselves. All that is required is time and effort. Libraries could also tap into the publishing arena by creating and publishing their own resources. Bibliographies, guides and other resources could be created and published easily and virtually.

E-BOOK WEB SERVICES

A different twist on e-books is the e-book Web service. This can be likened to an e-book library service. Ultimately readers pay for access to e-books. E-book Web services are perfect for academic and special-library markets as well as for offices that rely on ephemeral material or reference material. NetLibrary (http://www.netLibrary.com) is currently the biggest of these services. It was originally designed to provide access right to the end user, who would pay for it. This has since been scaled back and netLibrary considers libraries to be its primary client. Libraries purchase titles from netLibrary's collection of over 30,000 books and 250 publishers (and growing) in a variety of subject areas. With netLibrary, libraries purchase individual titles as they would with paper books. In addition to the purchase price, libraries must also purchase access. This can be a one-time cost or a percentage price over a period of time. So although you may "own" the title, unless you buy access, your patrons may not be able to read the book.

The purchased book is stored at netLibrary and patrons of the library need to register with netLibrary to sign out materials. NetLibrary will supply cataloguing copy with the titles purchased and patrons can then use a library's Web-based catalogue to go directly to the title at netLibrary. There they log in and then sign the title out. Currently only one sign-out at a time is allowed per purchased copy. If you wish more than one patron to be able to view a title at a time, then the library must purchase more copies. Features allow patrons to mark and print sections of the book. Titles can also be downloaded to a PC to be read offline using netLibrary's eBook Reader. NetLibrary can supply statistics on usage on the library's collection.

NetLibrary is working with several integrated library system (ILS) vendors directly including Innovative Interfaces Incorporated (III), SIRSI, DRA and epixtech on the integration of netLibrary into the ILS acquisitions modules. Table of contents links are planned from the MARC record to the fulltext. Eventually the goal is to integrate netLibrary with the ILS circulation module so that the patron has to be authenticated only once. That feature has yet to be announced by any vendor.

This is truly an interesting method of purchasing resources. It offers seamless access for the patron and virtual storage for the library. It works on the same model as purchasing access to electronic journals and enables libraries to push the resource directly to the desktop of the user. With more integration with the ILS, this type of service may eventually be seamless to the patron. Libraries pay netLibrary to maintain the title and do not have to worry about reshelving, damage or repairs. Overdues are eliminated–the books "expire" when the title is due.

Another resource that deals with delivering e-books in the same fashion over the Web but to the end-user directly is Questia (http://www.questia.com). Users pay a subscription fee for service ($19.95USD for one month, $149.95 USD for a year and $14.95USD for 48 hours). This fee allows users to view, copy and print from the selection of titles (30,000 in January 2001). Bypassing the library could be a risky business move. Will users pay for this service when they can go to their libraries and access the same title? Questia is bargaining that this feature, combined with soon-to-be-offered journal-article searching, will convince students to go to this service for information. Libraries thought that users would come to the library to use the Web instead of paying to surf at home. They shouldn't make the same mistake with this kind of service. Questia has a huge amount of venture capital and it plans to be around for a long time.

Another service like Questia is eBrary (http://www.ebrary.com). Set to launch in the second quarter of 2001, eBrary is also directing itself to the patrons but is also attempting to work with libraries. Its service is based on free searching of resources but payment on a piece basis for printing at 15 cents/page USD, 25 cents/page USD for copying, or a price set by individual publishers depending on the value of the document. Library partners do not have to pay for the service but do have to provide a link from their Website and promote the service through materials and training sessions. EBrary hopes to augment library services and will share 5% of each transaction originating with a library to offset printing costs. EBrary is hoping that libraries will be their best salespeople.

Will libraries be by-passed by services like Questia and eBrary or will patrons use library services like netLibrary or individually held e-books? Perhaps they will work in harmony like libraries and bookstores currently do, but perhaps not. Today's society is willing to pay for convenience. Questia is planning to offer a reference service that will provide subscribers with a one-stop service, in essence serve as a pay-for-service library. Libraries could very well be left behind for e-book services like Questia.

These are the most popular e-book solutions currently available but the reader should be aware they are not the only ones. There are more services arriving on the e-book scene everyday.

THE PARALLELS OF THE INTERNET, E-JOURNALS AND E-BOOKS

As libraries move money, staff resources and hard disk space to electronic resources, we have slowly been changing our paradigm away from that of an insular service. When libraries made the leap into the world of the Internet, our paradigm shifted quickly and irreversibly. The turning point was the decision by many libraries to start cataloguing the Web. Today many catalogues contain links to resources not owned by the library. In essence the catalogue no longer serves as an inventory device–it serves as a portal to the world outside the library. The Internet has also made possible remote access to the OPAC and other resources. It was and is expected that libraries will continue to offer a variety of services to patrons at their home and office via the Internet. We have pushed the library out of the front doors to the desktop of the patron. In so doing, we have substantially changed our interface with our patrons.

Many homes and offices have access to the Web. This connectivity, combined with our efforts to offer Web-based remote services, have left libraries out of the equation. Originally, we taught patrons to use the Web and how to surf for "quality" information. But as electronic costs came down and Internet service providers (ISPs) grew, we found that users did not come to the library to get on the Web. They could do it from their home or office without the help of the library. They know they have to be wary of Internet resources and the validity of some sites but this does not stop them from making the Web a primary resource for finding information. Now you can search, shop and do research (using a variety of library resources) on the Web.

The introduction of ejournals has allowed libraries to reclaim some credibility and usefulness. Libraries have once again been included in the process. Libraries have always been major customers for journal publishers and this is still the case with e-journals, which libraries have embraced. They offer a complement to Web services, and patrons have to go to a library's site to access the resource. Libraries can tie holdings from periodical databases to full text e-journals and offer a complete service via the Web. In essence, we have been able to pull the patron back into the fold with the introduction of e-journals.

What is interesting to note with e-journals is that the definition of "ownership" for a library has changed. With paper subscriptions we held the actual paper and thus "owned" the resource. Now with e-journals, we "own" access to the resource. If we discontinue our subscription, we discontinue our ownership. The patrons do not care if the library physically owns the material or not, as long as they have access to a wider variety of materials. We have pulled Web-based patrons back to the library because the library is the point of access. This is a fundamental change. As noted before, we are not the owners of the resource–we are the portals to the resource. Our profession needs to accept this new role and rise to the challenge to stay as a major portal for patrons.

CONCLUSION–GET INVOLVED

Libraries have lost ground with one service and gained with another. Electronic books will break the tie and determine our role for the future. Eventually publishers will move us to this model just like they are doing with electronic journals. Libraries will have no choice but to provide access to e-books. Are we up to the challenge? Are you and your library willing to embrace this technology to ensure your future as a viable solution for users?

The e-book evolution is shaping up to be quite a battle that will require libraries to stay on the forefront of the technology, keep the resources pushed to the desktop and walk away from the paper paradigm if they wish to stay viable. Our current paper collections must become archival projects. Electronic access will be demanded and we will have to comply. Electronic books are part of the electronic revolution. Libraries can either be part of the process or be left behind.

NOTES

1. David Dorman, "E-Books and Libraries: A Discussion of the Present and Future," *Viewpoints* 1, no. 3, http://www.demco.com.
2. Open eBook Forum, http://www.openebook.com/aboutOEBF.htm.
3. Ibid., http://www.openebook.com/who.asp.

APPENDIX.
EBOOK WEB SITES OF INTEREST

Electronic Books Information Sites

EBookAd.com http://www.ebookad.com/

EBookNet http://ebooknet.com/

Electronic Book Evaluation Project (including Librarian's EBook Newsletter) http://www.rrlc.org/ebook/ebookhome.html

Knowbetter.com http://www.knowbetter.com/default.htm

Portable E-book Readers

Everybook/N-Vision http://www.nvisiontek.com/

Franklin eBookMan http://www.franklin.com

Gemstar/RCA http://ebook-gemstar.com/

GoReader http://www.goreader.com

Palm http://www.palm.com/products/palmm100/

Reader Software

Adobe's Acrobat PDF/Glassbook http://www.adobe.com/products/ebookreader/main.html)

Microsoft Reader http://www.microsoft.com/reader/

Peanut Reader software http://www.peanutpress.com

E-Book Web Services

Ebrary http://www.ebrary.com

NetLibrary http://www.netlibrary.com

Questia http://www.questia.com

E Is for Everything:
The Extra-Ordinary,
Evolutionary [E-]Journal

Gerry McKiernan

SUMMARY. An ever-increasing number of e-journals are transcending the limitations of the paper medium by incorporating and integrating a wide variety of innovative electronic features and content. In this article, we examine the current evolution of the scholarly journal and review the emergence of functionalities that expand and extend the conventional electronic journal. We further explore additional e-journal enhancements and consider new forms and formats of scholarly communication likely to arise in the not-so-distant future. *[Article copies available for a fee from The Haworth Document Delivery Service: 1-800-HAWORTH. E-mail address: <getinfo@haworthpressinc.com> Website: <http://www.HaworthPress.com> © 2002 by The Haworth Press, Inc. All rights reserved.]*

KEYWORDS. Electronic journal, innovation, customization, multimedia, object-oriented

While e-journals are still primarily text, in a digital environment, text can be connected with other text, media, services, and systems, from other text, media, services and systems, with other . . .

Gerry McKiernan, MS, is Science and Technology Librarian and Bibliographer, Iowa State University Library, 152 Parks Library, Ames, IA 50011 (e-mail: gerrymck@iastate.edu).

[Haworth co-indexing entry note]: "E Is for Everything: The Extra-Ordinary, Evolutionary [E-]Journal." McKiernan, Gerry. Co-published simultaneously in *The Serials Librarian* (The Haworth Information Press, an imprint of The Haworth Press, Inc.) Vol. 41, No. 3/4, 2002, pp. 293-321; and: *E-Serials Cataloging: Access to Continuing and Integrating Resources via the Catalog and the Web* (ed: Jim Cole, and Wayne Jones) The Haworth Information Press, an imprint of The Haworth Press, Inc., 2002, pp. 293-321. Single or multiple copies of this article are available for a fee from The Haworth Document Delivery Service [1-800-HAWORTH, 9:00 a.m. - 5:00 p.m. (EST). E-mail address: getinfo@haworthpressinc.com].

EDITION

Electronic Manuscript Submission, Refereeing, and Review

The conventional means by which a manuscript is submitted for consideration and review is for an author to provide a journal editor with the requisite number of copies of the manuscript in paper. Authors are also usually required to submit an electronic copy of the manuscript prepared using standard word-processing software (e.g., Microsoft Word). Typically, these are sent to a journal's editorial office using the national and international postal system or a commercial package delivery service (e.g., FedEx). Upon receipt, the journal editor will read a paper copy of the manuscript, assess its relevance to the journal's scope and its overall quality, and if deemed appropriate for further consideration, distribute copies to members of the journal's editorial board or external reviewers to evaluate the manuscript and its suitability for potential publication. As with the original submission, a copy of the manuscript would be sent by the same method used by the manuscript's author: by post or by a commercial delivery service. Following a review period–typically lasting several weeks–reviewers will return the manuscript with their evaluations and recommendations for publication.[1] After all the reviews are returned and a final assessment has been made by the journal's editor, the author will be notified–often by post–of the manuscript's acceptance or rejection.

If accepted, the author may be required to edit the manuscript to satisfy reviewer and editor recommendations. The author will then resubmit the manuscript with the appropriate changes to the journal's editorial office, once again using conventional distribution services. After final review, the edited manuscript will be scheduled for publication, and in time, published in a journal issue. Overall, such processes will require several months to more than a year before the manuscript is eventually published as an article in the respected journal. Such publication delay can be attributed to several factors, including the inherent limitations of conventional delivery systems (e.g., postal services), the duration of the review period, and the page limits of conventional paper journals.

Recognizing the need to expedite the publication of candidate manuscripts, journal publishers are utilizing the inherent potential of the Internet and the World Wide Web to facilitate the submission, review, and publication of relevant manuscripts. The American Chemical Society (ACS) is among an increasing number of scientific publishers expediting manuscript submission. For example, authors who wish to contribute to *Biochemistry* (pubs.acs.org/journals/bichaw/), the ACS journal devoted to the understanding of biological phenomena in terms of molecular structure and function, are provided with various Web-based options that permit them to submit select types of manuscripts electronically.[2] Some ACS journals not only offer electronic submission, but provide Web-based manuscript review as well.[3] Some journals provide a Web-based report form for reviewer ratings and comments (e.g., *British Journal of Surgery*).[4]

BioMed Central (www.biomedcentral.com/), a collection of peer-reviewed biomedical e-journals, offers authors a variety of formats for submitting manuscripts (e.g., Microsoft Word, PDF, RTF), figures (e.g., EPS, PNG, JPEG) and additional materials (e.g., XLS).[5] For the electronic-only e-journal *Conservation Ecology*, authors are required to submit manuscripts by electronic mail.[6] To expedite the review process, the Institute of Physics (IoP) offers a Web-based service that enables potential manuscript reviewers to register with its journal referee services so that candidate reviewers can be easily identified.[7]

In recognition of the need to provide "comprehensive workflow management solutions," ScholarOne[SM] offers Web-based applications that enable scientific, technical, and medical publishers to expedite manuscript submission, peer review, production, and publication. Tools offered by ScholarOne[SM] have been used to create more than 120 journals, including those published by Blackwell Science, the IEEE (the Institute of Electrical and Electronics Engineers), the Institute of Food Technologists (IFT), the Society for Neuroscience, and the American Physiological Society.

In select cases, electronic submission and review of manuscripts has led to the accelerated publication of manuscripts, providing access to accepted papers prior to formal incorporation or publication in an electronic or print journal. Among the major journal publishers or services offering expedited article publication are the IDEAL Online Library (*IDEAL First*),[8] Springer-Verlag (*Online First*),[9] and Wiley InterScience (EarlyViews®).[10]

Virtual E-Journals

In an effort to reduce the Information Overload that readers may experience,[11] some publishers have created *virtual e-journals*. An excellent example of a virtual journal is the *Virtual Journal of Nanoscale Science and Technology (VJNS&T)*, a "weekly multijournal compilation of the latest research on nanoscale systems" published by the American Institute of Physics (AIP) in cooperation with the American Physical Society (APS).[12] This virtual e-journal provides an abstract for all articles in its collection as well as the full-text for most source journals. Articles in *VJNS&T* cover various facets of nanoscale science and technology (e.g., fabrication, process, structural properties, etc.) selected from e-journals published by AIP, APS, and several cooperating professional societies (e.g., Acoustical Society of America, the Optical Society of America, and SPIE–The International Journal of Optical Engineering).[13] Among *VJNS&T* source journals are *Applied Physics Letters*, *Physical Review B*, and *Physical Review Letters*.

Other virtual e-journals include *CV Surgery Online* (ahavj.ahajournals.org), published for the American Heart Association by Lippincott Williams & Wilkins in cooperation with HighWire Press™; *Virtual Journal of Biological Physics Research* (www.vjbio.org/), published by AIP and APS; and the *Virtual Journal of Helsinki Medical Research* (www.terkko.helsinki.fi/vjhmr/), a "monthly multijournal compilation of the latest research at the University of Helsinki," Finland, and the *Virtual Journal* component of *Science's STKE: Signal Transduction Knowledge Environment* (stke.sciencemag.org/), published by the American Society for the Advancement of Science (AAAS) in cooperation with participating publishers (see Figure 1).

Synoptic E-Journals

To further alleviate the burden on readers who seek to remain informed about current developments in ever-changing fields, some publishers offer electronic versions of synoptic journals. A synoptic journal may be defined as a journal that provides synopses or summaries of articles in a broad subject field (e.g., medicine) or specific disciplines within a field (e.g., cardiology). The Massachusetts Medical Society publishes several excellent examples of synoptic e-journals in the field of medicine in its *Journals Watch Online* series (www.jwatch.org/). Published with the assistance of HighWire Press™, the series provides access to synoptic journals in a variety of medical disciplines (e.g., cardiology, infectious diseases, neurology, etc.).

EGO-CENTRIC

Alerting Services

One of the most common value-added features offered by e-journals is automated notification or alerting services. Such current-awareness services typically send registered readers an e-mail message containing the table of contents of a newly published e-journal issue or the table of contents with associated abstracts, when available. With some services, a reader may have the option of receiving the full-text of articles. Such automated notification alleviates the need for a reader to continually revisit an e-journal to identify potentially relevant new content. With electronic notification, a reader can preview new content within an information system used on a routine basis for general purposes.

FIGURE 1. Home Page of *Science's STKE: Signal Transduction Knowledge Environment Virtual Journal*

If the new content is not relevant, the reader need not revisit the journal Website, thereby reducing the time required to maintain awareness of new developments.

Representative of the range of e-journal alerting options are those offered by the Web version of *MCEER Information Service News* (mceer.buffalo.edu/infoService/enews/), the monthly newsletter of the Multidisciplinary Center for Earthquake Engineering Research (MCEER) that reviews current events and literature in earthquake hazards mitigation and related fields. For this e-publication, subscribers can:

• receive notification that a new issue has been published
• receive the titles only of the monthly news for all items
• receive full text for articles and items, and titles for the remainder
• receive full text for meetings and calls for papers, and titles for the remainder

- receive full text, citations and items of interest, and titles of the remainder, or
- receive full text for all published materials.

Readers may choose to receive the entire contents of the monthly newsletter or only news for selected topics (e.g., "Advanced Materials," "Bridges," "Buildings," etc.). Content may be delivered in plain text or HTML format.

Personalized E-Journals

To reduce the Information Overload of readers, some e-journals enable readers to specify the journal titles to be read on a regular basis from a collection of available titles. For example, the Institute of Physics (www.iop.org/) allows readers to create a "Personal Main Menu" in which the reader can customize a main menu that includes only journal titles selected by the reader and not all titles subscribed to by his or her library. In addition, a reader can specify that only the table of contents for the current issue be linked and not those for the entire journal archive. In ScienceDirect®, the Elsevier Science collection of over 1,200 e-journals in the life, physical, technical, and social sciences, a reader can establish a "Personal Journal List" that focuses on his or her scientific specialty or field of interest. In addition, the service allows readers to include non-subscribed journal titles with institutionally subscribed titles, thereby providing a more comprehensive identification of potentially relevant literature.[14]

Through its *E-News* option (mceer.buffalo.edu/infoService/enews/), readers of the Web version of *MCEER Information Service News* can create a customized edition of the newsletter by selecting from among one or more broad topics from a predefined group (e.g., "Advanced Materials," "Bridges," "Buildings," etc.). This personalized version will offer the reader relevant news in a variety of categories (e.g., "Articles," "Call for Papers," "Items of Interest," etc.) for each of the selected topics (e.g., "Bridges," "Codes," "Insurance," etc.) (see Figure 2).

Font, Format, and Display Control

Personalization and customization of e-journals are not limited to the selection of e-journal titles or topics. The *Internet Journal of Chemistry* (IJC) (www.ijc.com/), for example, offers a variety of options for reader configuration of its content structure, reference link style, journal title format, author name order, footnote display, and other components and content.[15] While default options are available for a particular browser, platform, or hardware,

FIGURE 2. A Sample of *E-News*, a Customized Edition of the Web Version of *MCEER Information Service News*

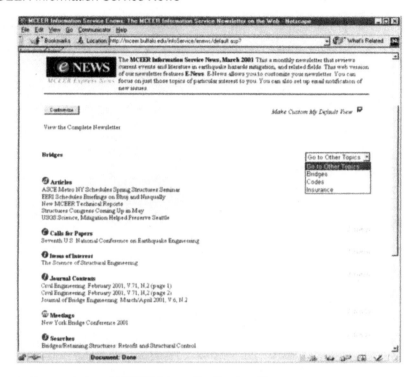

Reprinted by permission of *MCEER Information Services News.*

readers can configure the journal to enable individual article browsing, display article citations in a separate window, condense an article to save space, eliminate frame presentation, or display an article as a single page, among other options (see Figure 3).

Using its customization options, readers may choose to have the standard American Chemical Society (www.acs.org) abbreviation used for a journal title (e.g., *J. Am. Chem. Soc.*) or its full title (e.g., *Journal of the American Chemical Society*) in a reference citation, and opt to display an author's name as initial(s) and surname or surname and initial(s). Readers may also select from several standard scales or base units for displaying temperature, energy amounts, or length. In addition, readers may specify the size and display style of interactive features available within the journal (e.g., ball and stick, strands,

FIGURE 3. Schematic Depicting Optional Page Layouts for the *Internet Journal of Chemistry*

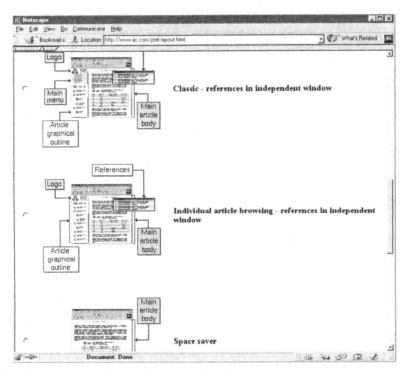

Reprinted by permission of *Internet Journal of Chemistry*.

wireframe) or display the icon for available graphics (e.g., chart, figure, or equation) or linked media (e.g., interactive chemical structure, graphs, or spectral data, VRML) within an article and its associated outline.

ELECTRIC

Indexing and Searching

A select number of e-journals have embraced the potential of the digital environment, providing novel and innovative access to their content. One, *J.UCS: The Journal of Universal Computer Science* (www.jucs.org), provides access to its articles using the alphanumeric subject category codes of the *ACM Computing Classification System*.[16] Articles are assigned one or more subject codes as well as keywords, and subject codes are hotlinked within an abstract, allowing a hyperlinked search of all articles assigned the same code. *J.UCS* is a joint publication of the KNOW Center in Graz, Austria, and Springer-Verlag. It covers all aspects of computer science and was one of the first electronic journals, published without interruption since its founding in 1995.

A second e-journal, the *Astrophysical Journal*, offers a "self-organized" visual index (simbad.u-strasbg.fr/ApJ/map.pl) to more than 16,000 recent articles (1994-2000) created by the application of a Kohonen Self-Organizing Map (SOM) algorithm. SOM is an artificial intelligence technology based on neural computing developed by Teuvo Kohonen of the Helsinki University of Technology. The algorithm automatically organizes indexing terms (or documents) and clusters them within a two-dimensional grid. [17] The keywords and subject headings used by the *Astrophysical Journal* to index articles published in the journal serve as the source vocabulary for the application. One may browse this visual index by clicking a primary category node (e.g., "Cosmo.") or secondary node (e.g., "Dark Matter") from this "bibliographic map." In a right-hand frame, the node number (e.g., "Node 23"), the total number of documents associated with the node (e.g., "97") and all indexing terms and phrases assigned to documents categorized within the node are displayed (see Figure 4).

The number of documents assigned for each index term or phrase relative to the number of documents in the retrieved set is indicated (e.g., "Cosmology: Dark Matter: 9/97"). The reader may retrieve citations and abstracts for all items associated with a node ("Get Documents") or display a detailed SOM, allowing him or her to browse the conceptual context of a term or phrase. Readers may also identify and select relevant standardized terms or phrases using a "keyword query" option. Once selected, an associated SOM is created with identical display or retrieval options as found in the main SOM. A Kohonen SOM self-organized visual index has also been created for *Astronomy and Astrophysics* and its *Supplement Series* (simbad.u-strasbg.fr/A+A/map.pl). [18]

The *Journal of Artificial Intelligence Research* (*JAIR*) (www.jair.org/) allows a reader to navigate a different kind of information map. Established in 1993, *JAIR* publishes research and survey articles and technical notes in all areas of artificial intelligence (AI). Within *JAIR*, a reader may search and browse a linear index by author or title, or manipulate and interact with a three-dimensional categorized "Information Space" created by a Java applet (see Figure 5). [19]

Within this Information Space, yellow squares represent articles published in the journal. "Each square is arranged equidistantly about a label describing a category to which the corresponding article has been assigned. The area of the circle around each category label is directly proportional to the number of articles assigned to that category." Viewpoints can be manipulated using appropriate shift or control keys and the mouse pointer. A mouse rollover of a square

FIGURE 4. The Kohonen SOM (Self-Organized Map) Index for the *Astrophysical Journal* (1994-2000) (left frame); The Indexing Terms and Phases for a Particular Node of the Index with the Associated Number of Articles (right frame)

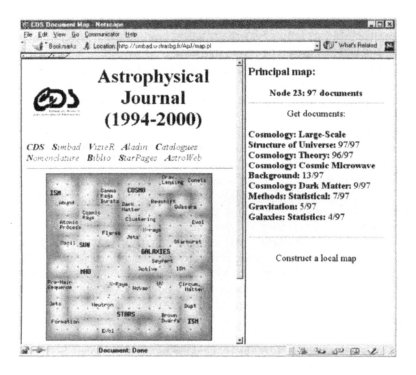

Reprinted by permission of CDS: Centre de Données Astronomiques de Strasbourg.

will display the title of the associated article above the square and the full author, title, volume, and pagination of the article within a left-handed frame within the applet. The reader may retrieve the full text of the article as a full or compressed PostScript file by selecting the preferred format from an additional Java applet window.

JAIR also provides a "keyphrase" index to its content (extractor.iit.nrc.ca/jair/keyphrases/) that has been automatically generated by text summarization software (http://extractor.iit.nrc.ca/).

FIGURE 5. "Information Space," the Three-Dimensional Index for the *Journal of Artificial Intelligence Research* (*JAIR*)

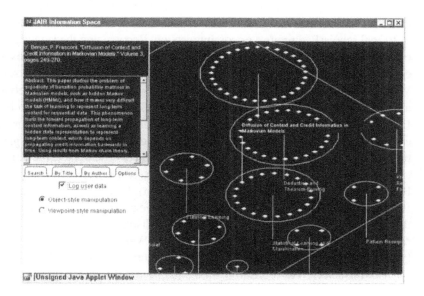

Reprinted by permission of *Journal of Artificial Intelligence Research* (*JAIR*).

Computer Code

To complement or supplement the contents of select articles, an increasing number of e-journals encourage authors to provide supplemental data or resources. One of the more noteworthy supplemental materials found is computer code or programs. A good example is the computer software provided as an appendix to a recent article in *Conservation Ecology* (www.consecol.org). The program, *Nonpoint*, allows a reader to simulate the interaction among key stakeholders in the management of a lake vulnerable to pollution. Actors in the simulation include scientists, economists, regulations, farmers, the lake and its environment, and the reader. In addition to the program, full documentation for the use of the program is provided.[20]

JAIR, the journal devoted to artificial intelligence research, also allows authors to include computer code with articles. For example, an article that describes a new system for induction of oblique decision trees named *OCI* includes an online appendix that is the C source code for the described system.[21]

Translation Services

Although English is the lingua franca of science and world trade and has become the de facto standard for Internet communication, it is not the only language of formal scholarly discourse or communication. Recognizing the language preferences of its readers, *Cultivate Interactive* (www.cultivate-int.org) enables readers to automatically translate an English-language article into one of several Western European languages in real time. *Cultivate Interactive* is a Web magazine funded under the Digital Heritage and Cultural Content program by the European Commission to report activities of CULTIVATE, the pan-European community of libraries, museums, archives, galleries, and non-profit organizations. For any article in the magazine, a reader may choose to have the introductory section translated into one of several Western European languages (i.e., French, German, Italian, Portuguese, or Spanish). In activating the translation from a drop-down menu at the bottom of the article, the first few paragraphs of the original English version are translated and displayed. Translations are machine-generated through WorldLingo™, a free Web-based translation service (worldlingo.com). Using the site's full service, text may be translated into another of the select Western European languages or other languages offered by the service.

Readers of the *Astrophysical Journal* can have the abstract of an article automatically translated by linking to BabelFish (babelfish.altavista.com), the translation service offered by AltaVista, through the Astronomy Abstract Service of the NASA Astrophysics Data System (ADS) (cdsads.u-strasbg.fr/).

EMPOWERING

Download Options

Before the era of e-journals, many researchers used bibliographic databases to identify publications potentially relevant to their research interests. To efficiently manage retrieved citations and abstracts they downloaded the associated records into a personal bibliographic management software package.[22] Acknowledging the value of personalized bibliographic databases, a number of e-journals offer readers an opportunity to download the bibliographic records associated with e-journals into one of these packages. For example, *bmj.com* (www.bmj.com) allows readers to use EndNote® (www.endnote.com/), Reference Manager® (www.isiresearchsoft.com/rm/rminfo.asp), ProCite® (www.procite.com/), or the Medlars (Medline®) format.

Within the e-journals published by the Institute of Physics (www.iop.org), readers can save the abstract in formats used by EndNote®, Reference Manager®, ProCite®, as well as BibTex.[23] In addition, files can be saved in HTML or plain text (ASCII). Comma Separated Variable (CSV) format files within an article can be also saved, allowing the reader to collect data from any table and import it to other table-oriented applications (e.g., Microsoft Excel).

Reader Participation

Unlike the print medium, the Web permits journal publishers to *dynamically* solicit and ascertain reader opinion about a variety of professional and publication issues. Using the Web, *bmj.com* solicited reader preferences about the publication of articles in its paper journal. Specifically, it requested that readers rate the importance of "readability" versus "appraisability" of proposed shortened articles. In a second questionnaire, it solicited reader opinions about nine paper versions (www.bmj.com/cgi/content/full/319/7220/DC1/1) with links to examples of the particular versions. Among these were a "traditionally structured short version with emphasis on methods," "journalistic style," and "diary style."

As a distributed, interactive environment, the Web can empower readers to develop resource collections of significant benefit to their community. For example, readers of the *MRS Internet Journal of Nitride Semiconductor Research* (nsr.mij.mrs.org) can contribute relevant references to journal articles, books, conference papers, or unpublished work, for inclusion in its Web-accessible database (nsr.mij.mrs.org/refs/Default.html).

Virtual Filing Cabinets

Recognizing that digital environments provide opportunities to manage digital resources more effectively and efficiently than possible in paper media, some e-journal publishers enable readers to create and maintain an electronic "filing cabinet" of relevant citations with links to abstracts and article full text. For example, the Institute of Physics (IoP), through its Electronic Journals service (www.iop.org/EJ/), allows readers to "keep an online list of papers of interest" or store articles for future review or use ("Filing Cabinet"). In addition, readers can append comments or annotations ("Personal Notes") to any article for placement in their Filing Cabinet. For the reader, these personal notes appear after the abstract on the abstract page of the article. Comments and annotations may be edited, amended, or deleted at any time.

Within the Electronic Journals service, IoP offers HyperCite™, a technology that provides a link to the abstracts of cited articles and offers access to their full text in select journals for valid subscribers (see below). As with its published journal articles, readers can annotate and file any cited article into a Filing Cabinet. Currently, the Filing Cabinet functionality is only available in the Electronic Journals "Enhanced" and "Remote" services.

The American Institute of Physics, through its Online Journal Publishing Service (OJPS), allows all readers to create an "Article Collection" by selecting articles from a journal table of contents or article abstract page. Those with a personal or an institutional journal subscription may also create a collection from a search results page.[24] Each entry in the collection includes a link to its abstract. Full-text access is provided as a full or sectioned HTML file, a PDF file, and a compressed PostScript file. Non-subscribers can purchase an article on a pay-per-view basis ("Order").

The collection is available indefinitely as long as it is accessed at least once in ninety days; a collection not accessed during this period is erased. Currently, there is no limit on the number of items that can be added to a collection. The reader may delete any or all items at any time. For future access and use, article collections must be formally named. A collection can be assigned several different names to reflect different aspects of its content. As collections are not password protected, readers are encouraged to create unique names to prevent unauthorized access.

Through its "My Folders" feature in its "My Profile" personalization function, readers of *Science's STKE: Signal Transduction Knowledge Environment* (stke.sciencemag.org) can store information from any section of the publication in folders. As with other personal electronic filing and storage services, journal data and information are maintained on the publisher"s server and not on the user"s local workstation.

ENTWINED

Reference Linking

For scholars, the citing of relevant literature in publications is the foundation of the scholarly communication process. Through cited works, authors document and substantiate their arguments and points of view. Utilizing the inherent capabilities of the digital environment, appropriately cited references potentially can be linked to their full text, and minimally to a corresponding abstract.

Using its HyperCite® linking technology, the Institute of Physics (www.iop.org) was one of the first publishers to offer extensive access from cited references to corresponding abstracts or full-text articles. Through this technology, IoP currently provides links to the online content of several major publishers and learned societies. Among these are the collections or services provided by the Institution of Electrical Engineers (INSPEC), Elsevier Engineering Information (Compendex®), the IDEAL Online Library, Springer-Verlag (LINK), the American Chemical Society (Chemport), the American Institute of Physics (Online Journal Publishing Service), and the CrossRef initiative, a collaborative reference-linking service managed by the Publishers International Linking Service, Inc. (PILA). CrossRef (www.crossref.org) is now the most comprehensive linking service, providing access to nearly 3 million article records for more than 3,800 journals from more than 70 publishers from its referral database.[25,26]

One CrossRef participating publisher, Elsevier Science, through its ScienceDirect® service, provides access to the full text of more than 1,200 e-journals. Within its articles, citations may link to an abstract or to the full text of the article in HTML and/or PDF format. In addition, some cited references provide a link to a "SummaryPlus" version of the article. SummaryPlus is an abridged format of the original article that includes not only its introductory sections (i.e., author statement, title, and abstract), but a content outline, thumbnail images of all figures with their captions, and all cited references. In some cases as with the original listing of references, these secondary level references will include links to an abstract, article full text, or a SummaryPlus version of the citation.

Citation Indexing

Simply stated, "a citation index is an ordered list of cited articles, each of which is accompanied by a listing of citing articles. The citing article is identified by a source citation, the cited article by a reference citation."[27] Developed a half century ago by Eugene Garfield in response to the inadequate and inappropriate subject characterization of journal articles typical of many conventional print indexes of the time, citation indexing today has become a standard technique by which conceptually related publications can be easily determined.

One of the major resources incorporated within *bmj.com* (www.bmj.com), the electronic journal of the British Medical Association, is *NetPrints*[TM], (clinmed.netprints.org/), a "repository of non-peer-reviewed original research" in clinical medicine and health research sponsored by the BMJ Publishing Group in collaboration with HighWire Press[TM]. *NetPrints*[TM] offers "CiteTrack," an e-mail alerting service that notifies a registered reader of new content that matches a keyword, subject, or author profile, or that cites a previous contribution in its collection.[28] Alerts include the full citation for all relevant items as well as their associated Web addresses.

Articles in the IDEAL Online Library (www.idealibrary.com) that have been cited by subsequent articles in its collection are indicated by a "Cited by" hotlink on the abstract page for the article. In linking to the associated "Cited by" page, a bibliographic list of the citing papers beneath an entry for the cited paper is displayed, as are hotlinks to the abstract, references, and the full text of the citing article. Access to the full text is provided to subscribing institutions.

Through its Electronic Journals service, the Institute of Physics (www.iop.org) offers readers an "Articles Citing this Article" page which displays a bibliographic list of articles that cite a currently viewed article in their references. Using its HyperCite® technology, links are provided from the citing references to their corresponding abstracts, if these are available in the IoP collection. If an institution subscribes to the citing journal, the citation for the citing article will include a hyperlink indicating that the full-text article is available ("IOP Article"). This hyperlink links to an abstract for the citing article from which its full text can be retrieved along with its associated citations. From this reference list, readers may further explore relevant literature by following these linked citations.

Relatedness

In addition to offering access to citing articles, the IDEAL Online Library (www.idealibrary.com) allows readers to automatically identify articles in its collection similar to the one currently under consideration ("IDEAL Related Articles"). In selecting this option, a citation list of all related articles is displayed. Each listed related article includes hotlinks to an associated abstract and to the corresponding full text. A hotlink to articles similar to each of these related articles ("More Like This") is also provided.

Science Magazine (www.sciencemag.org), the preeminent weekly published by the American Association for the Advancement of Science (AAAS) offers an analogous feature. As with the IDEAL Online Library, readers of this e-publication can only retrieve similar articles from the local collection. The collections of other e-journal publishers or related services are not linked to either. The parameters by which articles are determined to be related or similar is not explicitly specified.

Within PubMed Central (www.pubmedcentral.nih.gov), the NIH-sponsored repository for biological and medical research, readers are able to link to the abstract of an article in PubMed, a free version of Medline®, the premier bibliographic database covering the fields of medicine, nursing, dentistry, veterinary medicine, and related topics, produced by the U.S. National Library of Medicine and provided by the National Center for Biotechnology Information

(NCBI) (www.ncbi.nlm.nih.gov). Within PubMed, readers are able to view records similar to the one under review ("Related Articles"). A word-weighted algorithm utilizing title and abstract keywords as well as the assigned subject headings is used to determine and identify these similar articles.[29]

One of most innovative e-journals that enable readers to identify related articles across a *variety* of electronic collections is *Perspectives in Electronic Publishing* (*PeP*) (aims.ecs.soton.ac.uk/pep.nsf), an experimental e-journal developed by Steven Hitchcock of the University of Southampton. In addition to its original reviews and commentary, *PeP* provides access to an indexed collection of full-text, freely available articles, papers, and other publications devoted to the various aspects of electronic networked publishing. Through an enhanced Web technology, *PeP* provides "on-the-fly" links to significant keywords, phrases, and concepts *within the text* of a selected publication, thereby allowing the user to dynamically identify other papers in its collection relevant to a specific topic (see Figure 6).

EXPLORATIVE

Database Linking

In recent years, the availability of government-supported and commercial bibliographic databases via the Web has increased significantly. Recognizing their inherent benefit, an increasing number of e-journal publishers provide direct links from articles to these resources. For example, the IDEAL Online Library (www.idealibrary.com) includes a hotlink from an article abstract page in its collection to an item record within PubMed. Within this Medline® database, readers can link to a variety of complementary sources, notably several NCBI Entrez databases (www.ncbi.nlm.nih.gov/Database/index.html) that provide data on nucleotide sequences, protein sequences, macromolecular structures, and whole genomes. In addition, readers may "LinkOut" to full-text sources for this article and as well as related articles.

Through its HyperCite® technology, the Institute of Physics (www.iop.org) has established links to several major databases, notably *INSPEC, Compendex®,* and *MathSciNet Reviews*. Synergy (www.blackwell-synergy.com), the online journal service from Blackwell Science and Munksgaard, provides separate hotlinks for the authors of a paper directly to the PubMed Medline® database, enabling the reader to easily identify additional papers of potential interest.

FIGURE 6. The First Page of a Sample Article from *Perspectives in Electronic Publishing* (*PeP*) with Embedded, "On-the-Fly," Dynamic Links

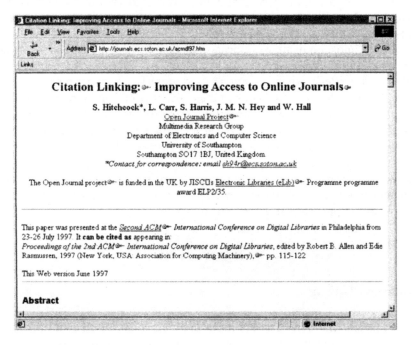

Reprinted by permission of *Perspectives in Electronic Publishing* (*PeP*).

Demonstrations

A variety of e-journals have incorporated multimedia components to augment reader understanding of article text.[30] Animation, streaming and non-streaming audio and video files, and three-dimensional interactive models are major examples of common multimedia. Among the e-journals with some of the most impressive animation is *Expert Reviews in Molecular Medicine* (www-ermm.cbcu.cam.ac.uk), an e-journal published by the University of Cambridge School of Clinical Medicine devoted to understanding health and disease at the cellular and molecular level. Using Flash technology, the journal offers a variety of animations that illustrate highly complex concepts and relationships addressed in select journal articles.[31]

Visual demonstrations are not limited to animation. A select number of e-journals include non-streaming or streaming video files to complement article content. For example, *Development* (usa.biologists.com/Development), the research journal published by the Company of Biologists that addresses all aspects of plant and animal development, includes embedded video clips for select articles. The journal offers a separate index to facilitate access to these files (usa.biologists.com/Development/movies/index.html). One of the most innovative of all electronic journals, the *Internet Journal of Chemistry* (www.ijc.com) embeds not only QuickTime™ (www.apple.com/quicktime) and MPEG (www.mpeg.org/MPEG/index.html) movie files, but also interactive graphs and tables.

Models

Of the various media types embedded within the *Internet Journal of Chemistry*, perhaps the most impressive are interactive chemical 3-D structures created with the Virtual Reality Markup Language (VRML) and with Chime, the chemical structure plug-in provided by MDL Information Systems (www.mdli.com). With Chime models, using the mouse pointer or mouse control options, readers can rotate the molecular model; display the structure as a wire frame, sticks, ball and sticks, or space fill, or other appropriate structure; change the rendering from three-dimensional to two-dimensional; change the coloring; or cluster components, among numerous options. VRM models have similar display and manipulation options (see Figure 7).

As previously noted, some e-journals permit authors to include computer code as supplemental material. Such code may be computer software that can be used to model interactions among systems or users, such as the *Nonpoint* program provided as an appendix to an article in *Conservation Ecology* (www.consecol.org).[32]

EXPRESSIVE

Discussion Forums

Electronic discussion lists were among the first scholarly uses of the Internet. Such professional forums enable individuals with similar interests to participate in a virtual discussion of relevant issues of mutual concern. Recognizing the potential value of such interactions, some e-journals have incorporated discussion forums within their journals. *Cultivate Interactive* (www.cultivate-int.org), for example, offers a discussion forum that allows individuals to discuss issues relating to the Telematics for Libraries program.

McLuhan Studies (www.chass.utoronto.ca/mcluhan-studies), the e-journal established to examine, discuss, and continue the work of Marshall

FIGURE 7. A Three-Dimensional Model of Benzene Used to Illustrate an Article in the *Internet Journal of Chemistry*. (The interactive model was created using VRML, the Virtual Reality Markup Language.)

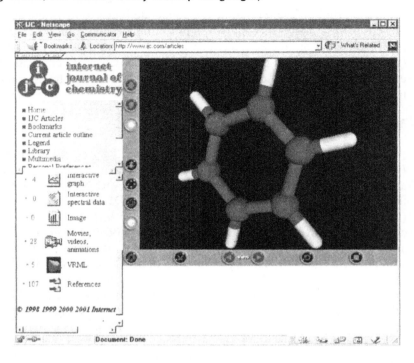

Reprinted by permission of *Internet Journal of Chemistry*.

McLuhan–"the visionary educator of mass media"–provides a discussion forum for this purpose. The *MRS Internet Journal of Nitride Semiconductor Research* (nsr.mij.mrs.org) offers forums on several general and specific topics related to its scope. These include one devoted to properties of nitride semiconductors, one devoted to substrates, one devoted to nichia blue lasers, and one on the doping of III-V nitride semiconductors, among others.

Science's STKE: Signal Transduction Knowledge Environment Virtual Journal also offers several highly specific and general forums (stke.sciencemag.org/cgi/forum). *Sociological Research Online* (www.socresonline.org.uk) through its "Pinboard" feature (www.socresonline.org.uk/pinboard) provides a variety of methods by which readers can communicate with each other as well as with the journal editor. *Expert Reviews in Molecular Medicine* (www-ermm.cbcu.cam.ac.uk) maintains a separate discussion group for each of its articles.[33]

Dynamic Articles

Unlike the print medium, the Web offers authors an opportunity to augment a previously published work with current findings and new observations. For example, in *STKE Reviews*, a section with *Science's STKE: Signal Transduction Knowledge Environment* (stke.sciencemag.org), authors can update reviews as circumstances warrant.

Reactive E-Journals

Journals have long encouraged readers to respond to articles and other components. Such responses typically have taken the form of letters to the editor or companion articles that support or oppose published items. In the digital environment, a number of publishers are continuing this tradition by providing Web-based forms to facilitate submissions. For example, *bmj.com* (www.bmj.com), through its "Rapid Responses" feature, allows readers to comment on articles, editorials, and other content, as well as on previously published letters. Responses received for the most recent seven, fourteen, and twenty-one days are accessible. The IDEAL Online Library (www.idealibrary.com) publishes a *Forum* column that provides critiques of published papers within the scope of its individual journals (e.g., *Animal Behaviour Forum* (www.academicpress.com/anbehav/forum)). Only the electronic version of a journal contains *Forum* articles.

In the journal *Conservation Ecology* (www.consecol.org), readers may comment on an article by using Web-based response or submission forms. Readers may submit brief comments ("Response Form") (e.g., www.consecol.org/Journal/cgi-bin/response_form.html?ms=100845) or contribute extensive commentary or full articles containing charts, tables, and graphics ("Response Upload Page") (www.consecol.org/Journal/cgi-bin/long_response_form.html?ms=100845). If a response is accepted for publication, it is linked to the original article and designated as a response.

One of the most innovative e-journals incorporating a variety of novel features, functionalities, and content is the *Journal of Interactive Media in Education (JIME)* (www-jime.open.ac.uk/), a journal that seeks to "foster a multidisciplinary and intellectually rigorous debate on the theoretical and practical aspects of interactive media in education." Through its "document-centered discourse interface," *JIME* enables readers, reviewers, and authors "to progressively enrich JIME documents with . . . interactive demonstrations, video and audio clips, evaluation instruments, discussions, and pointers to related or future work."[34] Within framed windows, readers may opt to display editor, reviewer, and public comments beside an original article.

User commentary on e-articles need not be limited to public discourse. Some e-journals allow users to create personalized private or public annotations for an article or an article section. For example, *J.UCS: Journal of Universal Computer Science* (www.jucs.org/jucs) allows readers to critique articles, note relevant references, and include an active Web address for public use. The *Internet Journal of Chemistry* (www.jic.com) permits readers to add private notes to individual sections of an article in a similar manner. By using select internal and external Web addresses, readers can create a highly personalized version of an article.

EXTRA

Database Access

In addition to linking articles to select databases, some e-journals provide direct access to public or restricted bibliographic databases. For example, *bmj.com* (www.bmj.com), through its homepage, provides links to the PubMed free version of Medline® as well as to an enhanced version (Medline® Plus) for members of the British Medical Association. The *MRS Internet Journal of Nitride Semiconductors* (nsr.mij.mrs.org) offers open access to its specialized database of more than 38,000 records that can be searched by subject, author, or year. In addition, a reader can access a list of all newly added references, browse an alphabetical "directory" of journals with links to bibliographic citations to the journal, a title listing of each record organized by journal chronologically, and a first-author index.[35] A bibliography of records in citation format arranged alphabetically by first author is also available.

Through its ScienceDirect® service (www.sciencedirect.com), Elsevier Science offers access to some of the most significant scholarly abstract and index databases. Among these are BIOSIS Previews®, the leading life science database; EMBASE, the international biomedical and pharmacological resource; Ei Compendex®, the premier engineering database, and INSPEC®, the leading English-language bibliographic information service that provides access to the world"s scientific and technical literature in physics, electrical engineering, electronics, communications, computers and computing, and information technology. Users may search an individual database or perform searches across several databases simultaneously.[36] In either case, access is limited to institutional subscribers.

E-Book Access

In the past few years, an increasing number of publishers have published monographic works on the Web. Among the most notable services are the *ACM Digital Library* (www.acm.org/dl), a digital collection of the Association for Computing Machinery that provides bibliographic information, abstracts, reviews, and the full text of ACM periodicals and proceedings and the publications of its affiliated organizations, and *IEEE/IEE Electronic Library* (IEL) (ieeexplore.ieee.org), a digital library that provides the full text of journals, conference proceedings, and other serial publications of the Institute of Electrical and Electronics Engineers and the Institution of Electrical Engineers, as well as IEEE standards.

More recently, the American Society of Agricultural Engineers (ASAE), the professional and technical organization dedicated to "the advancement of engineering applicable to agricultural, food, and biological systems," offers a *Technical Library* (asae.frymulti.com), full-text collections of select 2001 ASAE technical publications, including conference and technical proceedings, journals, monographs, and standards. The collections may be searched separately or concurrently by keyword, document number, author, title, or reference (see Figure 8).[37]

Through its LINK service (link.springer-ny.com/home.htm), Springer-Verlag offers access to monographic works (e.g., *Handbook of Environmental Chemistry*) and several of its monographic series (e.g., *Lecture Notes in Computer Science*).[38] These monographic works are browsable through a table of contents and displayed as PDF files. *BioMed Central* (www.biomedcentral.com), the collection of peer-reviewed biomedical e-journals, offers *New Science Primers*, two-page modules with a glossary that provide a synthesized account of a "central field in modern biology." Topics of published primers include the cell cycle, immunity, proteins, and cell signaling.[39]

Supplemental Data

In addition to offering computer code and software programs, some e-journals allow authors to include such supplemental materials as output files from programs, data sets, as well as text appendices. Within an article in *Internet Archaeology* (intarch.ac.uk), the "first fully refereed electronic journal for archaeology," readers may search data sets using a variety of specialized query forms.[40] Search results with relevant data are displayed in an HTML table. In some cases, links are provided from within tables to an interactive map. A reader can export data sets, including underlying geospatial data, to a local database or to a geographic information system (GIS).[41]

FIGURE 8. The Homepage of the *Technical Library* of the American Society for Agricultural Engineering (ASAE) with a Drop-Down Menu Listing the Available Full-Text Collections

Reprinted by permission of ASAE *Technical Library*

In some cases, supplemental material may only be available in the electronic version of a journal. A notable example is the supplemental material available in *Science* that "extends beyond the coverage of the print product to include information such as extended tables of data, explanatory figures, and details of experimental methods." [42]

EXPERIENCE

In one of the most insightful articles on the future of scientific journals, Bachrach reviews the potential of the e-journal in the context of scholarly activity and current technology. He perceptively notes that while "color graphics, animation, sound, and large data sets are now routine and essential components of the scientific method and process, all of these are [typically] omitted when it comes time to distribute the knowledge." In commenting on the inherent potential of the Internet, the Web, and associated programming languages and computer software, Bachrach notes that the "time has come for a dramatic, profound shift in how scientists should (and will) communicate in the future."[43]

Nearly a generation before this observation, and more recently, Lancaster outlined the inevitable replacement of print on paper by electronic publication.[44] As summarized by Shum,[45] Lancaster viewed the development of the journal as a continuum based on the utilization of computer technology:

- computers used for print production
- journal distributed in both print and electronic formats
- publication design is rooted in print, but articles are developed solely for electronic distribution
- interaction between authors and readers is possible; publications can evolve as a result of such interactions
- the inclusion of multimedia content
- both interactive participation and multimedia capabilities are supported

Not only did Lancaster concisely outline the general evolution of the electronic journal and other publications, he, and others, clearly anticipated the innovative e-journals of today. Among the novel features, functionalities, and content they identified were: accelerated publication; alerting services; user annotation and commentary; computer code and program supplements; data manipulation; electronic discussion forums; electronic manuscript submission; font, format, and display control; modeling; multimedia components; personalization; and reader participation.[46,47,48,49] In view of the increasing availability of these and similar components in e-journals, two additional stages may be proposed for the Lancaster continuum:

- linked access to select primary and secondary information sources and resources
- "anything being connected to anything"

In describing the underlying design of the *Internet Journal of Chemistry* (www.ijc.com), Bachrach and his colleagues not only delineate its overall structure and organization, but a complete reconceptualization of the electronic journal itself as well:

> In a sense, we are dramatically remaking the concept of . . . [the] scientific journal. The traditional print model has a single delivery mode of text and graphics, forever fixed upon the page, delivered in immutable form to isolated readers. In our model, the journal becomes a large inter-connected collection of objects, cross-linked and cross-referenced into a single web.[50]

For Bachrach and his co-authors, the journal is one "large object" made up of article objects, individual request objects, a server object, solution objects, page objects, and reference objects, and other objects that interact with each other, the network and the hardware environment to "create the "journal" that is delivered to each reader." [51] In this model, the reader is considered an object that dynamically participates in the creation of the journal.

At a general level, one may view the emerging innovative and novel e-journals as "object-oriented" journals in which component features, functionalities, and content are interconnected and cross-referenced into an interrelated, dynamic, interactive experience. At a higher level, the transformation of the electronic journal now underway may be viewed as a realization of the perceptive vision of Tim Berners-Lee, the creator of the World Wide Web:

> The vision I have . . . is about anything being connected to anything. It is a vision that provides us with new freedom, and allows us to grow faster than we ever could when we were fettered by the . . . systems into which we bound ourselves.[52]

NOTE

The author is most grateful to the following organizations and individuals for permission to reproduce selected screen prints from their respective Web sites: Figure 1: The American Association for the Advancement of Science (AAAS); Figure 2: Multidisciplinary Center for Earthquake Engineering Research (MCEER), *MCEER Information Service News*; Figure 3: Steven M. Bachrach, Editor-in-Chief, *Internet Journal of Chemistry*; Figure 4: Soizick Lesteven, Centre de Données Astronomiques de Strasbourg (CDS); Figure 5: Martha Pollack, Executive Editor, *Journal of Artificial Intelligence Research*; Figure 6: Steve Hitchcock, University of Southampton, Intelligence, Agents, Multimedia Research Group; Figure 7: Steven M. Bachrach, Editor-in-Chief, *Internet Journal of Chemistry*; Figure 8: Donna M. Hull, Director, Publications, American Society of Agricultural Engineers.

REGISTRY

EJI(sm): A Registry of Innovative E-Journal Features, Functionalities, and Content (http://www.public.iastate.edu/~CYBERSTACKS/EJI.htm) is a categorized registry of electronic journals, journal services, or "knowledge environments" that offer or provide innovative or novel access, organization, or navigational features, functionalities, or content. E-journals that include embedded multimedia components are listed in *M-Bed(sm): A Registry of Embedded Multimedia Electronic Journals* (http://www.public. iastate.edu/~CYBERSTACKS/M-Bed.htm).

REFERENCES

1. Paul Pavey, Steve Probets, and David Brailsford, "The Development of an On-Line Submission and Peer Review System" (paper presented at *Electronic Publishing in the Third Millennium*, the Fourth ICC/IFIP Conference on Electronic Publishing, August 17-19, 2000, Kaliningrad State University, Kalingrad, Russia). <http://www.espere.org/elpub2000.pdf> (20 May 2001).

2. American Chemical Society, "ACS Journals Manuscript Submission Site. Biochemistry," c2001. <http://pubs.acs.org/cgi-bin/submission_gen/index.pl?Journal=bichaw> (22 April 2001).

3. American Chemical Society. "Biochemistry. Manuscript Review," c2001. <http:// pubs.acs.org/cgi-bin/review/webreview.pl?bichaw> 20 May 2001.

4. British Journal of Surgery, "Referee's Report Form," c2001. <http://www. blackwellscience.com/~cgilib/jnlpage.bin?Journal=BJS&File=BJS&Page=authors/referee> (20 May 2001).

5. BioMedCentral, "Manuscript Submission," 2001. <http://www.biomedcentral.com/ manuscript/checklist.asp?man_id=New) (23 April 2001.)

6. Conservation Ecology, "Submitting a Manuscript," n. d. <http://www.consecol.org/ Journal/submit/instructions.html> (23 April 2001).

7. Institute of Physics, "Journal Referee Services and Information," 2001. <http:// www.iop.org/Journals/rsi/> (30 April 2001.)

8. IDEAL Online Library, "IDEALFirst," n.d. <http://www.apnet.com/www/ ideal/IDEALFirstinfo.htm> (5 May 2001).

9. Springer-Verlag, LINK Information, "Online First Publications," 2001. <http:// link.springer-ny.com/doi/online-first.htm> (5 May 2001).

10. Wiley InterScience, "Wiley InterScience Launches EarlyView® for Separate Journal Articles to Enhance Online Customer Convenience," 2000. <http://www3.inter-science.wiley.com/prrel_final_0501.html> (5 May 2001).

11. Orrin E. Klapp, *Overload and Boredom: Essays on the Quality of Life in the Information Society* (Westport, Conn.: Greenwood Press, 1986).

12. Virtual Journal of Science and Technology, "About the Virtual Journal of Nanoscale Science & Technology," 2001. <http://ojps.aip.org/journals/doc/VIRT01-home/about.jsp> (5 May 2001).

13. Virtual Journal of Science and Technology, "Participating Publishers & Journals," 2001. <http://ojps.aip.org/jhtml/vjs/partpub.jsp> (5 May 2001).

14. ScienceDirect, "10 Tips for Using ScienceDirect," 2001. <http:// www.science-direct.com/science/page/static/scidir/static_scidir_splash_use1.html> (8 May 2001).

15. Steven M. Bachrach, Anatoli Krassavine, and Darin C. Burleigh, "End-User Customized Chemistry Journal Articles," *Journal of Chemical Information and Computer Sciences* 39, no. 1 (1999): 84.

16. Association for Computing Machinery, "ACM Computing Classification System," c2000. <http://www.acm.org/class/1998/ccs98.html> (8 May 2001).

17. Teuvo Kohonen, *Self-Organizing Maps*. 3rd ed. (Berlin: Springer, 2001).

18. P. Poinçot, S. Lesteven, and F. Murtagh, "A Spatial User Interface to the Astronomical Literature," *Astronomy and Astrophysics. Supplement Series* (May 1998): 183-191. These maps created at CDS: Centre de Données Astronomiques de Strasbourg, Strasbourg, France.

19. MIT Artificial Intelligence Laboratory. Information Architecture, "The JAIR Information Space," 1998. <http://www.infoarch.ai.mit.edu/jair/jair-space.html> (9 May 2001).

20. Stephen Carpenter, William Brock, and Paul Hanson, "Ecological and Social Dynamics in Simple Models of Ecosystem Management. NonPoint Software Documentation," *Conservation Ecology* 3, no. 2, article 4 (December 1999). <www.consecol.org/Journal/vol3/iss2/art4/> (May 16 2001).

21. Sreerama K. Murthy, Simon Kasif, and Steven Salzberg, "A System for Induction of Oblique Decision Trees," *Journal of Artificial Intelligence Research* 2:1-32. <http://www.cs.cmu.edu/afs/cs/project/jair/pub/volume2/murthy94a.pdf> (20 May 2001)

22. Peter Evans, "Personal Research Assistants: A Review of 3 Major Personal Bibliographic Management Tools," *Biblio Tech Review*, 1998. <http://www.biblio-tech.com/html/pbms.html> (20 May 2001)

23. Dana Jacobsen, "BibText," 1996. <http://www.ecst.csuchico.edu/~jacobsd/bib/formats/bibtex.html> (19 May 2001).

24. American Institute of Physics. Online Journal Publishing Service, "How to Manage Your Article Collection," c2001. <http://ojps.aip.org/cgi-bin/help_system?KEY=OJPS&TYPE=OJPS/ARTCOLL> (12 May 2001).

25. CrossRef, "CrossRef:. The Central Source for Reference Linking," c2000. <www.cross.ref> (19 May 2001).

26. Ed Pentz, "CrossRef: A Collaborative Linking Network," *Issues in Science and Technology Librarianship*, 30 (Winter 2001). <http://www.library.ucsb.edu/istl/01-winter/article1.html> (19 May 2001).

27. Eugene Garfield, ""Science Citation Index"–A New Dimension in Indexing," *Science* 144 (3619) (May 8, 1964): 649-654. <http://www.garfield.library.upenn.edu/essays/v7p525y1984.pdf> (19 May 2001).

28. NetPrints, "Track the Topics, Authors and Articles Important to You with Our CiteTrack Service," c2001. <http://clinmed.netprints.org/help/citetrack/> (19 May 2001).

29. PubMed, "Computation of Related Articles," n.d. <http://www.ncbi.nlm.nih.gov:80/entrez/query/static/computation.html> (15 May 2001).

30. Gerry McKiernan, "The Static and the Dynamic: Embedded Multimedia in Electronic Journals." *Technicalities* 20, no. 4 (July/August 2000): 1, 11-14.

31. Expert Reviews in Molecular Medicine, "Animations and Movies," n.d. <http://www-ermm.cbcu.cam.ac.uk/animations.htm> (15 May 2001).

32. Carpenter, Brock, and Hanson, "Ecological and Social Dynamics."

33. Expert Reviews in Molecular Medicine, "Discussion Groups," n.d. <http://www-ermm.cbcu.cam.ac.uk/discuss.htm> (15 May 2001).

34. Simon Buckingham Shum and Tamara Sumner, "JIME: An Interactive Journal for Interactive Media," *FirstMonday* 6, no. 2 (February 2001). <http://www.firstmonday.org/issues/issue6_2/buckingham_shum/index.html> (16 May 2001).

35. MRS Internet Journal of Nitride Semiconductor Research, "MRS Internet Journal of Nitride Semiconductor Research References," c2001. <http://nsr.mij.mrs.org/refs/Default.html> (16 May 2001).

36. ScienceDirect, "A&I Databases on ScienceDirect," c2001. <www.sciencedirect.com/science/page/static/scidir/static_scidir_splash_prod4.html> (17 May 2001)

37. American Society of Agricultural Engineers. Technical Library, "Welcome to Our New ASAE Technical Library," c2000. <asae.frymulti.com/> (17 May 2001).

38. Springer-Verlag, "Available Books/Book Series in LINK," c2001. <link.springer.de/ol/bookser.htm> (17 May 2001).

39. New Science Press, "New Science Primers," c2001. <www.new-science-press.com/cells-primer.asp> (17 May 2001).

40. Martin Millett, Francisco Queiroga, Kris Strutt, Jeremy Taylor, and Steven Willis, "The Ave Valley, Northern Portugal: An Archaeological Survey of Iron Age and Roman Settlement Ave Valley Data Sets–Data Help," *Internet Archaeology* 9 (autumn/winter 2000). <intarch.ac.uk/journal/issue9/millett/data.html> (19 May 2001).

41. Ibid.

42. Science Magazine, "Supplemental Data," c2000. <www.sciencemag.org/feature/beyond/index.shtml> (17 May 2001).

43. Steven M. Bachrach, "Scientific Journals of the Future," in *The Transition from Paper: Where Are We Going and How Will We Get There?* ed. R. Stephen Berry and Anne Simon Moffat (Boston: American Academy of Arts & Sciences, 2001) <www.amacad.org/publications/trans.htm> (18 May 2001).

44. F.W. Lancaster, "The Paperless Society Revisited," *American Libraries* 16, no 8 (September 1985): 553.

45. Simon Buckingham Shum and Tamara Sumner, "JIME," <www.firstmonday.org/issues/issue6_2/buckingham_shum/index.html> (16 May 2001).

46. F. W. Lancaster, *Toward Paperless Information Systems* (New York: Academic Press, 1978).

47. Lancaster, "The Paperless Society Revisited," 553-555.

48. F.W. Lancaster, "Electronic Publishing," *Library Trends*, 37, no. 3 (winter 1989): 316-325.

49. F.W. Lancaster, "The Evolution of Electronic Publishing," *Library Trends*, 43, no. 4 (spring 1995): 518-527.

50. Bachrach, Krassavine, and Burleigh, "End-User Customized Chemistry Journal Articles," 84.

51. Ibid.

52. Tim Berners-Lee, *Weaving the Web: The Original Design and Ultimate Destiny of the World Wide Web by Its Inventor* (San Francisco: HarperSanFrancisco, 1999), 1-2.

Index

Note: This index is alphabetized in word-by-word order. Numbers are filed as numbers instead of as though they were spelled out, e.g., 590 files before 856. Prepositions in subheadings are ignored in filing. Page numbers are given in full form, e.g., 296-298.

For Product Safety Concerns and Information please contact our EU representative GPSR@taylorandfrancis.com Taylor & Francis Verlag GmbH, Kaufingerstraße 24, 80331 München, Germany

Batch number: 08164873

Printed by Printforce, the Netherlands